BASIC
ECONOMETRICS
A Computer Handbook
Using Shazam

For use with Gujarati:

BASIC ECONOMETRICS, 3rd Edition

Kenneth J. White
Steven A. Theobald
University of British Columbia

McGraw-HILL, INC.

New York St. Louis San Francisco Auckland Bogotá Caracas
Lisbon London Madrid Mexico City Milan Montreal New Delhi
San Juan Singapore Sydney Tokyo Toronto

BASIC ECONOMETRICS: A COMPUTER HANDBOOK USING SHAZAM
for use with Gujarati: BASIC ECONOMETRICS, Third Edition

If you have any questions about using this or other McGraw-Hill software programs,
please call our service hotline at 1-800-648-SERV, 9:00 A.M. to 5:00 P.M. Eastern Standard Time.

P/N 069865-1
Part of ISBN 0-07-069864-3

5 6 7 8 9 HAM HAM 0 9 8 7 6 5 4 3 2 1 0

PREFACE

This handbook is designed to show how to use the computer program SHAZAM to do the econometric examples discussed in Gujarati, *Basic Econometrics*, McGraw-Hill, Third Edition. Users should be warned that throughout this handbook, it is assumed that SHAZAM Version 7.0 is being used. Any earlier SHAZAM Version may not have all of the commands and options used here. It is possible to use *SHAZY:The SHAZAM Student Version* for many of the exercises in this book but SHAZY does not contain all the advanced features of SHAZAM. In particular, the ARIMA, COINT, HET, LOGIT, PC, PROBIT and TOBIT commands are not available in SHAZY. The EXACTDW option on the OLS command and the graphics options on the PLOT command are also not contained in SHAZY.

The authors wish to thank the following people for helpful contributions to this handbook. First, Damodar Gujarati, whose manuscript provided the basis for this book. Second, Tanya Jansma, Diana Whistler, and Donna Wong for contributions and advice during the project. Third, Linda Bui, Nancy Horsman, and Justin Wyatt for their contributions in preparing earlier versions of this book.

This handbook is a substantial revision of:

White, K.J. and Bui, L.T.M., *Basic Econometrics: A Computer Handbook Using SHAZAM*, McGraw-Hill, 1988, ISBN 0-07-834463-8.

Appropriate references for SHAZAM are:

SHAZAM User's Reference Manual Version 7.0, McGraw-Hill, 1993, ISBN 0-07-069862-7.

White, K.J., Boyd, J.A.J., Wong, S.D. and Whistler, D., *SHAZY: The SHAZAM Student Version*, McGraw-Hill, 1993, ISBN 0-07-833843-3.

TABLE OF CONTENTS

1. INTRODUCTION

The aim of this handbook is to teach readers how to use the econometric computer program SHAZAM. It is designed to accompany the third edition of the textbook *Basic Econometrics* by Damodar N. Gujarati (McGraw-Hill, 1994). As the reader of *Basic Econometrics* is taught the theoretical framework of econometrics, he or she is shown how to apply this knowledge using a computer, an essential tool in the actual practice of econometrics.

Chapters in this handbook correspond directly to those found in the text and follow them section by section. Every empirical example provided in the text is replicated using SHAZAM. In some instances, certain topics are explored in greater depth to allow for the demonstration of key SHAZAM commands.

When SHAZAM commands and options are first used, a basic description is provided. Although it is desirable, this approach does not require that the handbook be read in sequential order. Rather, the index, which cites the first time a command or option is used as well as any particularly useful demonstration, can be consulted when necessary.

SHAZAM is a comprehensive econometrics program that is easy to learn for beginners yet provides the necessary tools for the advanced econometrician. This handbook does not contain the complete set of SHAZAM commands. For a comprehensive description of SHAZAM, the reader is directed to the following:

> *SHAZAM User's Reference Manual Version 7.0*, McGraw-Hill, 1993, ISBN 0-07-069862-7.

Style Specifications of this Handbook:

This handbook observes the following style. The names of chapters, sections, examples, figures, variables and tables that refer to the text, *Basic Econometrics*, are italicized. Equation numbers are often cited and correspond directly to equations, proofs, formulas, or reported results found in the text. Computer file names discussed in the body text are printed in an italicized bold uppercase font (e.g. *DATAFILE*). All SHAZAM commands (and in this chapter, MS-DOS commands) used and the subsequent output are printed in an uppercase Courier font (e.g. PRINT YEAR X Y). Commands and options discussed in the body text are in a bold uppercase font. Note that command lines beginning with an asterisk ("*") are ignored by SHAZAM and are used as comment lines to help the reader follow the steps being taken. SHAZAM output is encased in a lightly shaded box. Finally, a summary of the SHAZAM commands, options, and temporary variables used are found, in alphabetical order, at the end of each chapter.

General Computer Operations:

This handbook is written in a general format. The programs were run on a personal computer with the MS-DOS operating system. However, SHAZAM operation is identical on most machines and operating systems. Readers should, though, be familiar with the use of files and text editors available for the type of operating system they are using. If problems arise, please consult your instructor or the *SHAZAM User's Reference Manual.*

Editing A File with MS-DOS:

It is often convenient to store data and commands in text files. A simple text editor is called TED (*PC Magazine* 7(19) (Nov. 1988)). To edit a file type:

    TED *filename*

where *filename* refers to the name of the file. Alternately, if MS-DOS Version 5.0 or greater is being used, you can also use its editor by typing:

    EDIT *filename*

Both these text editors contain easy to use on-screen menus. If neither of these editors are available, consult the documentation for your computer for more information.

Basic MS-DOS Commands:

(i) Storing Files

Most personal computers (PC's) come equipped with "hard drives" which are able to store information (i.e. files) even when the power is switched off. The hard drive on PC is usually called the "C:" drive.

Files can also be stored on 3.5" or 5.25" diskettes. The "floppy" drives in which the diskettes are inserted are usually called the "A:" or "B:" drives. Diskettes are useful if you are working on someone else's computer (say, in a computer lab) or when little space is available on your hard drive. Even if the hard drive is used, it is wise to "backup" files on diskettes.

(ii) Copying and Deleting Files

When using MS-DOS, files are copied using the MS-DOS **COPY** command and deleted using the **DEL** command.

The first command below will copy a file, say *FILE1*, from the C: drive (i.e. the hard drive) to a diskette in the A: drive (i.e. a floppy drive). The second command deletes *FILE1* from the C: drive.

```
C:\>COPY FILE1 A:
C:\>DEL FILE1
```

Similarly the next command will copy a file, say *FILE1*, from a diskette in A: drive to the C: drive.

```
C:\>COPY A:FILE1
```

(iii) Making Directories And Sub-directories

To is important to learn how directories and sub-directories work. The "root" directory is the position at which the computer starts at (usually denoted C:\). If you are working on a particular project, it is often convenient to store all the pertinent files in a separate directory. The **MD** command makes a directory. The **CD** command is used to change to a directory. The **CD..** command is used to move back to the previous directory.

The following commands start at the root directory, make a directory, say *JUNK*, move to that directory, copy the file *FILE1* from a diskette in A: drive, and move back to the root directory. Note that the backslash symbol "\" is used to map directories.

```
C:\>MD JUNK
C:\>CD JUNK
C:\JUNK\>COPY A:FILE1
C:\JUNK\>CD..
C:\>
```

Of course, it is possible to make directories in diskettes. The commands are identical. However, you must first move directly to the desired floppy drive. The following commands move from the C: drive to the A: drive.

```
C:\>A:
A:\>
```

(iv) Listing the Files and Sub-directories Contained in a Directory

The command **DIR** is used to list all the files in the current directory. Note that sub-directories listed are enclosed in square parentheses. The **DIR/W** command lists these files and sub-directories in columns. This is useful when there are so many files that the listing goes off the screen. In addition, the asterisk symbol "*" is used as a "wild card" in MS-DOS. In the following example:

```
C:\>DIR
C:\>DIR/W *.DAT
C:\>DIR/W S*.*
C:\>COPY *.DAT A:
```

the first **DIR** command lists all the files and directories in the root directory. The second command line lists, in columns, all the files ending with the extension *.DAT*. The third line lists all files beginning with the letter "S." The fourth line copies all the files ending with the extension *.DAT* to a diskette in the A: drive. Note though, that these files are also still contained in the current directory. Copying a file does not erase it from its source.

Running SHAZAM on MS-DOS:

There are many versions of SHAZAM available. Many student use SHAZY, the Student Version. The reference is:

SHAZY, The SHAZAM Student Version, McGraw-Hill, 1994, IBSN 0-07-833843-3.

There are two ways to run SHAZAM. The first is called the "interactive" method. First, go to the SHAZAM directory. If the student version of SHAZAM is used, a SHAZAM session is initiated by typing **SHAZY** and hitting the enter key.

```
C:\>CD SHAZAM
C:\SHAZAM\>SHAZY
```

SHAZAM will then ask for further instructions. SHAZAM commands are entered line by line and the output from the commands appear immediately on the screen. If you want to save the output from a screen to a file, type, as the first SHAZAM command:

```
FILE SCREEN filename
```

where *filename* is the name of the file you want the output to be sent to. If this file does not exist, it will be created automatically. The SHAZAM session is ended by typing the SHAZAM command **STOP**.

The interactive method is most suitable if something short and simple has to be computed. The disadvantage is that, if an error is made, many commands may have to be retyped.

The batch or "command file" method is a more popular and often more convenient approach to running SHAZAM. With this method, a complete set of commands are constructed using a text editor and saved in a file. The advantage to this method is that the command file can be edited if necessary and then reused.

The following is an example of simple SHAZAM command file, called say *EXER1.SHA*. (At this point, do not worry about what these commands actually do).

```
SAMPLE 1 10
READ(EXER1.DAT) Y X
PLOT Y X
STOP
```

The file inside the parentheses, *EXER1.DAT* is an example of a data file. This file contains data that SHAZAM will use to execute commands.

At the DOS prompt, the following commands move to the SHAZAM directory, make a sub-directory, say *ECON326*, and moves to this sub-directory. The command file *EXER1.SHA* and the data file, *EXER1.DAT* are then copied from a diskette in the A: drive. Since the "wild card" symbol ("*") is used, all files with the root "EXER1." and any extension will be copied. (An extension is the part of a file name that follows the dot "."). This command file is then run and the output sent to a file called, in this case, *EXER1.OUT*. Finally, the sub-directory "C:\SHAZAM\ECON326" is exited.

```
C:\>CD SHAZAM
C:\SHAZAM\>MD ECON326
C:\SHAZAM\>CD ECON326
C:\SHAZAM\ECON326\>COPY A:EXER1.*
C:\SHAZAM\ECON326\>SHAZY EXER1.SHA EXER1.OUT
C:\SHAZAM\ECON326\>CD..
C:\SHAZAM\>CD..
C:\>
```

Note that the above commands assume that SHAZAM is accessible from all directories and sub-directories on the hard drive (C:). See the SHAZAM installation instructions for more details.

If you have the command file *EXER1.SHA* on a diskette but, for some reason, do not want to copy it onto the hard drive, the following commands (replacing lines 4 and 5 above) will read the command file *EXER1.SHA* directly from the diskette (in this case from the A: drive) and store the output file *EXER1.OUT* on the hard drive.

```
C:\SHAZAM\ECON326\>COPY A:EXER1.DAT
C:\SHAZAM\ECON326\>SHAZY A:EXER1.SHA EXER1.OUT
```

Note that, when specifying where SHAZAM should search for the data files (see the **READ** command in Chapter 2), be sure to specify on which drive they are stored on. Above, it is assumed that the data must be copied onto the hard drive.

The above series of commands are worth studying. It is important to have a solid understanding of the use of directories and disk drives.

Running SHAZAM for WINDOWS:

The procedure for running SHAZAM for WINDOWS, SHAZAMW, is a little different from above. If you are at the DOS prompt, type:

```
C:\>WIN SHAZAMW
```

or, if you are in the WINDOWS environment, double click on the SHAZAM icon. Once the program has finished loading, at the SHAZAM prompt type the SHAZAM commands:

```
FILE INPUT EXER1.SHA
```

where again, *EXER1.SHA* is a SHAZAM command file. To store the output in a file, in this case, *EXER1.OUT*, the first line of the command file should contain the SHAZAM command:

```
FILE OUTPUT EXER1.OUT
FILE INPUT EXER1.SHA
```

If the output file *EXER1.OUT* does not exist, it will automatically be created.

Running SHAZAM for Macintosh Computers:

First, double click on the SHAZAM folder icon to open it. (Note that all your SHAZAM data files and SHAZAM command files should be inside the SHAZAM folder). To run SHAZAM, double click on the SHAZAM icon (it is a circle resembling a globe). (See the chapter "How to Run SHAZAM on Macintosh" in the *SHAZAM User's Reference Manual* for more details). When SHAZAM begins, you will see the SHAZAM prompt "TYPE COMMAND."

To run SHAZAM interactively, enter SHAZAM commands at the SHAZAM prompt and hit the return key. To end the run, type **STOP**.

If you have all your SHAZAM commands in a file, type:

```
FILE INPUT commandfilename
```

where *commandfilename* is the name of the command file. The output will appear on the screen. Once the SHAZAM run is finished, type **STOP**.

To send the output to a file while still having it appear on the screen, type:

```
FILE  SCREEN  outputfilename
FILE  INPUT  commandfilename
STOP
```

where *outputfilename* is the name of the file the output is to be sent to. To send the output to a file type:

```
FILE  OUTPUT  outputfilename
FILE  INPUT  commandfilename
STOP
```

A Comment on Rounding Errors:

At times, you may notice that some of the results reported in this handbook do not match exactly those printed in the *Basic Econometrics* text. To a large extent, this is due to rounding errors. Although rounding errors may appear to be a trivial problem, the cumulative effect of rounding errors can have a significant impact on numerical calculations. To illustrate this point, the following example has been created. In the first line, the four fractions are given in decimal form with significant figures. The fifth column gives the value of the product of the four numbers. In each successive row, one significant figure is dropped and the numbers are rounded. By comparing the products of the four numbers in each successive row, the effect of rounding errors can be seen.

2/13	6/13	9/13	10/13	PRODUCT
.1538462	.4615385	.6923077	.7692308	.037813820
.153846	.461539	.692308	.769231	.037813836
.15385	.46154	.69231	.76923	.037814962
.1538	.4615	.6923	.7692	.037797376
.154	.462	.692	.769	.037861266
.15	.46	.69	.77	.036659700
.2	.5	.7	.8	.056000000

Note the difference between the smallest and largest products given in the fifth column. There is a 48.094 percentage change between the numbers. It should now be clear that rounding errors can significantly alter numerical results. Therefore, a great deal of care should be taken to minimize their occurrence. In all SHAZAM runs, the maximum number of digits possible are retained in computer memory, even if they are not actually printed.

2. TWO-VARIABLE REGRESSION MODEL: SOME BASIC IDEAS

In *Chapter 2*, Gujarati introduces the two-variable regression model. This model has the property that the population regression line is simply the locus of points through the conditional mean of the dependent variable. To illustrate this using SHAZAM, the hypothetical data presented in *Section 2.1* will be used to reproduce the plots given in the text.

Begin by creating a data file to store the data from *Table 2.1* using a text editor available on your computer. Name the file *TABLE2.1* or follow file name rules for your computer. The data can be typed into the file in pairs of Y and X, one observation per line. This method is called the observation-by-observation method. An alternate method called the variable-by-variable method is explained later in this chapter. Note that SHAZAM requires a blank line following the last line in both data and command files.

File *TABLE2.1* should look like this:

```
55    80
60    80
65    80
70    80
75    80
65    100
70    100
74    100
80    100
85    100
88    100
79    120
84    120
90    120
94    120
98    120
80    140
93    140
95    140
103   140
108   140
113   140
115   140
102   160
107   160
110   160
116   160
118   160
125   160
110   180
115   180
120   180
130   180
135   180
```

140	180
120	200
136	200
140	200
144	200
145	200
135	220
137	220
140	220
152	220
157	220
160	220
162	220
137	240
145	240
155	240
165	240
175	240
189	240
150	260
152	260
175	260
178	260
180	260
185	260
191	260

Next, create a command file to hold your SHAZAM commands. Name your command file *CHAP2*. In order to have SHAZAM read, print, plot and calculate statistics on the data, six commands are needed:

SAMPLE, READ, PRINT, STAT, PLOT, and **STOP.**

The **SAMPLE** Command

The **SAMPLE** command is used to specify the desired sample range for the data. The format of the **SAMPLE** command is:

SAMPLE *beg end*

where *beg* and *end* are numbers specifying the beginning and ending observations. The **SAMPLE** command should not set a sample size larger than the number of observations available in the data.

There are 60 observations in *Table 2.1*. To use the entire range of observations, set the **SAMPLE** range to 1 through 60 with the following command:

```
SAMPLE 1 60
```

The READ Command

The **READ** command performs two functions: it inputs the data and it assigns variable names. The general format of the **READ** command is:

READ (*filename*) *vars* / *options*

where *filename* is the name of the data file, *vars* is a list of variable names, and *options* is a list of options. (The **BYVAR** option will be demonstrated later in this chapter). All of the variables listed on the **READ** command must have the same number of observations. Variable names can be a mixture of letters and numbers but the first character must be a letter. Spaces are not allowed within the name. Note that variable names can be no longer than 8 characters.

Recall that the data in *TABLE2.1* is organized in pairs of consumption and income variables, entered one observation per line. With the **READ** command, name the variables *CONSUME* and *INCOME* .

```
READ(TABLE2.1) CONSUME INCOME
```

The PRINT Command

The format of the **PRINT** command is:

PRINT *vars* / *options*

where *vars* is a list of variable names and *options* is a list of desired options (to be demonstrated later as required).

To print the data, use the following **PRINT** command:

```
PRINT CONSUME INCOME
```

Next, use the **STAT** command to obtain descriptive statistics for both *CONSUME* and *INCOME*.

The STAT Command

The **STAT** command computes means, standard deviations, variances, minimums, and maximums for the variables listed. The format for the **STAT** command is:

STAT *vars* / *options*

where *vars* is a list of variables and *options* is a list of desired options.

In this example, the **STAT** command should look like the following:

```
STAT CONSUME INCOME
```

Now use the **PLOT** command to plot the dependent variable, *CONSUME*, against the independent variable, *INCOME*.

The PLOT Command

The **PLOT** command will plot variables. In general, the format of the **PLOT** command is:

PLOT *depvars* *indep* / *options*

where *depvars* is a list of one or more dependent variables to be plotted against a single independent variable, *indep*, and *options* is a list of desired options.

Plot *CONSUME* against *INCOME* as follows:

```
PLOT CONSUME INCOME
```

Finally, use the **STOP** command to inform SHAZAM that it has reached the end of the command file.

```
                        The STOP Command

    The STOP command is used to indicate that SHAZAM is finished. The
    format of this command is:

    STOP
```

Recall that SHAZAM requires a blank line following a STOP command.

The complete command file (CHAP2) is as follows:

```
SAMPLE 1 60
READ(TABLE2.1) CONSUME INCOME
PRINT CONSUME INCOME
STAT CONSUME INCOME
PLOT CONSUME INCOME
STOP
```

After running this SHAZAM program, the following output is obtained:

```
|_SAMPLE 1 60
|_READ(TABLE2.1) CONSUME INCOME
   2 VARIABLES AND        60 OBSERVATIONS STARTING AT OBS        1
|_PRINT CONSUME INCOME
        CONSUME          INCOME
      55.00000        80.00000
      60.00000        80.00000
      65.00000        80.00000
      70.00000        80.00000
      75.00000        80.00000
      65.00000        100.0000
      70.00000        100.0000
      74.00000        100.0000
      80.00000        100.0000
      85.00000        100.0000
      88.00000        100.0000
      79.00000        120.0000
      84.00000        120.0000
      90.00000        120.0000
      94.00000        120.0000
      98.00000        120.0000
      80.00000        140.0000
      93.00000        140.0000
      95.00000        140.0000
      103.0000        140.0000
      108.0000        140.0000
      113.0000        140.0000
      115.0000        140.0000
      102.0000        160.0000
```

107.0000	160.0000
110.0000	160.0000
116.0000	160.0000
118.0000	160.0000
125.0000	160.0000
110.0000	180.0000
115.0000	180.0000
120.0000	180.0000
130.0000	180.0000
135.0000	180.0000
140.0000	180.0000
120.0000	200.0000
136.0000	200.0000
140.0000	200.0000
144.0000	200.0000
145.0000	200.0000
135.0000	220.0000
137.0000	220.0000
140.0000	220.0000
152.0000	220.0000
157.0000	220.0000
160.0000	220.0000
162.0000	220.0000
137.0000	240.0000
145.0000	240.0000
155.0000	240.0000
165.0000	240.0000
175.0000	240.0000
189.0000	240.0000
150.0000	260.0000
152.0000	260.0000
175.0000	260.0000
178.0000	260.0000
180.0000	260.0000
185.0000	260.0000
191.0000	260.0000

|_STAT CONSUME INCOME

NAME	N	MEAN	ST. DEV	VARIANCE	MINIMUM	MAXIMUM
CONSUME	60	121.20	36.458	1329.2	55.000	191.00
INCOME	60	173.67	57.812	3342.3	80.000	260.00

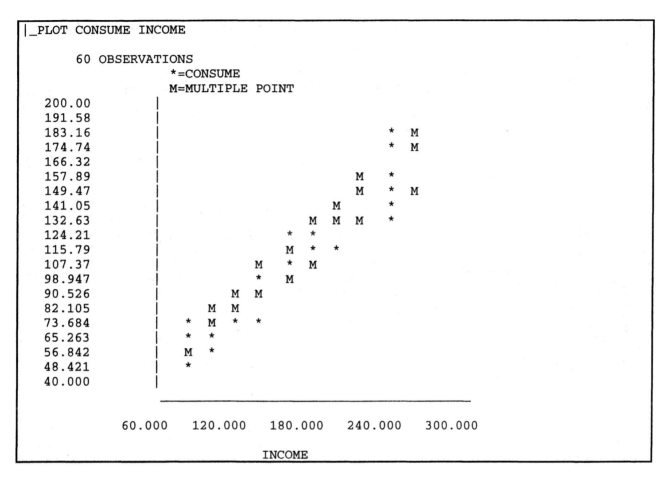

```
|_PLOT CONSUME INCOME

    60 OBSERVATIONS
                    *=CONSUME
                    M=MULTIPLE POINT
  200.00    |
  191.58    |
  183.16    |                              *    M
  174.74    |                              *    M
  166.32    |
  157.89    |                         M    *
  149.47    |                         M    *    M
  141.05    |                    M         *
  132.63    |               M    M    M    *
  124.21    |          *    *
  115.79    |          M    *    *
  107.37    |     M    *    M
  98.947    |          *    M
  90.526    |     M    M
  82.105    |   M    M
  73.684    | *    M    *    *
  65.263    | *    *
  56.842    | M    *
  48.421    | *
  40.000    |
            _____
        60.000   120.000   180.000   240.000   300.000

                         INCOME
```

The above plot is similar to *Figure 2.1* in the text. This type of plot is usually called a "line printer plot" since it only uses symbols which are available on a computer line printer. Because the resolution of a line printer plot is not very high, the symbol "M" is used to indicate that more than one data point is plotted.

High quality graphics can be obtained using GNUPLOT, a graphics program which is interfaced with SHAZAM. For more information on using GNUPLOT, see the *SHAZAM User's Reference Manual*.

Note that, in SHAZAM output, all command lines are printed with the prefix "|_".

To illustrate the use of the variable-**BY-VAR**iable method for reading data, the **BYVAR** option on the **READ** command will be used in this next example. Examine the data from *Tables 2.4* and *2.5* in the text. Both tables have the same X values but their Y values are different. Let the Y values from *Table 2.4* be named *Y1* and the Y values from *Table 2.5* be named *Y2*. Using a data file called *TAB2425*, type the data in variable **BY VAR**iable with the first observation of each variable beginning on a new line. Start with *Y1* on the first line followed by *Y2* on the second line and *X* on the third line. In this case, the data for each variable fits on one line, but the data for any variable may continue onto additional lines. However, as mentioned, the first observation of a variable must start on a new line. All variables read in must have the same number of observations corresponding to the **SAMPLE** command.

The data file for this example, 3 variables and 10 observations, should appear as:

```
70    65    90    95  110   115   120   140   155   150
55    88    90    80  118   120   145   135   145   175
80   100   120   140  160   180   200   220   240   260
```

The command file below will read in the data, assign variable names, print the variables to confirm that they were read in properly, compute some descriptive statistics, and plot the dependent variables, *Y1* and *Y2*, against the independent variable, *X*.

```
SAMPLE 1 10
READ (TAB2425) Y1 Y2 X / BYVAR
PRINT Y1 Y2 X
STAT Y1 Y2 X
PLOT Y1 Y2 X
STOP
```

The following is the output from the revised command file:

```
|_SAMPLE 1 10
|_READ (TAB2425) Y1 Y2 X / BYVAR
    3 VARIABLES AND        10 OBSERVATIONS STARTING AT OBS          1
|_PRINT Y1 Y2 X

        Y1              Y2              X
    70.00000        55.00000        80.00000
    65.00000        88.00000        100.0000
    90.00000        90.00000        120.0000
    95.00000        80.00000        140.0000
    110.0000        118.0000        160.0000
    115.0000        120.0000        180.0000
    120.0000        145.0000        200.0000
    140.0000        135.0000        220.0000
    155.0000        145.0000        240.0000
    150.0000        175.0000        260.0000
|_STAT Y1 Y2 X
NAME        N    MEAN        ST. DEV      VARIANCE     MINIMUM      MAXIMUM
Y1          10   111.00       31.429       987.78       65.000       155.00
Y2          10   115.10       36.534       1334.8       55.000       175.00
X           10   170.00       60.553       3666.7       80.000       260.00
```

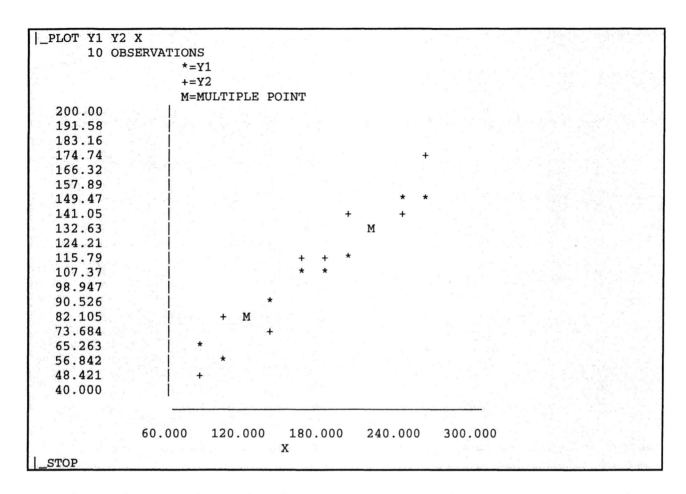

```
|_PLOT Y1 Y2 X
         10 OBSERVATIONS
                        *=Y1
                        +=Y2
                        M=MULTIPLE POINT
```

The above plot is similar to that shown in *Figure 2.3* of the text. Note that data from the first sample is represented by "*" while data from the second sample is represented by "+".

SHAZAM commands and options used in Chapter 2

PLOT *depvars   indep*

PRINT *vars*

READ (*filename*) *vars*   /   **BYVAR**

SAMPLE *beg   end*

STAT *vars*

STOP

3. TWO-VARIABLE REGRESSION MODEL: THE PROBLEM OF ESTIMATION

This chapter will demonstrate the method of Ordinary Least Squares (OLS). *Section 3.1* of the text discusses this method and applies it to the data found in *Table 3.1*. As in Chapter 2, the **SAMPLE, READ,** and **PRINT** commands will be used to enter and display the data. However, since there are only four observations in *Table 3.1*, it is easier to include the data in the command file rather than use a separate data file. This is done by eliminating the *filename* on the **READ** command and inserting the data on the four observations directly after the **READ** command. Once they are read in, these vectors of variables are now available for calculations with the **GENR** or **GEN1** commands.

The **GENR** and **GEN1** Commands

The **GENR** command will create new variables from old variables and perform a variety of data transformations. The **SAMPLE** command defines the observation range used in **GENR** commands. In general, the format of the **GENR** command is:

GENR   *newvar=equation*

where *newvar* is the name of the new variable to be created and *equation* is any arithmetic equation involving old variables, constants, and mathematical functions.

The **GEN1** command is used to create a scalar variable or constant. The **GEN1** command is equivalent to using a **SAMPLE 1 1** command with a **GENR** command to generate a variable with only one observation. The format of the **GEN1** command is:

GEN1   *newvar=equation*

The **LIST** option with the **READ** command prints the variables after they have been read. This is equivalent to using a **PRINT** command directly after the **READ** command. Printing data is advisable in that it checks that the data has been read in properly.

The following commands will replicate the information found in *Table 3.1*. Note that the "*" and "**" symbols with the **GENR** command are used to specify multiplication and exponentiation respectively.

```
SAMPLE 1 4
READ Y X / LIST
4 1
5 4
7 5
12 6
GENR YHAT1=1.572+1.357*X
GENR E1=Y-YHAT1
GENR E1E1=E1**2
GENR YHAT2=3+X
GENR E2=Y-YHAT2
GENR E2E2=E2**2
PRINT YHAT1 E1 E1E1
PRINT YHAT2 E2 E2E2
```

The SHAZAM output from the above commands follows.

```
|_SAMPLE 1 4
|_READ Y X / LIST
    2 VARIABLES AND         4 OBSERVATIONS STARTING AT OBS         1
       Y1               X1
     4.000000          1.000000
     5.000000          4.000000
     7.000000          5.000000
    12.00000           6.000000
|_GENR YHAT1=1.572+1.357*X
|_GENR E1=Y-YHAT1
|_GENR E1E1=E1**2
|_GENR YHAT2=3+X
|_GENR E2=Y-YHAT2
|_GENR E2E2=E2**2
|_PRINT YHAT1 E1 E1E1
      YHAT1             E1              E1E1
     2.928571          1.071429        1.147959
     7.000000         -2.000000        4.000000
     8.357143         -1.357143        1.841837
     9.714286          2.285714        5.224490
|_PRINT YHAT2 E2 E2E2
      YHAT2             E2              E2E2
     4.000000          0.0000000       0.0000000
     7.000000         -2.000000        4.000000
     8.000000         -1.000000        1.000000
     9.000000          3.000000        9.000000
```

As explained in the text, 1.572 and 1.357 are the OLS parameter estimates. The **OLS** command can be used to obtain these estimated coefficients directly. Many other useful statistics are also computed.

```
                          The OLS Command

  The OLS command will perform Ordinary Least Squares regressions and
  produce standard regression diagnostics. In addition, the OLS command
  has an extensive list of options that provides many features for estimation
  and testing of the linear regression model. The general format is:

  OLS  depvar  indeps  / options

  where depvar is the dependent variable, indeps is a list of independent
  variables, and options  is a list of desired options. A constant term is
  automatically included unless the NOCONSTANT option is specified.
  Standard output includes the R² and adjusted R² statistics, the variance of
  the estimate, standard errors and variance of the estimated coefficients,
  and elasticity at the sample means.
```

The general format is explained above. Standard output includes the R^2 and adjusted R^2 statistics.

The output from the **OLS** command follows.

```
|_OLS Y X
       4 OBSERVATIONS        DEPENDENT VARIABLE = Y
...NOTE..SAMPLE RANGE SET TO:     1,    4

 R-SQUARE =   0.6786     R-SQUARE ADJUSTED =     0.5179
VARIANCE OF THE ESTIMATE-SIGMA**2 =    6.1071
STANDARD ERROR OF THE ESTIMATE-SIGMA =    2.4713
SUM OF SQUARED ERRORS-SSE=    12.214
MEAN OF DEPENDENT VARIABLE =    7.0000
LOG OF THE LIKELIHOOD FUNCTION = -7.90838

VARIABLE     ESTIMATED   STANDARD    T-RATIO           PARTIAL STANDARDIZED ELASTICITY
   NAME      COEFFICIENT   ERROR       2 DF    P-VALUE CORR. COEFFICIENT  AT MEANS
X            1.3571       0.6605      2.055     0.176  0.824    0.8238      0.7755
CONSTANT     1.5714       2.917       0.5388    0.644  0.356    0.0000      0.2245
```

The **STAT** command will now be used to replicate the information found in *Table 3.1*.

The **SUMS=** option with the **STAT** command stores the sum of each variable listed as a vector in the variable specified. Note that the first element of this vector contains the sum of the first variable listed with the **STAT** command.

Elements can be extracted from vectors using the **GEN1** command. The position of a particular element is specified using parentheses. For example, the following command stores the third element of the vector *S* in the new variable *S3*.

```
GEN1 S3=S(3)
```

The "**?**" symbol placed in the first column of a command line suppresses the normal output of the command. Since only the sums of the various variables are of interest, the standard output will be suppressed here. Also, SHAZAM ignores all command lines beginning with the symbol "*****". Hence, this is a convenient way of including comment lines in the command file.

Recall that a **STOP** command is required to indicate that the SHAZAM run is finished.

The commands below continue with the example in *Section 3.1*.

```
?STAT Y1 X1 E1 E1E1 E2 E2E2 / SUMS=TOTALS
* All lines beginning with an asterisk are ignored by SHAZAM and can be used
* to include comments in the command file.
GEN1 SUMY1=TOTALS(1)
GEN1 SUMX1=TOTALS(2)
GEN1 SUME1=TOTALS(3)
GEN1 SUME1E1=TOTALS(4)
GEN1 SUME2=TOTALS(5)
GEN1 SUME2E2=TOTALS(6)
PRINT SUMY1 SUMX1 SUME1 SUME1E1 SUME2 SUME2E2
```

The output follows.

```
|_?STAT Y1 X1 E1 E1E1 E2 E2E2 / SUMS=TOTALS
|_* All lines beginning with an asterisk are ignored by SHAZAM and can be used
|_* to include comments in the command file.
|_GEN1 SUMY1=TOTALS(1)
|_GEN1 SUMX1=TOTALS(2)
|_GEN1 SUME1=TOTALS(3)
|_GEN1 SUME1E1=TOTALS(4)
|_GEN1 SUME2=TOTALS(5)
|_GEN1 SUME2E2=TOTALS(6)
|_PRINT SUMY1 SUMX1 SUME1 SUME1E1 SUME2 SUME2E2
   SUMY1
  28.00000
   SUMX1
  16.00000
   SUME1
 0.0000000
   SUME1E1
  12.21429
   SUME2
 0.0000000
   SUME2E2
  14.00000
```

The empirical example in *Section 3.6* takes a closer look at OLS estimation. First, the **OLS** command will be used to estimate the model. Then the formulas found in *Chapter*

3 will be used to estimate the model the "long way". While this may seem tedious, this exercise will both explore the fundamentals of OLS and provide the user with the opportunity to program each calculation.

The **PCOV** option with the **OLS** command Prints the **COV**ariance matrix of the estimated coefficients. This should not be confused with the covariance of *variables* matrix obtained when using the **PCOV** option with the **STAT** command.

The **MEAN=** option with the **STAT** command stores the **MEAN**s of the variables listed as a vector in the variable specified. The **PCPDEV** option Prints a CrossProduct matrix of the variables listed in **DEV**iations from the means and the **CPDEV=** option stores this matrix in the variable specified. Similarly, the **PCP** and **CP=** options Print and store the original **Cross Product** matrix.

The **MATRIX** command described below is introduced at this point so as to provide a method of extracting elements from a matrix. For a detailed look at the **MATRIX** command, see Chapter 9.

The **MATRIX** Command

The **MATRIX** command can be used to create and manipulate matrices. It is similar to the **GENR** command except it operates on matrices instead of vectors. In contrast to the GENR command, the **MATRIX** command ignores the current **SAMPLE** command. The general format is:

MATRIX *newmat=equation*

where *newmat* is the name of the new matrix to be created from an *equation*.

It is important to understand how to extract elements from a matrix or a vector. For example, the command:

```
MATRIX C=X(1,2)
```

extracts the element in row 1 and column 2 of the matrix **X**, and stores it in the new variable C. Using this method, elements from the crossproduct matrix of deviations can be extracted for later use.

The user should be aware of differences in the sum of squares notation between the Gujarati text and SHAZAM that may be somewhat confusing. Although Gujarati's notation will be followed, keep the differences in mind when reading SHAZAM output. In particular:

Sum of squares	Gujarati	SHAZAM
Total	TSS	SST
Explained (or Regression)	ESS	SSR
Residual (or Errors)	RSS	SSE

The following commands replicate the results reported in *Section 3.6*. These commands are worth studying since a key point of *Chapter 3* is understanding the formulas involved.

```
SAMPLE 1 10
READ(TABLE3.2) Y X
OLS Y X / PCOV
* Now the hard way.
STAT X Y / MEAN=M CPDEV=DEVM PCPDEV CP=CPM
GEN1 XBAR=M(1)
GEN1 YBAR=M(2)
MATRIX SIGMAXY=DEVM(1,2)
MATRIX SIGMAXX=DEVM(1,1)
MATRIX TSS=DEVM(2,2)
MATRIX SXX=CPM(1,1)
* Estimate the coefficients using equations (3.1.6) and (3.1.7).
GEN1 BETA2=SIGMAXY/SIGMAXX
GEN1 BETA1=YBAR-BETA2*XBAR
* Compute the regression variance using equation (3.3.5).
GENR YHAT=BETA1+BETA2*X
GENR EE=(Y-YHAT)**2
?STAT EE / SUMS=RSS
GEN1 SIGMA2=RSS/8
* Compute the variances for the estimated coefficients using equations
* (3.3.1) to (3.3.4).
GEN1 VARB2=SIGMA2/SIGMAXX
GEN1 VARB1=(SXX/(10*(SIGMAXX)))*SIGMA2
* Use Equation (3.3.9) to compute the covariance between B1 and B2.
GEN1 COVB1B2=-XBAR*VARB2
* Compute the R2 statistic using equation (3.5.5).
GEN1 R2=1-RSS/TSS
PRINT BETA1 VARB1 BETA2 VARB2 COVB1B2 SIGMA2 R2
STOP
```

The output follows.

```
|_SAMPLE 1 10
|_READ(TABLE3.2) Y X
   2 VARIABLES AND        10 OBSERVATIONS STARTING AT OBS        1

|_OLS Y X / PCOV

OLS ESTIMATION
     10 OBSERVATIONS      DEPENDENT VARIABLE = Y
...NOTE..SAMPLE RANGE SET TO:    1,   10

 R-SQUARE =   0.9621     R-SQUARE ADJUSTED =   0.9573
VARIANCE OF THE ESTIMATE-SIGMA**2 =    42.159
STANDARD ERROR OF THE ESTIMATE-SIGMA =   6.4930
SUM OF SQUARED ERRORS-SSE=    337.27
MEAN OF DEPENDENT VARIABLE =    111.00
LOG OF THE LIKELIHOOD FUNCTION = -31.7809

VARIABLE    ESTIMATED   STANDARD   T-RATIO         PARTIAL STANDARDIZED ELASTICITY
  NAME      COEFFICIENT  ERROR        8 DF   P-VALUE CORR. COEFFICIENT AT MEANS
X           0.50909    0.3574E-01   14.24    0.000 0.981    0.9808       0.7797
CONSTANT    24.455     6.414        3.813    0.005 0.803    0.0000       0.2203

VARIANCE-COVARIANCE MATRIX OF COEFFICIENTS
X           0.12775E-02
CONSTANT -0.21718          41.137
             X                CONSTANT

|_* Now the hard way.
|_STAT X Y / MEAN=M CPDEV=DEVM PCPDEV CP=CPM
NAME         N    MEAN       ST. DEV     VARIANCE     MINIMUM     MAXIMUM
X           10   170.00      60.553       3666.7       80.000      260.00
Y           10   111.00      31.429       987.78       65.000      155.00

CROSSPRODUCT MATRIX IN DEVIATIONS -       10 OBSERVATIONS

X          33000.
Y          16800.        8890.0
             X             Y
|_GEN1 XBAR=M(1)
|_GEN1 YBAR=M(2)
|_MATRIX SIGMAXY=DEVM(1,2)
|_MATRIX SIGMAXX=DEVM(1,1)
|_MATRIX TSS=DEVM(2,2)
|_MATRIX SXX=CPM(1,1)
|_* Estimate the coefficients using equations (3.1.6) and (3.1.7).
|_GEN1 BETA2=SIGMAXY/SIGMAXX
|_GEN1 BETA1=YBAR-BETA2*XBAR
|_* Compute the regression variance using equation (3.3.5).
|_GENR YHAT=BETA1+BETA2*X
|_GENR EE=(Y-YHAT)**2
|_?STAT EE / SUMS=RSS
|_GEN1 SIGMA2=RSS/8
|_* Compute the variances for the estimated coefficients using equations
|_* (3.3.1) to (3.3.4).
|_GEN1 VARB2=SIGMA2/SIGMAXX
|_GEN1 VARB1=(SXX/(10*(SIGMAXX)))*SIGMA2
|_* Use Equation (3.3.9) to compute the covariance between B1 and B2.
```

```
|_GEN1 COVB1B2=-XBAR*VARB2
|_* Compute the R2 statistic using equation (3.5.5).
|_GEN1 R2=1-RSS/TSS
|_PRINT BETA1 VARB1 BETA2 VARB2 COVB1B2 SIGMA2 R2
   BETA1
  24.45455
   VARB1
  41.13705
   BETA2
  0.5090909
   VARB2
  0.1277548E-02
   COVB1B2
 -0.2171832
   SIGMA2
  42.15909
   R2
  0.9620616
|_STOP
```

The following commands will estimate the coffee consumption example in *Section 3.7.*

```
SAMPLE 1 11
READ(TABLE3.4) Y X
OLS Y X
STOP
```

The output follows.

```
|_SAMPLE 1 11
|_READ(TABLE3.4) YEAR Y X
   3 VARIABLES AND       11 OBSERVATIONS STARTING AT OBS        1

|_OLS Y X

 OLS ESTIMATION
      11 OBSERVATIONS      DEPENDENT VARIABLE = Y
...NOTE..SAMPLE RANGE SET TO:    1,   11


 R-SQUARE =   0.6628    R-SQUARE ADJUSTED =   0.6253
VARIANCE OF THE ESTIMATE-SIGMA**2 =  0.16564E-01
STANDARD ERROR OF THE ESTIMATE-SIGMA =  0.12870
SUM OF SQUARED ERRORS-SSE=  0.14908
MEAN OF DEPENDENT VARIABLE =    2.2064
LOG OF THE LIKELIHOOD FUNCTION =  8.04811


VARIABLE     ESTIMATED    STANDARD    T-RATIO        PARTIAL STANDARDIZED ELASTICITY
  NAME       COEFFICIENT    ERROR       9 DF    P-VALUE CORR. COEFFICIENT  AT MEANS
X            -0.47953      0.1140      -4.206    0.002-0.814   -0.8141     -0.2197
CONSTANT      2.6911       0.1216      22.13     0.000 0.991    0.0000      1.2197
|_STOP
```

SHAZAM commands and options used in Chapter 3

GEN1 *newvar=equation*

GENR *newvar=equation*

MATRIX *newmat=equation*

OLS *depvar indeps / **PCOV**

PRINT *vars / options*

READ (*datafilename*) *vars / **LIST**

SAMPLE *beg end*

STAT / **CP= CPDEV= MEAN= PCOV PCP PCPDEV SUMS=**

STOP

4. THE NORMALITY ASSUMPTION: CLASSICAL NORMAL LINEAR REGRESSION

Chapter 4 discusses two topics. First is the assumption that the error terms, u_t, are normally distributed. If the residuals are normally distributed and the X variable is non-stochastic (fixed), then Y is a linear function of the errors, and is therefore, normally distributed. As is shown in equations (4.3.2) and (4.3.4), since the estimates of β_1 and β_2 are a linear function of Y, they will be normally distributed with $\mathrm{Var}(\beta_1)$ and $\mathrm{Var}(\beta_2)$. If the distribution of β_1 and β_2 can be shown to be normal and given that the residual variance is known, confidence intervals can be constructed using tables of the Normal distribution (see *Chapter 5* for the proofs involved). If the variance is not known, then the t-distribution can be used. However, if the residuals are not normal then neither the Normal or t-distribution is strictly valid. Hence, testing for the normality of the errors is important. Testing methods are discussed and illustrated in *Section 5.12*.

Section 4.4 discusses the Maximum Likelihood (ML) method of estimation. In ML estimation, the objective is to find the values of parameters most likely to have produced the dependent variable. It is assumed that the dependent variable follows a normal distribution. Earlier, the least squares method was examined where the parameters were chosen to minimize the sum of squared errors. It turns out that, when normality is assumed, the ML method is equivalent to OLS. However, in more advanced models such as those in the second half of the textbook, the two methods may yield different results.

ML estimation tries to find the values of β_1 and β_2 that maximize the log-likelihood function described in equation (5) of *Appendix 4A*. While this seems complicated, SHAZAM does all the work. In SHAZAM output, the log-likelihood function is labelled "LOG OF THE LIKELIHOOD FUNCTION." The value printed is computed using equation (5).

The 4 observations from *Table 3.1* will be used to illustrate the ML method. First, estimate the Ordinary Least Squares (OLS) regression using the commands below. Then examine the value of the "LOG OF THE LIKELIHOOD FUNCTION" printed in the output.

```
SAMPLE 1 4
READ(TABLE3.1) Y X
PRINT Y X
OLS Y X
```

The output follows.

```
|_SAMPLE 1 4
|_READ(TABLE3.1) Y X
    2 VARIABLES AND        4 OBSERVATIONS STARTING AT OBS        1
|_PRINT Y X
      Y                X
   4.000000        1.000000
   5.000000        4.000000
   7.000000        5.000000
  12.00000         6.000000

|_OLS Y X

OLS ESTIMATION
      4 OBSERVATIONS      DEPENDENT VARIABLE = Y


 R-SQUARE =  0.6786     R-SQUARE ADJUSTED =  0.5179
VARIANCE OF THE ESTIMATE =    6.1071
STANDARD ERROR OF THE ESTIMATE =    2.4713
MEAN OF DEPENDENT VARIABLE =    7.0000
LOG OF THE LIKELIHOOD FUNCTION = -7.90838

VARIABLE     ESTIMATED   STANDARD   T-RATIO    PARTIAL STANDARDIZED ELASTICITY
  NAME       COEFFICIENT   ERROR      2 DF       CORR.  COEFFICIENT  AT MEANS
X            1.3571      0.66047     2.0548     0.8238  0.82375      0.77551
CONSTANT     1.5714      2.9166      0.53879    0.3560  0.0          0.22449
```

The log-likelihood function will now be computed for the case posed in *Section 3.1*, where the regression line is assumed to be $Y = 3 + X$ (i.e. $\beta_1 = 3$ and $\beta_2 = 1$). In order to compute the log-likelihood function for this Least Squares estimation, the values for the coefficient for X and the constant term must be restricted to these values.

The **RESTRICT** Command

The **RESTRICT** option with the **OLS** command is used to set the coefficients to any values desired. The **RESTRICT** option requires the use of the **RESTRICT** and **END** commands. The general format for restricted Least Squares is:

OLS *depvar indeps /* **RESTRICT** *options*

RESTRICT *equation1*

RESTRICT *equation2*

...

END

> The **RESTRICT** option informs SHAZAM that the **RESTRICT** commands are to follow. More than one is allowed provided each is typed on a separate line. The *equation* is a linear function of the variables (that represent the coefficients) involved in the estimation. The **END** command marks the end of the list of **RESTRICT** commands.

Continuing with the above example, the following commands will estimate a restricted Least Squares model in which the coefficients for X and the constant term are restricted to being 1 and 3, respectively:

```
OLS Y X CONSTANT / RESTRICT
RESTRICT X=1
RESTRICT CONSTANT=3
END
```

The output follows.

```
|_OLS Y X / RESTRICT

 OLS ESTIMATION
        4 OBSERVATIONS       DEPENDENT VARIABLE = Y
|_RESTRICT X=1
|_RESTRICT CONSTANT=3
|_END

 R-SQUARE =  0.6316    R-SQUARE ADJUSTED =  0.7237
VARIANCE OF THE ESTIMATE =    3.5000
STANDARD ERROR OF THE ESTIMATE =    1.8708
MEAN OF DEPENDENT VARIABLE =    7.0000
LOG OF THE LIKELIHOOD FUNCTION = -8.18128

VARIABLE     ESTIMATED    STANDARD    T-RATIO     PARTIAL STANDARDIZED ELASTICITY
  NAME      COEFFICIENT    ERROR       4 DF        CORR.  COEFFICIENT  AT MEANS
X            1.0000     0.12071E-07  0.82841E+08 1.0000  0.60698      0.57143
CONSTANT     3.0000     0.68286E-07  0.43933E+08 1.0000  0.0          0.42857
```

Note, that the "STANDARD ERROR, T-RATIO, and PARTIAL CORRELATION" output does not have any useful interpretation in a model where the coefficients are restricted to exact values. In fact, the standard errors should theoretically be zero and the t-ratios should be infinity. SHAZAM results nearly show this. The remainder of the output can be used for the purposes below.

The value of the log-likelihood function of the restricted model (-8.18128) is lower than that of the unrestricted model (-7.90838) because the OLS estimates are Maximum Likelihood. That is, there can be no other set of coefficients specified which would yield a higher value of the log-likelihood function. In other words, it can be concluded that there is no better set of coefficients in the linear form of the model than those produced by OLS.

When comparing two regressions, it is often desirable to choose the one with the highest log-likelihood function. However, this comparison is only valid if both regressions have exactly the same form of the dependent variable. In particular, different formulas are used to compute the log of the likelihood function for regressions with different functional forms. This topic is discussed in more detail in Chapter 7. An example is provided in which the log-likelihood functions of four different models are compared. The models are linear, log-linear (the dependent variable is in logs), linear-log (the independent variables are in logs), and log-log (all variables are in logs).

SHAZAM commands and options used in Chapter 4

END
OLS *depvar indeps* / **RESTRICT**
PRINT *vars* / *options*
READ(*datafile*) *vars* / *options*
RESTRICT *coef=equation*
SAMPLE *beg end*

5 . TWO-VARIABLE REGRESSION INTERVAL ESTIMATION AND TESTING

This chapter shows how to estimate coefficient confidence intervals to test hypotheses about the coefficients. In addition, an example will show how to forecast and how to construct confidence intervals for the forecast. Finally, an analysis of the residuals will be performed.

In *Section 5.3*, Gujarati discusses confidence intervals for regression coefficients. Such confidence intervals can be constructed easily using the **CONFID** command.

The **CONFID** Command

SHAZAM can automatically compute **CONFID**ence intervals for any coefficient from a previous estimation with the **CONFID** command. In general, the **CONFID** command must be placed immediately after an estimation command (such as **OLS**). The general format is:

CONFID *coef1* *coef2* ... / *options*

where *coef1* and *coef2* are the names of the variables (representing the coefficients) and *options* is a list of available options.

When two coefficients are listed, the **CONFID** command will also print a **PLOT** of the confidence ellipse based on an **F**-distribution. (Gujarati discusses this topic in *Section 10.6*). The **NOFPLOT** is used to suppress the confidence ellipse from the output. Hence, the individual confidence intervals based on the t-distribution will be printed. Note that "**CONSTANT**" is used to specify the estimated coefficient for the constant term.

First, the **CONFID** command will be used to construct the confidence intervals (5.3.9) and (5.3.11). The "**?**" symbol will be used to suppress the **OLS** output previously presented in Chapter 3.

```
SAMPLE 1 10
READ(TABLE3.2) Y X
?OLS Y X
CONFID X CONSTANT / NOFPLOT
```

The output follows.

```
|_CONFID X CONSTANT / NOFPLOT
USING 95% AND 90% CONFIDENCE INTERVALS

CONFIDENCE INTERVALS BASED ON T-DISTRIBUTION WITH   8 D.F.
    - T CRITICAL VALUES =   2.306 AND   1.860
NAME    LOWER 2.5%    LOWER 5%    COEFFICENT    UPPER 5%    UPPER 2.5%    STD. ERROR
X          0.4267      0.4426      0.50909        0.5756      0.5915        0.036
CONSTANT   9.664       12.52       24.455         36.38       39.24         6.414
```

The lower and upper bounds for a 95% confidence interval are printed as "LOWER 2.5%" and "UPPER 2.5%." By default, SHAZAM prints both the 90% and 95% confidence intervals.

SHAZAM will now be used to construct the confidence intervals for the estimated coefficients and for the variance of the regression the "long way" (see *Sections 5.3* and *5.4*). Studying the command file below will help the user to understand what is involved in constructing confidence intervals.

The **COEF=** and **STDERR=** options on an **OLS** command store the vectors of the estimated **COEF**ficients and **ST**an**D**ard **ERR**ors in the variables specfied. The estimated constant term and its standard error are stored as the last elements of these vectors.

In the command file below, Temporary variables are used.

Temporary Variables

There are many temporary variables available on the **OLS** comand These variables contain useful statistics from the most recent regression command in the SHAZAM run. Note that all temporary variables begin with a **$**. Also, when a temporary variable is used in a **GEN1** or **GENR** command, its current value is printed.

The temporary variables **$DF** and **$SIG2** contain the degrees of freedom and the variance of the estimate (SIGMA**2)

```
?OLS Y X / COEF=BETAS STDERR=SE
PRINT BETAS SE
* Construct the 95% confidence intervals for the estimated coefficients. The
* 95% critical value for a two-sided t-distribution with 8 degrees of freedom
* is 2.306 (see Table D.2 in Appendix D). Since the vectors BETAS and SE are
* 2 observations long, change the SAMPLE range.
SAMPLE 1 2
GENR LOWER=BETAS-2.306*SE
GENR UPPER=BETAS+2.306*SE
PRINT LOWER BETAS UPPER
```

```
* Since the CONFID command does not do the calculations for the confidence
* interval for the variance of the estimate, construct a 95% confidence interval
* for the variance of the estimate (SIGMA**2).  The 95% critical values for a
* two-sided Chi-Square distribution with 8 degrees of freedom are 2.1797 and
* 17.5346 (see Table D.4).
GEN1 LOWSIG2=$DF*$SIG2/17.5346
GEN1 UPSIG2=$DF*$SIG2/2.1797
PRINT LOWSIG2 $SIG2 UPSIG2
```

The output (with the comment lines omitted) follows.

```
|_?OLS Y X / COEF=BETAS STDERR=SE
|_PRINT BETAS SE
   BETAS
 0.5090909        24.45455
   SE
 0.3574281E-01   6.413817
|_SAMPLE 1 2
|_GENR LOWER=BETAS-2.306*SE
|_GENR UPPER=BETAS+2.306*SE
|_PRINT LOWER BETAS UPPER
      LOWER           BETAS           UPPER
  0.4266680        0.5090909       0.5915138
   9.664283        24.45455        39.24481

|_GEN1 LOWSIG2=$DF*$SIG2/17.5346
..NOTE..CURRENT VALUE OF $DF  =     8.0000
..NOTE..CURRENT VALUE OF $SIG2=    42.159
|_GEN1 UPSIG2=$DF*$SIG2/2.1797
..NOTE..CURRENT VALUE OF $DF  =     8.0000
..NOTE..CURRENT VALUE OF $SIG2=    42.159
|_PRINT LOWSIG2 $SIG2 UPSIG2
   LOWSIG2
   19.23470
   $SIG2       42.15909
   UPSIG2
   154.7336
```

In *Section 5.7*, Gujarati tests the hypothesis that $\beta_2 = 0.3$. This can be done easily using the **TEST** command.

The **TEST** Command

The **TEST** command in SHAZAM is used for linear or nonlinear hypothesis testing on regression coefficients. Generally, the **TEST** command(s) must directly follow an estimation command. For a single hypothesis test, the general format is:

TEST *equation*

> where *equation* is an equation made up of combinations of variables (that represent the estimated coefficients) involved in the estimation. Each single hypothesis must be placed on a separate line.

The commands to test the hypothesis that $\beta_2 = 0.3$ are below. Recall that the sample range was set to observation 1 to 2. Hence, the **SAMPLE** command must be used to reset the sample to the full range of observations.

```
SAMPLE 1 10
?OLS Y X
TEST X=0.3
```

The output follows.

```
|_TEST X=.3
TEST VALUE =   0.20909      STD. ERROR OF TEST VALUE  0.35743E-01
T STATISTIC =   5.8498739     WITH    8 D.F.    P-VALUE= 0.00038
F STATISTIC =   34.221024     WITH    1 AND    8 D.F.  P-VALUE= 0.00038
WALD CHI-SQUARE STATISTIC =    34.221024     WITH    1 D.F.  P-VALUE= 0.00000
UPPER BOUND ON P-VALUE BY CHEBYCHEV INEQUALITY = 0.02922
```

The "T STATISTIC" above is identical to equation (5.7.4). Note, as well, that the p-value, the lowest significance level at which the null hypothesis can be rejected, is 0.038%.

The **ANOVA** option with the **OLS** command prints the **AN**alysis **O**f **VA**riance tables discussed in *Section 5.9*. Two F-Test statistics are provided. The "ANALYSIS OF VARIANCE - FROM MEAN" table from the **ANOVA** output includes an F-Test statistic (following equation (5.9.1)) testing if the slope coefficients are zero. This table corresponds to *Table 5.4* of the text. In addition, the "ANALYSIS OF VARIANCE - FROM ZERO" table provides an F-Test statistic testing the joint hypothesis that the slope coefficients and the intercept term are both equal to zero.

The pertinent output from the **ANOVA** option on the **OLS** command follows.

	ANALYSIS OF VARIANCE - FROM MEAN			
	SS	DF	MS	F
REGRESSION	8552.7	1.	8552.7	202.868
ERROR	337.27	8.	42.159	P-VALUE
TOTAL	8890.0	9.	987.78	0.000

	ANALYSIS OF VARIANCE - FROM ZERO			
	SS	DF	MS	F
REGRESSION	0.13176E+06	2.	65881.	1562.685
ERROR	337.27	8.	42.159	P-VALUE
TOTAL	0.13210E+06	10.	13210.	0.000

Section 5.10 of the text shows how to use regression coefficients for prediction. The following commands will construct the 95% confidence interval (5.10.5) for the true mean value of Y.

Note that the **SQRT(x)** function with the **GEN1** (or **GENR**) command computes the **SQ**uare **R**oo**T** of the number or variable inside the parentheses. As well, the temporary variable **$N**, representing the number of observations used in the estimation, will be used.

```
?STAT X / MEAN=M CPDEV=SLX
PRINT M SLX
GEN1 YHAT=BETA2+BETA1*100
GEN1 VARYHAT=$SIG2*(1/$N+((100-M)**2)/SLX)
GEN1 SEYHAT=SQRT(VARYHAT)
PRINT YHAT VARYHAT SEYHAT
GEN1 LOWERF=YHAT-2.306*SEYHAT
GEN1 UPPERF=YHAT+2.306*SEYHAT
PRINT LOWERF UPPERF
```

The output follows.

```
|_?STAT X / MEAN=M CPDEV=SLX
|_PRINT M SLX
    M
  170.0000
    SLX
  33000.00
|_GEN1 YHAT=BETAS(2)+BETAS(1)*100
|_GEN1 VARYHAT=$SIG2*(1/$N+((100-M)**2)/SLX)
..NOTE..CURRENT VALUE OF $SIG2=    42.159
..NOTE..CURRENT VALUE OF $N   =    10.000
|_GEN1 SEYHAT=SQRT(VARYHAT)
|_PRINT YHAT VARYHAT SEYHAT
    YHAT
   75.36364
    VARYHAT
   10.47590
    SEYHAT
   3.236649
|_GEN1 LOWERF=YHAT-2.306*SEYHAT
|_GEN1 UPPERF=YHAT+2.306*SEYHAT
|_PRINT LOWERF UPPERF
    LOWERF
   67.89992
    UPPERF
   82.82735
```

Section 5.10 also shows how to construct a confidence interval for an individual prediction. The commands below construct the 95% confidence interval (5.10.7) corresponding to $X_0 = 100$.

```
GEN1 VARY0=$SIG2*(1+1/$N+(100-M)**2/SLX)
GEN1 SEYHAT0=SQRT(VARY0)
GEN1 LOWF0=YHAT-2.306*SEYHAT0
GEN1 UPF0=YHAT+2.306*SEYHAT0
PRINT LOWF0 UPF0 SEYHAT0 VARY0
```

The output (with the printed current values of **$SIG2** and **$N** omitted) follows.

```
_GEN1 VARY0=$SIG2*(1+1/$N+(100-M)**2/SLX)
_GEN1 SEYHAT0=SQRT(VARY0)
_GEN1 LOWF0=YHAT-2.306*SEYHAT0
_GEN1 UPF0=YHAT+2.306*SEYHAT0
_PRINT LOWF0 UPF0 SEYHAT0 VARY0
   LOWF0
  58.63361
   UPF0
  92.09366
   SEYHAT0
  7.254997
   VARY0
  52.63499
```

The above prediction, or forecast, was performed the "long way". The **FC** command can be used to generate forecasts. This command will be demonstrated in Chapter 8.

In *Section 5.12*, the text discusses methods for testing the assumption that the disturbances, u_t , are normally distributed. The Jarque-Bera Lagrange Multiplier Test and a **G**oodness of Fit Test are performed using the data from the current example. These tests are performed by SHAZAM when the **LM** and **GF** options are used. Note that either the **LIST**, **RSTAT**, or **MAX** option must be used with the **GF** option.

When the **GF** option is specified, SHAZAM prints the **G**oodness of Fit Test for normality in the residuals. The residuals are ranked and put into several groups. The number of groups is automatically set by SHAZAM based on the sample size. In the output, the line beginning with "EXPECTED" contains the number of residuals that would be in each group if a perfectly normal distribution were achieved. A Chi-square test statistic (see equation (5.13.1)) is constructed to test whether the difference between the number of expected and observed is statistically significant. If the value is above the critical value for a Chi-square statistic (see *Table 4.D* in *Appendix D* for critical values), the normality assumption can be rejected.

As well, with the **GF** option, the coefficient of skewness and the coefficient of excess kurtosis are printed. A normal distribution is symmetric, neither skewed to the right nor left. If the coefficient of skewness is positive, the distribution is skewed to the right and, if negative, skewed to the left. The coefficient of excess kurtosis measures whether the distribution of the residuals has the regular bell-shaped curve of a normal distribution. A negative value indicates a relatively flatter distribution while a positive value indicates a more concentrated peaked distribution. If these test statistics are not statistically different from zero, then it can be concluded that the residuals do not exhibit skewness and/or excess kurtosis. The rule of thumb is that the test statistic must be more than two standard deviations from zero to allow for the conclusion that the residuals are either skewed and/or exhibit excess kurtosis.

The **LM** option gives the Jarque-Bera Lagrange Multiplier test for normality of the residuals (see equation (5.13.2)). If the test statistic exceeds the critical value for a Chi-square distribution with 2 degrees of freedom, there exists evidence for non-normal residuals.

```
OLS Y X / RSTAT LM GF
```

The pertinent output follows.

```
COEFFICIENT OF SKEWNESS =  -0.4724 WITH STANDARD DEVIATION OF 0.6870
COEFFICIENT OF EXCESS KURTOSIS =  -0.9963 WITH STANDARD DEVIATION OF 1.3342
     GOODNESS OF FIT TEST FOR NORMALITY OF RESIDUALS -  6 GROUPS
OBSERVED  0.0  2.0  3.0  4.0  1.0  0.0
EXPECTED  0.2  1.4  3.4  3.4  1.4  0.2
CHI-SQUARE =    1.0041 WITH  2 DEGREES OF FREEDOM
JARQUE-BERA ASYMPTOTIC LM NORMALITY TEST
CHI-SQUARE =    0.7769 WITH  2 DEGREES OF FREEDOM
```

SHAZAM commands and options used in Chapter 5

CONFID *coef1 coef2 ...* / **NOFPLOT**

GEN1 *newvar=equation*   with **SQRT(x)**

GENR *newvar=equation*

OLS *depvar indeps* / **COEF= STDERR= ANOVA GF LM**

PRINT *vars*

READ (*datafilename*) *vars* / *options*

SAMPLE *beg end*

STAT *vars* / **MEAN= CPDEV=**

TEST *equation*

Temporary variables used

$DF	Degrees of Freedom
$N	Number of obsevations in the estimation
$SIG2	Variance of the Estimate - SIGMA**2

6. EXTENSIONS OF THE TWO-VARIABLE LINEAR REGRESSION MODEL

Chapter 6 introduces various aspects of linear regression analysis using the two-variable regression model. The topics considered include regression through the origin, the question of units of measurement, and the functional form of the linear regression model.

Section 6.1 discusses regressions through the origin. The **NOCONSTANT** option with an estimation command (such as **OLS**) is used to suppress the constant term in the regression or when the user is supplying the constant. When the **NOCONSTANT** option is used, the Raw-Moment R^2 (see equation (6.1.9)) is printed.

The example below will be used to introduce the **TIME** command. This command provides a convenient way of specifying **SAMPLE** ranges when using time series data.

The **TIME** Command

The **TIME** command specifies the beginning year and frequency of the data for a time series so that an alternate form of the **SAMPLE** command can be used. The format is:

TIME *beg freq*

where *beg* is the beginning year and *freq* is the frequency of the data (for example, use 1 for annual data, 4 for quarterly data, and 12 for monthly data).

Note that, when using the **TIME** command, a dot "." must be included when specifying the **SAMPLE** range. For example, the first quarter of 1975 to the third quarter of 1990 would be specified as:

```
TIME 1975 4
SAMPLE 1975.1 1990.3
```

If annual data is used (as below), a zero must follow the dot.

The following commands will estimate the model and construct the confidence intervals found in the example in *Section 6.1*:

```
TIME 1971 1
SAMPLE 1971.0 1980.0
READ(TABLE6.1) YEAR Y X
OLS Y X / NOCONSTANT
* Construct the confidence interval for the estimated coefficient for X.
CONFID X
* Now estimate the model with a constant term.
OLS Y X
* Construct the confidence interval for the estimated coefficient for X
* from the model including a constant.
CONFID X
```

The output follows.

```
|_TIME 1971 1
|_SAMPLE 1971.0 1980.0
|_READ(TABLE6.1) YEAR Y X
   3 VARIABLES AND        10 OBSERVATIONS STARTING AT OBS        1

|_OLS Y X / NOCONSTANT

 OLS ESTIMATION
      10 OBSERVATIONS      DEPENDENT VARIABLE = Y
...NOTE..SAMPLE RANGE SET TO:    1,    10

 R-SQUARE =   0.7146     R-SQUARE ADJUSTED =    0.7146
VARIANCE OF THE ESTIMATE-SIGMA**2 =   381.91
STANDARD ERROR OF THE ESTIMATE-SIGMA =   19.542
SUM OF SQUARED ERRORS-SSE=   3437.1
MEAN OF DEPENDENT VARIABLE =   19.390
LOG OF THE LIKELIHOOD FUNCTION = -43.3884
RAW MOMENT R-SQUARE =   0.7825

VARIABLE    ESTIMATED   STANDARD   T-RATIO        PARTIAL STANDARDIZED ELASTICITY
  NAME      COEFFICIENT   ERROR      9 DF    P-VALUE CORR. COEFFICIENT  AT MEANS
X            1.0899      0.1916     5.690     0.000 0.885     0.8624      0.9522
|_* Construct the confidence interval for the estimated coefficient for X.
|_CONFID X
USING 95% AND 90% CONFIDENCE INTERVALS
CONFIDENCE INTERVALS BASED ON T-DISTRIBUTION WITH   9 D.F.
     - T CRITICAL VALUES =   2.262 AND    1.833
NAME    LOWER 2.5%   LOWER 5%    COEFFICENT    UPPER 5%    UPPER 2.5%    STD. ERROR
X          0.6566       0.7388      1.0899        1.441       1.523        0.192
|_* Now estimate the model with a constant term.
|_OLS Y X

 OLS ESTIMATION
      10 OBSERVATIONS      DEPENDENT VARIABLE = Y
...NOTE..SAMPLE RANGE SET TO:    1,    10

 R-SQUARE =   0.7155     R-SQUARE ADJUSTED =    0.6800
VARIANCE OF THE ESTIMATE-SIGMA**2 =   428.16
STANDARD ERROR OF THE ESTIMATE-SIGMA =   20.692
SUM OF SQUARED ERRORS-SSE=   3425.3
MEAN OF DEPENDENT VARIABLE =   19.390
```

```
LOG OF THE LIKELIHOOD FUNCTION = -43.3712

VARIABLE    ESTIMATED    STANDARD    T-RATIO          PARTIAL STANDARDIZED ELASTICITY
  NAME     COEFFICIENT    ERROR       8 DF    P-VALUE CORR.  COEFFICIENT  AT MEANS
X            1.0691       0.2383       4.486    0.002  0.846    0.8459      0.9340
CONSTANT     1.2797       7.689        0.1664   0.872  0.059    0.0000      0.0660
|_* Construct the confidence interval for the estimated coefficient for X
|_* from the model including a constant.
|_CONFID X
USING 95% AND 90% CONFIDENCE INTERVALS
CONFIDENCE INTERVALS BASED ON T-DISTRIBUTION WITH   8 D.F.
      - T CRITICAL VALUES =    2.306 AND    1.860
NAME    LOWER 2.5%    LOWER 5%    COEFFICENT    UPPER 5%    UPPER 2.5%    STD. ERROR
X          0.5195       0.6258       1.0691       1.512       1.619        0.238
```

In *Section 6.2*, Gujarati provides a numerical example in which the units of measurement for the dependent and independent variables are scaled. The commands below will replicate this example. Note that only columns 1, 2, and 4 are included in the data file *TABLE6.2*. The scaled variables in columns 3 and 5 of *Table 6.2* will be created using the **GENR** command.

```
TIME 1974 1
SAMPLE 1974.0 1983.0
READ (TABLE6.2) YEAR GPDIBILL GNPBILL
GENR GPDIMILL=GPDIBILL*1000
GENR GNPMILL=GNPBILL*1000
PRINT YEAR GPDIBILL GPDIMILL
PRINT YEAR GNPBILL GNPMILL
* Estimate the model (6.2.21) using the data in billions of dollars.
OLS GPDIBILL GNPBILL
* Estimate the model (6.2.22) using the data in millions of dollars.
OLS GPDIMILL GNPMILL
* Estimate the model (6.2.23) using the GDPI data in billions of dollars and
* the GNP data in millions of dollars.
OLS GPDIBILL GNPMILL
* Estimate the model (6.2.24) using the GDPI data in millions of dollars and
* the GNP data in billions of dollars.
OLS GPDIMILL GNPBILL
```

The output follows.

```
|_PRINT YEAR GPDIBILL GPDIMILL
    YEAR          GPDIBILL         GPDIMILL
  1974.000       195.5000         195500.0
  1975.000       154.8000         154800.0
  1976.000       184.5000         184500.0
  1977.000       214.2000         214200.0
  1978.000       236.7000         236700.0
  1979.000       236.3000         236300.0
  1980.000       208.5000         208500.0
  1981.000       230.9000         230900.0
  1982.000       194.3000         194300.0
  1983.000       221.0000         221000.0
```

```
|_PRINT YEAR GNPBILL GNPMILL
     YEAR            GNPBILL            GNPMILL
  1974.000         1246.300          1246300.
  1975.000         1231.600          1231600.
  1976.000         1298.200          1298200.
  1977.000         1369.700          1369700.
  1978.000         1438.600          1438600.
  1979.000         1479.400          1479400.
  1980.000         1475.000          1475000.
  1981.000         1512.200          1512200.
  1982.000         1480.000          1480000.
  1983.000         1534.700          1534700.
|_* Estimate the model (6.2.21) using the data in billions of dollars.

|_OLS GPDIBILL GNPBILL

OLS ESTIMATION
      10 OBSERVATIONS     DEPENDENT VARIABLE = GPDIBILL
...NOTE..SAMPLE RANGE SET TO:    1,    10


 R-SQUARE =   0.5641     R-SQUARE ADJUSTED =    0.5096
VARIANCE OF THE ESTIMATE-SIGMA**2 =    331.40
STANDARD ERROR OF THE ESTIMATE-SIGMA =    18.204
SUM OF SQUARED ERRORS-SSE=   2651.2
MEAN OF DEPENDENT VARIABLE =    207.67
LOG OF THE LIKELIHOOD FUNCTION = -42.0903


VARIABLE    ESTIMATED   STANDARD   T-RATIO          PARTIAL STANDARDIZED ELASTICITY
  NAME      COEFFICIENT   ERROR      8 DF   P-VALUE CORR. COEFFICIENT  AT MEANS
GNPBILL      0.17395    0.5406E-01   3.218     0.012 0.751      0.7511     1.1782
CONSTANT    -37.002      76.26      -0.4852    0.641-0.169      0.0000    -0.1782
|_* Estimate the model (6.2.22) using the data in millions of dollars.

|_OLS GPDIMILL GNPMILL

OLS ESTIMATION
      10 OBSERVATIONS     DEPENDENT VARIABLE = GPDIMILL
...NOTE..SAMPLE RANGE SET TO:    1,    10


 R-SQUARE =   0.5641     R-SQUARE ADJUSTED =    0.5096
VARIANCE OF THE ESTIMATE-SIGMA**2 =   0.33140E+09
STANDARD ERROR OF THE ESTIMATE-SIGMA =    18204.
SUM OF SQUARED ERRORS-SSE=  0.26512E+10
MEAN OF DEPENDENT VARIABLE =   0.20767E+06
LOG OF THE LIKELIHOOD FUNCTION = -111.168


VARIABLE    ESTIMATED   STANDARD   T-RATIO          PARTIAL STANDARDIZED ELASTICITY
  NAME      COEFFICIENT   ERROR      8 DF   P-VALUE CORR. COEFFICIENT  AT MEANS
GNPMILL      0.17395    0.5406E-01   3.218     0.012 0.751      0.7511     1.1782
CONSTANT    -37002.     0.7626E+05  -0.4852    0.641-0.169      0.0000    -0.1782
|_* Estimate the model (6.2.23) using the GDPI data in billions of dollars and
|_* the GNP data in millions of dollars.

|_OLS GPDIBILL GNPMILL

OLS ESTIMATION
      10 OBSERVATIONS     DEPENDENT VARIABLE = GPDIBILL
...NOTE..SAMPLE RANGE SET TO:    1,    10
```

```
R-SQUARE =   0.5641     R-SQUARE ADJUSTED =    0.5096
VARIANCE OF THE ESTIMATE-SIGMA**2 =    331.40
STANDARD ERROR OF THE ESTIMATE-SIGMA =   18.204
SUM OF SQUARED ERRORS-SSE=   2651.2
MEAN OF DEPENDENT VARIABLE =    207.67
LOG OF THE LIKELIHOOD FUNCTION = -42.0903


VARIABLE    ESTIMATED  STANDARD   T-RATIO       PARTIAL STANDARDIZED ELASTICITY
  NAME      COEFFICIENT  ERROR       8 DF   P-VALUE CORR. COEFFICIENT  AT MEANS
GNPMILL    0.17395E-03 0.5406E-04   3.218    0.012 0.751     0.7511     1.1782
CONSTANT   -37.002      76.26      -0.4852   0.641-0.169     0.0000    -0.1782
|_* Estimate the model (6.2.24) using the GDPI data in millions of dollars and
|_* the GNP data in billions of dollars.

|_OLS GPDIMILL GNPBILL

 OLS ESTIMATION
      10 OBSERVATIONS     DEPENDENT VARIABLE = GPDIMILL
...NOTE..SAMPLE RANGE SET TO:    1,   10


 R-SQUARE =   0.5641     R-SQUARE ADJUSTED =    0.5096
VARIANCE OF THE ESTIMATE-SIGMA**2 =   0.33140E+09
STANDARD ERROR OF THE ESTIMATE-SIGMA =    18204.
SUM OF SQUARED ERRORS-SSE=  0.26512E+10
MEAN OF DEPENDENT VARIABLE =   0.20767E+06
LOG OF THE LIKELIHOOD FUNCTION = -111.168


VARIABLE    ESTIMATED  STANDARD   T-RATIO       PARTIAL STANDARDIZED ELASTICITY
  NAME      COEFFICIENT  ERROR       8 DF   P-VALUE CORR. COEFFICIENT  AT MEANS
GNPBILL    173.95       54.06       3.218    0.012 0.751     0.7511     1.1782
CONSTANT   -37002.    0.7626E+05  -0.4852   0.641-0.169     0.0000    -0.1782
```

In *Sections 6.4* to *6.6,* Gujarati discusses how elasticities are measured in models where the dependent and independent variables are either both in logs or one is in levels while the other is in logs. *Table 6.5* summarizes the formulas involved. The following options with the **OLS** command are used to compute the elasticities for the various functional forms using these formulas:

Linear (at means)	no option is needed
Log-log	**LOGLOG**
Log-lin (at means of *indeps*)	**LOGLIN**
Lin-log (at means of *depvar*)	**LINLOG**

Note that the formula for the log-likelihood function for the **LOGLOG** and **LOGLIN** models is different than the one used for the linear and **LINLOG** models discussed in *Chapter 4* (see equation (5) in *Appendix 4A*). The **LOGLOG** and **LOGLIN** options compute the log-likelihood functions using the following formula:

$$-\frac{N}{2}\ln\left(2\pi\tilde{\sigma}^2\right)-\frac{N}{2}+\sum_{t=1}^{N}\ln Y_t \quad \text{where} \quad \tilde{\sigma}^2 = \frac{1}{N}\sum_{t=1}^{N}e_t^2$$

The **LOG(x)** function with the **GENR** command is used to take natural logs. Similarly, the **EXP(x)** function with the **GENR** command generates antilogs.

The coffee consumption example in *Section 6.4* is estimated in double log form. As mentioned above, since both the dependent and independent variables are in logs, the **LOGLOG** option must be used in order to compute the correct elasticities (and log-likelihood function).

```
TIME 1970 1
SAMPLE 1970.0 1980.0
READ(TABLE3.4) YEAR Y X
GENR LNY=LOG(Y)
GENR LNX=LOG(X)
OLS LNY LNX / LOGLOG
```

As the output will show, the elasticities are identical to the estimated coefficients.

```
|_OLS LNY LNX / LOGLOG

  OLS ESTIMATION
        11 OBSERVATIONS        DEPENDENT VARIABLE = LNY
...NOTE..SAMPLE RANGE SET TO:    1,    11
   R-SQUARE =   0.7448     R-SQUARE ADJUSTED =    0.7164
VARIANCE OF THE ESTIMATE-SIGMA**2 =  0.25148E-02
STANDARD ERROR OF THE ESTIMATE-SIGMA =  0.50148E-01
SUM OF SQUARED ERRORS-SSE= 0.22633E-01
MEAN OF DEPENDENT VARIABLE =  0.78728
LOG OF THE LIKELIHOOD FUNCTION(IF DEPVAR LOG) =  9.75588


VARIABLE    ESTIMATED   STANDARD   T-RATIO          PARTIAL STANDARDIZED ELASTICITY
  NAME      COEFFICIENT   ERROR       9 DF    P-VALUE CORR. COEFFICIENT  AT MEANS
LNX        -0.25305    0.4937E-01  -5.125    0.001-0.863    -0.8630      -0.2530
CONSTANT    0.77742    0.1524E-01   51.00    0.000 0.998     0.0000       0.7774
```

In the real GDP example from *Section 6.5*, the dependent variable is in logs and the independent variable is in levels. Hence, the **LOGLIN** option should be used.

In this model, a time trend, T, is included as an independent variable. The **TIME(x)** function with the **GENR** command creates a time index starting at x+1. Although using the *YEAR* variable would provide the same results (try it), the **TIME(x)** function will be demonstrated. Note that, if the *YEAR* variable did not exist, the command

```
GENR YEAR=TIME(1970)
```

would generate a variable which increases in increments of 1, starting at 1971 and ending at the end of the **SAMPLE** range.

The data for this example is found in the data file *EXER322.DAT*.

```
TIME 1972 1
SAMPLE 1972.0 1991.0
READ(EXER322.DAT) YEAR NOMGDP REALGDP
GENR T=TIME(0)
PRINT YEAR NOMGDP REALGDP T
GENR LNRGDP=LOG(REALGDP)
OLS LNRGDP T / COEF=COEF LOGLIN
PLOT LNRGDP T
GEN1 YHAT0=EXP(COEF(2))
GEN1 INSTANTR=COEF(1)*100
GEN1 COMPRATE=(EXP(COEF(1)-1))*100
PRINT YHAT0 INSTANTR COMPRATE
OLS REALGDP T
```

The output, including a plot replicating *Figure 6.4*, follows.

```
|_PRINT YEAR NOMGDP REALGDP T
      YEAR             NOMGDP           REALGDP            T
   1972.000          1207.000          3107.100        1.000000
   1973.000          1349.600          3268.600        2.000000
   1974.000          1458.600          3248.100        3.000000
   1975.000          1585.900          3221.700        4.000000
   1976.000          1768.400          3380.800        5.000000
   1977.000          1974.100          3533.300        6.000000
   1978.000          2232.700          3703.500        7.000000
   1979.000          2488.600          3796.800        8.000000
   1980.000          2708.000          3776.300        9.000000
   1981.000          3030.600          3843.100        10.00000
   1982.000          3149.600          3760.300        11.00000
   1983.000          3405.000          3906.600        12.00000
   1984.000          3777.200          4148.500        13.00000
   1985.000          4038.700          4279.800        14.00000
   1986.000          4268.600          4404.500        15.00000
   1987.000          4539.900          4539.900        16.00000
   1988.000          4900.400          4718.600        17.00000
   1989.000          5250.800          4838.000        18.00000
   1990.000          5522.200          4877.500        19.00000
   1991.000          5677.500          4821.000        20.00000
|_GENR LNRGDP=LOG(REALGDP)
|_OLS LNRGDP T / COEF=COEF LOGLIN

OLS ESTIMATION
      20 OBSERVATIONS        DEPENDENT VARIABLE = LNRGDP
...NOTE..SAMPLE RANGE SET TO:     1,    20

 R-SQUARE =   0.9738     R-SQUARE ADJUSTED =    0.9723
VARIANCE OF THE ESTIMATE-SIGMA**2 =   0.60644E-03
STANDARD ERROR OF THE ESTIMATE-SIGMA =   0.24626E-01
SUM OF SQUARED ERRORS-SSE=   0.10916E-01
```

```
MEAN OF DEPENDENT VARIABLE =    8.2732
LOG OF THE LIKELIHOOD FUNCTION(IF DEPVAR LOG) = -118.711
```

VARIABLE NAME	ESTIMATED COEFFICIENT	STANDARD ERROR	T-RATIO 18 DF	P-VALUE	PARTIAL CORR.	STANDARDIZED COEFFICIENT	ELASTICITY AT MEANS
T	0.24699E-01	0.9550E-03	25.86	0.000	0.987	0.9868	0.2593
CONSTANT	8.0139	0.1144E-01	700.5	0.000	1.000	0.0000	8.0139

```
|_PLOT LNRGDP T
      20 OBSERVATIONS
                       *=LNRGDP
                       M=MULTIPLE POINT
    8.5000        |
    8.4737        |                                      *  *  *
    8.4474        |                                   *
    8.4211        |
    8.3947        |                                *
    8.3684        |                             *
    8.3421        |                          *
    8.3158        |                       *
    8.2895        |
    8.2632        |                    *
    8.2368        |           *     *
    8.2105        |        *     *     *
    8.1842        |
    8.1579        |      *
    8.1316        |
    8.1053        |    *
    8.0789        |   *  *
    8.0526        |     *
    8.0263        | *
    8.0000        |
                  |_____
             0.000    5.000   10.000   15.000   20.000
                              T
|_GEN1 YHAT0=EXP(COEF:2)
|_GEN1 INSTANTR=COEF:1*100
|_GEN1 COMPRATE=(EXP(COEF:1)-1)*100
|_PRINT YHAT0 INSTANTR COMPRATE
   YHAT0
  3022.693
   INSTANTR
  2.469928
   COMPRATE
  2.500684

|_OLS REALGDP T

 OLS ESTIMATION
      20 OBSERVATIONS     DEPENDENT VARIABLE = REALGDP
...NOTE..SAMPLE RANGE SET TO:    1,   20


 R-SQUARE =   0.9674    R-SQUARE ADJUSTED =   0.9656
VARIANCE OF THE ESTIMATE-SIGMA**2 =   11861.
STANDARD ERROR OF THE ESTIMATE-SIGMA =   108.91
SUM OF SQUARED ERRORS-SSE=  0.21350E+06
MEAN OF DEPENDENT VARIABLE =   3958.7
LOG OF THE LIKELIHOOD FUNCTION = -121.135
```

VARIABLE NAME	ESTIMATED COEFFICIENT	STANDARD ERROR	T-RATIO 18 DF	P-VALUE	PARTIAL CORR.	STANDARDIZED COEFFICIENT	ELASTICITY AT MEANS
T	97.681	4.223	23.13	0.000	0.984	0.9836	0.2591
CONSTANT	2933.1	50.59	57.98	0.000	0.997	0.0000	0.7409

In the GNP-money supply example from *Section 6.5*, the dependent variable is in levels while the independent variable is in logs. Hence, the **LINLOG** option should be specified so that the correct formula is used when the elasticities at the means are computed.

The following commands will replicate the regression results from the GDP-money supply example.

```
TIME 1973 1
SAMPLE 1973.0 1987.0
READ(TABLE6.3) YEAR Y X
GENR LNX=LOG(X)
OLS Y LNX / LINLOG
```

The pertinent output follows.

```
|_OLS Y LNX / LINLOG

OLS ESTIMATION
     15 OBSERVATIONS     DEPENDENT VARIABLE = Y
...NOTE..SAMPLE RANGE SET TO:    1,   15

 R-SQUARE =   0.9831    R-SQUARE ADJUSTED =    0.9818
VARIANCE OF THE ESTIMATE-SIGMA**2 =    20047.
STANDARD ERROR OF THE ESTIMATE-SIGMA =    141.59
SUM OF SQUARED ERRORS-SSE=  0.26061E+06
MEAN OF DEPENDENT VARIABLE =    2790.9
LOG OF THE LIKELIHOOD FUNCTION = -94.5046
```

VARIABLE NAME	ESTIMATED COEFFICIENT	STANDARD ERROR	T-RATIO 13 DF	P-VALUE	PARTIAL CORR.	STANDARDIZED COEFFICIENT	ELASTICITY AT MEANS
LNX	2584.8	94.04	27.49	0.000	0.992	0.9915	0.9262
CONSTANT	-16329.	696.6	-23.44	0.000	-0.988	0.0000	-5.8509

For the *Illustrative Example* in *Section 6.6*, the output provided (6.6.2) includes an F-statistic testing the hypothesis that the slope coefficients are jointly equal to zero. Recall that this test statistic is printed when the **ANOVA** option with the **OLS** command is used. This F-statisitic is available following an **OLS** command, even without the **ANOVA** option, in the temporary variable $ANF. In this case, since there is only one slope coefficient, the F-statistic is equivalent to the square of the t-ratio (which tests that the coefficient for the *INVX* variable is zero). The commands below will verify this.

The **TRATIO=** option with an estimation command (such as **OLS**) stores the vector of **T-RATIO**s in the variable specified. As is the case with similar options, the t-ratio for the constant term is stored as the last element of the vector.

```
TIME 1950 1
SAMPLE 1950.0 1966.0
READ(TABLE6.4) YEAR Y X
GENR INVX=1/X
OLS Y INVX / TRATIO=TSTAT
* Compare the F-Statistic with the squared t-ratio of the slope coefficient.
GEN1 TSTAT2=TSTAT(1)**2
PRINT $ANF TSTAT2
```

The output follows.

```
|_OLS Y INVX / TRATIO=TSTAT

 OLS ESTIMATION
      17 OBSERVATIONS      DEPENDENT VARIABLE = Y
...NOTE..SAMPLE RANGE SET TO:    1,   17


 R-SQUARE =   0.3849    R-SQUARE ADJUSTED =   0.3439
VARIANCE OF THE ESTIMATE-SIGMA**2 =   2.6695
STANDARD ERROR OF THE ESTIMATE-SIGMA =  .1.6339
SUM OF SQUARED ERRORS-SSE=   40.043
MEAN OF DEPENDENT VARIABLE =   4.7882
LOG OF THE LIKELIHOOD FUNCTION = -31.4042

VARIABLE    ESTIMATED   STANDARD   T-RATIO         PARTIAL STANDARDIZED ELASTICITY
  NAME      COEFFICIENT   ERROR      15 DF   P-VALUE CORR. COEFFICIENT  AT MEANS
INVX         8.7243      2.848       3.064   0.008 0.620     0.6204      1.2983
CONSTANT    -1.4282      2.067      -0.6908  0.500-0.176     0.0000     -0.2983
|_* Compare the F-Statistic with the squared t-ratio of the slope coefficient.
|_GEN1 TSTAT2=TSTAT(1)**2
|_PRINT $ANF TSTAT2
    $ANF        9.385404
    TSTAT2
   9.385404
```

SHAZAM commands and options used in Chapter 6

CONFID *coef1 coef2 ... / options*

GEN1 *newvar=equation*

GENR *newvar=equation*   with **LOG**(x) **EXP**(x) **TIME**(x)

OLS *depvar indeps* / **NOCONSTANT COEF= TRATIO= LINLOG
LOGLOG LOGLIN ANOVA**

PLOT *depvar indeps* / *options*

PRINT *vars* / *options*

READ (*datafilename*) *vars* / *options*

SAMPLE *beg end*

STOP

TIME *beg freq*

Temporary variables used

$ANF   **ANOVA F**-Statistic

7. MULTIPLE REGRESSION ANALYSIS: THE PROBLEM OF ESTIMATION

Example 1 from *Section 7.6* is the first empirical example of a multiple regression provided in the text. First, the **OLS** command will be used to estimate this model. Second, the formulas discussed in the previous sections of the chapter will be used to estimate the model the "long way". While this procedure is not necessary since the **OLS** command is easier and faster, the method does illustrate the computations involved and verifies the output from the **OLS** command.

A new option, the **PCOR** option with the **STAT** command, will be used in the command file below. It Prints a **COR**relation matrix of the variables listed. The **COR=** option stores this matrix in the variable specified.

Occasionally, SHAZAM commands need to be longer than 80 columns. An ampersand (&) is used to continue a SHAZAM command line. For example, if a long equation were given on a **GENR** command, it could be continued onto the following line. The following example is taken from the commands below.

```
GEN1 VARB1=((1/13)+(X2BAR**2*SIGX3X3+X3BAR**2*SIGX2X2-2*X2BAR*X3BAR*SIGX2X3) &
/(SIGX2X2*SIGX3X3-SIGX2X3**2))*SIG2
```

SHAZAM will remove the & from the equation and put the two pieces together. The maximum length of a command including continuation lines is 4096 characters.

The following commands will replicate the results for *Example 7.1*. Note that, since this example carries over to *Section 7.7*, the **STOP** command is omitted.

```
TIME 1970 1
SAMPLE 1970.0 1982.0
READ (TABLE7.1) YEAR Y X2 X3
* Estimate the model "the easy way".
OLS Y X2 X3 / PCOV
* Now use the formulas from Section 7.4.
STAT Y X2 X3 / PCPDEV CPDEV=DEV MEAN=M
* Extract elements from the crossproduct matrix of variables listed in
* deviations from the means.
MATRIX SIGYX2=DEV(2,1)
MATRIX SIGX3X3=DEV(3,3)
MATRIX SIGYX3=DEV(3,1)
MATRIX SIGX2X3=DEV(3,2)
MATRIX SIGX2X2=DEV(2,2)
MATRIX SIGYY=DEV(1,1)
* Now estimate BETA2 using Equation (7.4.7).
GEN1 BETA2=(SIGYX2*SIGX3X3-SIGYX3*SIGX2X3)/(SIGX2X2*SIGX3X3-SIGX2X3**2)
* Estimate BETA3 using Equation (7.4.8).
GEN1 BETA3=(SIGYX3*SIGX2X2-SIGYX2*SIGX2X3)/(SIGX3X3*SIGX2X2-SIGX2X3**2)
* Estimate BETA1, the constant term.
```

```
GEN1 YBAR=M(1)
GEN1 X2BAR=M(2)
GEN1 X3BAR=M(3)
GEN1 BETA1=YBAR-BETA2*X2BAR-BETA3*X3BAR
PRINT BETA1 BETA2 BETA3
* Estimate the Regression variance, SIGMA**2, using formula (7.4.18).
GENR CONSTANT=1
GENR E=Y-(BETA1*CONSTANT+BETA2*X2+BETA3*X3)
GENR E2=E**2
?STAT E2 / SUMS=SSE
GEN1 SIG2=SSE/(13-3)
PRINT SSE SIG2
* Now compute the variances and standard errors of BETA2 using (7.4.11),
* of BETA3 using (7.4.14), and of BETA1 using (7.4.9).
GEN1 VARB2=(SIGX3X3/(SIGX2X2*SIGX3X3-SIGX2X3**2))*SIG2
GEN1 SEB2=SQRT(VARB2)
GEN1 VARB3=(SIGX2X2/(SIGX2X2*SIGX3X3-SIGX2X3**2))*SIG2
GEN1 SEB3=SQRT(VARB3)
GEN1 VARB1=((1/13)+(X2BAR**2*SIGX3X3+X3BAR**2*SIGX2X2-2*X2BAR*X3BAR*SIGX2X3) &
/(SIGX2X2*SIGX3X3-SIGX2X3**2))*SIG2
GEN1 SEB1=SQRT(VARB1)
PRINT VARB2 SEB2 VARB3 SEB3 VARB1 SEB1
* Use (7.4.17) to compute the covariance between BETA2 and BETA3.
?STAT X2 X3 / PCOR COR=CORMAT
MATRIX R23=CORMAT(1,2)
GEN1 COVB2B3=-R23*SIG2/((1-R23**2)*SQRT(SIGX2X2)*SQRT(SIGX3X3))
PRINT COVB2B3
* Now compute the R-square statistic using Equation (7.5.5).
GEN1 R2=(BETA2*SIGYX2+BETA3*SIGYX3)/SIGYY
PRINT R2
```

The output follows.

```
|_TIME 1970 1
|_SAMPLE 1970.0 1982.0
|_READ (TABLE7.1) YEAR Y X2 X3
   4 VARIABLES AND          13 OBSERVATIONS STARTING AT OBS          1
||_* Estimate the model "the easy way".
|_OLS Y X2 X3 / PCOV

 OLS ESTIMATION
      13 OBSERVATIONS        DEPENDENT VARIABLE = Y
...NOTE..SAMPLE RANGE SET TO:     1,    13


 R-SQUARE =   0.8766     R-SQUARE ADJUSTED =   0.8519
VARIANCE OF THE ESTIMATE-SIGMA**2 =   1.3703
STANDARD ERROR OF THE ESTIMATE-SIGMA =   1.1706
SUM OF SQUARED ERRORS-SSE=   13.703
MEAN OF DEPENDENT VARIABLE =   7.7569
LOG OF THE LIKELIHOOD FUNCTION = -18.7886


VARIABLE    ESTIMATED   STANDARD    T-RATIO        PARTIAL STANDARDIZED ELASTICITY
  NAME      COEFFICIENT   ERROR       10 DF     P-VALUE CORR. COEFFICIENT  AT MEANS
X2          -1.3925     0.3050      -4.565      0.001-0.822    -0.6614     -1.1945
X3           1.4700     0.1758       8.363      0.000 0.935     1.2116      1.2671
CONSTANT     7.1934     1.595        4.511      0.001 0.819     0.0000      0.9273
```

```
VARIANCE-COVARIANCE MATRIX OF COEFFICIENTS
X2         0.93036E-01
X3        -0.34419E-01  0.30901E-01
CONSTANT -0.38892      0.22412E-01   2.5434
           X2            X3          CONSTANT
|_* Now use the formulas from Section 7.4.
|_STAT Y X2 X3 / PCPDEV CPDEV=DEV MEAN=M
NAME       N   MEAN      ST. DEV       VARIANCE      MINIMUM      MAXIMUM
Y         13   7.7569     3.0419        9.2531        3.3000       13.460
X2        13   6.6538     1.4449        2.0877        4.9000       9.7000
X3        13   6.6862     2.5071        6.2856        3.1300       10.810

CROSSPRODUCT MATRIX IN DEVIATIONS -      13 OBSERVATIONS

Y          111.04
X2         6.1362       25.052
X3         72.025       27.905       75.428
            Y            X2           X3
|_* Extract elements from the crossproduct matrix of variables listed in
|_* deviations from the means.
|_MATRIX SIGYX2=DEV(2,1)
|_MATRIX SIGX3X3=DEV(3,3)
|_MATRIX SIGYX3=DEV(3,1)
|_MATRIX SIGX2X3=DEV(3,2)
|_MATRIX SIGX2X2=DEV(2,2)
|_MATRIX SIGYY=DEV(1,1)
|_* Now estimate BETA2 using Equation (7.4.7).
|_GEN1 BETA2=(SIGYX2*SIGX3X3-SIGYX3*SIGX2X3)/(SIGX2X2*SIGX3X3-SIGX2X3**2)
|_* Estimate BETA3 using Equation (7.4.8).
|_GEN1 BETA3=(SIGYX3*SIGX2X2-SIGYX2*SIGX2X3)/(SIGX3X3*SIGX2X2-SIGX2X3**2)
|_* Estimate BETA1, the constant term.
|_GEN1 YBAR=M(1)
|_GEN1 X2BAR=M(2)
|_GEN1 X3BAR=M(3)
|_GEN1 BETA1=YBAR-BETA2*X2BAR-BETA3*X3BAR
|_PRINT BETA1 BETA2 BETA3
    BETA1
   7.193357
    BETA2
  -1.392472
    BETA3
   1.470032
|_* Estimate the Regression variance, SIGMA**2, using formula (7.4.18).
|_GENR CONSTANT=1
|_GENR E=Y-(BETA1*CONSTANT+BETA2*X2+BETA3*X3)
|_GENR E2=E**2
|_?STAT E2 / SUMS=SSE
|_GEN1 SIG2=SSE/(13-3)
|_PRINT SSE SIG2
    SSE
   13.70316
    SIG2
   1.370316
|_* Now compute the variances and standard errors of BETA2 using (7.4.11),
|_* of BETA3 using (7.4.14), and of BETA1 using (7.4.9).
|_GEN1 VARB2=(SIGX3X3/(SIGX2X2*SIGX3X3-SIGX2X3**2))*SIG2
|_GEN1 SEB2=SQRT(VARB2)
|_GEN1 VARB3=(SIGX2X2/(SIGX2X2*SIGX3X3-SIGX2X3**2))*SIG2
```

```
|_GEN1 SEB3=SQRT(VARB3)
|_GEN1 VARB1=((1/13)+(X2BAR**2*SIGX3X3+X3BAR**2*SIGX2X2-2*X2BAR*X3BAR*SIGX2X3) &
| /(SIGX2X2*SIGX3X3-SIGX2X3**2))*SIG2
|_GEN1 SEB1=SQRT(VARB1)
|_PRINT VARB2 SEB2 VARB3 SEB3 VARB1 SEB1
    VARB2
 0.9303593E-01
    SEB2
 0.3050179
    VARB3
 0.3090064E-01
    SEB3
 0.1757858
    VARB1
  2.543353
    SEB1
  1.594789
|_* Use (7.4.17) to compute the covariance between BETA2 and BETA3.
|_?STAT X2 X3 / PCOR COR=CORMAT

  CORRELATION MATRIX OF VARIABLES -        13 OBSERVATIONS

X2          1.0000
X3          0.64193        1.0000
            X2             X3
|_MATRIX R23=CORMAT(1,2)
|_GEN1 COVB2B3=-R23*SIG2/((1-R23**2)*SQRT(SIGX2X2)*SQRT(SIGX3X3))
|_PRINT COVB2B3
    COVB2B3
-0.3441890E-01
|_* Now compute the R-square statistic using Equation (7.5.5).
|_GEN1 R2=(BETA2*SIGYX2+BETA3*SIGYX3)/SIGYY
|_PRINT R2
    R2
 0.8765896
```

Specification bias is the topic of *Section 7.7*. In order to examine the implications of omitted variable bias, the expected inflation rate variable, X_3, will be dropped from the "true" model described in equation (7.6.2). The new model, equation (7.7.6), will be estimated and the coefficient for X_2, b_{12}, will be saved.

```
* Estimate (7.7.6).and save the coefficient b12.
OLS Y X2 / COEF=C1
GEN1 B12=C1(2)
```

The output follows.

```
|_OLS Y X2 / COEF=C1

 OLS ESTIMATION
      13 OBSERVATIONS      DEPENDENT VARIABLE = Y
...NOTE..SAMPLE RANGE SET TO:    1,   13


 R-SQUARE =   0.0135     R-SQUARE ADJUSTED =   -0.0761
 VARIANCE OF THE ESTIMATE-SIGMA**2 =   9.9577
```

```
STANDARD ERROR OF THE ESTIMATE-SIGMA =    3.1556
SUM OF SQUARED ERRORS-SSE=   109.53
MEAN OF DEPENDENT VARIABLE =    7.7569
LOG OF THE LIKELIHOOD FUNCTION = -32.2996
```

VARIABLE NAME	ESTIMATED COEFFICIENT	STANDARD ERROR	T-RATIO 11 DF	P-VALUE	PARTIAL CORR.	STANDARDIZED COEFFICIENT	ELASTICITY AT MEANS
X2	0.24493	0.6305	0.3885	0.705	0.116	0.1163	0.2101
CONSTANT	6.1272	4.285	1.430	0.181	0.396	0.0000	0.7899

```
|_GEN1 B12=C1(1)
```

The coefficient for X_2 is now both positive and not statistically different from zero. These results confirm that, if a "true" model had been defined by a set of coefficients, omitting one or more of the independent variables from the model would have produced biased estimates.

The simple regression coefficient for X_2, b_{12}, is unbiased if $E(b_{12}) = \beta_2$. However, following formula (7.7.4), it will be shown below, that $E(b_{12}) = \beta_2 + \beta_2 b_{32}$.

```
* Estimate (7.7.7) and store the coefficient B32. Recall that BETA2 and BETA3
* are still defined from previous commands.
OLS X3 X2 / COEF=C2
GEN1 B32=C2(1)
PRINT BETA2 B32
* Now show that B12 from (7.7.6) is equal to BETA2+BETA3*B23.
GEN1 OTHERB12=BETA2+BETA3*B32
PRINT B12 OTHERB12
```

The output follows.

```
|_* Estimate (7.7.7) and store the coefficient B32. Recall that BETA2 and BETA3
|_* are still defined from the above commands.

|_OLS X3 X2 / COEF=C2

OLS ESTIMATION
     13 OBSERVATIONS        DEPENDENT VARIABLE = X3
...NOTE..SAMPLE RANGE SET TO:    1,   13

 R-SQUARE =   0.4121     R-SQUARE ADJUSTED =   0.3586
VARIANCE OF THE ESTIMATE-SIGMA**2 =   4.0314
STANDARD ERROR OF THE ESTIMATE-SIGMA =   2.0078
SUM OF SQUARED ERRORS-SSE=   44.346
MEAN OF DEPENDENT VARIABLE =   6.6862
LOG OF THE LIKELIHOOD FUNCTION = -26.4222
```

VARIABLE NAME	ESTIMATED COEFFICIENT	STANDARD ERROR	T-RATIO 11 DF	P-VALUE	PARTIAL CORR.	STANDARDIZED COEFFICIENT	ELASTICITY AT MEANS
X2	1.1139	0.4011	2.777	0.018	0.642	0.6419	1.1085
CONSTANT	-0.72528	2.727	-0.2660	0.795	-0.080	0.0000	-0.1085

```
|_GEN1 B32=C2(1)
|_PRINT BETA2 B32
   BETA2
```

```
   -1.392472
     B32
    1.113857
|_* Now show that B12 from (7.7.6) is equal to BETA2+BETA3*B23.
|_GEN1 OTHERB12=BETA2+BETA3*B32
|_PRINT B12 OTHERB12
     B12
   0.2449337
     OTHERB12
   0.2449337
```

In *Section 7.8*, the text discusses the problem of comparing the R^2 statistics from a linear model with that of a model in which the dependent and independent variables are in logs. When the **LOGLOG** option (or **LOGLIN** option in the case where the independent variables are in levels) is specified with the **RSTAT** option and the **OLS** command, SHAZAM prints the R^2 statistic Gujarati discusses. It is labelled in the output as "R-SQUARE BETWEEN ANTILOGS OBSERVED AND PREDICTED."

The **PREDICT=** option with the **OLS** command saves the **PREDICT**ed values of the dependent variable in the variable specified. In this example, these predicted values will be saved for later use.

The commands below will replicate the results for the coffee demand example reported in *Example 7.2*.

```
TIME 1970 1
SAMPLE 1970.0 1980.0
READ(TABLE3.4) YEAR Y X
GENR LNY=LOG(Y)
GENR LNX=LOG(X)
OLS Y X / PREDICT=YHAT
OLS LNY LNX / RSTAT LOGLOG PREDICT=LNYHAT
```

Note that some of the **RSTAT** output has been omitted from the output below since it is not of interest at this point.

```
|_OLS Y X / PREDICT=YHAT

 OLS ESTIMATION
      11 OBSERVATIONS      DEPENDENT VARIABLE = Y
...NOTE..SAMPLE RANGE SET TO:    1,    11


 R-SQUARE =    0.6628    R-SQUARE ADJUSTED =    0.6253
VARIANCE OF THE ESTIMATE-SIGMA**2 =   0.16564E-01
STANDARD ERROR OF THE ESTIMATE-SIGMA =   0.12870
SUM OF SQUARED ERRORS-SSE=   0.14908
MEAN OF DEPENDENT VARIABLE =    2.2064
LOG OF THE LIKELIHOOD FUNCTION =    8.04811
VARIABLE    ESTIMATED    STANDARD    T-RATIO          PARTIAL STANDARDIZED ELASTICITY
  NAME      COEFFICIENT   ERROR      9 DF     P-VALUE CORR. COEFFICIENT  AT MEANS
X          -0.47953      0.1140     -4.206    0.002-0.814    -0.8141     -0.2197
```

```
CONSTANT   2.6911      0.1216      22.13     0.000 0.991     0.0000      1.2197

|_OLS LNY LNX / RSTAT LOGLOG PREDICT=LNYHAT

 OLS ESTIMATION
     11 OBSERVATIONS       DEPENDENT VARIABLE = LNY
...NOTE..SAMPLE RANGE SET TO:    1,   11

 R-SQUARE =   0.7448     R-SQUARE ADJUSTED =   0.7164
VARIANCE OF THE ESTIMATE-SIGMA**2 =  0.25148E-02
STANDARD ERROR OF THE ESTIMATE-SIGMA =  0.50148E-01
SUM OF SQUARED ERRORS-SSE=  0.22633E-01
MEAN OF DEPENDENT VARIABLE =  0.78728
LOG OF THE LIKELIHOOD FUNCTION(IF DEPVAR LOG) =  9.75588

VARIABLE   ESTIMATED   STANDARD   T-RATIO          PARTIAL STANDARDIZED ELASTICITY
  NAME     COEFFICIENT   ERROR      9 DF   P-VALUE CORR. COEFFICIENT  AT MEANS
LNX       -0.25305     0.4937E-01  -5.125    0.001-0.863   -0.8630    -0.2530
CONSTANT   0.77742     0.1524E-01  51.00     0.000 0.998    0.0000     0.7774
R-SQUARE BETWEEN OBSERVED AND PREDICTED = 0.7448
R-SQUARE BETWEEN ANTILOGS OBSERVED AND PREDICTED = 0.7187
```

As the text notes, based on the R^2 statistics, the log-log model appears to have a better fit. As well, the log-likelihood function is larger in the log-log model.

The following commands will replicate the information found in *Table 7.2*.

```
GENR ANTIYHAT=EXP(LNYHAT)
GENR LNOFYHAT=LOG(YHAT)
PRINT YEAR Y YHAT LNYHAT ANTIYHAT LNY LNOFYHAT / WIDE
```

The output follows.

```
|_PRINT YEAR Y YHAT LNYHAT ANTIYHAT LNY LNOFYHAT / WIDE
  YEAR        Y        YHAT      LNYHAT     ANTIYHAT      LNY       LNOFYHAT
 1970.0    2.57000    2.32188    0.84355    2.3246     0.94390     0.84238
 1971.0    2.50000    2.33627    0.85361    2.3481     0.91629     0.84855
 1972.0    2.35000    2.34586    0.86054    2.3644     0.85441     0.85265
 1973.0    2.30000    2.34106    0.85705    2.3562     0.83290     0.85060
 1974.0    2.25000    2.32668    0.84686    2.3323     0.81093     0.84444
 1975.0    2.20000    2.33147    0.85021    2.3401     0.78845     0.84650
 1976.0    2.11000    2.17323    0.75794    2.1338     0.74668     0.77621
 1977.0    1.94000    1.82317    0.62727    1.8725     0.66268     0.60058
 1978.0    1.97000    2.02457    0.69408    2.0018     0.67803     0.70536
 1979.0    2.06000    2.11568    0.73128    2.0777     0.72270     0.74938
 1980.0    2.02000    2.13007    0.73768    2.0910     0.70309     0.75615
```

Although not done in the text, the above model will be estimated assuming a log-linear and linear-log functional form. Since the **LOGLOG, LOGLIN,** and **LINLOG** options are used where appropriate, the log-likelihood functions for the four models are comparable. As well, since the **RSTAT** option is used with the models where the dependent variable is in logs, the "R-SQUARE BETWEEN ANTILOGS OBSERVED AND PREDICTED" is computed. These can be compared to the R^2 of the models where the dependent variable is in levels.

```
OLS LNY X / RSTAT LOGLIN
OLS Y LNX / LINLOG
```

The output follows.

```
|_OLS LNY X / RSTAT LOGLIN

 OLS ESTIMATION
        11 OBSERVATIONS      DEPENDENT VARIABLE = LNY
...NOTE..SAMPLE RANGE SET TO:    1,   11

 R-SQUARE =   0.6971     R-SQUARE ADJUSTED =   0.6634
VARIANCE OF THE ESTIMATE-SIGMA**2 =   0.29851E-02
STANDARD ERROR OF THE ESTIMATE-SIGMA =   0.54636E-01
SUM OF SQUARED ERRORS-SSE=  0.26866E-01
MEAN OF DEPENDENT VARIABLE =   0.78728
LOG OF THE LIKELIHOOD FUNCTION(IF DEPVAR LOG) =   8.81299


VARIABLE    ESTIMATED   STANDARD   T-RATIO        PARTIAL STANDARDIZED ELASTICITY
  NAME      COEFFICIENT   ERROR       9 DF     P-VALUE CORR. COEFFICIENT  AT MEANS
X           -0.22028    0.4840E-01  -4.551     0.001-0.835    -0.8349     -0.2227
CONSTANT     1.0100     0.5163E-01  19.56      0.000 0.988     0.0000      1.0100


R-SQUARE BETWEEN OBSERVED AND PREDICTED = 0.6971
R-SQUARE BETWEEN ANTILOGS OBSERVED AND PREDICTED = 0.6787

|_OLS Y LNX / LINLOG

 OLS ESTIMATION
        11 OBSERVATIONS      DEPENDENT VARIABLE = Y
...NOTE..SAMPLE RANGE SET TO:    1,   11

 R-SQUARE =   0.7112     R-SQUARE ADJUSTED =   0.6791
VARIANCE OF THE ESTIMATE-SIGMA**2 =   0.14185E-01
STANDARD ERROR OF THE ESTIMATE-SIGMA =   0.11910
SUM OF SQUARED ERRORS-SSE=  0.12766
MEAN OF DEPENDENT VARIABLE =   2.2064
LOG OF THE LIKELIHOOD FUNCTION =   8.90117

VARIABLE    ESTIMATED   STANDARD   T-RATIO        PARTIAL STANDARDIZED ELASTICITY
  NAME      COEFFICIENT   ERROR       9 DF     P-VALUE CORR. COEFFICIENT  AT MEANS
LNX         -0.55206    0.1173      -4.708     0.001-0.843    -0.8433     -0.2502
CONSTANT     2.1848     0.3620E-01  60.36      0.000 0.999     0.0000      0.9902
```

The relevant statistics from the above estimations follow.

Functional Form	Comparable R^2	Comparable LLF
Linear	0.6628	8.04811
Linear-log	0.7112	8.90117
Log-Log	0.7187	9.75588
Log-linear	0.6787	8.81299

The log-log model seems most appropriate given that it has both the highest R^2 and log-likelihood function.

The command file below will replicate the results for the Cobb-Douglas Production Function example in *Section 7.10*.

```
TIME 1958 1
SAMPLE 1958.0 1972.0
READ(TABLE7.3) Y X2 X3
GENR LNY=LOG(Y)
GENR LNX2=LOG(X2)
GENR LNX3=LOG(X3)
OLS LNY LNX2 LNX3 / LOGLOG
```

The output follows.

```
|_OLS LNY LNX2 LNX3 / LOGLOG

 OLS ESTIMATION
      15 OBSERVATIONS       DEPENDENT VARIABLE = LNY
...NOTE..SAMPLE RANGE SET TO:     1,    15

 R-SQUARE =   0.8890     R-SQUARE ADJUSTED =   0.8705
VARIANCE OF THE ESTIMATE-SIGMA**2 =  0.55965E-02
STANDARD ERROR OF THE ESTIMATE-SIGMA =  0.74810E-01
SUM OF SQUARED ERRORS-SSE=  0.67158E-01
MEAN OF DEPENDENT VARIABLE =    10.097
LOG OF THE LIKELIHOOD FUNCTION(IF DEPVAR LOG) = -132.166

VARIABLE    ESTIMATED   STANDARD   T-RATIO           PARTIAL STANDARDIZED ELASTICITY
  NAME      COEFFICIENT   ERROR      12 DF    P-VALUE CORR. COEFFICIENT   AT MEANS
LNX2       1.4988       0.5398      2.777     0.017 0.625   0.3727        1.4988
LNX3       0.48986      0.1020      4.800     0.000 0.811   0.6443        0.4899
CONSTANT  -3.3385       2.450      -1.363     0.198-0.366   0.0000       -3.3385
```

The command file below will produce the plots shown in *Figure 7.6* and replicate the estimation results reported for *Example 7.4* in *Section 7.11*.

```
SAMPLE 1 10
READ(TABLE7.4) OUTPUT TCOST

* Replicate Figure 7.6.
GENR AC=TCOST / OUTPUT
GENR TCLAG=LAG(TCOST)
GENR MC=TCOST-TCLAG
PLOT TCOST OUTPUT
PLOT AC MC OUTPUT
* Now estimate (7.11.6).
GENR OUTPUT2=OUTPUT**2
GENR OUTPUT3=OUTPUT**3
OLS TCOST OUTPUT OUTPUT2 OUTPUT3
```

The output follows.

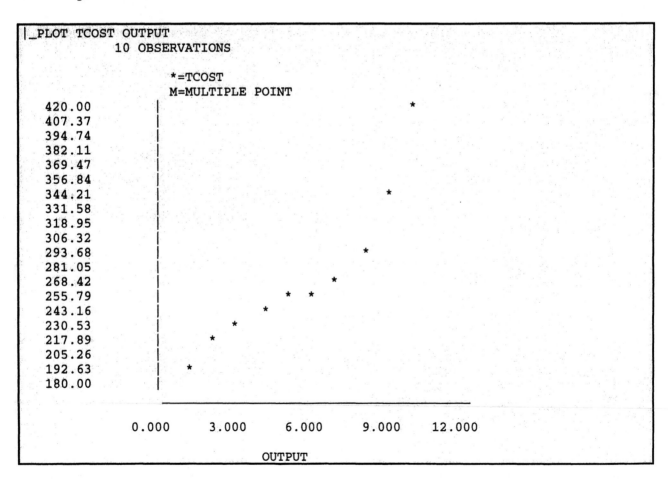

```
|_PLOT AC MC OUTPUT

      10 OBSERVATIONS
                   *=AC
                   +=MC
                   M=MULTIPLE POINT
      200.00    |
      189.47    |    M
      178.95    |
      168.42    |
      157.89    |
      147.37    |
      136.84    |
      126.32    |
      115.79    |
      105.26    |      *
      94.737    |
      84.211    |
      73.684    |       *
      63.158    |                              +
      52.632    |           *            *
      42.105    |             *  *
      31.579    |     +             *    *  *  *
      21.053    |                       +
      10.526    |       +      +      +
  -0.99476E-13  |          +      +
                _____

           0.000    3.000    6.000    9.000    12.000
                            OUTPUT
|_* Now estimate (7.11.6).
|_GENR OUTPUT2=OUTPUT**2
|_GENR OUTPUT3=OUTPUT**3

|_OLS TCOST OUTPUT OUTPUT2 OUTPUT3

      10 OBSERVATIONS      DEPENDENT VARIABLE = TCOST
...NOTE..SAMPLE RANGE SET TO:     1,   10


 R-SQUARE =    0.9983     R-SQUARE ADJUSTED =    0.9975
VARIANCE OF THE ESTIMATE-SIGMA**2 =    10.791
STANDARD ERROR OF THE ESTIMATE-SIGMA =   3.2849
SUM OF SQUARED ERRORS-SSE=    64.744
MEAN OF DEPENDENT VARIABLE =    276.10
LOG OF THE LIKELIHOOD FUNCTION = -23.5287
```

VARIABLE NAME	ESTIMATED COEFFICIENT	STANDARD ERROR	T-RATIO 6 DF	P-VALUE	PARTIAL CORR.	STANDARDIZED COEFFICIENT	ELASTICITY AT MEANS
OUTPUT	63.478	4.779	13.28	0.000	0.983	2.9202	1.2645
OUTPUT2	-12.962	0.9857	-13.15	0.000	-0.983	-6.7302	-1.8074
OUTPUT3	0.93959	0.5911E-01	15.90	0.000	0.988	4.9072	1.0294
CONSTANT	141.77	6.375	22.24	0.000	0.994	0.0000	0.5135

SHAZAM commands and options used in Chapter 7

GEN1 *newvar=equation*   with **SQRT**(x)

GENR *newvar=equation* with **LOG**(x) **EXP**(x) **LAG**(x)

MATRIX *newmat=equation*

OLS *depvar indeps* / **COEF= PCOV LINLOG LOGLIN LOGLOG**
                         PREDICT= RSTAT

PLOT *depvars* *indep* / *options*

PRINT *vars* / **WIDE**

READ(*datafile*) *vars* / *options*

SAMPLE *beg end*

STAT *vars* / **PCPDEV CPDEV= MEAN= PCOR COR= SUMS=**

TIME *beg freq*

&   Continuation of SHAZAM Command to another line

?   Suppression of Output

8. MULTIPLE REGRESSION ANALYSIS: THE PROBLEM OF INFERENCE

Chapter 8 applies the ideas of interval estimation and hypothesis testing developed in *Chapter 5* to models involving three or more variables.

In *Section 8.2, Example 8.1*, personal consumption expenditure, *PCE*, is regressed on personal disposable income, *PDI*, and a time trend, *TIME*. The commands below replicate the results found in equation (8.2.2).

```
TIME 1956 1
SAMPLE 1956.0 1970.0
READ(TABLE8.1) PCE PDI TIME
OLS PCE PDI TIME / ANOVA
```

The output follows.

```
|_OLS PCE PDI TIME / ANOVA

 OLS ESTIMATION
      15 OBSERVATIONS      DEPENDENT VARIABLE = PCE
...NOTE..SAMPLE RANGE SET TO:     1,    15

 R-SQUARE =   0.9988    R-SQUARE ADJUSTED =   0.9986
VARIANCE OF THE ESTIMATE-SIGMA**2 =   6.4308
STANDARD ERROR OF THE ESTIMATE-SIGMA =   2.5359
SUM OF SQUARED ERRORS-SSE=   77.169
MEAN OF DEPENDENT VARIABLE =   367.69
LOG OF THE LIKELIHOOD FUNCTION = -33.5687

                       ANALYSIS OF VARIANCE - FROM MEAN
                       SS          DF          MS                    F
REGRESSION          65965.         2.       32983.              5128.879
ERROR               77.169        12.       6.4308              P-VALUE
TOTAL               66042.        14.       4717.3                0.000

                       ANALYSIS OF VARIANCE - FROM ZERO
                       SS          DF          MS                    F
REGRESSION       0.20939E+07       3.     0.69798E+06         108537.897
ERROR               77.169        12.       6.4308              P-VALUE
TOTAL            0.20940E+07      15.     0.13960E+06            0.000
```

VARIABLE NAME	ESTIMATED COEFFICIENT	STANDARD ERROR	T-RATIO 12 DF	PARTIAL P-VALUE	CORR.	STANDARDIZED COEFFICIENT	ELASTICITY AT MEANS
PDI	0.72659	0.4874E-01	14.91	0.000	0.974	0.8236	0.7959
TIME	2.7363	0.8486	3.225	0.007	0.681	0.1782	0.0595
CONSTANT	53.160	13.03	4.081	0.002	0.762	0.0000	0.1446

Recall that the p-values reported by SHAZAM are two-tailed (see *Section 5.8* of the text). That is, the p-values reported indicate the probability of obtaining t-values greater than or less than those estimated.

The **CONFID** command will be used to construct the 95% confidence intervals reported in *Section 8.4*.

```
|_CONFID PDI TIME CONSTANT
USING 95% AND 90% CONFIDENCE INTERVALS

CONFIDENCE INTERVALS BASED ON T-DISTRIBUTION WITH  12 D.F.
     - T CRITICAL VALUES =   2.179 AND   1.782
NAME     LOWER 2.5%   LOWER 5%   COEFFICENT   UPPER 5%   UPPER 2.5%   STD. ERROR
PDI        0.6204      0.6397      0.72659     0.8135      0.8328       0.049
TIME       0.8872      1.224       2.7363      4.248       4.585        0.849
CONSTANT   24.78       29.95       53.160      76.37       81.54       13.026
```

Notice that the F-test statistic (8.5.6) reported in the text is printed when the **ANOVA** option is used with the **OLS** command. The **TEST** command will be used below to compute this statistic.

If a joint test is required that involves several hypotheses, these should be grouped together with a blank **TEST** command to introduce them and an **END** command to mark the end of the group. The general command format for a joint hypothesis test is:

TEST

TEST   *equation 1*

TEST   *equation 2*

...

END

The output for the current example follows.

```
|_TEST
|_TEST PDI=0
|_TEST TIME=0
|_END
F STATISTIC =     5128.8792     WITH     2 AND    12 D.F.  P-VALUE= 0.00000
WALD CHI-SQUARE STATISTIC =    10257.758     WITH     2 D.F.  P-VALUE= 0.00000
UPPER BOUND ON P-VALUE BY CHEBYCHEV INEQUALITY = 0.00019
```

Before estimating equation (8.5.14) where the time trend is dropped, statistics from equation (8.2.2) which are stored in temporary variables must be saved. They are needed for constructing the F-statistic of equation (8.5.17). Recall that in Chapter 3, the differences between SHAZAM and the text in the notation of the sum of squared statistics are discussed. A brief review may help prevent confusion below. In particular, the temporary variables **$SSR**, **$SSE**, and **$SST** represent the regression, error, and total sum of squares, respectively.

```
GEN1 Q3=$SSR
GEN1 Q4=$SSE
GEN1 Q5=$SST
GEN1 R2NEW=$R2
* Now estimate (8.5.14).
OLS PCE PDI / ANOVA
* Test Beta2=0.
TEST PDI=0
```

The output follows.

```
|_GEN1 Q3=$SSR
..NOTE..CURRENT VALUE OF $SSR =    65965.
|_GEN1 Q4=$SSE
..NOTE..CURRENT VALUE OF $SSE =    77.169
|_GEN1 Q5=$SST
..NOTE..CURRENT VALUE OF $SST =    66042.
|_GEN1 R2NEW=$R2
..NOTE..CURRENT VALUE OF $R2  =    0.99883
|_* Now estimate (8.5.14).
|_OLS PCE PDI / ANOVA

 OLS ESTIMATION
      15 OBSERVATIONS    DEPENDENT VARIABLE = PCE
...NOTE..SAMPLE RANGE SET TO:    1,   15


 R-SQUARE =   0.9978    R-SQUARE ADJUSTED =   0.9977
VARIANCE OF THE ESTIMATE-SIGMA**2 =   11.080
STANDARD ERROR OF THE ESTIMATE-SIGMA =   3.3286
SUM OF SQUARED ERRORS-SSE=   144.03
MEAN OF DEPENDENT VARIABLE =   367.69
LOG OF THE LIKELIHOOD FUNCTION = -38.2491


                   ANALYSIS OF VARIANCE - FROM MEAN
                    SS         DF         MS              F
REGRESSION        65898.       1.       65898.        5947.715
ERROR             144.03      13.       11.080        P-VALUE
TOTAL             66042.      14.       4717.3         0.000

                   ANALYSIS OF VARIANCE - FROM ZERO
                    SS         DF         MS              F
REGRESSION     0.20939E+07     2.     0.10469E+07     94492.412
ERROR             144.03      13.       11.080        P-VALUE
TOTAL          0.20940E+07    15.     0.13960E+06      0.000


VARIABLE    ESTIMATED    STANDARD    T-RATIO          PARTIAL STANDARDIZED ELASTICITY
  NAME     COEFFICIENT    ERROR      13 DF   P-VALUE CORR. COEFFICIENT  AT MEANS
PDI         0.88125     0.1143E-01    77.12   0.000 0.999    0.9989      0.9653
CONSTANT    12.762       4.682        2.726   0.017 0.603    0.0000      0.0347
* Test Beta2=0.
|_TEST PDI=0
TEST VALUE =   0.88125     STD. ERROR OF TEST VALUE  0.11427E-01
T STATISTIC =    77.121431     WITH    13 D.F.     P-VALUE= 0.00000
F STATISTIC =    5947.7151     WITH     1 AND    13 D.F.  P-VALUE= 0.00000
WALD CHI-SQUARE STATISTIC =    5947.7151     WITH     1 D.F.  P-VALUE= 0.00000
UPPER BOUND ON P-VALUE BY CHEBYCHEV INEQUALITY = 0.00017
```

Note that the output labelled "ANALYSIS OF VARIANCE - FROM MEAN" corresponds to *Table 8.5* and the F-statistic reported corresponds to equation (8.5.15).

Now, construct the F-statistic (8.5.17) testing the incremental contribution of *TIME* after allowing for the contribution of *PDI*. First follow equation (8.5.16). Then use equation (8.5.19) where the R^2 statistics are used.

```
* Construct (8.5.17).
GEN1 Q1=$SSR
GEN1 Q2=Q3-Q1
GEN1 R2OLD=$R2
PRINT Q1 Q2 Q3 Q4 Q5 / WIDE
GEN1 FSTAT2=(Q2/1)/(Q4/12)
PRINT FSTAT1
* Compute (8.5.17) using the R-Squares (i.e. (5.5.19))
GEN1 FSTAT2=((R2NEW-R2OLD)/1)/((1-R2NEW)/($N-3))
PRINT FSTAT2
```

The output follows.

```
|_* Construct (8.5.17).
|_GEN1 Q1=$SSR
..NOTE..CURRENT VALUE OF $SSR =     65898.
|_GEN1 Q2=Q3-Q1
|_GEN1 R2OLD=$R2
..NOTE..CURRENT VALUE OF $R2   =  0.99782
|_PRINT Q1 Q2 Q3 Q4 Q5 / WIDE
    Q1          Q2          Q3          Q4          Q5
  65898.23    66.86562    65965.10    77.16902    66042.27
|_GEN1 FSTAT1=(Q2/1)/(Q4/12)
|_PRINT FSTAT1
    FSTAT1
   10.39779
|_* Compute (8.5.17) using the R-Squares (i.e. (5.5.19))
|_GEN1 FSTAT2=((R2NEW-R2OLD)/1)/((1-R2NEW)/($N-3))
..NOTE..CURRENT VALUE OF $N   =    15.000
|_PRINT FSTAT2
    FSTAT2
   10.39779
```

Note , as mentioned in the text, that the F-statistic above is the square of the t-ratio of the *TIME* variable from equation (8.2.2).

In *Example 2*, from *Section 8.6*, Y is regressed on X, X^2, and X^3, where Y is total cost and X is output. The hypothesis that the coefficients of the X^2 and X^3 terms are the same (8.6.6) is tested below. That is, does $\beta_3 = \beta_4$?

The necessary commands and pertinent output follow. (See Chapter 7 for the full output).

```
SAMPLE 1 10
READ(TABLE7.4) X Y
GENR X2=X**2
GENR X3=X**3
OLS Y X X2 X3
TEST X2=X3
```

```
|_TEST X2=X3
TEST VALUE =  -13.901      STD. ERROR OF TEST VALUE   1.0442
T STATISTIC =  -13.312955     WITH    6 D.F.     P-VALUE= 0.00001
F STATISTIC =    177.23477     WITH    1 AND    6 D.F.  P-VALUE= 0.00001
WALD CHI-SQUARE STATISTIC =    177.23477     WITH    1 D.F.  P-VALUE= 0.00000
UPPER BOUND ON P-VALUE BY CHEBYCHEV INEQUALITY = 0.00564
```

In *Example 8.3* of *Section 8.7*, a restricted Cobb-Douglas production function, assuming constant returns to scale, is estimated (8.7.13). An unrestricted model is then estimated and the results are used to test the above restriction (see equation (8.7.14)). The commands below replicate the results provided in the text.

```
TIME 1958 1
SAMPLE 1958.0 1972.0
READ(TABLE7.3) Y X2 X3
GENR LNY=LOG(Y)
GENR LNX2=LOG(X2)
GENR LNX3=LOG(X3)
* Construct the new variables for (8.7.13) and estimate the model.
GENR LNYX2=LNY-LNX2
GENR LNX3X2=LNX3-LNX2
OLS LNYX2 LNX3X2 / LOGLOG
* Test the null hypothesis that the production function exhibits constant
* returns to scale (8.7.14).
?OLS LNY LNX2 LNX3 / LOGLOG
TEST LNX2+LNX3=1
```

The output follows.

```
|_OLS LNYX2 LNX3X2 / LOGLOG

 OLS ESTIMATION
      15 OBSERVATIONS      DEPENDENT VARIABLE = LNYX2

 R-SQUARE =    0.7685    R-SQUARE ADJUSTED =    0.7507
 VARIANCE OF THE ESTIMATE-SIGMA**2 =  0.70365E-02
 STANDARD ERROR OF THE ESTIMATE-SIGMA =  0.83884E-01
 SUM OF SQUARED ERRORS-SSE=  0.91475E-01
 MEAN OF DEPENDENT VARIABLE =    4.4371
 LOG OF THE LIKELIHOOD FUNCTION(IF DEPVAR LOG) = -49.5924
```

VARIABLE NAME	ESTIMATED COEFFICIENT	STANDARD ERROR	T-RATIO 13 DF	P-VALUE	PARTIAL CORR.	STANDARDIZED COEFFICIENT	ELASTICITY AT MEANS
LNX3X2	0.61298	0.9330E-01	6.570	0.000	0.877	0.8767	0.6130
CONSTANT	1.7086	0.4159	4.108	0.001	0.752	0.0000	1.7086

```
|_* Test the null hypothesis that the production function exhibits constant
|_* returns to scale (8.7.14).
|_?OLS LNY LNX2 LNX3 / LOGLOG
|_TEST LNX2+LNX3=1
TEST VALUE =   0.98863      STD. ERROR OF TEST VALUE  0.47428
T STATISTIC =    2.0844583     WITH   12 D.F.    P-VALUE= 0.05915
F STATISTIC =    4.3449663     WITH    1 AND   12 D.F.  P-VALUE= 0.05915
WALD CHI-SQUARE STATISTIC =    4.3449663     WITH    1 D.F.  P-VALUE= 0.03712
UPPER BOUND ON P-VALUE BY CHEBYCHEV INEQUALITY = 0.23015
```

In *Example 8.4* from *Section 8.7*, Y is regressed on X_2, X_3, X_4 and X_5, where Y is per capita consumption of chicken, X_2 is the real disposable income, X_3 is the real retail price of chicken per pound, X_4 is the real retail price for pork per pound, and X_5 is the real retail price for beef per pound. The main idea in this example is to constrain the model by assuming that pork and beef prices do not affect chicken consumption. Both the constrained and unconstrained models are estimated. The hypothesis that $\beta_4 = \beta_5 = 0$ is then tested.

The temporary variable $K represents the total number of coefficients in the regression, *including* the constant term.

The following commands replicate the results provided in *Example 8.4*. Note that the data for this example is found in the data file *EXER723.DAT*.

```
TIME 1960 1
SAMPLE 1960.0 1982.0
READ(EXER723.DAT) YEAR Y X2 X3 X4 X5 X6/ LIST
GENR LNY=LOG(Y)
GENR LNX2=LOG(X2)
GENR LNX3=LOG(X3)
GENR LNX4=LOG(X4)
GENR LNX5=LOG(X5)
* Test the joint hypothesis that the coefficients for X4 and X5 are jointly
* equal to zero (8.7.21). First estimate (8.7.23) then use the TEST command.
OLS LNY LNX2 LNX3 LNX4 LNX5 / LOGLOG
TEST
TEST LNX4=0
TEST LNX5=0
END
* Now construct the test statistic using (8.7.10).
GEN1 R2UR=$R2
GEN1 K=$K
GEN1 N=$N
GEN1 M=2
* Estimate (8.7.24) and save the R-Square statistic.
OLS LNY LNX2 LNX3 / LOGLOG
GEN1 R2R=$R2
GEN1 F=((R2UR-R2R)/M)/((1-R2UR)/(N-K))
PRINT F
```

The output follows.

```
|_* Test the joint hypothesis that the coefficients for X4 and X5 are jointly
|_* equal to zero (8.7.21). First estimate (8.7.23) then use the TEST command.

|_OLS LNY LNX2 LNX3 LNX4 LNX5 / LOGLOG

 OLS ESTIMATION
      23 OBSERVATIONS       DEPENDENT VARIABLE = LNY
...NOTE..SAMPLE RANGE SET TO:    1,   23

 R-SQUARE =   0.9823     R-SQUARE ADJUSTED =   0.9784
VARIANCE OF THE ESTIMATE-SIGMA**2 =  0.76127E-03
STANDARD ERROR OF THE ESTIMATE-SIGMA =  0.27591E-01
SUM OF SQUARED ERRORS-SSE=  0.13703E-01
MEAN OF DEPENDENT VARIABLE =   3.6639
LOG OF THE LIKELIHOOD FUNCTION(IF DEPVAR LOG) = -31.5100
```

VARIABLE NAME	ESTIMATED COEFFICIENT	STANDARD ERROR	T-RATIO 18 DF	P-VALUE	PARTIAL CORR.	STANDARDIZED COEFFICIENT	ELASTICITY AT MEANS
LNX2	0.34256	0.8327E-01	4.114	0.001	0.696	1.0406	0.3426
LNX3	-0.50459	0.1109	-4.550	0.000	-0.731	-0.5964	-0.5046
LNX4	0.14855	0.9967E-01	1.490	0.153	0.331	0.3007	0.1485
LNX5	0.91105E-01	0.1007	0.9046	0.378	0.209	0.1844	0.0911
CONSTANT	2.1898	0.1557	14.06	0.000	0.957	0.0000	2.1898

```
|_TEST
|_TEST LNX4=0
|_TEST LNX5=0
|_END
F STATISTIC =    1.1392446     WITH    2 AND   18 D.F.  P-VALUE= 0.34208
WALD CHI-SQUARE STATISTIC =    2.2784893     WITH    2 D.F.  P-VALUE= 0.32006
UPPER BOUND ON P-VALUE BY CHEBYCHEV INEQUALITY = 0.87777
|_* Now construct the test statistic using (8.7.10).
|_GEN1 R2UR=$R2
..NOTE..CURRENT VALUE OF $R2  =   0.98231
|_GEN1 K=$K
..NOTE..CURRENT VALUE OF $K   =   5.0000
|_GEN1 N=$N
..NOTE..CURRENT VALUE OF $N   =   23.000
|_GEN1 M=2
|_* Estimate (8.7.24) and save the R-Square statistic.

|_OLS LNY LNX2 LNX3 / LOGLOG

 OLS ESTIMATION
      23 OBSERVATIONS       DEPENDENT VARIABLE = LNY
...NOTE..SAMPLE RANGE SET TO:    1,   23

 R-SQUARE =   0.9801     R-SQUARE ADJUSTED =   0.9781
VARIANCE OF THE ESTIMATE-SIGMA**2 =  0.77187E-03
STANDARD ERROR OF THE ESTIMATE-SIGMA =  0.27783E-01
SUM OF SQUARED ERRORS-SSE=  0.15437E-01
MEAN OF DEPENDENT VARIABLE =   3.6639
LOG OF THE LIKELIHOOD FUNCTION(IF DEPVAR LOG) = -32.8807
```

VARIABLE NAME	ESTIMATED COEFFICIENT	STANDARD ERROR	T-RATIO 20 DF	P-VALUE	PARTIAL CORR.	STANDARDIZED COEFFICIENT	ELASTICITY AT MEANS
LNX2	0.45153	0.2469E-01	18.28	0.000	0.971	1.3716	0.4515
LNX3	-0.37221	0.6347E-01	-5.865	0.000	-0.795	-0.4400	-0.3722
CONSTANT	2.0328	0.1162	17.50	0.000	0.969	0.0000	2.0328

```
|_GEN1 R2R=$R2
..NOTE..CURRENT VALUE OF $R2  =  0.98007
|_GEN1 F=((R2UR-R2R)/M)/((1-R2UR)/(N-K))
|_PRINT F
    F
  1.139245
```

Section 8.8 discusses testing for structural stability using an equation modeling British personal savings rates as a function of personal income. However, it may be the case that the structure of the model is not stable over the entire sample range of 1946 to 1963. A Chow Test is constructed testing whether there exists a structural break between the reconstruction period (1946 to 1954) following World War II and the post-reconstruction period (1955 to 1963). First, the **CHOWONE=** option with the **DIAGNOS** command will be used to compute the Chow Test statistic. The "long way" will then be used.

The **DIAGNOS** Command

SHAZAM can perform a number of diagnostic tests after estimating a single equation regression model. The **DIAGNOS** command generally must follow an **OLS** command. The format is:

DIAGNOS / *options*

where *options* is a list of desired options.

The **CHOWONE** option specifies the breakpoint for the Chow test. That is, it specifies the number of observations in the first group. (The **CHOWTEST** option reports the test statistics for every breakpoint).

```
TIME 1946 1
SAMPLE 1946.0 1963.0
READ(TABLE8.8) YEAR SAVINGS INCOME
OLS SAVINGS INCOME
DIAGNOS / CHOWONE=9
* Now construct the Chow F-Test statistic the "long way" following (8.8.4).
GEN1 S1=$SSE
GEN1 DF1=$K
GEN1 DF2=$N-2*$K
SAMPLE 1946.0 1954.0
OLS SAVINGS INCOME
GEN1 S2=$SSE
SAMPLE 1955.0 1963.0
OLS SAVINGS INCOME
GEN1 S3=$SSE
SAMPLE 1946.0 1963.0
GEN1 S4=S2+S3
```

```
GEN1 S5=S1-S4
PRINT S4 S5 DF1 DF2
GEN1 CHOWF=(S5/DF1)/(S4/DF2)
PRINT CHOWF
```

The output follows.

```
|_OLS SAVINGS INCOME

OLS ESTIMATION
      18 OBSERVATIONS     DEPENDENT VARIABLE = SAVINGS
...NOTE..SAMPLE RANGE SET TO:     1,    18

 R-SQUARE =    0.9185     R-SQUARE ADJUSTED =    0.9134
VARIANCE OF THE ESTIMATE-SIGMA**2 =  0.35764E-01
STANDARD ERROR OF THE ESTIMATE-SIGMA =  0.18911
SUM OF SQUARED ERRORS-SSE=  0.57223
MEAN OF DEPENDENT VARIABLE =  0.77333
LOG OF THE LIKELIHOOD FUNCTION =  5.49644

VARIABLE     ESTIMATED     STANDARD     T-RATIO          PARTIAL STANDARDIZED ELASTICITY
  NAME       COEFFICIENT   ERROR         16 DF  P-VALUE CORR. COEFFICIENT  AT MEANS
INCOME       0.11785       0.8774E-02   13.43    0.000 0.958    0.9584      2.3992
CONSTANT    -1.0821        0.1452       -7.455   0.000-0.881    0.0000     -1.3992
|_DIAGNOS / CHOWONE=9

DEPENDENT VARIABLE = SAVINGS          18 OBSERVATIONS
REGRESSION COEFFICIENTS
   0.117845048596       -1.08207148733

SEQUENTIAL CHOW AND GOLDFELD-QUANDT TESTS
   N1   N2    SSE1        SSE2         CHOW     PVALUE    G-Q       DF1  DF2 PVALUE
    9    9 0.13965     0.19312       5.0371    0.022 0.7231         7    7 0.340

              CHOW TEST - F DISTRIBUTION WITH DF1=    2 AND DF2=  14
|_* Now construct the Chow F-Test statistic the "long way" following (8.8.4).
|_GEN1 S1=$SSE
..NOTE..CURRENT VALUE OF $SSE =  0.57223
|_GEN1 DF1=$K
..NOTE..CURRENT VALUE OF $K    =   2.0000
|_GEN1 DF2=$N-2*$K
..NOTE..CURRENT VALUE OF $N    =  18.000
..NOTE..CURRENT VALUE OF $K    =   2.0000
|_SAMPLE 1946.0 1954.0

|_OLS SAVINGS INCOME

OLS ESTIMATION
       9 OBSERVATIONS     DEPENDENT VARIABLE = SAVINGS
...NOTE..SAMPLE RANGE SET TO:     1,     9

 R-SQUARE =    0.3092     R-SQUARE ADJUSTED =    0.2105
VARIANCE OF THE ESTIMATE-SIGMA**2 =  0.19950E-01
STANDARD ERROR OF THE ESTIMATE-SIGMA =  0.14124
SUM OF SQUARED ERRORS-SSE=  0.13965
MEAN OF DEPENDENT VARIABLE =  0.26778
```

```
LOG OF THE LIKELIHOOD FUNCTION =  5.97582

VARIABLE    ESTIMATED   STANDARD    T-RATIO        PARTIAL STANDARDIZED ELASTICITY
  NAME      COEFFICIENT   ERROR        7 DF    P-VALUE CORR. COEFFICIENT AT MEANS
INCOME      0.47028E-01 0.2657E-01   1.770      0.120 0.556    0.5561      1.9943
CONSTANT  -0.26625      0.3054      -0.8719     0.412-0.313    0.0000     -0.9943
|_GEN1 S2=$SSE
..NOTE..CURRENT VALUE OF $SSE =  0.13965
|_SAMPLE 1955.0 1963.0

|_OLS SAVINGS INCOME

 OLS ESTIMATION
         9 OBSERVATIONS     DEPENDENT VARIABLE = SAVINGS
...NOTE..SAMPLE RANGE SET TO:   10,   18

 R-SQUARE =   0.9131    R-SQUARE ADJUSTED =   0.9007
VARIANCE OF THE ESTIMATE-SIGMA**2 =  0.27589E-01
STANDARD ERROR OF THE ESTIMATE-SIGMA =  0.16610
SUM OF SQUARED ERRORS-SSE=  0.19312
MEAN OF DEPENDENT VARIABLE =   1.2789
LOG OF THE LIKELIHOOD FUNCTION =  4.51704

VARIABLE    ESTIMATED   STANDARD    T-RATIO        PARTIAL STANDARDIZED ELASTICITY
  NAME      COEFFICIENT   ERROR        7 DF    P-VALUE CORR. COEFFICIENT AT MEANS
INCOME      0.15045     0.1755E-01   8.575      0.000 0.956    0.9555      2.3685
CONSTANT   -1.7502      0.3576      -4.895      0.002-0.880    0.0000     -1.3685
|_GEN1 S3=$SSE
..NOTE..CURRENT VALUE OF $SSE =  0.19312
|_SAMPLE 1946.0 1963.0
|_GEN1 S4=S2+S3
|_GEN1 S5=S1-S4
|_PRINT S4 S5 DF1 DF2
    S4
  0.3327711
    S5
  0.2394554
    DF1
   2.000000
    DF2
   14.00000
|_GEN1 CHOWF=(S5/DF1)/(S4/DF2)
|_PRINT CHOWF
    CHOWF
   5.037060
```

As the output shows, both methods produce identical Chow Test F-statistics.

Section 8.9 shows how to test the functional form of a regression. In particular, choosing between linear and log-linear regression models is discussed. The commands below follow the step by step procedure described. Note that the data for this example is found in the file *EXER720.DAT*.

```
TIME 1971 4
SAMPLE 1971.3 1975.2
READ(EXER720.DAT) YEAR QUARTER Y X2 X3 X4 X5
* Construct the MWD test statistic.
* Estimate the linear model (8.9.3) and save the predicted values, YHAT.
OLS Y X2 X3 / PREDICT=YF
PRINT $ANF
* Estimate the log-linear model (8.9.4). Save the predicted values, LNYHAT.
GENR LNX2=LOG(X2)
GENR LNX3=LOG(X3)
GENR LNY=LOG(Y)
OLS LNY LNX2 LNX3 / PREDICT=LNYF
PRINT $ANF
* Construct Z1.
GENR Z1=LOG(YF)-LNYF
* Regress Y on the X's and Z1 (8.9.5). Reject the null hypothesis that Y is a
* linear function of regressors if the t-ratio for the coefficient for Z1
* is statistically different from zero.
OLS Y X2 X3 Z1
PRINT $ANF
* Since the coefficient for Z1 is not statistically significant, we can not
* reject the hypothesis that the true model is linear.
* Now assume that the true model is log-linear.
* Construct Z2.
GENR Z2=EXP(LNYF)-YF
* Regress the log of Y on the logs of the X's and Z2 (8.9.6). Reject the
* alternate hypothesis that LNY is a linear function of logs of the regressors
* if the t-ratio for the coefficient for Z2 is statistically significant.
OLS LNY LNX2 LNX3 Z2
PRINT $ANF
* Since the coefficient for Z2 is statistically significant (at 12% level),
* the hypothesis that the true is log-linear can be rejected at a 12% level
* of confidence.
```

The output follows.

```
|_* Construct the MWD test statistic.
|_* Estimate the linear model (8.9.3) and save the predicted values, YHAT.
|_OLS Y X2 X3 / PREDICT=YF

 OLS ESTIMATION
      16 OBSERVATIONS        DEPENDENT VARIABLE = Y
...NOTE..SAMPLE RANGE SET TO:    3,    18

 R-SQUARE =   0.7706    R-SQUARE ADJUSTED =   0.7354
VARIANCE OF THE ESTIMATE-SIGMA**2 =  0.11044E+07
STANDARD ERROR OF THE ESTIMATE-SIGMA =   1050.9
SUM OF SQUARED ERRORS-SSE=  0.14357E+08
MEAN OF DEPENDENT VARIABLE =   7645.0
LOG OF THE LIKELIHOOD FUNCTION = -132.360

VARIABLE    ESTIMATED   STANDARD   T-RATIO        PARTIAL STANDARDIZED ELASTICITY
  NAME      COEFFICIENT   ERROR     13 DF    P-VALUE CORR. COEFFICIENT AT MEANS
X2          -3782.2      572.5     -6.607    0.000-0.878    -0.9957    -1.5371
X3           2815.3      947.5      2.971    0.011 0.636     0.4478     1.2638
CONSTANT     9734.2      2888.      3.371    0.005 0.683     0.0000     1.2733
```

```
|_PRINT $ANF
   $ANF       21.84067
|_* Estimate the log-linear model (8.9.4). Save the predicted values, LNYHAT.
|_GENR LNX2=LOG(X2)
|_GENR LNX3=LOG(X3)
|_GENR LNY=LOG(Y)

|_OLS LNY LNX2 LNX3 / PREDICT=LNYF

 OLS ESTIMATION
      16 OBSERVATIONS      DEPENDENT VARIABLE = LNY
...NOTE..SAMPLE RANGE SET TO:     3,    18


 R-SQUARE =    0.7292     R-SQUARE ADJUSTED =    0.6875
VARIANCE OF THE ESTIMATE-SIGMA**2 =  0.29428E-01
STANDARD ERROR OF THE ESTIMATE-SIGMA =  0.17155
SUM OF SQUARED ERRORS-SSE=  0.38257
MEAN OF DEPENDENT VARIABLE =    8.9022
LOG OF THE LIKELIHOOD FUNCTION =  7.16447
```

VARIABLE NAME	ESTIMATED COEFFICIENT	STANDARD ERROR	T-RATIO 13 DF	PARTIAL P-VALUE CORR.	STANDARDIZED COEFFICIENT	ELASTICITY AT MEANS
LNX2	-1.7607	0.2982	-5.904	0.000-0.853	-0.9749	-0.2215
LNX3	1.3398	0.5273	2.541	0.025 0.576	0.4195	0.1849
CONSTANT	9.2278	0.5684	16.23	0.000 0.976	0.0000	1.0366

```
|_PRINT $ANF
   $ANF       17.50066
|_* Construct Z1.
|_GENR Z1=LOG(YF)-LNYF
|_* Regress Y on the X's and Z1 (8.9.5). Reject the null hypothesis that Y is a
|_* linear function of regressors if the t-ratio for the coefficient for Z1
|_* is statistically different from zero.

|_OLS Y X2 X3 Z1

 OLS ESTIMATION
      16 OBSERVATIONS      DEPENDENT VARIABLE = Y
...NOTE..SAMPLE RANGE SET TO:     3,    18


 R-SQUARE =    0.7707     R-SQUARE ADJUSTED =    0.7133
VARIANCE OF THE ESTIMATE-SIGMA**2 =  0.11963E+07
STANDARD ERROR OF THE ESTIMATE-SIGMA =   1093.8
SUM OF SQUARED ERRORS-SSE=  0.14356E+08
MEAN OF DEPENDENT VARIABLE =    7645.0
LOG OF THE LIKELIHOOD FUNCTION = -132.360
```

VARIABLE NAME	ESTIMATED COEFFICIENT	STANDARD ERROR	T-RATIO 12 DF	PARTIAL P-VALUE CORR.	STANDARDIZED COEFFICIENT	ELASTICITY AT MEANS
X2	-3783.1	597.3	-6.334	0.000-0.877	-0.9960	-1.5374
X3	2817.7	993.3	2.837	0.015 0.634	0.4482	1.2649
Z1	85.319	4117.	0.2072E-01	0.984 0.006	0.0029	0.0001
CONSTANT	9727.6	3023.	3.218	0.007 0.681	0.0000	1.2724

```
|_PRINT $ANF
   $ANF       13.44104
|_* Since the coefficient for Z1 is not statistically significant, we can not
|_* reject the hypothesis that the true model is linear.
|_* Now assume that the true model is log-linear.
|_* Construct Z2.
```

```
|_GENR Z2=EXP(LNYF)-YF
|_* Regress the log of Y on the logs of the X's and Z2 (8.9.6). Reject the
|_* alternate hypothesis that LNY is a linear function of logs of the regressors
|_* if the t-ratio for the coefficient for Z2 is statistically significant.

|_OLS LNY LNX2 LNX3 Z2

 OLS ESTIMATION
       16 OBSERVATIONS      DEPENDENT VARIABLE = LNY
...NOTE..SAMPLE RANGE SET TO:     3,    18

 R-SQUARE =    0.7798     R-SQUARE ADJUSTED =    0.7248
VARIANCE OF THE ESTIMATE-SIGMA**2 =   0.25920E-01
STANDARD ERROR OF THE ESTIMATE-SIGMA =   0.16100
SUM OF SQUARED ERRORS-SSE=   0.31103
MEAN OF DEPENDENT VARIABLE =    8.9022
LOG OF THE LIKELIHOOD FUNCTION =  8.82050


VARIABLE    ESTIMATED   STANDARD    T-RATIO          PARTIAL STANDARDIZED ELASTICITY
  NAME      COEFFICIENT   ERROR      12 DF    P-VALUE CORR. COEFFICIENT  AT MEANS
LNX2        -1.9699      0.3069     -6.419    0.000-0.880   -1.0907      -0.2478
LNX3         1.5892      0.5172      3.073    0.010 0.664    0.4976       0.2194
Z2          -0.12938E-03 0.7788E-04 -1.661    0.123-0.432   -0.2477      0.0008
CONSTANT     9.1486      0.5356      17.08    0.000 0.980    0.0000       1.0277
|_PRINT $ANF
   $ANF      14.16645
|_*
|_* Since the coefficient for Z2 is statistically significant (at 12% level),
|_* the hypothesis that the true is log-linear can be rejected at a 12% level
|_* of confidence.
```

Section 8.10 shows how to make predictions based on a multiple regression. The **FC** command will be used to replicate the results provided.

The **FC** Command

The **FC** command uses a set of regression coefficients for a single equation and a set of data to compute predicted values of the dependent variable. The procedure is exactly the same as that used to compute predicted, or ForeCasted, values in regressions. The advantage of the **FC** command is that the estimated coefficients can be taken form a previous regression and predicted values can be generated over any chosen set of observations.

In general, the format of the **FC** command, when the estimated coefficients from the immediately preceding regression are used, is:

FC / *options*

where *options* is a list of desired options.

The **BEG=** and **END=** options with the **FC** command are used to specify the sample range of the forecast.

In the current example, the data from *Table 8.1* is used to estimate a set of coefficients (8.10.1). The sample range of the data used is 1956 to 1970. A set of values for the independent variables for 1971 is assumed. These values are plugged into the estimated regression equation and, based on the regression results using the 1956 to 1970 data, a prediction is made.

The values of the independent variables to be used for prediction have to be added to the end of the original vector of independent variables. That is, 1 observation is added to the variables *PCE*, *PDI*, and *TIME*.

The **DIM** command can be used to specify the length of a variable (i.e. a vector).

The **DIM** Command

The **DIM** command **DIM**ensions a vector or matrix before any data is defined. The format is:

DIM *var   size   var   size ...*

where *var* is the name of the vector or matrix to be dimensioned, and *size* is either one or two numbers to indicate the size of *var*. If only one number is given, SHAZAM assumes that *var* is a vector. If two numbers are given, SHAZAM assumes that *var* is a matrix and that the first number given specifies the number of rows and the second the number of columns.

If a previously undefined variable is read in without having been **DIM**ensioned, the **SAMPLE** range on the **READ** command determines its length.

Since the file *TABLE8.1* contains only 15 observations for the variables, the **SAMPLE** range must be 15 observations long when inputting the file with the **READ** command. Thus, the **DIM** command must be used to dimension the variables to be 16 observations long so that the 16th observation can be added to them. By changing the **SAMPLE** range, the **GENR** command can be used to add the assumed values of the variables to the end of the vectors. The **OLS** command will then estimate the model using the first 15 observations. The **FC** command then uses the estimated coefficients to construct a forecast assuming the values of $567 million for *PDI* and 16 for *TIME*.

```
DIM PCE 16 PDI 16 TIME 16
TIME 1956 1
SAMPLE 1956.0 1970.0
READ(TABLE8.1) PCE PDI TIME
SAMPLE 1971.1 1971.0
GENR PCE=0
GENR PDI=567
GENR TIME=16
SAMPLE 1956.0 1971.0
PRINT PCE PDI TIME
SAMPLE 1956.0 1970.0
OLS PCE PDI TIME
FC / LIST BEG=1971.0 END=1971.0
```

The output follows.

```
|_SAMPLE 1956.0 1971.0
|_PRINT PCE PDI TIME
      PCE             PDI             TIME
   281.4000        309.3000        1.000000
   288.1000        316.1000        2.000000
   290.0000        318.8000        3.000000
   307.3000        333.0000        4.000000
   316.1000        340.3000        5.000000
   322.5000        350.5000        6.000000
   338.4000        367.2000        7.000000
   353.3000        381.2000        8.000000
   373.7000        408.1000        9.000000
   397.7000        434.8000        10.00000
   418.1000        458.9000        11.00000
   430.1000        477.5000        12.00000
   452.7000        499.0000        13.00000
   469.1000        513.5000        14.00000
   476.9000        533.2000        15.00000
   0.0000000       567.0000        16.00000
|_SAMPLE 1956.0 1970.0

|_OLS PCE PDI TIME

.OLS ESTIMATION
      15 OBSERVATIONS     DEPENDENT VARIABLE = PCE
...NOTE..SAMPLE RANGE SET TO:     1,    15


 R-SQUARE =   0.9988    R-SQUARE ADJUSTED =    0.9986
VARIANCE OF THE ESTIMATE-SIGMA**2 =    6.4308
STANDARD ERROR OF THE ESTIMATE-SIGMA =   2.5359
SUM OF SQUARED ERRORS-SSE=    77.169
MEAN OF DEPENDENT VARIABLE =    367.69
LOG OF THE LIKELIHOOD FUNCTION = -33.5687
```

VARIABLE NAME	ESTIMATED COEFFICIENT	STANDARD ERROR	T-RATIO 12 DF	P-VALUE	PARTIAL CORR.	STANDARDIZED COEFFICIENT	ELASTICITY AT MEANS
PDI	0.72659	0.4874E-01	14.91	0.000	0.974	0.8236	0.7959
TIME	2.7363	0.8486	3.225	0.007	0.681	0.1782	0.0595
CONSTANT	53.160	13.03	4.081	0.002	0.762	0.0000	0.1446

```
|_FC / LIST BEG=1971.0 END=1971.0

DEPENDENT VARIABLE = PCE              1 OBSERVATIONS
REGRESSION COEFFICIENTS
   0.726593526870      2.73627658975       53.1603117330
    OBS.    OBSERVED     PREDICTED    CALCULATED  STD. ERROR
    NO.      VALUE         VALUE       RESIDUAL
    16    0.00000        508.92        -508.92       3.176          *    I
```

The following commands will compute the Likelihood Ratio test discussed in
Appendix 8A. Recall that the Log of the Likelihood Function is available in the
temporary variable $LLF. First, the unrestricted model is estimated and the value of the
log-likelihood function, ULLF, is saved. The variable X_3 is dropped and this restricted
model is estimated. The value of log-likelihood function, RLLF, is saved. The LR Test
statistic is constructed by taking the difference between ULLF and RLLF and multiplying
it by 2 (equation (3)). This produces a Chi-square test statistic with 1 degree of freedom.

```
TIME 1971 4
SAMPLE 1971.3 1975.2
READ(EXER720.DAT) YEAR QUARTER Y X2 X3 X4 X5
* Estimate the unrestricted log-likelihood function, ULLF.
OLS Y X2 X3
GEN1 ULLF=$LLF
* Estimate the restricted log-likelihood function, RLLF.
OLS Y X2
GEN1 RLLF=$LLF
* Construct the LR Test statistic.
GEN1 LAMBDA=2*(ULLF-RLLF)
PRINT LAMBDA
```

The output follows.

```
|_* Estimate the unrestricted log-likelihood function, ULLF.
|_?OLS Y X2 X3
|_GEN1 ULLF=$LLF
..NOTE..CURRENT VALUE OF $LLF =  -132.36
|_* Estimate the restricted log-likelihood function, RLLF.
|_?OLS Y X2
|_GEN1 RLLF=$LLF
..NOTE..CURRENT VALUE OF $LLF =  -136.51
|_* Construct the LR Test statistic.
|_GEN1 LAMBDA=2*(ULLF-RLLF)
|_PRINT LAMBDA
   LAMBDA
   8.291959
```

The 95% critical value for a Chi-Square distribution with 1 degree of freedom is 3.84.
Since the value of 8.291959 is larger than a 3.84, the null hypothesis that the price of
carnations, X_3, has no effect on the demand for roses can be rejected.

Since the text cites the p-value, SHAZAM will be used to compute it. That is, with a Chi-Square distribution, we need to find the area to the right of the calculated test statistic. This is done with the **DISTRIB** command.

The **DISTRIB** Command

The **DISTRIB** command will compute the probability density function (PDF) and cumulative density function (CDF) for certain distributions. In particular, this is useful when appropriate statistical tables are unavailable. The general form is:

DISTRIB *vars* / *options*

where *vars* is a list of variables and *options* is a list of options that are required on the specified type of distribution.

The **TYPE=** option with the **DISTRIB** command specifies the type of distribution. If the type is not specified, SHAZAM assumes **TYPE=NORMAL**. Other useful choices include **CHI, F**, and **T**. The **DF=** option is required when **CHI** or **T** is selected. The **DF1=** and **DF2=** options are required when **TYPE=F** is selected. These options specify the Degrees of Freedom.

```
DISTRIB LAMBDA / TYPE=CHI DF=1
```

The output follows.

```
|_DISTRIB LAMBDA / TYPE=CHI DF=1
CHI-SQUARE PARAMETERS- DF=    1.0000
MEAN=    1.0000      VARIANCE=    2.0000      MODE=   0.00000

                  DATA          PDF          CDF          1-CDF
     LAMBDA
 ROW      1      8.2920     0.21928E-02 0.99602      0.39821E-02
```

The column marked "1-CDF" is the p-value for the test statistic *LAMBDA*. Hence, the p-value of obtaining a Chi-Square value of 8.292 or greater is 0.00398. Clearly, this bolsters the above conclusion that the null hypothesis should be rejected.

SHAZAM commands and options used in Chapter 8

CONFID *coef1 coef2 ...* / *options*

DIAGNOS / CHOWONE= CHOWTEST

DIM *var size var size*

DISTRIB *vars* / **TYPE= DF= DF1= DF2=**

END

FC / BEG= END= LIST

GEN1 *newvar=equation*

GENR *newvar=equation* with **LOG**(x) **TIME**(x) **EXP**(x)

OLS *depvar indeps* / **ANOVA LOGLOG PREDICT=**

PRINT *vars* / **WIDE**

READ(*datafile*) *vars* / *options*

SAMPLE *beg end*

TEST *equation*

TIME *beg freq*

? Suppression of Output

Temporary variables used

$ANF	ANOVA F-Statistic
$K	Number of coefficients
$LLF	Log of the Likelihood Function
$N	Number of observations used in the estimation
$R2	R-Square
$SSE	Sum of Squared Errors
$SSR	Regression - SS
$SST	Total - SS

9. THE MATRIX APPROACH TO THE LINEAR REGRESSION MODEL

This chapter uses matrix algebra to demonstrate the concepts of regression analysis that have been presented in previous chapters.

Section 9.3 of the text provides an illustrated example of the matrix method using the coffee-consumption data from *Chapter 3*.

The first step is to construct the **X** matrix of independent variables described in equation (9.1.6). First, the independent variables will be read from the data file *TABLE3.2*. Second, a vector of ones (representing the constant term) will be generated using the **GENR** command. Once all the columns of the **X** matrix have been created, the **MATRIX** command will be used to construct a new matrix from these vectors.

The following operators are valid on the **MATRIX** command:

-	Negation
*	Multiplication
+	Addition
-	Subtraction
'	Transposition
/	Hadamard Division
@	Kronecker Multiplication
|	Concatenation

Regular matrix rules apply on the **MATRIX** command. Therefore, when multiplying with "*", the first matrix to be multiplied must have the same number of columns as the second matrix has rows. Addition and subtraction of matrices are done element by element, so only matrices with the same dimensions may be added to and subtracted from one another. Kronecker multiplication can be done with matrices of any dimension. Concatenation puts two matrices together side by side, so both must have the same number of rows.

The following commands will create the **X** matrix.

```
SAMPLE 1 10
READ(TABLE3.2) Y X2
* Create a constant term.
GENR X1=1
* Construct the X matrix.
MATRIX X=(X1|X2)
PRINT X
```

The output follows.

```
|_SAMPLE 1 10
|_READ(TABLE3.2) Y X2
   2 VARIABLES AND        10 OBSERVATIONS STARTING AT OBS        1

|_* Create a constant term using the GENR command.
|_GENR X1=1
|_* Construct the X matrix.
|_MATRIX X=(X1|X2)
|_PRINT X
   X
   10 BY     2 MATRIX
   1.000000       80.00000
   1.000000       100.0000
   1.000000       120.0000
   1.000000       140.0000
   1.000000       160.0000
   1.000000       180.0000
   1.000000       200.0000
   1.000000       220.0000
   1.000000       240.0000
   1.000000       260.0000
```

The **INV(***matrix***)** function with the **MATRIX** command computes the inverse of *matrix*.

Now, using equation (9.3.11), following the steps in *Section 9.3*, estimate the OLS coefficients.

```
MATRIX XPX=X'X
PRINT XPX
MATRIX XPY=X'Y
PRINT XPY
MATRIX XPXINV=INV(XPX)
PRINT XPXINV
MATRIX BETA=XPXINV*XPY
PRINT BETA
```

The output follows.

```
|_MATRIX XPX=X'X
|_PRINT XPX
   XPX
   2 BY      2 MATRIX
   10.00000       1700.000
   1700.000       322000.0
|_MATRIX XPY=X'Y
|_PRINT XPY
   XPY
   1110.000       205500.0
|_MATRIX XPXINV=INV(XPX)
```

```
|_PRINT XPXINV
   XPXINV
   2 BY     2 MATRIX
 0.9757576      -0.5151515E-02
-0.5151515E-02   0.3030303E-04
|_MATRIX BETA=XPXINV*XPY
|_PRINT BETA
   BETA
   24.45455       0.5090909
```

Now compute the variance-covariance matrix using equation (9.3.13). First, the residual sum of squared errors (e'e) must be constructed using equation (9.3.18). The variance of the regression can then be computed using equation (9.3.14). Since the variance-covariance matrix is not provided in the text, use the **PCOV** option with the **OLS** command to verify the results. Note that the **PCOV** option will print this matrix even though the normal **OLS** output is suppressed using the "?" symbol.

```
MATRIX YPY=Y'Y
PRINT YPY
MATRIX BETAXPY=BETA'XPY
PRINT BETAXPY
MATRIX EPE=YPY-BETAXPY
PRINT EPE
GEN1 N=10
GEN1 K=2
MATRIX SIG2=EPE/(N-K)
PRINT SIG2
MATRIX COVMAT=SIG2*XPXINV
PRINT COVMAT
?OLS Y X2 / PCOV
```

The output follows.

```
|_MATRIX YPY=Y'Y
|_PRINT YPY
   YPY
   132100.0
|_MATRIX BETAXPY=BETA'XPY
|_PRINT BETAXPY
   BETAXPY
   131762.7
|_MATRIX EPE=YPY-BETAXPY
|_PRINT EPE
   EPE
   337.2727
|_GEN1 N=10
|_GEN1 K=2
|_MATRIX SIG2=EPE/(N-K)
|_PRINT SIG2
   SIG2
   42.15909
|_MATRIX COVMAT=SIG2*XPXINV
```

```
|_P COVMAT
    COVMAT
    2 BY      2 MATRIX
   41.13705      -0.2171832
 -0.2171832        0.1277548E-02
|_?OLS Y X2 / PCOV

VARIANCE-COVARIANCE MATRIX OF COEFFICIENTS
X2          0.12775E-02
CONSTANT -0.21718        41.137
            X2               CONSTANT
```

Equation (9.4.2), in *Section 9.4*, shows how to compute the R^2 statistic using matrix algebra. The following commands replicate the results provided in the text.

```
?STAT Y / MEAN=YBAR
MATRIX NYBAR2=N*YBAR**2
PRINT NYBAR2
MATRIX R2=(BETAXPY-NYBAR2)/(YPY-NYBAR2)
PRINT R2
```

The output follows.

```
|_?STAT Y / MEAN=YBAR
|_MATRIX NYBAR2=N*YBAR**2
|_PRINT NYBAR2
    NYBAR2
   123210.0
|_MATRIX R2=(BETAXPY-NYBAR2)/(YPY-NYBAR2)
|_PRINT R2
    R2
  0.9620616
```

Section 9.9 uses the multiple regression model presented in *Section 8.10* to demonstrate individual prediction using matrix algebra. First, using the data from the file *TABLE8.1*, construct the **X** matrix and the **Y** vector. Then use equation (9.3.11) to estimate the OLS coefficients. Note that the vector named *ONE* is a vector of ones and acts as the constant term.

```
SAMPLE 1 15
READ(TABLE8.1) Y X2 X3
GENR ONE=1
MATRIX X=(ONE|X2|X3)
PRINT X
MATRIX BETAHAT=INV(X'X)*X'Y
PRINT BETAHAT
```

The output follows.

```
|_PRINT X
    X
  15 BY        3 MATRIX
   1.000000        309.3000        1.000000
   1.000000        316.1000        2.000000
   1.000000        318.8000        3.000000
   1.000000        333.0000        4.000000
   1.000000        340.3000        5.000000
   1.000000        350.5000        6.000000
   1.000000        367.2000        7.000000
   1.000000        381.2000        8.000000
   1.000000        408.1000        9.000000
   1.000000        434.8000        10.00000
   1.000000        458.9000        11.00000
   1.000000        477.5000        12.00000
   1.000000        499.0000        13.00000
   1.000000        513.5000        14.00000
   1.000000        533.2000        15.00000
|_MATRIX BETAHAT=INV(X'X)*X'Y
|_PRINT BETAHAT
    BETAHAT
   53.16031        0.7265935       2.736277
```

Before using equation (9.9.5) to compute the individual prediction, the vector x_{1971} must be constructed. It will be inputed directly from the command file using the **READ** command.

The **ROWS=** and **COLS=** options with the **READ** command specify the number of **ROWS** and **COLumnS** when a matrix is being read in. Recall that the **LIST** option with the **READ** command prints all the data inputed.

```
READ X0 / ROWS=3 COLS=1 LIST
1
567
16
* Compute YHAT1971 (9.9.6).
MATRIX YHAT1971=X0'BETAHAT
PRINT YHAT1971
```

The output follows.

```
|_READ X0 / ROWS=3 COLS=1 LIST
    1 VARIABLES AND          3 OBSERVATIONS STARTING AT OBS        1
      X0
   1.000000
   567.0000
   16.00000
|_* Compute YHAT1971 (9.9.6).
|_MATRIX YHAT1971=X0'BETAHAT
|_PRINT YHAT1971
    YHAT1971
   508.9193
```

The following commands use equations (9.9.8) to (9.9.15) to compute the variance of the mean prediction and 95% confidence interval as well as the variance of the individual prediction and 95% confidence interval.

```
* Compute the variance of the regression using (9.3.14). As well, following the
* text, print (X'X)^-1
MATRIX SIG2=(Y'Y-BETAHAT'X'Y)/(15-3)
MATRIX XPXINV=INV(X'X)
PRINT SIG2 XPXINV
* Compute the variance (9.9.10) and the standard error (9.9.11) of the mean
* prediction.
MATRIX VARY1971=SIG2*X0'XPXINV*X0
GEN1 SEY1971=SQRT(VARY1971)
PRINT VARY1971 SEY1971
* Construct the 95% confidence interval on the mean response (9.9.12).
GEN1 LOWER=YHAT1971-2.179*SEY1971
GEN1 UPPER=YHAT1971+2.179*SEY1971
PRINT LOWER YHAT1971 UPPER
* Compute the variance of the individual prediction (9.9.15).
MATRIX VARINDIV=SIG2*(1+X0'XPXINV*X0)
GEN1 SEINDIV=SQRT(VARINDIV)
PRINT VARINDIV SEINDIV
* Construct the 95% confidence interval for individual prediction (8.10.7).
GEN1 LOWIND=YHAT1971-2.179*SEINDIV
GEN1 UPIND=YHAT1971+2.179*SEINDIV
PRINT LOWIND YHAT1971 UPIND
```

The output follows.

```
|_* Compute the variance of the regression using (9.3.14). As well, following the
|_* text, print (X'X)^-1
|_MATRIX SIG2=(Y'Y-BETAHAT'X'Y)/(15-3)
|_MATRIX XPXINV=INV(X'X)
|_P SIG2 XPXINV
    SIG2
  6.430752
   XPXINV
   3 BY     3 MATRIX
  26.38578      -0.9818386E-01   1.653178
 -0.9818386E-01  0.3694853E-03 -0.6328756E-02
  1.653178      -0.6328756E-02  0.1119740
|_* Compute the variance (9.9.10) and the standard error (9.9.11) of the mean
|_* prediction.
|_MATRIX VARY1971=SIG2*X0'XPXINV*X0
|_GEN1 SEY1971=SQRT(VARY1971)
|_PRINT VARY1971 SEY1971
   VARY1971
  3.657991
   SEY1971
  1.912588
|_* Construct the 95% confidence interval on the mean response (9.9.12).
|_GEN1 LOWER=YHAT1971-2.179*SEY1971
|_GEN1 UPPER=YHAT1971+2.179*SEY1971
```

```
|_PRINT LOWER YHAT1971 UPPER
    LOWER
   504.7517
    YHAT1971
   508.9193
    UPPER
   513.0868
|_* Compute the variance of the individual prediction (9.9.15).
|_MATRIX VARINDIV=SIG2*(1+X0'XPXINV*X0)
|_GEN1 SEINDIV=SQRT(VARINDIV)
|_PRINT VARINDIV SEINDIV
    VARINDIV
   10.08874
    SEINDIV
   3.176278
|_* Construct the 95% confidence interval for individual prediction (8.10.7).
|_GEN1 LOWIND=YHAT1971-2.179*SEINDIV
|_GEN1 UPIND=YHAT1971+2.179*SEINDIV
|_PRINT LOWIND YHAT1971 UPIND
    LOWIND
   501.9982
    YHAT1971
   508.9193
    UPIND
   515.8404
```

Section 9.10 summarizes the matrix approach to linear regressions. The model regresses per capita consumption expenditure, Y, on per capita disposable income, X_2, a time trend, X_3, and a constant. Understanding the steps involved in the commands below is the key to *Chapter 9*.

Instead of using the **MEAN=** option with the **STAT** command, the mean of a variable will be computed by multiplying the vector of the variable by a transposed vector of ones. (Note that the vector *ONE*, representing the constant term, can be used). In this operation, a 1 by n matrix is multiplied by an n by 1 matrix. The result is a single number in which the elements of the variable vector is summed. Dividing the result by n, the number of observations, generates the mean of the variable.

The following commands replicate the steps and results shown in *Section 9.10*.

```
SAMPLE 1 15
READ(TABLE9.4) Y X2 X3
GENR ONE=1
MATRIX X=(ONE|X2|X3)
GEN1 N=15
GEN1 K=3
PRINT X
* Use matrix algebra to compute the means of Y, X2, and X3.
MATRIX YBAR=(Y'ONE)/N
MATRIX X2BAR=(X2'ONE)/N
MATRIX X3BAR=(X3'ONE)/N
PRINT YBAR X2BAR X3BAR
* Use matrix algebra to compute the sums of the squared deviations from the
```

```
* means for the variables.
MATRIX DEVYY=((Y-YBAR)**2)'ONE
MATRIX DEVX2X2=((X2-X2BAR)**2)'ONE
MATRIX DEVX3X3=((X3-X3BAR)**2)'ONE
PRINT DEVYY DEVX2X2 DEVX3X3
* Compute X'X (9.10.3), X'Y (9.10.4), and (X'X)^-1 (9.10.5).
MATRIX XPX=X'X
MATRIX XPY=X'Y
MATRIX XPXINV=INV(XPX)
PRINT XPX XPY XPXINV
* Now compute the estimated coefficients (9.10.6).
MATRIX BETAHAT=XPXINV*XPY
PRINT BETAHAT
* Compute the residual sum of squares (9.10.7) and the regression
* variance (9.10.8)
MATRIX RSS=Y'Y-BETAHAT'XPY
GEN1 SIG2HAT=RSS/(N-K)
PRINT RSS SIG2HAT
* Construct the var-cov matrix (9.10.9).
MATRIX VARCOV=SIG2HAT*XPXINV
PRINT VARCOV
* Compute the explained sum of squares (9.10.10) and the total sum of squares
* (9.10.11).
MATRIX ESS=BETAHAT'XPY-N*YBAR**2
MATRIX TSS=Y'Y-N*YBAR**2
PRINT ESS TSS
* Compute the R-Square statistic (9.10.12).
MATRIX R2=ESS/TSS
PRINT R2
* Compute the adjusted R-Square statistic using (7.8.4)
MATRIX ADJR2=1-(1-R2)*(N-1)/(N-K)
PRINT ADJR2
* As Gujarati notes, the diagonal of the var-cov matrix, COV, contains the
* estimated variances of the coefficients. Compute the standard errors and the
* t-ratios of the estimated coefficients (9.10.14).
MATRIX B1=BETAHAT(1)
MATRIX B2=BETAHAT(2)
MATRIX B3=BETAHAT(3)
MATRIX SEB1=SQRT(VARCOV(1,1))
MATRIX TB1=B1/SEB1
MATRIX SEB2=SQRT(VARCOV(2,2))
MATRIX TB2=B2/SEB2
MATRIX SEB3=SQRT(VARCOV(3,3))
MATRIX TB3=B3/SEB3
PRINT B1 SEB1 TB1
PRINT B2 SEB2 TB2
PRINT B3 SEB3 TB3
* Construct the F-test statistic testing that B2=B3=0 (9.10.15).
GEN1 F=(ESS/2)/SIG2HAT
PRINT F
* Use the estimated parameters to make a forecast (9.10.16).
READ X71 / ROWS=3 COLS=1 LIST
1
2610
16
MATRIX FC1971=X71'BETAHAT
PRINT FC1971*
* Compute the variance of YHAT1971 (9.10.18).
```

```
MATRIX VARY71=SIG2HAT*(X71'XPXINV*X71)
MATRIX SEY71=SQRT(VARY71)
PRINT VARY71 SEY71
* Use (9.9.13) to compute the variance for the individual prediction.
MATRIX VARIND=SIG2HAT*(1+X71'XPXINV*X71)
MATRIX SEIND=SQRT(VARIND)
PRINT VARIND SEIND
* Use the PCOR option with the STAT command to print the correlation matrix
* (9.10.20).
?STAT Y X2 X3 / PCOR
```

The output follows.

```
|_GENR ONE=1
|_MATRIX X=(ONE|X2|X3)
|_GEN1 N=15
|_GEN1 K=3
|_PRINT X
   X
   15 BY     3 MATRIX
   1.000000        1839.000        1.000000
   1.000000        1844.000        2.000000
   1.000000        1831.000        3.000000
   1.000000        1881.000        4.000000
   1.000000        1883.000        5.000000
   1.000000        1910.000        6.000000
   1.000000        1969.000        7.000000
   1.000000        2016.000        8.000000
   1.000000        2126.000        9.000000
   1.000000        2239.000        10.00000
   1.000000        2336.000        11.00000
   1.000000        2404.000        12.00000
   1.000000        2487.000        13.00000
   1.000000        2535.000        14.00000
   1.000000        2595.000        15.00000
|_* Use matrix algebra to compute the means of Y, X2, and X3.
|_MATRIX YBAR=(Y'ONE)/N
|_MATRIX X2BAR=(X2'ONE)/N
|_MATRIX X3BAR=(X3'ONE)/N
|_PRINT YBAR X2BAR X3BAR
   YBAR
   1942.333
   X2BAR
   2126.333
   X3BAR
   8.000000
|_* Use matrix algebra to compute the sums of the squared deviations from the
|_* means for the variables.
|_MATRIX DEVYY=((Y-YBAR)**2)'ONE
|_MATRIX DEVX2X2=((X2-X2BAR)**2)'ONE
|_MATRIX DEVX3X3=((X3-X3BAR)**2)'ONE
|_PRINT DEVYY DEVX2X2 DEVX3X3
   DEVYY
   830121.3
   DEVX2X2
   1103111.
```

```
    DEVX3X3
   280.0000

|_* Compute X'X (9.10.3), X'Y (9.10.4), and (X'X)^-1 (9.10.5).
|_MATRIX XPX=X'X
|_MATRIX XPY=X'Y
|_MATRIX XPXINV=INV(XPX)
|_P XPX XPY XPXINV
    XPX
    3 BY     3 MATRIX
   15.00000        31895.00       120.0000
   31895.00     0.6892251E+08     272144.0
   120.0000        272144.0       1240.000
    XPY
   29135.00     0.6290582E+08     247934.0
    XPXINV
    3 BY     3 MATRIX
   37.23277       -0.2250812E-01   1.336707
 -0.2250812E-01   0.1371546E-04  -0.8319407E-03
   1.336707       -0.8319407E-03   0.5403457E-01
|_* Now compute the estimated coefficients (9.10.6).
|_MATRIX BETAHAT=XPXINV*XPY
|_PRINT BETAHAT
    BETAHAT
   300.2863        0.7419808       8.043563
|_* Compute the residual sum of squares (9.10.7) and the regression
|_* variance (9.10.8)
|_MATRIX RSS=Y'Y-BETAHAT'XPY
|_GEN1 SIG2HAT=RSS/(N-K)
|_P RSS SIG2HAT
    RSS
   1976.855
    SIG2HAT
   164.7379
|_* Construct the var-cov matrix (9.10.9).
|_MATRIX VARCOV=SIG2HAT*XPXINV
|_PRINT VARCOV
    VARCOV
    3 BY     3 MATRIX
   6133.650       -3.707941        220.2063
  -3.707941      0.2259457E-02   -0.1370522
   220.2063       -0.1370522       8.901545
|_* Compute the explained sum of squares (9.10.10) and the total sum of squares
|_* (9.10.11).
|_MATRIX ESS=BETAHAT'XPY-N*YBAR**2
|_MATRIX TSS=Y'Y-N*YBAR**2
|_PRINT ESS TSS
    ESS
   828144.5
    TSS
   830121.3
|_* Compute the R-Square statistic (9.10.12).
|_MATRIX R2=ESS/TSS
|_PRINT R2
    R2
   0.9976186
|_* Compute the adjusted R-Square statistic using (7.8.4).
|_MATRIX ADJR2=1-(1-R2)*(N-1)/(N-K)
```

```
|_PRINT ADJR2
   ADJR2
 0.9972217
|_* As Gujarati notes, the diagonal of the var-cov matrix, COV, contains the
|_* estimated variances of the coefficients. Compute the standard errors and the
|_* t-ratios of the estimated coefficients (9.10.14).
|_MATRIX B1=BETAHAT(1)
|_MATRIX B2=BETAHAT(2)
|_MATRIX B3=BETAHAT(3)
|_MATRIX SEB1=SQRT(VARCOV(1,1))
|_MATRIX TB1=B1/SEB1
|_MATRIX SEB2=SQRT(VARCOV(2,2))
|_MATRIX TB2=B2/SEB2
|_MATRIX SEB3=SQRT(VARCOV(3,3))
|_MATRIX TB3=B3/SEB3
|_PRINT B1 SEB1 TB1
    B1
   300.2863
    SEB1
   78.31763
    TB1
   3.834210
|_PRINT B2 SEB2 TB2
    B2
  0.7419808
    SEB2
  0.4753374E-01
    TB2
   15.60956
|_PRINT B3 SEB3 TB3
    B3
   8.043563
    SEB3
   2.983546
    TB3
   2.695974
|_* Construct the F-test statistic testing that B2=B3=0 (9.10.15).
|_GEN1 F=(ESS/2)/SIG2HAT
|_PRINT F
    F
   2513.521
|_* Use the estimated parameters to make a forecast (9.10.16).
|_READ X71 / ROWS=3 COLS=1 LIST
    1 VARIABLES AND         3 OBSERVATIONS STARTING AT OBS          1
      X71
   1.000000
   2610.000
   16.00000
|_MATRIX FC1971=X71'BETAHAT
|_PRINT FC1971
    FC1971
   2365.553
|_* Compute the variance of YHAT1971 (9.10.18).
|_MATRIX VARY71=SIG2HAT*(X71'XPXINV*X71)
|_MATRIX SEY71=SQRT(VARY71)
|_PRINT VARY71 SEY71
    VARY71
   48.64263
```

```
    SEY71
   6.974427
|_* Use (9.9.13) to compute the variance for the individual prediction.
|_MATRIX VARIND=SIG2HAT*(1+X71'XPXINV*X71)
|_MATRIX SEIND=SQRT(VARIND)
|_PRINT VARIND SEIND
    VARIND
   213.3806
    SEIND
   14.60755
|_* Use the PCOR option with the STAT command to print the correlation matrix
|_* (9.10.20).
|_?STAT Y X2 X3 / PCOR

 CORRELATION MATRIX OF VARIABLES -        15 OBSERVATIONS

Y         1.0000
X2        0.99809       1.0000
X3        0.97430       0.96639       1.0000
          Y             X2            X3
```

SHAZAM commands and options used in Chapter 9

GEN1 *newvar=equation*   with **SQRT**(x)

GENR *newvar=equation*

MATRIX *newmat=equation* with **INV**(*matrix*) **SQRT**(x)

OLS *depvar indeps* / **PCOV**

PRINT *vars* / *options*

READ(*datafile*) *vars* / **ROWS=** **COLS=** **LIST**

SAMPLE *beg end*

STAT *vars* / **MEAN=** **PCOR**

? Suppression of Output

10. MULTICOLLINEARITY

Chapter 10 is the first of three chapters describing the problems that arise in regression estimation when certain assumptions of the classical linear model are violated. This chapter looks at the problem of multicollinearity, a problem that occurs when some or all of the explanatory variables are intercorrelated.

An example of obvious multicollinearity is provided in *Section 10.1*. Hypothetical data is supplied where one variable, X_3, is simply five times the variable X_2. Hence, they are perfectly collinear. Another variable, X_3^*, also appears to be correlated with X_2, although it is no longer perfectly collinear. The **PCOR** option with the **STAT** command is used below to compute the correlation between X_3 and X_3^*. Note that the data is included directly in the command file.

```
SAMPLE 1 5
READ X2 X3 X3STAR / LIST
10 50 52
15 75 75
18 90 97
24 120 129
30 150 152
STAT X2 X3 X3STAR / PCOR
```

The pertinent output follows.

```
CORRELATION MATRIX OF VARIABLES -          5 OBSERVATIONS

X2           1.0000                      .
X3           1.0000         1.0000
X3STAR       0.99588        0.99588      1.0000
             X2             X3           X3STAR
```

As the above output confirms, the collinearity between X_2 and X_3 is perfect. As well, the coefficient of correlation between X_3 and X_3^* is 0.99588, reflecting the fact that, while not perfectly collinear, they are nevertheless highly correlated.

The empirical example in *Section 10.5* demonstrates that, in the presence of severe multicollinearity, OLS estimators and their standard errors become highly sensitive to even slight changes in the data. The commands below will first use the data from *Table 10.3* to estimate equation (10.5.4). Then equation (10.5.5) will be estimated using the data from *Table 10.4*. In addition, the correlation coefficient between the X_2 and X_3 variables (i.e. r_{23}) and the covariance between the coefficients for X_2 and X_3 will be computed.

```
SAMPLE 1 5
READ(TABLE10.3) Y X2 X3
STAT Y X2 X3 / PCOR
OLS Y X2 X3 / PCOV
READ(TABLE10.4) Y NEWX2 NEWX3
STAT Y NEWX2 NEWX3 / PCOR
OLS Y NEWX2 NEWX3 / PCOV
```

The pertinent output follows.

```
|_STAT Y X2 X3 / PCOR
NAME          N    MEAN        ST. DEV      VARIANCE     MINIMUM      MAXIMUM
Y             5    3.0000      1.5811       2.5000       1.0000       5.0000
X2            5    4.0000      3.1623       10.000       0.00000      8.0000
X3            5    6.8000      6.8702       47.200       0.00000      16.000

 CORRELATION MATRIX OF VARIABLES -          5 OBSERVATIONS

Y         1.0000
X2        0.90000       1.0000
X3        0.50632       0.55234       1.0000
             Y             X2            X3

|_OLS Y X2 X3 / PCOV

 OLS ESTIMATION
        5 OBSERVATIONS      DEPENDENT VARIABLE = Y
...NOTE..SAMPLE RANGE SET TO:     1,    .5


 R-SQUARE =    0.8101     R-SQUARE ADJUSTED =    0.6202
VARIANCE OF THE ESTIMATE-SIGMA**2 =  0.94939
STANDARD ERROR OF THE ESTIMATE-SIGMA =  0.97437
SUM OF SQUARED ERRORS-SSE=   1.8988
MEAN OF DEPENDENT VARIABLE =    3.0000
LOG OF THE LIKELIHOOD FUNCTION = -4.67413
```

VARIABLE NAME	ESTIMATED COEFFICIENT	STANDARD ERROR	T-RATIO 2 DF	P-VALUE	PARTIAL CORR.	STANDARDIZED COEFFICIENT	ELASTICITY AT MEANS
X2	0.44634	0.1848	2.415	0.137	0.863	0.8927	0.5951
X3	0.30488E-02	0.8507E-01	0.3584E-01	0.975	0.025	0.0132	0.0069
CONSTANT	1.1939	0.7737	1.543	0.263	0.737	0.0000	0.3980

```
VARIANCE-COVARIANCE MATRIX OF COEFFICIENTS
X2         0.34155E-01
X3        -0.86834E-02   0.72362E-02
CONSTANT  -0.77572E-01  -0.14472E-01    0.59858
              X2            X3            CONSTANT
|_STAT Y NEWX2 NEWX3 / PCOR
NAME          N    MEAN        ST. DEV      VARIANCE     MINIMUM      MAXIMUM
Y             5    3.0000      1.5811       2.5000       1.0000       5.0000
NEWX2         5    4.0000      3.1623       10.000       0.00000      8.0000
NEWX3         5    6.8000      6.8702       47.200       0.00000      16.000
```

```
CORRELATION MATRIX OF VARIABLES -          5 OBSERVATIONS

Y           1.0000
NEWX2       0.90000        1.0000
NEWX3       0.78249        0.82852        1.0000
              Y              NEWX2          NEWX3


|_OLS Y NEWX2 NEWX3 / PCOV

 OLS ESTIMATION
        5 OBSERVATIONS      DEPENDENT VARIABLE = Y
...NOTE..SAMPLE RANGE SET TO:     1,     5


 R-SQUARE =   0.8143     R-SQUARE ADJUSTED =   0.6286
VARIANCE OF THE ESTIMATE-SIGMA**2 =  0.92838
STANDARD ERROR OF THE ESTIMATE-SIGMA =  0.96352
SUM OF SQUARED ERRORS-SSE=   1.8568
MEAN OF DEPENDENT VARIABLE =    3.0000
LOG OF THE LIKELIHOOD FUNCTION = -4.61818


VARIABLE    ESTIMATED   STANDARD    T-RATIO         PARTIAL STANDARDIZED ELASTICITY
  NAME      COEFFICIENT   ERROR      2 DF    P-VALUE CORR. COEFFICIENT  AT MEANS
NEWX2       0.40135     0.2721       1.475   0.278 0.722    0.8027      0.5351
NEWX3       0.27027E-01 0.1252       0.2158  0.849 0.151    0.1174      0.0613
CONSTANT    1.2108      0.7480       1.619   0.247 0.753    0.0000      0.4036


VARIANCE-COVARIANCE MATRIX OF COEFFICIENTS
NEWX2       0.74019E-01
NEWX3      -0.28228E-01  0.15682E-01
CONSTANT   -0.10413      0.62728E-02  0.55954
              NEWX2          NEWX3         CONSTANT
```

At the end of *Section 10.5*, Gujarati notes that in the presence of high collinearity, individual regression coefficients cannot be estimated precisely. Rather, he notes, linear combinations of these coefficients can be estimated more precisely. The sums of the partial slope coefficients and their standard errors cited can be computed using the **TEST** command as follows.

```
?OLS Y X2 X3
TEST X2+X3
?OLS Y NEWX2 NEWX3
TEST NEWX2+NEWX3
```

The output follows.

```
|_?OLS Y X2 X3
|_TEST X2+X3
TEST VALUE =  0.44939     STD. ERROR OF TEST VALUE  0.15500
T STATISTIC =   2.8993399    WITH    2 D.F.    P-VALUE= 0.10122
F STATISTIC =   8.4061719    WITH    1 AND    2 D.F.  P-VALUE= 0.10122
WALD CHI-SQUARE STATISTIC =   8.4061719     WITH    1 D.F.  P-VALUE= 0.00374
UPPER BOUND ON P-VALUE BY CHEBYCHEV INEQUALITY = 0.11896
```

```
|_?OLS Y NEWX2 NEWX3
|_TEST NEWX2+NEWX3
TEST VALUE =  0.42838      STD. ERROR OF TEST VALUE  0.18233
T STATISTIC =   2.3494054    WITH    2 D.F.     P-VALUE= 0.14324
F STATISTIC =   5.5197056    WITH    1 AND    2 D.F.  P-VALUE= 0.14324
WALD CHI-SQUARE STATISTIC =    5.5197056     WITH    1 D.F.   P-VALUE= 0.01880
UPPER BOUND ON P-VALUE BY CHEBYCHEV INEQUALITY = 0.18117
```

The example in *Section 10.6* uses the hypothetical data from *Table 10.5* to regress consumption, Y, on income, X_2, and wealth, X_3.

First, estimate the equation (10.6.1) and the F-statistic (10.6.2). Recall that this F-statistic, testing that the slope coefficients are jointly equal to zero, is printed when the **ANOVA** option is used with the **OLS** command. It is also available in the temporary variable **$ANF**.

```
SAMPLE 1 10
READ(TABLE10.5) Y X2 X3
OLS Y X2 X3 / ANOVA
```

The output follows.

```
|_OLS Y X2 X3 / ANOVA

 OLS ESTIMATION
      10 OBSERVATIONS      DEPENDENT VARIABLE = Y
...NOTE..SAMPLE RANGE SET TO:     1,    10

 R-SQUARE =   0.9635    R-SQUARE ADJUSTED =    0.9531
VARIANCE OF THE ESTIMATE-SIGMA**2 =    46.349
STANDARD ERROR OF THE ESTIMATE-SIGMA =   6.8080
SUM OF SQUARED ERRORS-SSE=   324.45
MEAN OF DEPENDENT VARIABLE =    111.00
LOG OF THE LIKELIHOOD FUNCTION = -31.5871


                    ANALYSIS OF VARIANCE - FROM MEAN
                     SS          DF          MS             F
REGRESSION        8565.6         2.        4282.8         92.402
ERROR             324.45         7.        46.349        P-VALUE
TOTAL             8890.0         9.        987.78         0.000

                    ANALYSIS OF VARIANCE - FROM ZERO
                     SS          DF          MS             F
REGRESSION      0.13178E+06      3.        43925.        947.697
ERROR             324.45         7.        46.349        P-VALUE
TOTAL           0.13210E+06     10.        13210.         0.000

VARIABLE   ESTIMATED    STANDARD    T-RATIO       PARTIAL STANDARDIZED ELASTICITY
  NAME    COEFFICIENT    ERROR        7 DF     P-VALUE CORR. COEFFICIENT  AT MEANS
X2         0.94154       0.8229       1.144     0.290 0.397    1.8140      1.4420
X3        -0.42435E-01 0.8066E-01   -0.5261     0.615-0.195   -0.8340     -0.6652
CONSTANT   24.775        6.752        3.669     0.008 0.811    0.0000      0.2232
```

As the output shows, the individual t-ratios for the coefficients indicate that β_2 and β_3 are individually not statistically different from zero, yet the value of the F-statistic, 92.402, implies that the hypothesis that β_2 and β_3 are jointly equal to zero, can be rejected. Hence, the two variables are so highly correlated that isolating the individual impact of either income or wealth on consumption is impossible.

When the **CONFID** command is used and two variables (representing the coefficients) are specified, a joint confidence ellipse (*Figure 10.3*) is printed. The following command plots the joint confidence interval to test the hypothesis that $\beta_2 = \beta_3 = 0$.

CONFID X3 X2

The output follows.

```
|_CONFID X3 X2
USING 95% AND 90% CONFIDENCE INTERVALS

CONFIDENCE INTERVALS BASED ON T-DISTRIBUTION WITH    7 D.F.
      - T CRITICAL VALUES =    2.365 AND    1.895
NAME     LOWER 2.5%     LOWER 5%      COEFFICENT    UPPER 5%     UPPER 2.5%     STD. ERROR
X3         -0.2332        -0.1953     -0.42435E-01   0.1104        0.1483         0.081
X2         -1.005         -0.6179      0.94154       2.501         2.888          0.823
CONFIDENCE REGION PLOT FOR X3         AND X2
 USING F DISTRIBUTION WITH 2 AND      7 D.F.       F-VALUE =    4.740


        205 OBSERVATIONS
                      M=MULTIPLE POINT
   0.30000          |
   0.26842          |
   0.23684          |
   0.20526          | M
   0.17368          | MM
   0.14211          | M+M                          +
   0.11053          |  *MM*
   0.78947E-01      |   MMM
   0.47368E-01      |  *MM*
   0.15789E-01      |   MMM
  -0.15789E-01      |   *MMM
  -0.47368E-01      |   MMM*
  -0.78947E-01      |    MMM
  -0.11053          |    MMMM
  -0.14211          |    MMM
  -0.17368          |   *MM*
  -0.20526          |    MMM
  -0.23684          |   +          M+M
  -0.26842          |            *MM
  -0.30000          |             MM

                    _____

              -2.000       0.000       2.000       4.000       6.000


                             X2
```

The next part of this example regresses wealth on income (10.6.3), consumption on income (10.6.4), and consumption on wealth (10.6.5).

```
OLS X3 X2
OLS Y X2
OLS Y X3
```

The output follows.

```
|_OLS X3 X2

 OLS ESTIMATION
      10 OBSERVATIONS      DEPENDENT VARIABLE = X3
...NOTE..SAMPLE RANGE SET TO:    1,   10

 R-SQUARE =   0.9979    R-SQUARE ADJUSTED =   0.9977
VARIANCE OF THE ESTIMATE-SIGMA**2 =    890.41
STANDARD ERROR OF THE ESTIMATE-SIGMA =   29.840
SUM OF SQUARED ERRORS-SSE=   7123.3
MEAN OF DEPENDENT VARIABLE =    1740.0
LOG OF THE LIKELIHOOD FUNCTION = -47.0321

VARIABLE    ESTIMATED   STANDARD   T-RATIO        PARTIAL STANDARDIZED ELASTICITY
  NAME     COEFFICIENT   ERROR       8 DF    P-VALUE CORR. COEFFICIENT  AT MEANS
X2          10.191      0.1643      62.04     0.000 0.999    0.9990      0.9957
CONSTANT    7.5455      29.48       0.2560    0.804 0.090    0.0000      0.0043

|_OLS Y X2

 OLS ESTIMATION
      10 OBSERVATIONS      DEPENDENT VARIABLE = Y
...NOTE..SAMPLE RANGE SET TO:    1,   10

 R-SQUARE =   0.9621    R-SQUARE ADJUSTED =   0.9573
VARIANCE OF THE ESTIMATE-SIGMA**2 =    42.159
STANDARD ERROR OF THE ESTIMATE-SIGMA =   6.4930
SUM OF SQUARED ERRORS-SSE=   337.27
MEAN OF DEPENDENT VARIABLE =    111.00
LOG OF THE LIKELIHOOD FUNCTION = -31.7809

VARIABLE    ESTIMATED   STANDARD   T-RATIO        PARTIAL STANDARDIZED ELASTICITY
  NAME     COEFFICIENT   ERROR       8 DF    P-VALUE CORR. COEFFICIENT  AT MEANS
X2          0.50909     0.3574E-01  14.24     0.000 0.981    0.9808      0.7797
CONSTANT    24.455      6.414       3.813     0.005 0.803    0.0000      0.2203

|_OLS Y X3

 OLS ESTIMATION
      10 OBSERVATIONS      DEPENDENT VARIABLE = Y
...NOTE..SAMPLE RANGE SET TO:    1,   10
```

```
 R-SQUARE =    0.9567     R-SQUARE ADJUSTED =     0.9513
VARIANCE OF THE ESTIMATE-SIGMA**2 =    48.140
STANDARD ERROR OF THE ESTIMATE-SIGMA =    6.9383
SUM OF SQUARED ERRORS-SSE=    385.12
MEAN OF DEPENDENT VARIABLE =    111.00
LOG OF THE LIKELIHOOD FUNCTION = -32.4443


VARIABLE    ESTIMATED    STANDARD    T-RATIO          PARTIAL STANDARDIZED ELASTICITY
  NAME     COEFFICIENT    ERROR        8 DF    P-VALUE CORR. COEFFICIENT  AT MEANS
X3         0.49764E-01 0.3744E-02    13.29     0.000 0.978     0.9781     0.7801
CONSTANT    24.411       6.874        3.551    0.007 0.782     0.0000     0.2199
```

As the text notes, the results for (10.6.5), where the income variable is dropped, show that wealth now has a significant impact on consumption, whereas the results for (10.6.1), where both income and wealth are included, indicate that wealth has no significant effect on consumption. In addition, the results for regressions (10.6.4) and (10.6.5) show that, in the presence of strong multicollinearity, dropping the highly collinear variable often makes the other variable statistically significant.

Section 10.7 discusses the use of eigenvalues and condition numbers as a method of diagnosing multicollinearity. The **PC** command can be used to compute these statistics.

The PC Command

The **PC** command extracts **P**rincipal **C**omponents from a set of data and the eigenvalues of either the cross-product matrix, the scaled cross-product matrix, the cross-product-deviation matrix, or the correlation matrix. Some multicollinearity tests are also possible. In general, the format of the **PC** command is:

PC *vars / options*

where *vars* is a list of variables and *options* a list of desired options.

The **PCOLLIN** option with the **PC** command prints the conditional numbers (k) and conditional indexes (CI) cited in the text. The **SCALE** option is used to scale the **X'X** matrix as needed. The **SCALE** option scales the **X'X** matrix by dividing each element of the **X'X** matrix by summed X^2, leaving 1 on the diagonal.

Using the data from *Table 7.3*, the commands below will replicate the results provided in *Appendix 7A.7*.

```
SAMPLE 1 15
READ(TABLE7.3) Y X2 X3
GENR LNX2=LOG(X2)
GENR LNX3=LOG(X3)
* Generate a constant term.
GENR X1=1
PC X1 LNX2 LNX3 / SCALE PCOLLIN
```

The output follows.

```
|_PC X1 LNX2 LNX3 / SCALE PCOLLIN
 PRINCIPAL COMPONENTS ON     3 VARIABLES        MAXIMUM OF     3 FACTORS RETAINED
EIGENVALUES
   2.9996        0.37545E-03  0.24219E-04

SUM OF EIGENVALUES =    3.0000

CUMULATIVE PERCENTAGE OF EIGENVALUES
  0.99987        0.99999        1.0000

VARIANCE REDUCTION BENCHMARK FUNCTION
  100.00         99.999         93.939

CONDITION NUMBERS
  1.0000         7989.3         0.12385E+06

CONDITION INDEXES
  1.0000         89.383         351.92

VARIANCE PROPORTIONS
     X1          LNX2          LNX3
  1  0.00001     0.00000       0.00004
  2  0.04907     0.00691       0.59592
  3  0.95092     0.99308       0.40404
```

SHAZAM commands and options used in Chapter 10

CONFID *coef1 coef2 ... / options*

GENR *newvar=equation* with **LOG**(x)

OLS *depvar indeps /* **ANOVA PCOV**

PC *vars /* **PCOLLIN SCALE**

READ(*datafile*) *vars /* **LIST**

SAMPLE *beg end*

STAT *vars /* **PCOR**

TEST *equation*

? Suppression of Output

11. HETEROSCEDASTICITY

Chapter 11 discusses the problem of heteroscedasticity. Recall that one of the assumptions of the classic linear regression model is that the disturbances, u_t, all have the same variance, σ^2. That is, the disturbances are homoscedastic. If heteroscedasticity is ignored, the usual OLS estimates will be incorrect and may, in fact, underestimate the value of the true variance. This chapter introduces a number of methods for detecting heteroscedasticity as well as some possible remedial measures.

Section 11.4 provides the results of a Monte Carlo study to demonstrate the consequences of using OLS in the presence of heteroscedasticity. The following output is from a Monte Carlo study using the commands found in the appendix of this chapter. Note that, following the Davidson and McKinnon study from which the example was taken, 20,000 repetitions were performed.

```
****** EXECUTION BEGINNING FOR DO LOOP  # =           1
    ALPHA
  0.5000000
      MSTDOLS         MSTDOLS2          MSTDGLS
  0.2877274       0.2795223        0.2566996
  0.1677158       0.1393328        0.1224295
****** EXECUTION BEGINNING FOR DO LOOP  # =           1
    ALPHA
  1.000000
      MSTDOLS         MSTDOLS2          MSTDGLS
  0.2497476       0.2510425        0.1855230
  0.1455774       0.1076707        0.6189193E-01
****** EXECUTION BEGINNING FOR DO LOOP  # =           1
    ALPHA
  2.000000
      MSTDOLS         MSTDOLS2          MSTDGLS
  0.2032698       0.2238895        0.1104565
  0.1184856       0.7925631E-01    0.1033545E-01
****** EXECUTION BEGINNING FOR DO LOOP  # =           1
    ALPHA
  3.000000
      MSTDOLS         MSTDOLS2          MSTDGLS
  0.1763885       0.2095821        0.6229506E-01
  0.1028165       0.6817711E-01    0.1652825E-02
****** EXECUTION BEGINNING FOR DO LOOP  # =           1
    ALPHA
  4.000000
      MSTDOLS         MSTDOLS2          MSTDGLS
  0.1583048       0.1982720        0.2486748E-01
  0.9227560E-01   0.6254821E-01    0.4056996E-03
```

Note that the standard errors printed in the first rows correspond to $\hat{\beta}_2$ and the second rows correspond to $\hat{\beta}_1$. The above results are very close to those reported in the text.

The topic of *Section 11.5* is the detection of heteroscedasticity. Several methods are used to determine whether there exists a systematic relationship between the error term from the OLS regression and different forms of the independent variable. The data found in *Table 11.1* is used to provide empirical examples for some of these tests.

Park Test: Equation (11.5.3) is estimated and the residuals are transformed into logs and squared. These logged and squared residuals are then regressed on the logged independent variable and a constant (equation (11.5.4)). If the coefficient for the logged independent variable is statistically different from zero, there is evidence of heteroscedasticity in the error terms.

```
SAMPLE 1 9
READ(TABLE11.1) AVCOMP AVPROD
* Equation (11.5.3).
OLS AVCOMP AVPROD / RESID=E1
* The Park Test (11.5.4).
GENR LNE1SQ=LOG(E1**2)
GENR LNAVPROD=LOG(AVPROD)
OLS LNE1SQ LNAVPROD / LOGLOG
```

The output follows.

```
|_* Equation (11.5.3).

|_OLS AVCOMP AVPROD / RESID=E1

 OLS ESTIMATION
        9 OBSERVATIONS        DEPENDENT VARIABLE = AVCOMP
...NOTE..SAMPLE RANGE SET TO:     1,    9


 R-SQUARE =    0.4375    ·R-SQUARE ADJUSTED =    0.3571
VARIANCE OF THE ESTIMATE-SIGMA**2 =  0.11372E+06
STANDARD ERROR OF THE ESTIMATE-SIGMA =   337.23
SUM OF SQUARED ERRORS-SSE=  0.79605E+06
MEAN OF DEPENDENT VARIABLE =    4161.7
LOG OF THE LIKELIHOOD FUNCTION = -64.0263


VARIABLE   ESTIMATED    STANDARD    T-RATIO          PARTIAL STANDARDIZED ELASTICITY
  NAME     COEFFICIENT    ERROR      7 DF   P-VALUE CORR. COEFFICIENT  AT MEANS
AVPROD     0.23296     0.9984E-01   2.333   0.052 0.661     0.6614      0.5213
CONSTANT   1992.3       936.5       2.127   0.071 0.627     0.0000      0.4787
|_* The Park Test (11.5.4).
|_GENR LNE1SQ=LOG(E1**2)
|_GENR LNAVPROD=LOG(AVPROD)

|_OLS LNE1SQ LNAVPROD / LOGLOG

 OLS ESTIMATION
        9 OBSERVATIONS        DEPENDENT VARIABLE = LNE1SQ
...NOTE..SAMPLE RANGE SET TO:     1,    9


 R-SQUARE =    0.0599    R-SQUARE ADJUSTED =   -0.0744
VARIANCE OF THE ESTIMATE-SIGMA**2 =    2.1503
```

```
STANDARD ERROR OF THE ESTIMATE-SIGMA =    1.4664
SUM OF SQUARED ERRORS-SSE=   15.052
MEAN OF DEPENDENT VARIABLE =    10.238
LOG OF THE LIKELIHOOD FUNCTION(IF DEPVAR LOG) = -107.226
```

VARIABLE NAME	ESTIMATED COEFFICIENT	STANDARD ERROR	T-RATIO 7 DF	P-VALUE	PARTIAL CORR.	STANDARDIZED COEFFICIENT	ELASTICITY AT MEANS
LNAVPROD	-2.8010	4.196	-0.6676	0.526	-0.245	-0.2447	-2.8010
CONSTANT	35.817	38.32	0.9347	0.381	0.333	0.0000	35.8173

Since the coefficient for *LNAVPROD* is not statistically different from zero, it can be concluded that the error variance is not heteroscedastic.

Glejser Test: The Glejser test is performed by regressing the absolute values of the OLS residuals on various forms of the independent variable thought to be closely associated with σ^2. If the coefficient for the independent variable or any of its transformations is statistically different from zero, it may be concluded that heteroscedasticity is present in the model. Note that the **ABS(x)** function with the **GENR** command is used to take absolute values.

```
GENR ABE=ABS(E1)
*  |e|  = B1 + B2*X + v
OLS ABE AVPROD
*  |e|  = B1 + B2*SQRT(X) + v
GENR SQRTAVP=SQRT(AVPROD)
OLS ABE SQRTAVP
*  |e|  = B1 + B2*(1/X) + v
GENR INVAP=1/AVPROD
OLS ABE INVAP
*  |e|  = B1 + B2*(1/SQRT(X)) + v
GENR SQTINVAP=SQRT(INVAP)
OLS ABE SQTINVAP
```

The output follows.

```
|_*  |e|  = B1 + B2*X + v

|_OLS ABE AVPROD

 OLS ESTIMATION
       9 OBSERVATIONS       DEPENDENT VARIABLE = ABE


 R-SQUARE =   0.0128    R-SQUARE ADJUSTED =  -0.1282
VARIANCE OF THE ESTIMATE-SIGMA**2 =    51982.
STANDARD ERROR OF THE ESTIMATE-SIGMA =   227.99
SUM OF SQUARED ERRORS-SSE=  0.36387E+06
MEAN OF DEPENDENT VARIABLE =    217.93
LOG OF THE LIKELIHOOD FUNCTION = -60.5034
```

VARIABLE NAME	ESTIMATED COEFFICIENT	STANDARD ERROR	T-RATIO 7 DF	P-VALUE	PARTIAL CORR.	STANDARDIZED COEFFICIENT	ELASTICITY AT MEANS
AVPROD	-0.20340E-01	0.6750E-01	-0.3013	0.772	-0.113	-0.1132	-0.8691
CONSTANT	407.35	633.1	0.6434	0.540	0.236	0.0000	1.8691

```
|_* |e| = B1 + B2*SQRT(X) + v
|_GENR SQRTAVP=SQRT(AVPROD)

|_OLS ABE SQRTAVP

 OLS ESTIMATION
        9 OBSERVATIONS      DEPENDENT VARIABLE = ABE
...NOTE..SAMPLE RANGE SET TO:      1,     9

 R-SQUARE =    0.0110    R-SQUARE ADJUSTED =   -0.1303
VARIANCE OF THE ESTIMATE-SIGMA**2 =    52078.
STANDARD ERROR OF THE ESTIMATE-SIGMA =    228.21
SUM OF SQUARED ERRORS-SSE=  0.36454E+06
MEAN OF DEPENDENT VARIABLE =    217.93
LOG OF THE LIKELIHOOD FUNCTION = -60.5118
```

VARIABLE NAME	ESTIMATED COEFFICIENT	STANDARD ERROR	T-RATIO 7 DF	P-VALUE	PARTIAL CORR.	STANDARDIZED COEFFICIENT	ELASTICITY AT MEANS
SQRTAVP	-3.7098	13.31	-0.2788	0.788	-0.105	-0.1048	-1.6398
CONSTANT	575.30	1284.	0.4480	0.668	0.167	0.0000	2.6398

```
|_* |e| = B1 + B2*(1/X) + v
|_GENR INVAP=1/AVPROD

|_OLS ABE INVAP

 OLS ESTIMATION
        9 OBSERVATIONS      DEPENDENT VARIABLE = ABE
...NOTE..SAMPLE RANGE SET TO:      1,     9

 R-SQUARE =    0.0062    R-SQUARE ADJUSTED =   -0.1358
VARIANCE OF THE ESTIMATE-SIGMA**2 =    52332.
STANDARD ERROR OF THE ESTIMATE-SIGMA =    228.76
SUM OF SQUARED ERRORS-SSE=  0.36632E+06
MEAN OF DEPENDENT VARIABLE =    217.93
LOG OF THE LIKELIHOOD FUNCTION = -60.5337
```

VARIABLE NAME	ESTIMATED COEFFICIENT	STANDARD ERROR	T-RATIO 7 DF	P-VALUE	PARTIAL CORR.	STANDARDIZED COEFFICIENT	ELASTICITY AT MEANS
INVAP	0.12988E+07	0.6239E+07	0.2082	0.841	0.078	0.0784	0.6487
CONSTANT	76.552	683.4	0.1120	0.914	0.042	0.0000	0.3513

```
|_* |e| = B1 + B2*(1/SQRT(X)) + v

|_GENR SQTINVAP=SQRT(INVAP)

|_OLS ABE SQTINVAP

 OLS ESTIMATION
        9 OBSERVATIONS      DEPENDENT VARIABLE = ABE
...NOTE..SAMPLE RANGE SET TO:      1,     9

 R-SQUARE =    0.0076    R-SQUARE ADJUSTED =   -0.1341
VARIANCE OF THE ESTIMATE-SIGMA**2 =    52254.
STANDARD ERROR OF THE ESTIMATE-SIGMA =    228.59
SUM OF SQUARED ERRORS-SSE=  0.36578E+06
MEAN OF DEPENDENT VARIABLE =    217.93
LOG OF THE LIKELIHOOD FUNCTION = -60.5270
```

VARIABLE NAME	ESTIMATED COEFFICIENT	STANDARD ERROR	T-RATIO 7 DF	P-VALUE	PARTIAL CORR.	STANDARDIZED COEFFICIENT	ELASTICITY AT MEANS
SQTINVAP	29686.	0.1279E+06	0.2320	0.823	0.087	0.0874	1.4188
CONSTANT	-91.280	1335.	-0.6839E-01	0.947	-0.026	0.0000	-0.4188

Since none of the estimated coefficients for *AVPROD* nor any of its transformations are statistically different from zero, the Glejser test suggests that heteroscedasticity is not present in this model.

Spearman's Rank Correlation Test: This is another test which may be used to detect the presence of heteroscedasticity. The data found in *Table 11.2* is used for this example. The first step is to regress average annual return, *AVRET*, on its standard deviations, *SDAVRET*. The absolute value of the estimated residuals and *SDAVRET* are then used to compute the Spearman's rank correlation coefficient. The **PRANKCOR** option with the **STAT** command Prints a matrix of Spearman's **RANK CORrelation** coefficients between two variables. The **RANKCOR=** option stores this matrix in the variable specified. Finally, the t-statistic (11.5.6) is constructed. If the t-statistic does not exceed the t-appropriate critical value, the null hypothesis of heteroscedasticity can be rejected.

The **DISTRIB** command will be used to compute the p-value of the test statistic. Recall that the p-value is found under the heading "1-CDF" in the output. Note that **TYPE=** is set to **T** and **DF=** to 8.

```
* Spearman's Rank Correlation TEST
SAMPLE 1 10
READ(TABLE11.2) AVRET SDAVRET
OLS AVRET SDAVRET / RESID=E2
GENR ABE2=ABS(E2)
STAT SDAVRET ABE2 / RANKCOR=R PRANKCOR
* Compute equation (11.5.6).
MATRIX TSTAT=(R(2,1)*SQRT($N-2))/(SQRT(1-R(2,1)**2))
PRINT TSTAT
DISTRIB TSTAT / TYPE=T DF=8
```

The output follows.

```
|_* Spearman's Rank Correlation TEST

|_OLS AVRET SDAVRET / RESID=E2

 OLS ESTIMATION
      10 OBSERVATIONS       DEPENDENT VARIABLE = AVRET
...NOTE..SAMPLE RANGE SET TO:    1,   10

 R-SQUARE =    0.9165    R-SQUARE ADJUSTED =    0.9061
VARIANCE OF THE ESTIMATE-SIGMA**2 =   0.47642
STANDARD ERROR OF THE ESTIMATE-SIGMA =   0.69023
SUM OF SQUARED ERRORS-SSE=    3.8113
MEAN OF DEPENDENT VARIABLE =    12.970
LOG OF THE LIKELIHOOD FUNCTION = -9.36637
```

```
VARIABLE    ESTIMATED    STANDARD    T-RATIO          PARTIAL STANDARDIZED ELASTICITY
  NAME     COEFFICIENT    ERROR        8 DF    P-VALUE CORR. COEFFICIENT  AT MEANS
SDAVRET    0.45896      0.4897E-01   9.372      0.000 0.957    0.9574      0.5513
CONSTANT   5.8194       0.7935       7.333      0.000 0.933    0.0000      0.4487
|_GENR ABE2=ABS(E2)
|_STAT SDAVRET ABE2 / RANKCOR=R PRANKCOR
NAME       N     MEAN         ST. DEV      VARIANCE      MINIMUM       MAXIMUM
SDAVRET    10    15.580       4.6984       22.075        10.200        21.700
ABE2       10    0.45613      0.43854      0.19231       0.26929E-01   1.2411

SPEARMAN RANK CORRELATION MATRIX -          10 OBSERVATIONS

SDAVRET     1.0000
ABE2        0.33333        1.0000
               SDAVRET        ABE2
|_* Compute equation (11.5.6).
|_MATRIX TSTAT=(R(2,1)*SQRT($N-2))/(SQRT(1-R(2,1)**2))
..NOTE..CURRENT VALUE OF $N   =    10.000
|_PRINT TSTAT
    TSTAT
  1.000000
|_DISTRIB TSTAT / TYPE=T DF=8
T DISTRIBUTION DF=    8.0000
VARIANCE=    1.3333        H=    1.0000


              DATA        PDF        CDF        1-CDF
   TSTAT
ROW     1    1.0000      0.22761    0.82670    0.17330
```

Since the t-statistic is below the 90% critical value (p-value = 0.1733), it can be concluded that there is no evidence of a systematic relationship between the explanatory variable and the absolute values of the residuals. This suggests that there is no heteroscedasticity in the model.

The **HET** option with the **DIAGNOS** command runs a series of tests for heteroscedasticity. This option will be demonstrated using the data from *Table 11.1*.

```
SAMPLE 1 9
?OLS AVCOMP AVPROD
DIAGNOS / HET
```

The pertinent output follows.

```
HETEROSKEDASTICITY TESTS
  E**2 ON YHAT:           CHI-SQUARE =    0.008 WITH 1 D.F.
  E**2 ON YHAT**2:        CHI-SQUARE =    0.014 WITH 1 D.F.
  E**2 ON LOG(YHAT**2):   CHI-SQUARE =    0.003 WITH 1 D.F.
  E**2 ON X (B-P-G) TEST:      CHI-SQUARE =    0.008 WITH  1 D.F.
  E**2 ON LAG(E**2)  ARCH TEST: CHI-SQUARE =    2.173 WITH  1 D.F.
  LOG(E**2) ON X (HARVEY) TEST: CHI-SQUARE =    0.203 WITH  1 D.F.
  ABS(E) ON X (GLEJSER) TEST:  CHI-SQUARE =    0.147 WITH  1 D.F.
```

Again, the above test statistics reject the hypothesis that the model is heteroscedastic. They are similar to the tests discussed above except they follow a Chi-square distribution.

Goldfeld-Quandt Test: In this test, it is assumed that the regression variance, σ^2, is related to one of the independent variables, say X. The first step is to rank the observations based on the values of X. If it is assumed that σ^2 is positively related to X, the observations are sorted beginning with the lowest value of X. The idea is to have the larger residual sum of squares as the numerator in equation (11.5.10) so that the test statistic is greater than 1. If this is the case, the critical values from the upper points of the F-distribution (i.e. from the right-hand-side tail) are used (see the tables in the *Appendix*). If the test statistic is less than one, the critical values from the left side of the F-distribution are the ones to consult. Often, texts do not provide tables of these critical values. This dilemma can be avoided by looking at the p-value of the test statistic (or by simply inverting the test statistic and its degrees of freedom if it is smaller than 1).

The **SORT** Command

The **SORT** command can be used to sort data. A variable which will be used to sort the data must be specified. When completed, all observations of the specified variables will be arranged in ascending order according to the ranking of the sort variable. The general format of the **SORT** command is:

SORT *sortvar vars / options*

where *sortvar* is the name of the sorting variable, *vars* is a list of the variables to be sorted and *options* is a list of desired options.

The **DESC** option with the **SORT** command is used to sort the data in descending rather than ascending order. The **LIST** option prints the all the sorted data.

In the second step, a group of central observations of the sorted data is omitted. The third step involves running two regressions using the first and the second group of observations. The residual sum of squares from each regression are then used to compute the test statistic (11.5.10).

The data found in *Table 11.3* is used in *Example 11.3* to illustrate the Goldfeld-Quandt (GQ) test.

```
SAMPLE 1 30
READ(TABLE11.3) Y X
SORT X Y / LIST
SAMPLE 1 13
OLS Y X
GEN1 RSS1=$SSE
GEN1 DFDENOM=$DF
SAMPLE 18 30
OLS Y X
GEN1 RSS2=$SSE
GEN1 DFNUM=$DF
* Equation (11.5.10).
GEN1 LAMBDA=(RSS2/DFNUM)/(RSS1/DFDENOM)
PRINT LAMBDA
DISTRIB LAMBDA / TYPE=F DF1=DFNUM DF2=DFDENOM
```

The output follows.

```
| SORT X Y / LIST
        X                    Y
  80.00000            55.00000
  85.00000            70.00000
  90.00000            75.00000
  100.0000            65.00000
  105.0000            74.00000
  110.0000            80.00000
  115.0000            84.00000
  120.0000            79.00000
  125.0000            90.00000
  130.0000            98.00000
  140.0000            95.00000
  145.0000            108.0000
  150.0000            113.0000
  160.0000            110.0000
  165.0000            125.0000
  180.0000            115.0000
  185.0000            130.0000
  190.0000            135.0000
  200.0000            120.0000
  205.0000            140.0000
  210.0000            144.0000
  220.0000            152.0000
  225.0000            140.0000
  230.0000            137.0000
  240.0000            145.0000
  245.0000            175.0000
  250.0000            189.0000
  260.0000            180.0000
  265.0000            178.0000
  270.0000            191.0000
DATA HAS BEEN SORTED BY VARIABLE X

| SAMPLE 1 13
```

```
|_OLS Y X

 OLS ESTIMATION
     13 OBSERVATIONS      DEPENDENT VARIABLE = Y
...NOTE..SAMPLE RANGE SET TO:     1,    13


 R-SQUARE =   0.8887    R-SQUARE ADJUSTED =    0.8785
VARIANCE OF THE ESTIMATE-SIGMA**2 =    34.288
STANDARD ERROR OF THE ESTIMATE-SIGMA =    5.8556
SUM OF SQUARED ERRORS-SSE=   377.17
MEAN OF DEPENDENT VARIABLE =    83.538
LOG OF THE LIKELIHOOD FUNCTION = -40.3365


VARIABLE    ESTIMATED    STANDARD    T-RATIO         PARTIAL STANDARDIZED ELASTICITY
  NAME     COEFFICIENT    ERROR       11 DF   P-VALUE CORR. COEFFICIENT  AT MEANS
X           0.69677     0.7437E-01    9.370   0.000 0.943   0.9427       0.9592
CONSTANT    3.4094       8.705        0.3917  0.703 0.117   0.0000       0.0408
|_GEN1 RSS1=$SSE
..NOTE..CURRENT VALUE OF $SSE =    377.17
|_GEN1 DFDENOM=$DF
..NOTE..CURRENT VALUE OF $DF  =    11.000
|_SAMPLE 18 30

|_OLS Y X

 OLS ESTIMATION
      13 OBSERVATIONS      DEPENDENT VARIABLE = Y
...NOTE..SAMPLE RANGE SET TO:    18,    30


 R-SQUARE =   0.7681    R-SQUARE ADJUSTED =    0.7470
VARIANCE OF THE ESTIMATE-SIGMA**2 =    139.71
STANDARD ERROR OF THE ESTIMATE-SIGMA =    11.820
SUM OF SQUARED ERRORS-SSE=   1536.8
MEAN OF DEPENDENT VARIABLE =    155.85
LOG OF THE LIKELIHOOD FUNCTION = -49.4675


VARIABLE    ESTIMATED    STANDARD    T-RATIO         PARTIAL STANDARDIZED ELASTICITY
  NAME     COEFFICIENT    ERROR       11 DF   P-VALUE CORR. COEFFICIENT  AT MEANS
X           0.79414      0.1316       6.035   0.000 0.876   0.8764       1.1798
CONSTANT   -28.027      30.64        -0.9147  0.380-0.266   0.0000      -0.1798
|_GEN1 RSS2=$SSE
..NOTE..CURRENT VALUE OF $SSE =    1536.8
|_GEN1 DFNUM=$DF
..NOTE..CURRENT VALUE OF $DF  =    11.000
|_* Equation (11.5.10).
|_GEN1 LAMBDA=(RSS2/DFNUM)/(RSS1/DFDENOM)
|_PRINT LAMBDA
   LAMBDA
   4.074595
|_DISTRIB LAMBDA / TYPE=F DF1=DFNUM DF2=DFDENOM
F DISTRIBUTION- DF1=    11.000     DF2=    11.000
MEAN=    1.2222    VARIANCE=   0.77601     MODE=    0.69231


             DATA        PDF        CDF       1-CDF
   LAMBDA
ROW     1    4.0746    0.12824E-01 0.98591     0.14090E-01
```

Since the test statistic λ exceeds the F[11, 11] 5% critical value, it can be concluded that the error variance is heteroscedastic. However, this conclusion is not possible at the 1% level of significance (p-value = 0.014).

This GQ test can also be performed using the **CHOWTEST** option with the **DIAGNOS** command. The **GQOBS=** option with the **CHOWTEST** option is used to specify the number of central observations to be omitted for the GQ test. The default is zero.

```
SAMPLE 1 30
SORT X Y
?OLS Y X
DIAGNOS / CHOWTEST GQOBS=4
```

The output follows.

```
| DIAGNOS / CHOWTEST GQOBS=4

DEPENDENT VARIABLE = Y                    30 OBSERVATIONS
REGRESSION COEFFICIENTS
    0.637784557616         9.29030743957


HARVEY-COLLIER  [1977] RECURSIVE T-TEST =            0.2565  WITH    27 D.F.
HARVEY-PHILLIPS [1974] HETEROSKEDASTICITY TEST =     4.8390  WITH M =     9

BACKWARDS

HARVEY-COLLIER  [1977] RECURSIVE T-TEST =            1.1691  WITH    27 D.F.
HARVEY-PHILLIPS [1974] HETEROSKEDASTICITY TEST =     0.2078  WITH M =     9

SEQUENTIAL CHOW AND GOLDFELD-QUANDT TESTS
  N1   N2      SSE1         SSE2        CHOW      PVALUE      G-Q        DF1    DF2 PVALUE
   3   27    16.667       2208.7      0.79339      0.463  0.0000        -1     23 0.000
   4   26   188.57        2155.9      0.92385E-01  0.912  0.0000         0     22 0.000
   5   25   189.77        2151.4      0.11082      0.896  0.1629         1     21 0.309
   6   24   200.51        2151.1      0.52768E-01  0.949  0.8988         2     20 0.577
   7   23   208.55        2148.7      0.21504E-01  0.979  0.5729         3     19 0.360
   8   22   229.15        2098.0      0.18982      0.828  0.4364         4     18 0.219
   9   21   244.80        2098.0      0.10175      0.904  0.3452         5     17 0.122
  10   20   292.91        2067.7      0.29374E-02  0.997  0.3037         6     16 0.074
  11   19   301.51        2054.3      0.29582E-01  0.971  0.2751         7     15 0.046
  12   18   341.67        2012.4      0.39320E-01  0.961  0.2695         8     14 0.034
  13   17   377.17        1906.9      0.43846      0.650  0.2663         9     13 0.027
  14   16   394.23        1902.3      0.36557      0.697  0.2518        10     12 0.018
  15   15   443.79        1635.5      1.7621       0.192  0.2454        11     11 0.014
  16   14   593.74        1628.6      0.81216      0.455  0.2472        12     10 0.013
  17   13   595.30        1536.8      1.3966       0.265  0.2426        13      9 0.011
  18   12   601.50        1329.0      2.9003       0.073  0.2818        14      8 0.019
  19   11   894.69        1266.5      1.2031       0.316  0.2590        15      7 0.013
  20   10   897.41        1204.0      1.6067       0.220  0.2689        16      6 0.017
  21    9   902.16        1072.6      2.5439       0.098  0.3144        17      5 0.033
  22    8   913.89         838.80     4.5130       0.021  0.2753        18      4 0.024
  23    7  1034.2          837.01     3.4036       0.049  0.8451        19      3 0.343
  24    6  1251.0          724.44     2.5384       0.098  0.7353        20      2 0.279
  25    5  1359.1          168.55     7.0924       0.003  1.313         21      1 0.607
```

| 26 | 4 | 1624.2 | 124.29 | 4.5552 | 0.020 0.0000 | 22 | 0 0.000 |
| 27 | 3 | 2210.9 | 37.500 | 0.65185 | 0.529 0.0000 | 23 | -1 0.000 |

CHOW TEST - F DISTRIBUTION WITH DF1=   2 AND DF2= 26

Note that the GQ statistic printed at N1=15 N2=15 is actually the inverse of the test statistic computed above. This is because SHAZAM uses RSS1 as the numerator and RSS2 as the denominator in formula (11.5.10). If it is assumed that the variance is positively related to the value of the sort variable, the **DESC** option with the **SORT** command can be used. Of course, as mentioned above, one can merely invert the test statistic and the degrees of freedom if it is less than one. However, this problem can be avoided by simply looking at the p-value which, as the above output confirms, is identical using both forms of the GQ formula.

The Breusch-Pagan Test: *Example 11.4* outlines the steps involved in performing the Breusch-Pagan (BP) test. The data from *Table 11.3* is used for this example.

Note that, in Step II, the estimated variance is computed by dividing the residual sum of the squares by the number of observations, N, not by N-K. This gives the Maximum-Likelihood estimate of the variance. The **DN** option on the **OLS** command is used so that SHAZAM **D**ivides the residual sum of squares by **N**, not N-K.

```
SAMPLE 1 30
OLS Y X / RESID=E DN
GEN1 VAR=$SIG2
PRINT VAR
GENR E2=E**2
GENR P=E2/VAR
OLS P X
* Equation (11.5.19).
GEN1 THETA=0.5*$SSR
PRINT THETA
DISTRIB THETA / TYPE=CHI DF=1
```

The output follows.

```
|_OLS Y X / RESID=E DN

 OLS ESTIMATION
      30 OBSERVATIONS      DEPENDENT VARIABLE = Y
...NOTE..SAMPLE RANGE SET TO:    1,    30


 R-SQUARE =   0.9466    R-SQUARE ADJUSTED =   0.9447
VARIANCE OF THE ESTIMATE-SIGMA**2 =   78.705
STANDARD ERROR OF THE ESTIMATE-SIGMA =    8.8716
SUM OF SQUARED ERRORS-SSE=   2361.2
MEAN OF DEPENDENT VARIABLE =    119.73
LOG OF THE LIKELIHOOD FUNCTION = -108.054
```

```
                              ASYMPTOTIC
VARIABLE    ESTIMATED   STANDARD   T-RATIO       PARTIAL STANDARDIZED ELASTICITY
  NAME      COEFFICIENT   ERROR    --------   P-VALUE CORR. COEFFICIENT  AT MEANS
X            0.63778    0.2765E-01  23.07      0.000 0.975    0.9730     0.9224
CONSTANT     9.2903     5.054        1.838     0.066 0.328    0.0000     0.0776
|_GEN1 VAR=$SIG2
..NOTE..CURRENT VALUE OF $SIG2=    78.705
|_PRINT VAR
    VAR
   78.70511
|_GENR E2=E**2
|_GENR P=E2/VAR

|_OLS P X

 OLS ESTIMATION
       30 OBSERVATIONS     DEPENDENT VARIABLE = P
...NOTE..SAMPLE RANGE SET TO:    1,   30


 R-SQUARE =   0.1757    R-SQUARE ADJUSTED =   0.1463
VARIANCE OF THE ESTIMATE-SIGMA**2 =   1.7468
STANDARD ERROR OF THE ESTIMATE-SIGMA =   1.3217
SUM OF SQUARED ERRORS-SSE=   48.910
MEAN OF DEPENDENT VARIABLE =   1.0000
LOG OF THE LIKELIHOOD FUNCTION = -49.8999

VARIABLE    ESTIMATED   STANDARD   T-RATIO       PARTIAL STANDARDIZED ELASTICITY
  NAME      COEFFICIENT   ERROR     28 DF     P-VALUE CORR. COEFFICIENT  AT MEANS
X           0.10063E-01 0.4119E-02  2.443      0.021 0.419    0.4192     1.7426
CONSTANT   -0.74261     0.7529     -0.9863     0.332-0.183    0.0000    -0.7426
|_* Equation (11.5.19).
|_GEN1 THETA=0.5*$SSR
..NOTE..CURRENT VALUE OF $SSR =   10.428
|_PRINT THETA
    THETA
   5.214011
|_DISTRIB THETA / TYPE=CHI DF=1
CHI-SQUARE PARAMETERS- DF=   1.0000
MEAN=   1.0000    VARIANCE=   2.0000    MODE=   0.00000

             DATA       PDF        CDF        1-CDF
  THETA
 ROW    1    5.2140    0.12886E-01 0.97759    0.22406E-01
```

As the text notes, the value of the test statistic, θ, is above the 5% Chi-square critical value with one degree of freedom, implying that the hypothesis of heteroscedasticity cannot be rejected. However, θ is not above the 1% Chi-square critical value. Thus, hypothesis of heteroscedasticity can be rejected at the 1% level of significance (p-value = 0.0224).

The White Test: This test involves estimating the model using OLS. The estimated residuals are squared and are regressed on the original independent variables, their squared values, and interactive terms if more than one explanatory variable is included. The R^2 statistic from this auxiliary regression is multiplied by N, the number of observations in the regression. The resulting test statistic follows a Chi-square distribution with p degrees of freedom where p is the number of regressors in the auxiliary regression not including the constant term. If the test statistic is above the appropriate critical value, it can be concluded that there is evidence that heteroscedasticity exists in the model.

The data for this example is found in the file *EXAMP115.DAT*. Details and variable descriptions are included at the end of the file.

```
SAMPLE 1 41
READ(EXAMP115.DAT) GOVREV TRADE GNP LOWDUMMY
GENR LNGOVREV=LOG(GOVREV)
GENR LNGNP=LOG(GNP)
GENR LNTRADE=LOG(TRADE)
* Equation (11.5.23).
OLS LNGOVREV LNTRADE LNGNP / RESID=UHAT LOGLOG
* Equation (11.5.24).
GENR LNTRADE2=LNTRADE**2
GENR LNGNP2=LNGNP**2
GENR UHAT2=UHAT**2
GENR LNTRGNP=LNTRADE*LNGNP
OLS UHAT2 LNTRADE LNGNP LNTRADE2 LNGNP2 LNTRGNP
* Construct the test statistic using (11.5.22) and compute the p-value.
GEN1 CHISTAT=$N*$R2
DISTRIB CHISTAT / TYPE=CHI DF=5
```

The output follows.

```
|_* Equation (11.5.23).
|_OLS LNGOVREV LNTRADE LNGNP / RESID=UHAT LOGLOG

 OLS ESTIMATION
     41 OBSERVATIONS       DEPENDENT VARIABLE = LNGOVREV
...NOTE..SAMPLE RANGE SET TO:    1,   41

 R-SQUARE =   0.6161    R-SQUARE ADJUSTED =    0.5959
VARIANCE OF THE ESTIMATE-SIGMA**2 =  0.41718
STANDARD ERROR OF THE ESTIMATE-SIGMA =  0.64589
SUM OF SQUARED ERRORS-SSE=   15.853
MEAN OF DEPENDENT VARIABLE =   2.9080
LOG OF THE LIKELIHOOD FUNCTION(IF DEPVAR LOG) = -157.924

VARIABLE    ESTIMATED   STANDARD   T-RATIO        PARTIAL STANDARDIZED ELASTICITY
  NAME     COEFFICIENT   ERROR      38 DF   P-VALUE CORR. COEFFICIENT  AT MEANS
LNTRADE    0.89566      0.2002     4.474    0.000 0.587    0.4534      0.8957
LNGNP     -0.72595      0.1049    -6.921    0.000-0.747   -0.7014     -0.7260
CONSTANT   4.0496       0.8676     4.668    0.000 0.604    0.0000      4.0496
_* Construct the test statistic using (11.5.22) and compute the p-value.
|_GENR LNTRADE2=LNTRADE**2
|_GENR LNGNP2=LNGNP**2
|_GENR UHAT2=UHAT**2
|_GENR LNTRGNP=LNTRADE*LNGNP
```

```
|_OLS UHAT2 LNTRADE LNGNP LNTRADE2 LNGNP2 LNTRGNP

OLS ESTIMATION
     41 OBSERVATIONS      DEPENDENT VARIABLE = UHAT2
...NOTE..SAMPLE RANGE SET TO:    1,   41


 R-SQUARE =   0.1148    R-SQUARE ADJUSTED =  -0.0117
VARIANCE OF THE ESTIMATE-SIGMA**2 =  0.30627
STANDARD ERROR OF THE ESTIMATE-SIGMA =  0.55341
SUM OF SQUARED ERRORS-SSE=   10.719
MEAN OF DEPENDENT VARIABLE =  0.38665
LOG OF THE LIKELIHOOD FUNCTION = -30.6752


VARIABLE    ESTIMATED    STANDARD    T-RATIO         PARTIAL STANDARDIZED ELASTICITY
  NAME     COEFFICIENT    ERROR       35 DF    P-VALUE CORR. COEFFICIENT AT MEANS
LNTRADE    2.5629        2.113        1.213    0.233 0.201    2.3962    22.8660
LNGNP      0.69184       1.173        0.5899   0.559 0.099    1.2344    10.4293
LNTRADE2  -0.40810       0.2608      -1.565    0.127-0.256   -2.4928   -12.8325
LNGNP2    -0.49085E-01 0.8944E-01 -0.5488     0.587-0.092   -1.0343    -4.4322
LNTRGNP    0.14943E-02 0.1463     0.1021E-01  0.992 0.002    0.0131     0.0780
CONSTANT  -5.8417        5.002       -1.168    0.251-0.194    0.0000   -15.1085
|_* Construct the test statistic using (11.5.22) and the p-value.
|_GEN1 CHISTAT=$N*$R2
..NOTE..CURRENT VALUE OF $N   =    41.000
..NOTE..CURRENT VALUE OF $R2  =   0.11476
|_DISTRIB CHISTAT / TYPE=CHI DF=5
CHI-SQUARE PARAMETERS- DF=   5.0000
MEAN=   5.0000       VARIANCE=   10.000     MODE=    3.0000


            DATA        PDF        CDF        1-CDF
  CHISTAT
  ROW    1    4.7050    0.12911    0.54706    0.45294
```

Since the test statistic falls below the 25% critical value (in fact, the p-value is 0.45294), it can be concluded that there is no heteroscedasticity.

Section 11.6 introduces two remedial measures for models suffering from heteroscedasticity. The first is the method of Weighted Least Squares (WLS). If the variances of the individual errors are known, WLS can be used to obtain estimates which are BLUE (Best Linear Unbiased Estimator).

The **WEIGHT=** option with the **OLS** command specifies a variable to be used as the weight for **WEIGHT**ed Least Squares. Each observation of the dependent and independent variables (including the constant term) are multiplied by the square root of the weight variable.

First, equation (11.6.2) will be estimated by weighting the variables the "long way". Then, for comparison, the **WEIGHT=** option will be used.

```
SAMPLE 1 9
READ(TABLE11.4) Y X SIGMA
* Run the unweighted OLS regression (11.6.3).
OLS Y X
* Construct the weighted variables and constant term.
GENR Y1=Y/SIGMA
GENR X1=X/SIGMA
GENR CONST=1/SIGMA
* Equation (11.6.2).
OLS Y1 X1 CONST / NOCONSTANT
* To follow the WLS methodology used here, take the inverse of the square
* of the weight variable.
GENR INVSIG2=1/(SIGMA**2)
OLS Y X / WEIGHT=INVSIG2
```

The output follows.

```
|_* Run the unweighted OLS regression (11.6.3).

|_OLS Y X

 OLS ESTIMATION
       9 OBSERVATIONS      DEPENDENT VARIABLE = Y
...NOTE..SAMPLE RANGE SET TO:    1,    9

 R-SQUARE =   0.9383    R-SQUARE ADJUSTED =    0.9295
VARIANCE OF THE ESTIMATE-SIGMA**2 =    12473.
STANDARD ERROR OF THE ESTIMATE-SIGMA =    111.68
SUM OF SQUARED ERRORS-SSE=    87313.
MEAN OF DEPENDENT VARIABLE =    4161.7
LOG OF THE LIKELIHOOD FUNCTION = -54.0806
```

VARIABLE NAME	ESTIMATED COEFFICIENT	STANDARD ERROR	T-RATIO 7 DF	P-VALUE	PARTIAL CORR.	STANDARDIZED COEFFICIENT	ELASTICITY AT MEANS
X	148.77	14.42	10.32	0.000	0.969	0.9687	0.1787
CONSTANT	3417.8	81.14	42.12	0.000	0.998	0.0000	0.8213

```
|_* Equation (11.6.2).

|_OLS Y1 X1 CONST / NOCONSTANT

 OLS ESTIMATION
       9 OBSERVATIONS      DEPENDENT VARIABLE = Y1
...NOTE..SAMPLE RANGE SET TO:    1,    9

 R-SQUARE =   0.9645    R-SQUARE ADJUSTED =    0.9595
VARIANCE OF THE ESTIMATE-SIGMA**2 =    0.18270E-01
STANDARD ERROR OF THE ESTIMATE-SIGMA =    0.13517
SUM OF SQUARED ERRORS-SSE=    0.12789
MEAN OF DEPENDENT VARIABLE =    4.3735
LOG OF THE LIKELIHOOD FUNCTION =    6.37168
RAW MOMENT R-SQUARE =    0.9993
```

```
VARIABLE     ESTIMATED  STANDARD    T-RATIO           PARTIAL STANDARDIZED ELASTICITY
  NAME       COEFFICIENT  ERROR        7 DF    P-VALUE CORR. COEFFICIENT  AT MEANS
X1             154.15     16.96       9.090    0.000 0.960     0.4633      0.1706
CONST          3406.6     80.98       42.07    0.000 0.998     1.1658      0.8312
|_* To follow the WLS methodology used here, take the inverse of the square
|_* of the weight variable.
|_GENR INVSIG2=1/(SIGMA**2)

|_OLS Y X / WEIGHT=INVSIG2


 OLS ESTIMATION
        9 OBSERVATIONS       DEPENDENT VARIABLE = Y
...NOTE..SAMPLE RANGE SET TO:     1,    9
SUM OF LOG(SQRT(ABS(WEIGHT)))   = -0.37221


  R-SQUARE =    0.9219     R-SQUARE ADJUSTED =    0.9107
VARIANCE OF THE ESTIMATE-SIGMA**2 =    15409.
STANDARD ERROR OF THE ESTIMATE-SIGMA =   124.13
SUM OF SQUARED ERRORS-SSE=  0.10786E+06
MEAN OF DEPENDENT VARIABLE =    4039.4
LOG OF THE LIKELIHOOD FUNCTION = -55.4040

VARIABLE     ESTIMATED  STANDARD    T-RATIO           PARTIAL STANDARDIZED ELASTICITY
  NAME       COEFFICIENT  ERROR        7 DF    P-VALUE CORR. COEFFICIENT  AT MEANS
X              154.15     16.96       9.090    0.000 0.960     0.9602      0.1566
CONSTANT       3406.6     80.98       42.07    0.000 0.998     0.0000      0.8434
```

As is expected, the results using the **WEIGHT=** option are identical to the "long way". Note that the R^2 statistic printed in the text is the Raw-Moment R^2. SHAZAM automatically prints the Raw-Moment R^2 (see the output) when the **NOCONSTANT** option is used. However, the R^2 printed with the **WEIGHT=** option is now based on the original data.

The other remedial measure that is discussed is the use of White's heteroscedasticity-consistent variances and standard errors. The **HETCOV** option with the **OLS** command uses White's **HET**eroscedastic-Consistent **COV**ariance matrix estimation to correct the estimates for an unknown form of heteroscedasticity.

The data needed to replicate the results reported in *Example 11.7* was taken from *Table 14.1* in W. Greene's *Econometric Analysis* , *Second Edition* (Macmillan, 1993).

```
SAMPLE 1 50
READ(WHITE.DAT) EXP INCOME
GENR INCOME2=INCOME**2
OLS EXP INCOME INCOME2
OLS EXP INCOME INCOME2 / HETCOV
```

The output follows.

```
| OLS EXP INCOME INCOME2

 OLS ESTIMATION
      50 OBSERVATIONS      DEPENDENT VARIABLE = EXP
...NOTE..SAMPLE RANGE SET TO:     1,    50


 R-SQUARE =    0.6553     R-SQUARE ADJUSTED =    0.6407
VARIANCE OF THE ESTIMATE-SIGMA**2 =    3212.5
STANDARD ERROR OF THE ESTIMATE-SIGMA =    56.679
SUM OF SQUARED ERRORS-SSE=   0.15099E+06
MEAN OF DEPENDENT VARIABLE =    373.26
LOG OF THE LIKELIHOOD FUNCTION = -271.270


VARIABLE    ESTIMATED   STANDARD    T-RATIO          PARTIAL STANDARDIZED ELASTICITY
  NAME      COEFFICIENT   ERROR      47 DF    P-VALUE CORR. COEFFICIENT  AT MEANS
INCOME      -1834.2      829.0      -2.213    0.032-0.307   -2.0381      -3.7389
INCOME2      1587.0      519.1       3.057    0.004 0.407    2.8163       2.5074
CONSTANT     832.91      327.3       2.545    0.014 0.348    0.0000       2.2315

| OLS EXP INCOME INCOME2 / HETCOV

 OLS ESTIMATION
      50 OBSERVATIONS      DEPENDENT VARIABLE = EXP
...NOTE..SAMPLE RANGE SET TO:     1,    50

USING HETEROSKEDASTICITY-CONSISTENT COVARIANCE MATRIX

 R-SQUARE =    0.6553     R-SQUARE ADJUSTED =    0.6407
VARIANCE OF THE ESTIMATE-SIGMA**2 =    3212.5
STANDARD ERROR OF THE ESTIMATE-SIGMA =    56.679
SUM OF SQUARED ERRORS-SSE=   0.15099E+06
MEAN OF DEPENDENT VARIABLE =    373.26
LOG OF THE LIKELIHOOD FUNCTION = -271.270


VARIABLE    ESTIMATED   STANDARD    T-RATIO          PARTIAL STANDARDIZED ELASTICITY
  NAME      COEFFICIENT   ERROR      47 DF    P-VALUE CORR. COEFFICIENT  AT MEANS
INCOME      -1834.2      1243.      -1.476    0.147-0.210   -2.0381      -3.7389
INCOME2      1587.0      830.0       1.912    0.062 0.269    2.8163       2.5074
CONSTANT     832.91      460.9       1.807    0.077 0.255    0.0000       2.2315
```

There are several other assumptions on the pattern of heteroscedasticity that are discussed at the end of *Section 11.6*. Using the data from *Table 11.4*, the following commands will estimate the models, based on these different assumptions, using WLS. (No output is provided).

```
* Assumption 1 - Equation (11.6.6).
GENR INVX2=(1/X)**2
OLS Y X / WEIGHT=INVX2
* Assumption 2 - Equation (11.6.8).
GENR INVX=1/X
OLS Y X / WEIGHT=INVX
* Assumption 3 - Equation (11.6.11).
?OLS Y X / PREDICT=PREDY
GENR INVPREDY=1/(PREDY**2)
OLS Y X / WEIGHT=INVPREDY
```

```
* Assumption 4 - Equation (11.6.12).
GENR LNY=LOG(Y)
GENR LNX=LOG(X)
OLS LNY LNX / LOGLOG
```

Example 11.8 in *Section 11.7* illustrates some of the various methods used for detecting heteroscedasticity and some of the remedial measures that can be taken.

```
SAMPLE 1 18
READ(TABLE11.5) SALES RD PROFITS
* Equation (11.7.1).
OLS RD SALES / RESID=E
* Park Test (equation (11.7.2)).
GENR E2=E**2
GENR LNE2=LOG(E2)
GENR LNSALES=LOG(SALES)
OLS LNE2 LNSALES
* Glejser Tests:
* Equation (11.7.3).
GENR ABSE=ABS(E)
OLS ABSE SALES
* Equation (11.7.4).
GENR SQTSALES=SQRT(SALES)
OLS ABSE SQTSALES
* Equation (11.7.5).
GENR INVSALES=1/SALES
OLS ABSE INVSALES
* Use WLS to estimate model (11.7.6)
GENR W=(1/SALES)
OLS RD SALES / WEIGHT=W
```

The output follows.

```
|_* Equation (11.7.1).
|_OLS RD SALES / RESID=E

 OLS ESTIMATION
      18 OBSERVATIONS      DEPENDENT VARIABLE = RD
...NOTE..SAMPLE RANGE SET TO:    1,    18


 R-SQUARE =   0.4783     R-SQUARE ADJUSTED =   0.4457
VARIANCE OF THE ESTIMATE-SIGMA**2 =  0.76129E+07
STANDARD ERROR OF THE ESTIMATE-SIGMA =   2759.2
SUM OF SQUARED ERRORS-SSE=  0.12181E+09
MEAN OF DEPENDENT VARIABLE =    3056.9
LOG OF THE LIKELIHOOD FUNCTION = -167.089


VARIABLE    ESTIMATED   STANDARD   T-RATIO        PARTIAL STANDARDIZED ELASTICITY
  NAME      COEFFICIENT   ERROR     16 DF   P-VALUE CORR. COEFFICIENT   AT MEANS
SALES     0.31900E-01 0.8329E-02   3.830    0.001 0.692    0.6916       0.9369
CONSTANT   192.99       991.0      0.1947   0.848 0.049    0.0000       0.0631
|_* Park Test (equation (11.7.2)).
|_GENR E2=E**2
|_GENR LNE2=LOG(E2)
|_GENR LNSALES=LOG(SALES)
```

```
|_OLS LNE2 LNSALES

 OLS ESTIMATION
      18 OBSERVATIONS      DEPENDENT VARIABLE = LNE2
...NOTE..SAMPLE RANGE SET TO:    1,   18


 R-SQUARE =    0.0779     R-SQUARE ADJUSTED =     0.0203
VARIANCE OF THE ESTIMATE-SIGMA**2 =    7.2556
STANDARD ERROR OF THE ESTIMATE-SIGMA =    2.6936
SUM OF SQUARED ERRORS-SSE=   116.09
MEAN OF DEPENDENT VARIABLE =    13.366
LOG OF THE LIKELIHOOD FUNCTION = -42.3168
```

VARIABLE NAME	ESTIMATED COEFFICIENT	STANDARD ERROR	T-RATIO 16 DF	P-VALUE	PARTIAL CORR.	STANDARDIZED COEFFICIENT	ELASTICITY AT MEANS
LNSALES	0.70143	0.6033	1.163	0.262	0.279	0.2791	0.5745
CONSTANT	5.6877	6.635	0.8572	0.404	0.210	0.0000	0.4255

```
|_* Glejser Tests:
|_* Equation (11.7.3).
|_GENR ABSE=ABS(E)

|_OLS ABSE SALES

 OLS ESTIMATION
      18 OBSERVATIONS      DEPENDENT VARIABLE = ABSE
...NOTE..SAMPLE RANGE SET TO:    1,   18


 R-SQUARE =    0.2150     R-SQUARE ADJUSTED =     0.1659
VARIANCE OF THE ESTIMATE-SIGMA**2 =   0.35708E+07
STANDARD ERROR OF THE ESTIMATE-SIGMA =    1889.7
SUM OF SQUARED ERRORS-SSE=   0.57133E+08
MEAN OF DEPENDENT VARIABLE =    1650.4
LOG OF THE LIKELIHOOD FUNCTION = -160.276
```

VARIABLE NAME	ESTIMATED COEFFICIENT	STANDARD ERROR	T-RATIO 16 DF	P-VALUE	PARTIAL CORR.	STANDARDIZED COEFFICIENT	ELASTICITY AT MEANS
SALES	0.11939E-01	0.5704E-02	2.093	0.053	0.464	0.4636	0.6494
CONSTANT	578.57	678.7	0.8525	0.407	0.208	0.0000	0.3506|_*

```
|_* Equation (11.7.4).
|_GENR SQTSALES=SQRT(SALES)

|_OLS ABSE SQTSALES

 OLS ESTIMATION
      18 OBSERVATIONS      DEPENDENT VARIABLE = ABSE
...NOTE..SAMPLE RANGE SET TO:    1,   18


 R-SQUARE =    0.2599     R-SQUARE ADJUSTED =     0.2136
VARIANCE OF THE ESTIMATE-SIGMA**2 =   0.33663E+07
STANDARD ERROR OF THE ESTIMATE-SIGMA =    1834.8
SUM OF SQUARED ERRORS-SSE=   0.53862E+08
MEAN OF DEPENDENT VARIABLE =    1650.4
LOG OF THE LIKELIHOOD FUNCTION = -159.745
```

VARIABLE NAME	ESTIMATED COEFFICIENT	STANDARD ERROR	T-RATIO 16 DF	P-VALUE	PARTIAL CORR.	STANDARDIZED COEFFICIENT	ELASTICITY AT MEANS
SQTSALES	7.9720	3.363	2.370	0.031	0.510	0.5098	1.3072
CONSTANT	-507.02	1008.	-0.5032	0.622	-0.125	0.0000	-0.3072

```
|_* Equation (11.7.5).
|_GENR INVSALES=1/SALES

|_OLS ABSE INVSALES

 OLS ESTIMATION
       18 OBSERVATIONS      DEPENDENT VARIABLE = ABSE
...NOTE..SAMPLE RANGE SET TO:     1,    18

 R-SQUARE =   0.1405    R-SQUARE ADJUSTED =   0.0868
VARIANCE OF THE ESTIMATE-SIGMA**2 =  0.39093E+07
STANDARD ERROR OF THE ESTIMATE-SIGMA =   1977.2
SUM OF SQUARED ERRORS-SSE=  0.62548E+08
MEAN OF DEPENDENT VARIABLE =    1650.4
LOG OF THE LIKELIHOOD FUNCTION = -161.091


VARIABLE     ESTIMATED   STANDARD    T-RATIO          PARTIAL STANDARDIZED ELASTICITY
  NAME       COEFFICIENT   ERROR      16 DF     P-VALUE CORR. COEFFICIENT  AT MEANS
INVSALES -0.19925E+08 0.1232E+08   -1.617      0.125-0.375     -0.3749     -0.3776
CONSTANT    2273.7       604.7       3.760      0.002 0.685      0.0000      1.3776
|_* Equation (11.7.6) - WLS.|_*
|_GENR W=(1/SALES)

|_OLS RD SALES / WEIGHT=W

 OLS ESTIMATION
       18 OBSERVATIONS      DEPENDENT VARIABLE = RD
...NOTE..SAMPLE RANGE SET TO:     1,    18
SUM OF LOG(SQRT(ABS(WEIGHT)))   =  -5.1715

 R-SQUARE =   0.6258    R-SQUARE ADJUSTED =   0.6024
VARIANCE OF THE ESTIMATE-SIGMA**2 =  0.16836E+07
STANDARD ERROR OF THE ESTIMATE-SIGMA =   1297.5
SUM OF SQUARED ERRORS-SSE=  0.26938E+08
MEAN OF DEPENDENT VARIABLE =     929.67
LOG OF THE LIKELIHOOD FUNCTION = -158.680


VARIABLE     ESTIMATED   STANDARD    T-RATIO          PARTIAL STANDARDIZED ELASTICITY
  NAME       COEFFICIENT   ERROR      16 DF     P-VALUE CORR. COEFFICIENT  AT MEANS
SALES     0.36798E-01 0.7114E-02    5.172      0.000 0.791      0.7910      1.2653
CONSTANT    -246.68      381.1     -0.6472      0.527-0.160      0.0000     -0.2653
```

APPENDIX FOR CHAPTER 11

The following commands estimate the Davidson-MacKinnon Monte Carlo study following the specifications outlined in *Section 11.4*. These commands are worth studying as this is a good example of a Monte Carlo experiment.

The **NOR(x)** function with the **GENR** command generates normally distributed random numbers with standard deviation x. The **UNI(x)** function with the **GENR** command generates uniformly distributed random numbers with the range (0,x).

The **DO** Command

The **DO** command is used to create **DO**-loops. **DO**-loops provide repeat operations. The format of the **DO**-loop is best shown by the following example.

```
READ(SOMEFILE) VAR1 VAR2 VAR3 VAR4 VAR5
DO #=1,5
GENR LNVAR#=LOG(VAR#)
PLOT LNVAR# VAR#
ENDO
```

This example creates 5 new variables (*LNVAR1* to *LNVAR5*) by taking the log of each variable. Each logged variable is then plotted against the original variable. In the example above, the **DO**-loop facility provides a numerical character substitution for the symbol #. Any of the symbols # % ? $!, may be used with the **DO** command. Note that an **ENDO** must be used to **EN**d the **DO**-loop.

Note that the **DO** command cannot be used with the student version of SHAZAM, SHAZY.

The number of repetitions can be set by specifying the variable *NREP* to the amount desired. The text example used 20,000 repetitions. However, that many repetitions may use quite a bit of computer time. 1000 may be a large enough number. Here, 20,000 repetitions are used.

```
SAMPLE 1 100
GENR X=UNI(1)
* Specify the number of replications for the Monte Carlo experiment.
GEN1 NREP=20000
* Specify values for alpha
SAMPLE 1 5
READ ALPHA / BYVAR LIST
```

```
0.5   1   2   3   4
* The SET NODOECHO command prevents repetitive printing of DO-loop
* commands.
SET NODOECHO
* Use a DO-loop to repeat operations for each value of ALPHA
DO %=1,5
* Generate standard errors.
SAMPLE 1 100
GENR SE=SQRT(X**ALPHA:%)*
* Initialize variables to save results
SAMPLE 1 2
GENR MSTDOLS=0
GENR MSTDOLS2=0
GENR MSTDGLS=0
* Now use a second-level DO-loop to do the NREP replications of the Monte
* Carlo experiment for a given value of ALPHA.
DO #=1,NREP
SAMPLE 1 100
* Generate errors that are normally distributed with heteroscedastic variance.
* The NOR function is used to generate normally distributed random numbers.
* To generate normal random numbers with standard deviation x the general
* command format is:
* GENR var=NOR(x)
GENR E=NOR(1)*SE
* Generate the Y's as specified in 11.4.1
GENR Y=1+X+E*
* Run OLS and save the standard errors.Generate a constant term using the GENR
* command. Use the ? prefix to suppress the output from the estimation.
GENR CONST=1
?OLS Y CONST X / NOCONSTANT STDERR=STDOLS
* Run OLS again but this time using the HETCOV option which corrects the
* standard errors for heteroscedasticity.
?OLS Y CONST X / NOCONSTANT HETCOV STDERR=STDOLS2
* Now use GLS with a diagonal OMEGA matrix. This is implemented by weighted OLS.
GENR VINV=1/(SE*SE)
?OLS Y CONST X / NOCONSTANT WEIGHT=VINV STDERR=STDGLS
* Sum the results
SAMPLE 1 2
GENR MSTDOLS=MSTDOLS+STDOLS
GENR MSTDOLS2=MSTDOLS2+STDOLS2
GENR MSTDGLS=MSTDGLS+STDGLS
* The ENDO command ends the list of commands for the estimations for each
* replication of the Monte Carlo study.
ENDO
* Now analyze the results for a given value of ALPHA.
PRINT ALPHA:%
* Now get the average standard errors.
SAMPLE 1 2
GENR MSTDOLS=MSTDOLS/NREP
GENR MSTDOLS2=MSTDOLS2/NREP
GENR MSTDGLS=MSTDGLS/NREP
PRINT MSTDOLS MSTDOLS2 MSTDGLS
* Use an ENDO command to finish the outer DO-loop.
ENDO
```

The output is provided at the beginning of this chapter.

SHAZAM commands and options used in Chapter 11.

DIAGNOS / **CHOWTEST GQOBS= HET**

DISTRIB *vars* / **DF= DF1= DF2= TYPE=CHI TYPE=F TYPE=T**

DO

ENDO

GEN1 *newvar=equation*

GENR *newvar=equation* with **ABS**(x) **INV**(x) **NOR**(x) **LOG**(x) **SQRT**(x) **UNI**(x)

MATRIX *newmat=equation*

OLS *depvar indeps* / **DN HETCOV LOGLOG NOCONSTANT PREDICT=
RESID= STDERR= WEIGHT=**

PRINT *vars* / *options*

READ(*datafile*) *vars* / **BYVAR LIST**

SAMPLE *beg end*

SET NODOECHO

SORT *sortvar vars* / **LIST**

STAT *vars* / **PRANKCOR RANKCOR=**

? Suppression of Output

Temporary variables used.

$DF	Degrees of Freedom
$N	Number of observations in the estimation
$R2	R-Square
$SSR	Regression Sum of Squares
$SIG2	Variance of the Estimate - sigma**2
$SSE	Sum of Squared Errors - sse

12. AUTOCORRELATION

The topic of *Chapter 12* is autocorrelation in regression models. Autocorrelation occurs when the error terms, u_t, in the population regression function are correlated. If this is the case, the classical linear regression model assumption that $E(u_i, u_j) = 0$, where $i \neq j$, is violated. As a result, OLS estimates are no longer BLUE (Best Linear Unbiased Estimator). While OLS estimates are still unbiased and consistent, they are no longer efficient (i.e. minimum variance). In this chapter, a number of techniques designed for detecting the presence of autocorrelation will be examined. Some remedial measures will then be introduced.

Section 12.4 uses the data found in *Table 12.1* to demonstrate how OLS is likely to underestimate σ^2 and the variances of the estimated coefficients. Equation (12.4.3) describes the "true" model, where $\beta_1 = 1$ and $\beta_2 = 0.8$. Equation (12.4.5), $u_t = 0.7u_{t-1} + \varepsilon_t$, describes the nature of the autocorrelation where ε_t satisfies all the OLS assumptions and is normally distributed with zero mean and variance equal to one. Random numbers assuming a normal distribution, with a zero mean and a variance equal to one, were generated (see the second column of *Table 12.1*). They will serve as values for ε that are to be plugged into equation (12.4.5). The values of u_t that result are used to generate 10 sample observations of Y. A sample regression (12.4.6) is then estimated by regressing these values of Y on the fixed values of X.

```
SAMPLE 1 11
READ(TABLE12.1) X E U
SAMPLE 2 11
* Generate the variable Y found in Table 12.2.
GENR Y=1+.8*X+U
PRINT X U Y
* Figure 12.5.
PLOT U X
* Estimate equation (12.4.6). Save the predicted values for use ahead.
OLS Y X / PREDICT=YHAT
```

The output follows.

```
|_PRINT X U Y
        X                 U                 Y
   1.000000          3.964000          5.764000
   2.000000          4.801000          7.401000
   3.000000          5.815700          9.215700
   4.000000          3.747990          7.947990
   5.000000          2.555593          7.555593
   6.000000          2.084915          7.884915
   7.000000          1.171441          7.771441
   8.000000          2.118008          9.518008
   9.000000          1.723606          9.923606
  10.00000          0.2495241         9.249524
```

```
|_* Figure 12.5.
|_PLOT U X

      10 OBSERVATIONS
                    *=U
                    M=MULTIPLE POINT
     6.0000      |
     5.6842      |              *
     5.3684      |
     5.0526      |
     4.7368      |          *
     4.4211      |
     4.1053      |
     3.7895      |        *
     3.4737      |              *
     3.1579      |
     2.8421      |
     2.5263      |                *
     2.2105      |
     1.8947      |                  *         *
     1.5789      |                              *
     1.2632      |
    0.94737      |                     *
    0.63158      |
    0.31579      |
  -0.13323E-14   |                                *

              _____

           0.000     3.000     6.000     9.000    12.000

                                X
|_* Estimate equation (12.4.6). Save the predicted values for use ahead.

|_OLS Y X / PREDICT=YHAT

 OLS ESTIMATION
       10 OBSERVATIONS       DEPENDENT VARIABLE = Y
...NOTE..SAMPLE RANGE SET TO:     2,    11

 R-SQUARE =    0.5419     R-SQUARE ADJUSTED =    0.4847
VARIANCE OF THE ESTIMATE-SIGMA**2 =   0.81138
STANDARD ERROR OF THE ESTIMATE-SIGMA =   0.90077
SUM OF SQUARED ERRORS-SSE=    6.4911
MEAN OF DEPENDENT VARIABLE =     8.2232
LOG OF THE LIKELIHOOD FUNCTION = -12.0286
```

VARIABLE NAME	ESTIMATED COEFFICIENT	STANDARD ERROR	T-RATIO 8 DF	P-VALUE	PARTIAL CORR.	STANDARDIZED COEFFICIENT	ELASTICITY AT MEANS
X	0.30509	0.9917E-01	3.076	0.015	0.736	0.7361	0.2041
CONSTANT	6.5452	0.6153	10.64	0.000	0.966	0.0000	0.7959

In the plot above, the errors, u_t, are plotted against X. The distinct pattern in the plotted residuals indicates that autocorrelation is present.

In *Figure 12.6*, the "true" population regression function is plotted alongside the sample regression function.

```
* Plot Figure 12.6.
GENR TRUEPRF=1+.8*X
PLOT YHAT TRUEPRF X
```

The output follows.

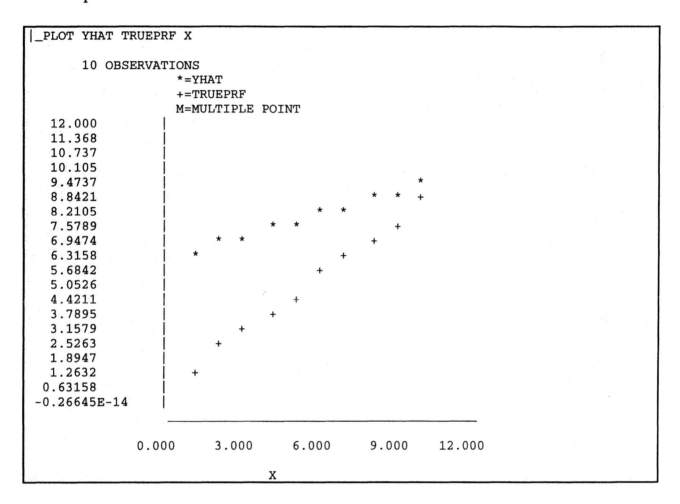

```
|_PLOT YHAT TRUEPRF X

    10 OBSERVATIONS
                       *=YHAT
                       +=TRUEPRF
                       M=MULTIPLE POINT
  12.000        |
  11.368        |
  10.737        |
  10.105        |
  9.4737        |                                       *
  8.8421        |                              *   *   +
  8.2105        |                       *   *
  7.5789        |               *   *                +
  6.9474        |       *   *                    +
  6.3158        |   *                        +
  5.6842        |                        +
  5.0526        |
  4.4211        |                    +
  3.7895        |               +
  3.1579        |       +
  2.5263        |   +
  1.8947        |
  1.2632        |   +
 0.63158        |
-0.26645E-14    |
                _____

            0.000     3.000     6.000     9.000     12.000

                              X
```

The above plot shows that the fitted regression line ("*") overestimates the true intercept and underestimates the true slope.

The next step in this example is to generate 10 sample values of Y with zero autocorrelation (see *Table 12.3*). These values are then used to estimate equation (12.4.7).

```
* Generate a "Y" variable with zero autocorrelation.
GENR Y=1+.8*X+E
PRINT E Y
* Estimate equation (12.4.7).
OLS Y X
```

The output follows.

```
|_PRINT E Y
       E                    Y
  0.4640000          2.264000
  2.026200           4.626200
  2.455000           5.855000
 -0.3230000          3.877000
 -0.6800000E-01      4.932000
  0.2960000          6.096000
 -0.2880000          6.312000
  1.298000           8.698000
  0.2410000          8.441000
 -0.9570000          8.043000
|_* Estimate equation (12.4.7).

|_OLS Y X


OLS ESTIMATION
      10 OBSERVATIONS         DEPENDENT VARIABLE = Y
...NOTE..SAMPLE RANGE SET TO:    2,   11


 R-SQUARE =    0.7997      R-SQUARE ADJUSTED =    0.7747
VARIANCE OF THE ESTIMATE-SIGMA**2 =  0.97526
STANDARD ERROR OF THE ESTIMATE-SIGMA =  0.98755
SUM OF SQUARED ERRORS-SSE=    7.8021
MEAN OF DEPENDENT VARIABLE =    5.9144
LOG OF THE LIKELIHOOD FUNCTION = -12.9484
```

VARIABLE NAME	ESTIMATED COEFFICIENT	STANDARD ERROR	T-RATIO 8 DF	P-VALUE	PARTIAL CORR.	STANDARDIZED COEFFICIENT	ELASTICITY AT MEANS
X	0.61454	0.1087	5.652	0.000	0.894	0.8943	0.5715
CONSTANT	2.5345	0.6746	3.757	0.006	0.799	0.0000	0.4285

The above parameter estimates are clearly closer to the true values. As anticipated, the variances of the regression and the estimated coefficients have increased.

Section 12.5 introduces several methods that can be used to test for the presence of autocorrelation. The graphical method considers plots of the residuals. As the text notes, plotting $\hat{u}_t$ can provide useful information.

The **LIST** option with the **OLS** command lists the residuals and the predicted values of the dependent variable and plots the residuals (as well as printing some of the residual statistics discussed ahead). The **HATDIAG=** option will be described below.

```
TIME 1960 1
SAMPLE 1960.0 1991.0
READ(TABLE5.6) YEAR Y X
OLS Y X / RESID=U HATDIAG=HT LIST
```

The output follows.

```
|_OLS Y X / RESID=U HATDIAG=HT LIST

 OLS ESTIMATION
      32 OBSERVATIONS      DEPENDENT VARIABLE = Y
 ...NOTE..SAMPLE RANGE SET TO:     1,    32


 R-SQUARE =    0.9465    R-SQUARE ADJUSTED =    0.9447
 VARIANCE OF THE ESTIMATE-SIGMA**2 =    6.8231
 STANDARD ERROR OF THE ESTIMATE-SIGMA =    2.6121
 SUM OF SQUARED ERRORS-SSE=    204.69
 MEAN OF DEPENDENT VARIABLE =    93.613
 LOG OF THE LIKELIHOOD FUNCTION = -75.0985
```

VARIABLE NAME	ESTIMATED COEFFICIENT	STANDARD ERROR	T-RATIO 30 DF	P-VALUE	PARTIAL CORR.	STANDARDIZED COEFFICIENT	ELASTICITY AT MEANS
X	0.80944	0.3514E-01	23.04	0.000	0.973	0.9729	0.8067
CONSTANT	18.091	3.311	5.465	0.000	0.706	0.0000	0.1933

OBS. NO.	OBSERVED VALUE	PREDICTED VALUE	CALCULATED RESIDUAL	
1	68.700	71.110	-2.4100	* I
2	70.700	73.134	-2.4336	* I
3	73.200	75.076	-1.8763	* I
4	75.000	77.343	-2.3427	* I
5	77.900	79.933	-2.0329	* I
6	79.600	81.633	-2.0327	* I
7	82.900	83.414	-0.51352	*I
8	84.900	85.032	-0.13241	*
9	88.200	87.137	1.0630	I *
10	89.700	87.461	2.2393	I *
11	91.200	88.432	2.7679	I *
12	93.000	90.779	2.2205	I *
13	95.800	93.046	2.7541	I *
14	98.000	94.989	3.0114	I *
15	97.000	93.532	3.4684	I *
16	97.700	95.312	2.3877	I *
17	100.80	97.579	3.2212	I *
18	102.30	98.874	3.4261	I *
19	103.40	99.360	4.0405	I *
20	102.00	98.469	3.5308	I *
21	99.500	97.903	1.5975	I *
22	98.700	98.955	-0.25482	*
23	100.00	99.036	0.96423	I *
24	100.50	100.65	-0.15465	*
25	100.40	102.76	-2.3592	* I
26	101.30	103.97	-2.6734	* I
27	104.40	105.75	-1.3541	* I
28	104.30	106.64	-2.3445	* I
29	104.40	107.45	-3.0540	* I
30	103.00	106.73	-3.7255	* I
31	103.20	106.89	-3.6874	* I
32	103.90	107.21	-3.3111	* I

```
 DURBIN-WATSON = 0.1380     VON NEUMANN RATIO = 0.1425    RHO =   0.94038
 RESIDUAL SUM = -0.25446E-12   RESIDUAL VARIANCE =    6.8231
 SUM OF ABSOLUTE ERRORS=    73.386
 R-SQUARE BETWEEN OBSERVED AND PREDICTED = 0.9465
 RUNS TEST:     5 RUNS,    14 POS,     0 ZERO,    18 NEG   NORMAL STATISTIC = -4.2922
```

The above plot of the residuals replicates the plot found in *Figure 12.7*. A pattern of positive autocorrelation is evident (see *Figure 12.3a*).

The text describes a method for computing the "standardized" residuals following a procedure developed by Draper and Smith (*Applied Regression Analysis , Second Edition*, Wiley, 1981). However, according to Draper and Smith, dividing the residuals by $\hat{\sigma}$, the standard error of the estimate, computes the "Unit Normal Deviate Form" of the residuals not the standardized form. The correct formula used to compute the standardized residuals is:

$$\hat{\sigma}_t = \hat{\sigma}\sqrt{1 - h_t} \qquad\qquad \text{where } h_t = X_t(X'X)^{-1}X'$$

In advanced textbooks, the h_t are often called the diagonals of the **HAT** matrix. SHAZAM computes and saves the **DIAG**onals of the **HAT** matrix when the **HATDIAG=** option with the **OLS** command is used. Recall that this was done in the previous set of commands.

The commands below compute the information found in *Table 12.4* as well as the standardized residuals described above.

```
GENR LAGU=LAG(U)
GENR UDFU=U/(SQRT($SIG2))
GENR SIGT=SQRT($SIG2*(1-HT))
GENR STDRESID=U/SIGT
* Table 12.4.
PRINT YEAR U UDFU LAGU STDRESID
```

The output follows.

```
|_* Table 12.4.
|_PRINT YEAR U UDFU LAGU STDRESID
     YEAR            U             UDFU             LAGU           STDRESID
   1960.000      -2.409992      -0.9226231       0.0000000        -1.013376
   1961.000      -2.433599      -0.9316605      -2.409992         -1.008791
   1962.000      -1.876261      -0.7182937      -2.433599         -0.7683884
   1963.000      -2.342701      -0.8968619      -1.876261         -0.9476700
   1964.000      -2.032918      -0.7782668      -2.342701         -0.8126941
   1965.000      -2.032748      -0.7782016      -2.032918         -0.8073413
   1966.000      -0.5135216     -0.1965927      -2.032748         -0.2027674
   1967.000      -0.1324071     -0.5068972E-01  -0.5135216        -0.5204987E-01
   1968.000       1.063042       0.4069669      -0.1324071         0.4159725
   1969.000       2.239265       0.8572631       1.063042          0.8757168
   1970.000       2.767933       1.059655        2.239265          1.080752
   1971.000       2.220550       0.8500983       2.767933          0.8646905
   1972.000       2.754110       1.054363        2.220550          1.071282
   1973.000       3.011447       1.152880        2.754110          1.171643
   1974.000       3.468444       1.327833        3.011447          1.349081
   1975.000       2.387670       0.9140775       3.468444          0.9290864
   1976.000       3.221231       1.233191        2.387670          1.255743
```

1977.000	3.426122	1.311631	3.221231	1.337908
1978.000	4.040457	1.546818	3.426122	1.579020
1979.000	3.530844	1.351721	4.040457	1.377991
1980.000	1.597454	0.6115570	3.530844	0.6229789
1981.000	-0.2548220	-0.9755412E-01	1.597454	-0.9952077E-01
1982.000	0.9642337	0.3691399	-0.2548220	0.3766288
1983.000	-0.1546517	-0.5920570E-01	0.9642337	-0.6058282E-01
1984.000	-2.359203	-0.9031793	-0.1546517	-0.9287735
1985.000	-2.673367	-1.023451	-2.359203	-1.056113
1986.000	-1.354141	-0.5184090	-2.673367	-0.5381332
1987.000	-2.344528	-0.8975613	-1.354141	-0.9348341
1988.000	-3.053971	-1.169159	-2.344528	-1.221698
1989.000	-3.725472	-1.426231	-3.053971	-1.485929
1990.000	-3.687361	-1.411641	-3.725472	-1.471671
1991.000	-3.311138	-1.267611	-3.687361	-1.323245

A high quality plot of the residuals and the standardized residuals (*Figure 12.7*) will be made using GNUPLOT, a graphics program interfaced with SHAZAM. (See the *SHAZAM User's Reference Manual* for more details on GNUPLOT).

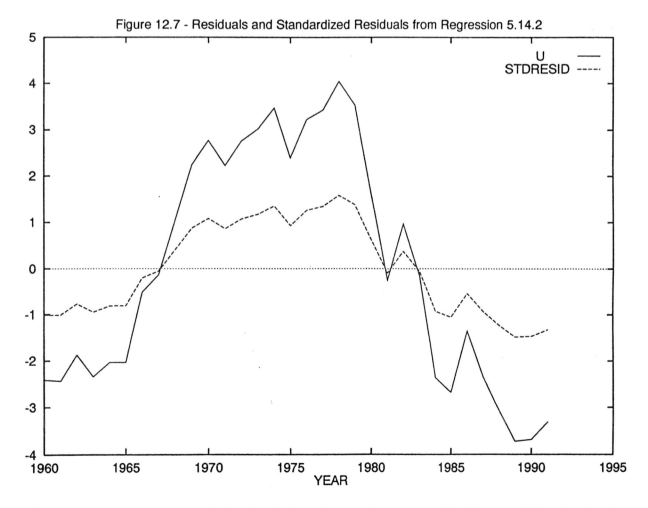

Figure 12.7 - Residuals and Standardized Residuals from Regression 5.14.2

As the text notes, patterns in both of the above plots resemble *Figure 12.1d*, indicating that the residuals from the model are not random.

The residuals will now be plotted against their lagged values (*Figure 12.8*).

```
* Figure 12.8
SAMPLE 1961.0 1991.0
PLOT U LAGU
```

The output follows.

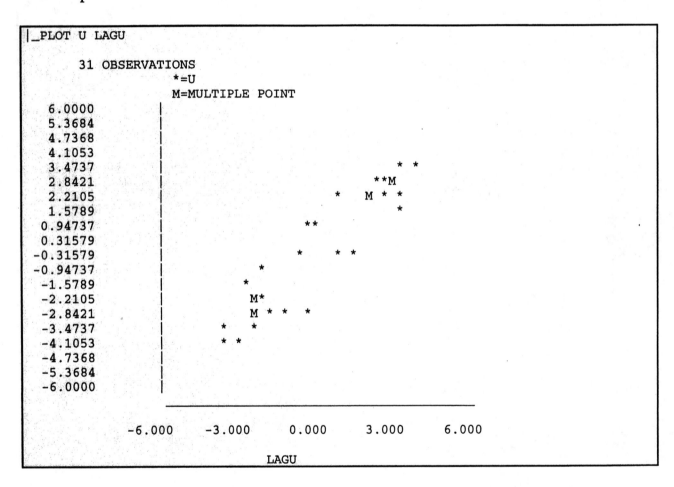

The above plot strongly resembles a pattern similar to *Figure 12.3a,* indicating that the model exhibits positive autocorrelation.

The remaining parts of *Section 12.5* focus on various statistics that are used to test for the presence of autocorrelation.

The **RSTAT** option with the **OLS** command prints Residual summary **STAT**istics. The output includes the Durbin-Watson statistic and related residual test statistics. The **RSTAT** option is automatically turned on when the **LIST** option is used with the **OLS** command.

The Runs Test: When the **RSTAT** or **LIST** options are used with the **OLS** command, a Runs Test statistic is printed. It is computed as follows:

$$\frac{n - E(n)}{\sigma_n} \qquad \text{where}$$

$$E(n) = \frac{2N_1N_2}{N_1 + N_2} + 1 \quad \text{and} \quad \sigma_n^2 = \frac{2N_1N_2(2N_1N_2 - N_1 - N_2)}{(N_1 + N_2)^2(N_1 + N_2 - 1)}$$

Under the null hypothesis of independence and assuming $N_1 > 10$ and $N_2 > 10$, the runs test statistic has an asymptotic standard normal distribution. *Table 6* of the Appendix can be consulted for critical values if N_1 or N_2 are within the range of the values listed .

The Durbin-Watson Statistic: As mentioned above, the Durbin-Watson statistic (D-W) is printed when the **RSTAT** or **LIST** option is used with an **OLS** command. As the text mentions, the full versions of SHAZAM (i.e. not SHAZY) print the p-value for the D-W statistic when the **EXACTDW** option is used with an **OLS** command.

```
SAMPLE 1960.0 1991.0
OLS Y X / RSTAT EXACTDW
```

The pertinent output follows. (See above for the full output).

```
DURBIN-WATSON STATISTIC   =    0.13804
DURBIN-WATSON P-VALUE =     0.000000
RUNS TEST:    5 RUNS,   14 POS,     0 ZERO,    18 NEG   NORMAL STATISTIC = -4.2922
```

The D-W statistic is clearly below the d_L bound indicating positive autocorrelation. As well, given that its p-value is zero (up to at least six decimal places), the null hypothesis that there is no positive autocorrelation must clearly be rejected. Furthermore, given N1 = 14 and N2 = 18 for the Runs Test, the critical values, or upper and lower bounds, found in *Table 6* in the *Appendix* of the text allow for the conclusion that the sequence of residuals is not random.

The Breusch-Godfrey Test:This test statistic is constructed by regressing the OLS residuals on a series of lagged values and the explanatory variables from the OLS regression (including the constant term). As equation (12.5.13) notes, the R^2 statistic is multiplied by (N-P), the number of observations minus the number of lagged periods considered in the auxiliary regression. The resulting statistic follows a Chi-square distribution with P degrees of freedom. If the test statistic exceeds the appropriate critical value at a chosen level of significance, the null hypothesis that the coefficients for the lagged residuals are jointly equal to zero can be rejected.

Following the text, the residuals will be lagged five periods.

```
GENR LAG1U=LAG(U)
GENR LAG2U=LAG(U,2)
GENR LAG3U=LAG(U,3)
GENR LAG4U=LAG(U,4)
GENR LAG5U=LAG(U,5)
SAMPLE 1965.0 1991.0
OLS U X LAG1U LAG2U LAG3U LAG4U LAG5U
GEN1 BGSTAT=$R2*$N
PRINT BGSTAT
* Compute the p-value.
DISTRIB BGSTAT / TYPE=CHI DF=5
```

The output follows.

```
|_OLS U X LAG1U LAG2U LAG3U LAG4U LAG5U

 OLS ESTIMATION
      27 OBSERVATIONS      DEPENDENT VARIABLE = U
 ...NOTE..SAMPLE RANGE SET TO:     6,    32


 R-SQUARE =    0.9082     R-SQUARE ADJUSTED =    0.8807
VARIANCE OF THE ESTIMATE-SIGMA**2 =   0.80405
STANDARD ERROR OF THE ESTIMATE-SIGMA =   0.89669
SUM OF SQUARED ERRORS-SSE=    16.081
MEAN OF DEPENDENT VARIABLE =    0.41094
LOG OF THE LIKELIHOOD FUNCTION = -31.3157


VARIABLE     ESTIMATED    STANDARD    T-RATIO          PARTIAL STANDARDIZED ELASTICITY
  NAME       COEFFICIENT    ERROR      20 DF   P-VALUE CORR. COEFFICIENT  AT MEANS
X          -0.31283E-01 0.2592E-01   -1.207   0.242-0.261    -0.1164    -7.4211
LAG1U        0.95404     0.2006        4.756   0.000 0.729     0.9322     1.0639
LAG2U       -0.17321     0.2761       -0.6273  0.538-0.139    -0.1644    -0.2142
LAG3U        0.12115     0.2752        0.4403  0.664 0.098     0.1104     0.1700
LAG4U        0.39706     0.2726        1.457   0.161 0.310     0.3567     0.5793
LAG5U       -0.45613     0.1990       -2.292   0.033-0.456    -0.4103    -0.6628
CONSTANT     3.0759      2.518         1.222   0.236 0.264     0.0000     7.4849
|_GEN1 BGSTAT=$R2*$N
..NOTE..CURRENT VALUE OF $R2   =   0.90825
..NOTE..CURRENT VALUE OF $N    =   27.000
|_PRINT BGSTAT
   BGSTAT
   24.52264
|_* Compute the p-value.
|_DISTRIB BGSTAT / TYPE=CHI DF=5
CHI-SQUARE PARAMETERS- DF=    5.0000
MEAN=   5.0000     VARIANCE=   10.000     MODE=    3.0000


              DATA       PDF        CDF       1-CDF
   BGSTAT
 ROW     1    24.523    0.76404E-04 0.99983    0.17224E-03
```

Recall that the p-value is found under the heading 1-CDF in the **DISTRIB** output.

The Breusch-Godfrey statistic is above the appropriate Chi-square critical value, even the 1% level of significance (p-value = 0.00017). Thus, the null hypothesis that there is no autocorrelation of any order can be rejected.

Section 12.6 describes some remedial methods of estimation that can be used. The first step is to determine the value of rho (ρ).

The Berenblutt-Webb Test is introduced as a method to test the hypothesis that $\rho = 1$ (i.e. perfect positive autocorrelation of order 1). Following equation (12.6.11), the commands below compute the g statistic.

```
* The Berenblutt-Webb Test.
SAMPLE 1960.0 1991.0
GENR DELTAY=Y-LAG(Y)
GENR DELTAX=X-LAG(X)
?OLS Y X
GEN1 RSS1=$SSE
SAMPLE 1961.0 1991.0
OLS DELTAY DELTAX / NOCONSTANT
GEN1 RSS2=$SSE
GEN1 G=RSS2/RSS1
PRINT G
```

The output follows.

```
|_OLS DELTAY DELTAX / NOCONSTANT

 OLS ESTIMATION
       31 OBSERVATIONS       DEPENDENT VARIABLE = DELTAY
...NOTE..SAMPLE RANGE SET TO:    2,    32

 R-SQUARE =    0.5932     R-SQUARE ADJUSTED =    0.5932
VARIANCE OF THE ESTIMATE-SIGMA**2 =   0.93979
STANDARD ERROR OF THE ESTIMATE-SIGMA =   0.96943
SUM OF SQUARED ERRORS-SSE=    28.194
MEAN OF DEPENDENT VARIABLE =    1.1355
LOG OF THE LIKELIHOOD FUNCTION = -42.5164
RAW MOMENT R-SQUARE =    0.7420

VARIABLE    ESTIMATED   STANDARD    T-RATIO         PARTIAL STANDARDIZED ELASTICITY
  NAME      COEFFICIENT   ERROR        30 DF    P-VALUE CORR. COEFFICIENT  AT MEANS
DELTAX      0.83242     0.8962E-01   9.289      0.000 0.861      0.7269      1.0547
|_GEN1 RSS2=$SSE
..NOTE..CURRENT VALUE OF $SSE =    28.194
|_GEN1 G=RSS2/RSS1
|_PRINT G
   G
  0.1377367
```

Since the value of 0.1377 lies below the D-W lower bounds d_L (even at a 1% level of significance), the hypothesis that $\rho = 1$ cannot be rejected.

Equations (12.6.18) and (12.6.20) report estimation results where ρ was computed using the Cochrane-Orcutt (C-O) Two Step procedure (see footnote 33 for the formula) and the D-W Two Step procedure (described in equation (12.6.19)), respectively.

When the **RSTAT** or **LIST** options are used with the **OLS** command, a value of ρ is computed using the Cochrane-Orcutt Two-Step procedure. This value of ρ is stored in the temporary variable **$RHO**.

The **AUTO** Command

The **AUTO** command provides features for estimation of models with autocorrelated errors. The general formula is:

AUTO *depvar   indeps   /   options*

where *depvar* is the dependent variable, *indeps* is a list of independent variables, and *options* is a list of desired options.

With the **AUTO** command, the default estimation method for a model with AR(1) errors is the Cochrane-Orcutt iterative estimation. The **RHO=** option with the **AUTO** command allows the user to specify any value of ρ for the regression.

When the **AUTO** command is used, SHAZAM automatically includes the first observation in the estimation using the Prais-Winsten transformation. The **DROP** option is used to drop the first observation (as is done in (12.6.18)).

The following commands estimate equations (12.6.18) and (12.6.20).

```
SAMPLE 1960.0 1991.0
?OLS Y X / RSTAT
GEN1 RHO2STEP=$RHO
* Equation (12.6.18).
AUTO Y X / RHO=RHO2STEP RSTAT DROP
* Estimate rho using the D-W 2 Step procedure (the coefficient on the lagged Y
* in equation (12.6.19)).
GENR LAGX=LAG(X)
GENR LAGY=LAG(Y)
SAMPLE 1961.0 1991.0
OLS Y LAGY X LAGX / DLAG
```

The output follows.

```
|_SAMPLE 1960.0 1991.0
|_?OLS Y X / RSTAT
|_GEN1 RHO2STEP=$RHO
..NOTE..CURRENT VALUE OF $RHO =  0.94038
|_* Equation (12.6.18).

|_AUTO Y X / RHO=RHO2STEP RSTAT DROP

DEPENDENT VARIABLE =  Y
..NOTE..R-SQUARE,ANOVA,RESIDUALS DONE ON ORIGINAL VARS

LEAST SQUARES ESTIMATION                31 OBSERVATIONS

                   ASYMPTOTIC  ASYMPTOTIC  ASYMPTOTIC
          ESTIMATE  VARIANCE    ST.ERROR    T-RATIO
RHO        0.94038   0.00373     0.06109    15.39389


 R-SQUARE =  0.9929     R-SQUARE ADJUSTED =    0.9926
VARIANCE OF THE ESTIMATE-SIGMA**2 =  0.93835
STANDARD ERROR OF THE ESTIMATE-SIGMA =  0.96868
SUM OF SQUARED ERRORS-SSE=   27.212
MEAN OF DEPENDENT VARIABLE =    93.613
LOG OF THE LIKELIHOOD FUNCTION = -41.9670

VARIABLE  ESTIMATED  STANDARD  T-RATIO        PARTIAL STANDARDIZED ELASTICITY
  NAME    COEFFICIENT  ERROR    29 DF  P-VALUE CORR. COEFFICIENT  AT MEANS
X         0.71514     0.1569    4.558   0.000  0.646   0.8595      0.7128
CONSTANT  28.734      18.57     1.547   0.133  0.276   0.0000      0.3069

DURBIN-WATSON = 1.5886    VON NEUMANN RATIO = 1.6415    RHO =  0.20465
RESIDUAL SUM =  0.15099E-13  RESIDUAL VARIANCE =  0.93835
SUM OF ABSOLUTE ERRORS=   24.341
R-SQUARE BETWEEN OBSERVED AND PREDICTED = 0.9921
RUNS TEST:   16 RUNS,   16 POS,    0 ZERO,   15 NEG  NORMAL STATISTIC = -0.1770
DURBIN H STATISTIC (ASYMPTOTIC NORMAL) =   1.2117
 MODIFIED FOR AUTO ORDER=1
|_* Estimate rho using the D-W 2 Step procedure (the coefficient on the lagged Y
|_* in equation (12.6.19)).
|_GENR LAGX=LAG(X)
..NOTE.LAG VALUE IN UNDEFINED OBSERVATIONS SET TO ZERO
|_GENR LAGY=LAG(Y)
..NOTE.LAG VALUE IN UNDEFINED OBSERVATIONS SET TO ZERO
|_SAMPLE 1961.0 1991.0

|_OLS Y LAGY X LAGX / DLAG

 OLS ESTIMATION
      31 OBSERVATIONS      DEPENDENT VARIABLE = Y
...NOTE..SAMPLE RANGE SET TO:    2,   32

 R-SQUARE =  0.9922     R-SQUARE ADJUSTED =    0.9913
VARIANCE OF THE ESTIMATE-SIGMA**2 =  0.92396
STANDARD ERROR OF THE ESTIMATE-SIGMA =  0.96123
SUM OF SQUARED ERRORS-SSE=   24.947
MEAN OF DEPENDENT VARIABLE =    94.416
LOG OF THE LIKELIHOOD FUNCTION = -40.6198
```

```
VARIABLE    ESTIMATED    STANDARD    T-RATIO           PARTIAL STANDARDIZED ELASTICITY
  NAME      COEFFICIENT    ERROR      27 DF    P-VALUE CORR. COEFFICIENT  AT MEANS
LAGY          0.94223    0.6998E-01   13.46     0.000  0.933    1.0178      0.9309
X             0.73352    0.1578       4.649     0.000  0.667    0.8938      0.7318
LAGX         -0.71216    0.1681      -4.236     0.000 -0.632   -0.9130     -0.6997
CONSTANT      3.4879     2.089        1.670     0.107  0.306    0.0000      0.0369

DURBIN-WATSON = 1.7664     VON NEUMANN RATIO = 1.8253     RHO =  0.10083
RESIDUAL SUM =  0.80036E-12  RESIDUAL VARIANCE =  0.92396
SUM OF ABSOLUTE ERRORS=   23.444
R-SQUARE BETWEEN OBSERVED AND PREDICTED = 0.9922
RUNS TEST:   12 RUNS,    15 POS,    0 ZERO,   16 NEG  NORMAL STATISTIC = -1.6400
DURBIN H STATISTIC (ASYMPTOTIC NORMAL) =  0.60954
```

Note that the coefficients for the constant terms reported above differ from those reported in the text. This is because SHAZAM estimates β_1 directly instead of β_1^* (see equation (12.6.15)).

Although the text reports the D-W d statistic, this statistic is not appropriate for models containing lagged values of the dependent variable. In such a case, the Durbin-h statistic (described in *Chapter 17*) is the appropriate statistic to be considering. The **RSTAT** option with the **AUTO** command prints the Durbin-h statistic. The **DLAG** option with the **OLS** command also prints the Durbin-h statistic. Note that the lagged dependent variable *must* be the first independent variable listed. (See Chapter 17 for more details).

Section 12.7 provides an illustrated example using the quarterly data found in *Table 12.7*. First, equation (12.7.1) is estimated. Note that the variables are in natural logs.

```
TIME 1962 4
SAMPLE 1962.1 1967.4
READ(TABLE12.7) YEAR HWI UNRATE
* Transform variables into natural logs.
GENR LNHWI=LOG(HWI)
GENR LNUN=LOG(UNRATE)
* Equation (12.7.1).
OLS LNHWI LNUN / LOGLOG RSTAT
```

The output follows.

```
|_* Equation (12.7.1).

|_OLS LNHWI LNUN / LOGLOG RSTAT

 OLS ESTIMATION
     24 OBSERVATIONS     DEPENDENT VARIABLE = LNHWI
...NOTE..SAMPLE RANGE SET TO:    1,   24

 R-SQUARE =   0.9550     R-SQUARE ADJUSTED =    0.9530
VARIANCE OF THE ESTIMATE-SIGMA**2 =  0.33773E-02
STANDARD ERROR OF THE ESTIMATE-SIGMA =  0.58115E-01
```

```
SUM OF SQUARED ERRORS-SSE=  0.74302E-01
MEAN OF DEPENDENT VARIABLE =    4.9226
LOG OF THE LIKELIHOOD FUNCTION(IF DEPVAR LOG) = -82.8653

VARIABLE    ESTIMATED   STANDARD   T-RATIO        PARTIAL STANDARDIZED ELASTICITY
  NAME      COEFFICIENT   ERROR      22 DF   P-VALUE CORR. COEFFICIENT  AT MEANS
LNUN        -1.5375      0.7114E-01  -21.61   0.000-0.977    -0.9772     -1.5375
CONSTANT     7.3084      0.1110       65.82   0.000 0.997     0.0000      7.3084

DURBIN-WATSON = 0.9108    VON NEUMANN RATIO = 0.9504    RHO =  0.54571
RESIDUAL SUM =  0.13045E-13  RESIDUAL VARIANCE =  0.33773E-02
SUM OF ABSOLUTE ERRORS=   1.1162
R-SQUARE BETWEEN OBSERVED AND PREDICTED = 0.9550
R-SQUARE BETWEEN ANTILOGS OBSERVED AND PREDICTED = 0.9563
RUNS TEST:    4 RUNS,   13 POS,    0 ZERO,   11 NEG  NORMAL STATISTIC = -3.7492
```

Since the D-W statistic computed above falls below the d_L bound at the 5% level of significance, it can be concluded that positive autocorrelation is present in the model.

In the remaining examples using the data from *Table 12.7*, the variables (for some reason) are transformed to base 10 logs. The variables can be converted by dividing the natural logs of the variables by the natural log of 10.

```
GENR LNHWI=LNHWI/LOG(10)
GENR LNUN=LNUN/LOG(10)
```

The commands below illustrate the methods discussed in the text for computing ρ. Note that, when the **RSTAT** option is used with the **OLS** command, the D-W statistic is available in the temporary variable **$DW**.

```
* Cochrane-Orcutt 2 Step:
GEN1 RHO2STEP=$RHO
* Durbin-Watson d:
GEN1 RHODW=1-($DW/2)
* Theil-Nagar d:
GEN1 RHOTHEIL=($N**2*(1-$DW/2)+$K**2)/($N**2-$K**2)
* Cochrane-Orcutt Iterative method:
AUTO LNHWI LNUN
* Durbin-Watson Two Step.
GENR LAGLNHWI=LAG(LNHWI)
GENR LAGLNUN=LAG(LNUN)
SAMPLE 1962.2 1967.4
OLS LNHWI LAGLNHWI LNUN LAGLNUN / COEF=CF DLAG
GEN1 RHODW2=CF(1)
PRINT RHO2STEP RHODW RHOTHEIL RHODW2
```

The pertinent output follows. Although the estimation of the model using the Cochrane-Orcutt iterated value of ρ is not included in the text, it is included below.

```
|_AUTO LNHWI LNUN

DEPENDENT VARIABLE =  LNHWI
..NOTE..R-SQUARE,ANOVA,RESIDUALS DONE ON ORIGINAL VARS

LEAST SQUARES ESTIMATION              24 OBSERVATIONS
BY COCHRANE-ORCUTT TYPE PROCEDURE WITH CONVERGENCE = 0.00100

      ITERATION          RHO              LOG L.F.              SSE
         1             0.00000           55.2944           0.14014E-01
         2             0.54571           59.3588           0.98418E-02
         3             0.57223           59.3530           0.98288E-02
         4             0.57836           59.3489           0.98279E-02
         5             0.57999           59.3476           0.98278E-02
         6             0.58044           59.3472           0.98277E-02

  LOG L.F. =     59.3472       AT RHO =      0.58044

                    ASYMPTOTIC   ASYMPTOTIC   ASYMPTOTIC
          ESTIMATE   VARIANCE    ST.ERROR     T-RATIO
RHO        0.58044    0.02763     0.16622      3.49203

 R-SQUARE =   0.9685     R-SQUARE ADJUSTED =    0.9670
VARIANCE OF THE ESTIMATE-SIGMA**2 =  0.44672E-03
STANDARD ERROR OF THE ESTIMATE-SIGMA =  0.21136E-01
SUM OF SQUARED ERRORS-SSE=  0.98277E-02
MEAN OF DEPENDENT VARIABLE =   2.1379
LOG OF THE LIKELIHOOD FUNCTION =  59.3472

VARIABLE   ESTIMATED   STANDARD   T-RATIO            PARTIAL STANDARDIZED ELASTICITY
  NAME     COEFFICIENT  ERROR     22 DF    P-VALUE CORR. COEFFICIENT  AT MEANS
LNUN       -1.4712     0.1251    -11.76    0.000-0.929   -0.9351     -0.4638
CONSTANT    3.1303     0.8490E-01  36.87   0.000 0.992    0.0000      1.4642


|_PRINT RHO2STEP RHODW RHOTHEIL RHODW2
    RHO2STEP
  0.5457087
    RHODW
  0.5446165
    RHOTHEIL
  0.5554180
    RHODW2
  0.7951696
```

The Theil-Nagar estimation of ρ will be used to estimate equations (12.7.2) and (12.7.3). Note that the first observation is dropped in (12.7.2). Recall that, with the **AUTO** command, the first observation is automatically included using the Prais-Winsten transformation. Hence, the **DROP** option with the **AUTO** command must be used to replicate the results reported in equation (12.7.2).

```
SAMPLE 1962.1 1967.4
* Equation (12.7.2).
AUTO LNHWI LNUN / RSTAT DROP RHO=RHOTHEIL
* Equation (12.7.3)
AUTO LNHWI LNUN / RSTAT RHO=RHOTHEIL
```

The output follows.

```
|_AUTO LNHWI LNUN / RSTAT DROP RHO=RHOTHEIL

DEPENDENT VARIABLE =   LNHWI
..NOTE..R-SQUARE,ANOVA,RESIDUALS DONE ON ORIGINAL VARS

LEAST SQUARES ESTIMATION              23 OBSERVATIONS

                   ASYMPTOTIC   ASYMPTOTIC   ASYMPTOTIC
          ESTIMATE   VARIANCE    ST.ERROR     T-RATIO
RHO       0.55542    0.03007     0.17339      3.20320

 R-SQUARE =   0.9685    R-SQUARE ADJUSTED =    0.9670
VARIANCE OF THE ESTIMATE-SIGMA**2 =  0.46697E-03
STANDARD ERROR OF THE ESTIMATE-SIGMA =  0.21609E-01
SUM OF SQUARED ERRORS-SSE=  0.98063E-02
MEAN OF DEPENDENT VARIABLE =   2.1379
LOG OF THE LIKELIHOOD FUNCTION =  56.6070

VARIABLE   ESTIMATED   STANDARD   T-RATIO        PARTIAL STANDARDIZED ELASTICITY
  NAME     COEFFICIENT   ERROR      21 DF   P-VALUE CORR. COEFFICIENT  AT MEANS
LNUN       -1.4672      0.1328     -11.04   0.000-0.924    -0.9325     -0.4625
CONSTANT    3.1285      0.8856E-01  35.33   0.000 0.992     0.0000      1.4634

DURBIN-WATSON = 1.7744    VON NEUMANN RATIO = 1.8551    RHO =  0.04455
RESIDUAL SUM =  0.14100E-13  RESIDUAL VARIANCE =  0.46697E-03
SUM OF ABSOLUTE ERRORS=  0.38884
R-SQUARE BETWEEN OBSERVED AND PREDICTED = 0.9670
RUNS TEST:   12 RUNS,   11 POS,    0 ZERO,   12 NEG  NORMAL STATISTIC = -0.2045
DURBIN H STATISTIC (ASYMPTOTIC NORMAL) =  0.38466
 MODIFIED FOR AUTO ORDER=1
|_* Equation (12.7.3).

|_AUTO LNHWI LNUN / RSTAT RHO=RHOTHEIL

DEPENDENT VARIABLE =   LNHWI
..NOTE..R-SQUARE,ANOVA,RESIDUALS DONE ON ORIGINAL VARS

LEAST SQUARES ESTIMATION              24 OBSERVATIONS

                   ASYMPTOTIC   ASYMPTOTIC   ASYMPTOTIC
          ESTIMATE   VARIANCE    ST.ERROR     T-RATIO
RHO       0.55542    0.02881     0.16974      3.27210

 R-SQUARE =   0.9684    R-SQUARE ADJUSTED =    0.9670
VARIANCE OF THE ESTIMATE-SIGMA**2 =  0.44706E-03
STANDARD ERROR OF THE ESTIMATE-SIGMA =  0.21144E-01
SUM OF SQUARED ERRORS-SSE=  0.98353E-02
```

```
MEAN OF DEPENDENT VARIABLE =   2.1379
LOG OF THE LIKELIHOOD FUNCTION =  59.3590


VARIABLE    ESTIMATED   STANDARD    T-RATIO        PARTIAL STANDARDIZED ELASTICITY
  NAME     COEFFICIENT    ERROR      22 DF    P-VALUE CORR. COEFFICIENT AT MEANS
LNUN       -1.4800       0.1198     -12.35    0.000-0.935    -0.9407    -0.4665
CONSTANT    3.1361       0.8128E-01  38.58    0.000 0.993     0.0000     1.4669


DURBIN-WATSON = 1.8285    VON NEUMANN RATIO = 1.9080   RHO =   0.05554
RESIDUAL SUM =  0.30893E-02  RESIDUAL VARIANCE =   0.44749E-03
SUM OF ABSOLUTE ERRORS=  0.39390
R-SQUARE BETWEEN OBSERVED AND PREDICTED = 0.9684
RUNS TEST:   12 RUNS,   11 POS,    0 ZERO,   13 NEG  NORMAL STATISTIC = -0.3854
DURBIN H STATISTIC (ASYMPTOTIC NORMAL) =  0.48991
 MODIFIED FOR AUTO ORDER=1
```

Section 12.8 introduces the Autoregressive Conditional Heteroscedasticity (ARCH) model. ARCH models recognize the presence of successive periods of relative volatility and stability and allow for the conditional variance to evolve over time as a function of past errors.

The text tests for the presence of ARCH by regressing the squared OLS residuals on their lagged values and a constant (12.8.4). A test statistic is constructed by multiplying the R^2 from this auxiliary regression by the number of observations in the auxiliary regression (not the number of observations in the original model). The test statistic follows a Chi-square distribution with p degrees of freedom where p is the number of periods the squared residuals are lagged in the auxiliary regression. If the test statistic is above the appropriate Chi-square critical value, it can be concluded that the error variance is serially correlated.

```
TIME 1960 1
SAMPLE ..960.0 1991.0
READ(TABLE5.6) YEAR Y X
OLS Y X / RESID=U
GENR U2=U**2
GENR LAGU2=LAG(U2)
SAMPLE 1961.0 1991.0
OLS U2 LAGU2 / RSTAT DLAG
* Construct the Chi-Square test statistic (12.8.5) and its p-value.
GEN1 CHISTAT=$N*$R2
PRINT CHISTAT
DISTRIB CHISTAT / TYPE=CHI DF=1
```

The output follows.

```
|_OLS U2 LAGU2 / RSTAT DLAG
      ?
 OLS ESTIMATION
     31 OBSERVATIONS       DEPENDENT VARIABLE = U2
...NOTE..SAMPLE RANGE SET TO:    2,    32

 R-SQUARE =    0.4665     R-SQUARE ADJUSTED =    0.4481
```

```
VARIANCE OF THE ESTIMATE-SIGMA**2 =    11.725
STANDARD ERROR OF THE ESTIMATE-SIGMA =    3.4242
SUM OF SQUARED ERRORS-SSE=    340.03
MEAN OF DEPENDENT VARIABLE =    6.4157
LOG OF THE LIKELIHOOD FUNCTION = -81.1105


VARIABLE    ESTIMATED   STANDARD    T-RATIO          PARTIAL STANDARDIZED ELASTICITY
  NAME      COEFFICIENT   ERROR      29 DF    P-VALUE CORR. COEFFICIENT  AT MEANS
LAGU2        0.69464     0.1379      5.036     0.000 0.683    0.6830      0.6766
CONSTANT     2.0746      1.059       1.959     0.060 0.342    0.0000      0.3234


DURBIN-WATSON = 1.6663    VON NEUMANN RATIO = 1.7218    RHO =  0.16651
RESIDUAL SUM = -0.43299E-14  RESIDUAL VARIANCE =    11.725
SUM OF ABSOLUTE ERRORS=    86.114
R-SQUARE BETWEEN OBSERVED AND PREDICTED = 0.4665
RUNS TEST:    13 RUNS,    15 POS,    0 ZERO,    16 NEG  NORMAL STATISTIC = -1.2742
DURBIN H STATISTIC (ASYMPTOTIC NORMAL) =    1.4477
|_* Construct the Chi-Square test statistic (12.8.5) and its p-value.
|_GEN1 CHISTAT=$N*$R2
..NOTE..CURRENT VALUE OF $N   =    31.000
..NOTE..CURRENT VALUE OF $R2  =   0.46650
|_PRINT CHISTAT
   CHISTAT
   14.46140
|_DISTRIB CHISTAT / TYPE=CHI DF=1
CHI-SQUARE PARAMETERS- DF=    1.0000
MEAN=    1.0000    VARIANCE=    2.0000    MODE=  0.00000


            DATA        PDF        CDF       1-CDF
  CHISTAT
  ROW     1    14.461    0.75954E-04 0.99986     0.14306E-03
```

As the p-value of 0.000143 reflects, the test statistic allows for the conclusion that the error variance is serially correlated.

SHAZAM prints the above statistic when the **HET** option with the **DIAGNOS** command is used.

```
SAMPLE 1960.0 1991.0
?OLS Y X
DIAGNOS / HET
```

The pertinent output follows.

```
HETEROSKEDASTICITY TESTS
   E**2 ON YHAT:          CHI-SQUARE =    4.086 WITH 1 D.F.
   E**2 ON YHAT**2:       CHI-SQUARE =    4.268 WITH 1 D.F.
   E**2 ON LOG(YHAT**2): CHI-SQUARE =    3.868 WITH 1 D.F.
   E**2 ON X (B-P-G) TEST:    CHI-SQUARE =    4.086 WITH    1 D.F.
   E**2 ON LAG(E**2)  ARCH TEST: CHI-SQUARE =   14.461 WITH    1 D.F.
   LOG(E**2) ON X (HARVEY) TEST: CHI-SQUARE =    0.317 WITH    1 D.F.
   ABS(E) ON X (GLEJSER) TEST:   CHI-SQUARE =    1.110 WITH    1 D.F.
```

Although the text does not provide an example, an ARCH model will be estimated using the current data.

The **HET** Command

The **HET** command implements maximum likelihood estimation of models which require corrections for heteroscedastic errors. The general format is:

HET *depvar indeps (exogs) / options*

where *depvar* is the dependent variable, *indeps* is a list of independent variables, *exogs* is an optional list of exogenous variables in the variance equation, and *options* is a list of desired options.

The **MODEL=** option is used to specify the form of heteroscedasticity. In this case, **MODEL=ARCH**. The **ARCH=** option specifies the order of the ARCH process. See the *SHAZAM User's Reference Manual* for more details.

The command below will estimate an ARCH model of order 1 for equation (12.8.1).

```
HET Y X / MODEL=ARCH ARCH=1
```

The output follows.

```
|_HET Y X / MODEL=ARCH ARCH=1
...NOTE..SAMPLE RANGE SET TO:      1,      32

ARCH        HETEROSKEDASTICITY MODEL        32 OBSERVATIONS
            ANALYTIC DERIVATIVES

  QUASI-NEWTON METHOD USING BFGS UPDATE FORMULA

INITIAL STATISTICS :

TIME =    0.000 SEC.   ITER. NO.     1 FUNCTION EVALUATIONS        1
LOG-LIKELIHOOD FUNCTION=   -72.84132
COEFFICIENTS
   0.8094427        18.09149        2.074606        0.6946406        2.529164
GRADIENT
   -92.45094        -1.139276       -0.1204507      -0.1786868E-01  -0.2935791E-01


TIME =    0.060 SEC.   ITER. NO.    16 FUNCTION EVALUATIONS       35
LOG-LIKELIHOOD FUNCTION=   -68.75629
COEFFICIENTS
   0.8314941        14.54203        0.4291552        1.228591        0.5466446E-01
GRADIENT
```

```
  -169.2822        -1.720591        0.1548738        -0.7815015        -0.1218408

FINAL STATISTICS :

TIME =    0.110 SEC.    ITER. NO.    25 FUNCTION EVALUATIONS     44
LOG-LIKELIHOOD FUNCTION=    -67.69098
COEFFICIENTS
   0.8100409        16.05770        0.4391117        1.018999        0.6892564E-03
GRADIENT
  -0.1316102       -0.1668796E-02 -0.1138042E-02   0.1075411E-02 -0.9709998E-03

*** WARNING - STATIONARITY CONSTRAINTS NOT SATISFIED

SQUARED CORR. COEF. BETWEEN OBSERVED AND PREDICTED    0.94650

ASY. COVARIANCE MATRIX OF PARAMETER ESTIMATES IS ESTIMATED USING
THE INFORMATION MATRIX

LOG OF THE LIKELIHOOD FUNCTION = -67.6910

                              ASYMPTOTIC
VARIABLE    ESTIMATED   STANDARD    T-RATIO             PARTIAL STANDARDIZED ELASTICITY
  NAME      COEFFICIENT   ERROR     --------   P-VALUE CORR. COEFFICIENT   AT MEANS
            MEAN EQUATION:
X            0.81004    0.9855E-02   82.20     0.000 0.998     0.9736       0.8073
CONSTANT    16.058      0.8910       18.02     0.000 0.961     0.0000       0.1715
            VARIANCE EQUATION:
ALPHA_        0.43911    0.2549       1.723     0.085 0.31
ALPHA_        1.0190     0.3379       3.016     0.003 0.50
DELTA_        0.68926E-03 477.9       0.1442E-05 1.000 0.00
```

Note that the above estimation violates the assumption that α_2 in the variance equation (defining the form of heteroscedasticity assumed) is $0 \leq \alpha_2 \leq 1$. Thus, interpret the above results with caution.

SHAZAM commands and options used in Chapter 12

AUTO *depvar indeps* / **DROP RHO= RSTAT**

DIAGNOS / **HET**

DISTRIB *vars* / **DF= TYPE=CHI**

GEN1 *newvar=equation*

GENR *newvar=equation* with **LAG**(x) **LAG**(x,n) **LOG**(x) **SQRT**(x)

HET *depvar indeps (exogs)* / **MODEL=ARCH ARCH=1**

OLS *depvar indeps* / **COEF= DLAG EXACTDW HATDIAG= LOGLOG**
$\qquad\qquad\qquad$ **NOCONSTANT PREDICT= RESID= RSTAT LIST**

PLOT *depvars indep* / *options*

PRINT *vars* / *options*

READ(*datafile*) *vars* / *options*

SAMPLE *beg end*

TIME *beg freq*

? Suppression of Output

Temporary variables used

$DW	Durbin-Watson statistic
$K	Number of Coefficients
$N	Number of observations used in the estimation
$RHO	Residual Autocorrelation Coefficient
$R2	R-square
$SIG2	Variance of the Estimate - SIGMA**2
$SSE	Sum of Squared Errors - SSE

13. ECONOMETRIC MODELLING I : TRADITIONAL ECONOMETRIC METHODOLOGY

Chapter 13 looks at some of the difficulties that may arise when specifying an econometric model. Specifically, the problems and consequences associated with equation specification errors are outlined. This chapter will illustrate some of the techniques discussed to test for model misspecification.

Section 13.4 uses the total cost function introduced in *Chapter 7* to test for incorrect functional form. In particular, the calculated residual errors from OLS regressions are analyzed.

Using the functional forms described in equations (13.4.4) to (13.4.6) (linear, quadratic, and cubic total cost functions), three OLS regressions are estimated, saving the residuals for later use. As well, the predicted values, the R^2 statistic, and the number of regressors, K, from the linear model are saved for use ahead.

Note that the number of coefficients from an estimation are available in the temporary variable **$K**. In addition, recall that the **LIST** option with the **OLS** command prints the Durbin-Watson statistic and lists and plots the residuals.

The following replicate the results provided in *Table 13.1*.

```
SAMPLE 1 10
READ(TABLE7.4) OUTPUT TCOST
GENR OUTPUT2=OUTPUT**2
GENR OUTPUT3=OUTPUT**3
* Linear Model (13.4.6)
OLS TCOST OUTPUT / PREDICT=TCOSHAT1 RESID=E1 LIST
GEN1 R2OLD=$R2
GEN1 KOLD=$K
* Quadratic Model - (13.4.5)
OLS TCOST OUTPUT OUTPUT2 /  RESID=E2 LIST
* Cubic Model - (13.4.4)
OLS TCOST OUTPUT OUTPUT2 OUTPUT3 /  RESID=E3 LIST
```

The output follows.

```
|_OLS TCOST OUTPUT / PREDICT=TCOSHAT1 RESID=E1 LIST

OLS ESTIMATION
     10 OBSERVATIONS      DEPENDENT VARIABLE = TCOST
...NOTE..SAMPLE RANGE SET TO:    1,    10
```

```
 R-SQUARE =    0.8409     R-SQUARE ADJUSTED =    0.8210
VARIANCE OF THE ESTIMATE-SIGMA**2 =    775.32
STANDARD ERROR OF THE ESTIMATE-SIGMA =   27.845
SUM OF SQUARED ERRORS-SSE=   6202.5
MEAN OF DEPENDENT VARIABLE =   276.10
LOG OF THE LIKELIHOOD FUNCTION = -46.3400
```

VARIABLE NAME	ESTIMATED COEFFICIENT	STANDARD ERROR	T-RATIO 8 DF	P-VALUE	PARTIAL CORR.	STANDARDIZED COEFFICIENT	ELASTICITY AT MEANS
OUTPUT	19.933	3.066	6.502	0.000	0.917	0.9170	0.3971
CONSTANT	166.47	19.02	8.752	0.000	0.952	0.0000	0.6029

OBS. NO.	OBSERVED VALUE	PREDICTED VALUE	CALCULATED RESIDUAL		
1	193.00	186.40	6.6000		I*
2	226.00	206.33	19.667		I *
3	240.00	226.27	13.733		I *
4	244.00	246.20	-2.2000		*
5	257.00	266.13	-9.1333		* I
6	260.00	286.07	-26.067	*	I
7	274.00	306.00	-32.000	*	I
8	297.00	325.93	-28.933	*	I
9	350.00	345.87	4.1333		I*
10	420.00	365.80	54.200		I *

```
DURBIN-WATSON = 0.7157    VON NEUMANN RATIO = 0.7952    RHO =  0.76336
RESIDUAL SUM = -0.20606E-12  RESIDUAL VARIANCE =    775.32
SUM OF ABSOLUTE ERRORS=   196.67
R-SQUARE BETWEEN OBSERVED AND PREDICTED = 0.8409
RUNS TEST:    3 RUNS,    5 POS,    0 ZERO,    5 NEG  NORMAL STATISTIC = -2.0125
|_GEN1 R2OLD=$R2
..NOTE..CURRENT VALUE OF $R2  = 0.84089
|_GEN1 KOLD=$K
..NOTE..CURRENT VALUE OF $K   =   2.0000
|_* Quadratic Model - (13.4.5)

|_OLS TCOST OUTPUT OUTPUT2 /  RESID=E2 LIST


 OLS ESTIMATION
        10 OBSERVATIONS     DEPENDENT VARIABLE = TCOST
...NOTE..SAMPLE RANGE SET TO:    1,   10


 R-SQUARE =    0.9284     R-SQUARE ADJUSTED =    0.9079
VARIANCE OF THE ESTIMATE-SIGMA**2 =    398.80
STANDARD ERROR OF THE ESTIMATE-SIGMA =   19.970
SUM OF SQUARED ERRORS-SSE=   2791.6
MEAN OF DEPENDENT VARIABLE =   276.10
LOG OF THE LIKELIHOOD FUNCTION = -42.3483
```

VARIABLE NAME	ESTIMATED COEFFICIENT	STANDARD ERROR	T-RATIO 7 DF	P-VALUE	PARTIAL CORR.	STANDARDIZED COEFFICIENT	ELASTICITY AT MEANS
OUTPUT	-8.0250	9.809	-0.8181	0.440	-0.295	-0.3692	-0.1599
OUTPUT2	2.5417	0.8691	2.925	0.022	0.742	1.3198	0.3544
CONSTANT	222.38	23.49	9.468	0.000	0.963	0.0000	0.8054

```
     OBS.      OBSERVED      PREDICTED    CALCULATED
     NO.        VALUE         VALUE        RESIDUAL
      1        193.00        216.90       -23.900              *      I
      2        226.00        216.50        9.5000                     I  *
      3        240.00        221.18        18.817                     I       *
      4        244.00        230.95        13.050                     I    *
      5        257.00        245.80        11.200                     I    *
      6        260.00        265.73       -5.7333                     *I
      7        274.00        290.75       -16.750               *     I
      8        297.00        320.85       -23.850              *      I
      9        350.00        356.03       -6.0333                *  I
     10        420.00        396.30        23.700                     I        *
```

DURBIN-WATSON = 1.0385   VON NEUMANN RATIO = 1.1539   RHO = 0.34783
RESIDUAL SUM = -0.13145E-12 RESIDUAL VARIANCE =   398.80
SUM OF ABSOLUTE ERRORS=   152.53
R-SQUARE BETWEEN OBSERVED AND PREDICTED = 0.9284
RUNS TEST: 4 RUNS,   5 POS,   0 ZERO,   5 NEG   NORMAL STATISTIC = -1.3416
|_* Cubic Model - (13.4.4)

|_OLS TCOST OUTPUT OUTPUT2 OUTPUT3 / RESID=E3 LIST

OLS ESTIMATION
       10 OBSERVATIONS   DEPENDENT VARIABLE = TCOST
...NOTE..SAMPLE RANGE SET TO: 1,   10

 R-SQUARE =   0.9983   R-SQUARE ADJUSTED =   0.9975
VARIANCE OF THE ESTIMATE-SIGMA**2 =   10.791
STANDARD ERROR OF THE ESTIMATE-SIGMA =   3.2849
SUM OF SQUARED ERRORS-SSE=   64.744
MEAN OF DEPENDENT VARIABLE =   276.10
LOG OF THE LIKELIHOOD FUNCTION = -23.5287

VARIABLE	ESTIMATED	STANDARD	T-RATIO		PARTIAL	STANDARDIZED	ELASTICITY
NAME	COEFFICIENT	ERROR	6 DF	P-VALUE	CORR.	COEFFICIENT	AT MEANS
OUTPUT	63.478	4.779	13.28	0.000	0.983	2.9202	1.2645
OUTPUT2	-12.962	0.9857	-13.15	0.000	-0.983	-6.7302	-1.8074
OUTPUT3	0.93959	0.5911E-01	15.90	0.000	0.988	4.9072	1.0294
CONSTANT	141.77	6.375	22.24	0.000	0.994	0.0000	0.5135

```
     OBS.      OBSERVED      PREDICTED    CALCULATED
     NO.        VALUE         VALUE        RESIDUAL
      1        193.00        193.22       -0.22238                   *
      2        226.00        224.39        1.6075                    I *
      3        240.00        240.91       -0.91469                   *I
      4        244.00        248.43       -4.4263               *    I
      5        257.00        252.57        4.4350                    I       *
      6        260.00        258.97        1.0317                    I *
      7        274.00        273.27        0.72634                   I*
      8        297.00        301.12       -4.1186               *    I
      9        350.00        348.14        1.8592                    I  *
     10        420.00        419.98        0.22378E-01                *
```

```
DURBIN-WATSON = 2.7002    VON NEUMANN RATIO = 3.0002    RHO = -0.35049
RESIDUAL SUM =  0.11809E-12  RESIDUAL VARIANCE =   10.791
SUM OF ABSOLUTE ERRORS=   19.364
R-SQUARE BETWEEN OBSERVED AND PREDICTED = 0.9983
RUNS TEST:    6 RUNS,    6 POS,    0 ZERO,    4 NEG  NORMAL STATISTIC =   0.1405
```

As the text notes, the Durbin-Watson statistic for the linear and quadratic models allow for the conclusion of positive correlation in the residual errors. The patterns of the residual plots for these two models clearly bolster the conclusion that the linear and quadratic cost functions have been misspecified. Note, though, that no pattern is apparent from the plotted residuals of the cubic cost function. (See also *Figure 13.1* of the text).

The next test for model misspecification discussed in the text is the Ramsey RESET test. This test is used to determine whether there exists a relationship between the residual errors and the predicted values of the dependent variable. If so, this would suggest that the R^2 statistic should increase. If this increase is statistically significant, there is evidence that the model may be misspecified.

In the text, the squared and cubed predicted values from the linear model are added as regressors to the model (see equation (13.4.7)). Equation (13.5.18) describes the F-test statistic to be constructed, where "old" refers to the basic linear model and "new" to the model where the squared and cubed predicted values are added.

The **RESET** option with the **DIAGNOS** command automatically performs this test. First, the "long way" will be used.

The following commands replicate *Figure 13.2*, the output for equation (13.49), and the reported F-statistic (13.4.10).

```
PLOT E1 TCOSHAT1
GENR TCOSHAT2=TCOSHAT1**2
GENR TCOSHAT3=TCOSHAT1**3
OLS TCOST OUTPUT TCOSHAT2 TCOSHAT3
GEN1 R2NEW=$R2
GEN1 KNEW=$K
PRINT R2OLD R2NEW KOLD KNEW $N
GEN1 F=((R2NEW-R2OLD)/(KNEW-KOLD))/((1-R2NEW)/($N-KNEW))
PRINT F
```

The output follows.

```
|_PLOT E1 TCOSHAT1

      10 OBSERVATIONS
                 *=E1
                 M=MULTIPLE POINT
   60.000       |
   53.684       |                                    *
   47.368       |
   41.053       |
   34.737       |
   28.421       |
   22.105       |
   15.789       |      *
   9.4737       |        *
   3.1579       |   *                        *
  -3.1579       |          *
  -9.4737       |            *
 -15.789        |
 -22.105        |
 -28.421        |              *
 -34.737        |                *    *
 -41.053        |
 -47.368        |
 -53.684        |
 -60.000        |
                 _____
            180.000   240.000   300.000   360.000   420.000

                              TCOSHAT1
|_GENR TCOSHAT2=TCOSHAT1**2
|_GENR TCOSHAT3=TCOSHAT1**3

|_OLS TCOST OUTPUT TCOSHAT2 TCOSHAT3

OLS ESTIMATION
      10 OBSERVATIONS       DEPENDENT VARIABLE = TCOST
...NOTE..SAMPLE RANGE SET TO:     1,    10


 R-SQUARE =    0.9983     R-SQUARE ADJUSTED =    0.9975
VARIANCE OF THE ESTIMATE-SIGMA**2 =    10.791
STANDARD ERROR OF THE ESTIMATE-SIGMA =   3.2849
SUM OF SQUARED ERRORS-SSE=    64.744
MEAN OF DEPENDENT VARIABLE =   276.10
LOG OF THE LIKELIHOOD FUNCTION = -23.5287
```

VARIABLE NAME	ESTIMATED COEFFICIENT	STANDARD ERROR	T-RATIO 6 DF	P-VALUE	PARTIAL CORR.	STANDARDIZED COEFFICIENT	ELASTICITY AT MEANS
OUTPUT	476.55	33.39	14.27	0.000	0.986	21.9230	9.4931
TCOSHAT2	-0.91865E-01	0.6192E-02	-14.84	0.000	-0.987	-46.7112	-26.4547
TCOSHAT3	0.11863E-03	0.7463E-05	15.90	0.000	0.988	25.9144	10.2100
CONSTANT	2140.2	132.0	16.22	0.000	0.989	0.0000	7.7516

```
|_GEN1 R2NEW=$R2
..NOTE..CURRENT VALUE OF $R2  =   0.99834
|_GEN1 KNEW=$K
..NOTE..CURRENT VALUE OF $K   =    4.0000
|_PRINT R2OLD R2NEW KOLD KNEW $N
```

```
    R2OLD
 0.8408909
    R2NEW
 0.9983392
    KOLD
  2.000000
    KNEW
  4.000000
    $N          10.00000
|_GEN1 F=((R2NEW-R2OLD)/(KNEW-KOLD))/((1-R2NEW)/($N-KNEW))
..NOTE..CURRENT VALUE OF $N   =   10.000
|_PRINT F
    F
  284.4035
```

Now the **RESET** option with the **DIAGNOS** command will be used to compute the Ramsey **RESET** test statistics. This option runs three regressions. The first includes the squared predicted values. The second regression (as above) includes the squared and cubed predicted values. The third includes the squared, cubed, and fourth power of the predicted values. The **RESET** output includes a set of F-statistics that test whether the coefficients on the predicted value variables are zero. In other words, it tests to see if the increase in the new R^2 term is statistically significant.

Recall that a **DIAGNOS** command must be preceded by an estimation command.

```
?OLS TCOST OUTPUT
DIAGNOS / RESET
```

The pertinent output follows.

```
|_DIAGNOS / RESET

DEPENDENT VARIABLE = TCOST            10 OBSERVATIONS
REGRESSION COEFFICIENTS
    19.9333333333        166.466666667


RAMSEY RESET SPECIFICATION TESTS USING POWERS OF YHAT
 RESET(2)=    8.5529     - F WITH DF1=  1 AND DF2=   7
 RESET(3)=    284.40     - F WITH DF1=  2 AND DF2=   6
 RESET(4)=    165.83     - F WITH DF1=  3 AND DF2=   5
```

Note that the F-statistic computed for "RESET(3)" is identical to the one reported in the text. Since the F-statistic is far above the 99% critical value for an F-distribution with 2 and 6 degrees of freedom, it again can be concluded that the linear model is misspecified.

Next, an alternate to the Ramsey RESET Test, the Lagrange Multiplier (LM) Test for adding variables is performed.

Recall that the residual errors from the restricted (i.e. linear) regression have previously been stored in the vector *E1*. First estimate the regression (13.4.14). Then compute the LM Test statistic and its p-value.

```
OLS E1 OUTPUT OUTPUT2 OUTPUT3
GEN1 LM=$N*$R2
PRINT LM
DISTRIB LM / TYPE=CHI DF=2
```

The output follows.

```
|_OLS E1 OUTPUT OUTPUT2 OUTPUT3

 OLS ESTIMATION
      10 OBSERVATIONS      DEPENDENT VARIABLE = E1
...NOTE..SAMPLE RANGE SET TO:    1,   10

 R-SQUARE =   0.9896    R-SQUARE ADJUSTED =   0.9843
VARIANCE OF THE ESTIMATE-SIGMA**2 =   10.791
STANDARD ERROR OF THE ESTIMATE-SIGMA =   3.2849
SUM OF SQUARED ERRORS-SSE=   64.744
MEAN OF DEPENDENT VARIABLE = -0.20606E-13
LOG OF THE LIKELIHOOD FUNCTION = -23.5287

VARIABLE    ESTIMATED   STANDARD   T-RATIO          PARTIAL STANDARDIZED ELASTICITY
  NAME      COEFFICIENT   ERROR       6 DF   P-VALUE CORR. COEFFICIENT  AT MEANS
OUTPUT      43.544        4.779      9.112   0.000 0.966    5.0220**********
OUTPUT2    -12.962        0.9857    -13.15   0.000-0.983  -16.8727**********
OUTPUT3     0.93959       0.5911E-01 15.90   0.000 0.988   12.3024**********
CONSTANT   -24.700        6.375      -3.874  0.008-0.845    0.0000**********
|_GEN1 LM=$N*$R2
..NOTE..CURRENT VALUE OF $N   =   10.000
..NOTE..CURRENT VALUE OF $R2  =  0.98956
|_PRINT LM
   LM
  9.895617
|_DISTRIB LM / TYPE=CHI DF=2
CHI-SQUARE PARAMETERS- DF=   2.0000
MEAN=   2.0000     VARIANCE=   4.0000     MODE=  0.00000

              DATA       PDF        CDF        1-CDF
   LM
ROW    1    9.8956   0.35495E-02 0.99290    0.70989E-02
```

Recall, from Chapter 8, that the p-value is found in the column marked "1-CDF." The LM test statistic allows for the rejection of the restricted regression (i.e. the linear total cost function) at the 1% significance level (p-value = 0.0071).

Section 13.5 examines measurement errors. Measurement of the dependent and independent variables may be a source of error in a regression estimation. The data for the consumption function example will be used to illustrate this point. First, the effect of measurement errors in the dependent variable will be shown. With this type of error, coefficient estimates will not be biased. However, the standard errors will be large (i.e. inefficient).

The data in *Table 13.2* has been created so that the following properties hold:

$E(u) = 0$, $E(\varepsilon) = 0$, $Cov(X, \varepsilon) = 0$, $Cov(u, \varepsilon) = 0$, $Var(u) = 0$, and $Var(\varepsilon) = 36$.

The true form of the model is given as $Y^* = 25 + 0.6X + u$. Also, $X = X^* + \omega$. (See the notes for *Table 13.2*).

Columns 1 (Y^*), 4 (X), and 5 (ε) from *Table 13.2* are not included in the data file **TABLE13.2**. They will be generated below.

```
SAMPLE 1 10
READ(TABLE13.2) XSTAR Y W U
GENR X=XSTAR+W
GENR YSTAR=25+.6*XSTAR+U
GENR E=Y-YSTAR
* Print Table 13.2.
PRINT YSTAR XSTAR Y X E W U / WIDE
* Compute the variances and covariances listed in the notes for Table 13.2.
STAT X E W U XSTAR / PCOV
```

The output follows.

```
|_PRINT YSTAR XSTAR Y X E W U / WIDE
   YSTAR        XSTAR         Y           X           E           W              U
75.46660      80.00000    67.60110    80.09400   -7.865500    0.9400000E-01   2.466600
74.98010      100.0000    75.44380    91.57210    0.463700   -8.427900      -10.01990
102.8242      120.0000   109.6956    122.1406     6.871400    2.140600        5.824200
125.7651      140.0000   129.4159    145.5969     3.650800    5.596900       16.76510
106.5035      160.0000   104.2388    168.5579    -2.264700    8.557900      -14.49650
131.4318      180.0000   125.8319    171.4793    -5.599900   -8.520700       -1.568200
149.3693      200.0000   153.9926    203.5366     4.623300    3.536600        4.369300
143.8628      220.0000   152.9208    222.8533     9.058000    2.853300      -13.13720
177.5218      240.0000   176.3344    232.9880    -1.187400   -7.012000        8.521800
182.2748      260.0000   174.5252    261.1813    -7.749600    1.181300        1.274800
|_* Compute the variances and covariances listed in the notes for Table 13.2.
|_STAT X E W U XSTAR / PCOV
NAME      N     MEAN        ST. DEV     VARIANCE     MINIMUM     MAXIMUM
X        10    170.00        60.850      3702.7        80.094      261.18
E        10    0.10000E-04    6.0000       36.000       -7.8655      9.0580
W        10    0.66613E-16    6.0000       36.000       -8.5207      8.5579
U        10    0.26645E-15   10.000       100.00       -14.496      16.765
XSTAR    10    170.00        60.553      3666.7        80.000      260.00
```

```
 COVARIANCE MATRIX OF VARIABLES -          10 OBSERVATIONS

X         3702.7
E         11.134        36.000
W         36.001        11.133        36.000
U        -0.42623E-03  -0.33295E-03   0.18219E-04   100.00
XSTAR     3666.7        0.77778E-03   0.11111E-02  -0.44444E-03   3666.7
             X             E             W             U           XSTAR
```

Note that the **STAT** command output confirms the assumptions made regarding the variances, covariances, and expected values for the data (see the footnotes for *Table 13.2*).

Next, estimate the regressions (13.5.11) and (13.5.12).

```
* Estimate (13.5.11).
OLS YSTAR XSTAR
* Estimate (13.5.12).
OLS Y XSTAR
```

The output follows.

```
|_* Estimate (13.5.11).

|_OLS YSTAR XSTAR

 OLS ESTIMATION
      10 OBSERVATIONS       DEPENDENT VARIABLE = YSTAR
...NOTE..SAMPLE RANGE SET TO:     1,    10

 R-SQUARE =    0.9296     R-SQUARE ADJUSTED =    0.9208
VARIANCE OF THE ESTIMATE-SIGMA**2 =    112.50
STANDARD ERROR OF THE ESTIMATE-SIGMA =    10.607
SUM OF SQUARED ERRORS-SSE=    900.00
MEAN OF DEPENDENT VARIABLE =    127.00
LOG OF THE LIKELIHOOD FUNCTION = -36.6885

VARIABLE    ESTIMATED    STANDARD    T-RATIO          PARTIAL STANDARDIZED ELASTICITY
  NAME      COEFFICIENT    ERROR       8 DF    P-VALUE CORR. COEFFICIENT   AT MEANS
XSTAR       0.60000      0.5839E-01   10.28     0.000 0.964    0.9641       0.8031
CONSTANT    25.000       10.48        2.386     0.044 0.645    0.0000       0.1969
|_* Estimate (13.5.12).

|_OLS Y XSTAR

 OLS ESTIMATION
      10 OBSERVATIONS       DEPENDENT VARIABLE = Y
...NOTE..SAMPLE RANGE SET TO:     1,    10

 R-SQUARE =    0.9066     R-SQUARE ADJUSTED =    0.8949
VARIANCE OF THE ESTIMATE-SIGMA**2 =    153.00
STANDARD ERROR OF THE ESTIMATE-SIGMA =    12.369
SUM OF SQUARED ERRORS-SSE=    1224.0
```

```
MEAN OF DEPENDENT VARIABLE =   127.00
LOG OF THE LIKELIHOOD FUNCTION = -38.2259
```

VARIABLE NAME	ESTIMATED COEFFICIENT	STANDARD ERROR	T-RATIO 8 DF	P-VALUE	PARTIAL CORR.	STANDARDIZED COEFFICIENT	ELASTICITY AT MEANS
XSTAR	0.60000	0.6809E-01	8.812	0.000	0.952	0.9522	0.8031
CONSTANT	25.000	12.22	2.046	0.075	0.586	0.0000	0.1969

The output above shows that the estimates are not biased. That is, the coefficients for the "true" consumption function (13.5.11) are identical to those estimated in (13.5.5), where Y (the observed income) instead of Y^* (the true income) was used. However, note that the variances are larger than those obtained when no measurement error exists. Keep in mind, as Gujarati notes, that the coefficients are identical because the sample was generated to match the assumptions of the measurement error model.

It will now be shown that, when measurement errors occur in the independent variable, the coefficient estimates are no longer unbiased. The regression using Y^* and X - *the true Y regressed on the observed X* - is estimated to illustrate this.

```
* Estimate (13.5.13).
OLS YSTAR X
```

The output follows.

```
|_* Estimate (13.5.13).

|_OLS YSTAR X

 OLS ESTIMATION
       10 OBSERVATIONS        DEPENDENT VARIABLE = YSTAR
...NOTE..SAMPLE RANGE SET TO:    1,   10

 R-SQUARE =   0.9205     R-SQUARE ADJUSTED =   0.9106
VARIANCE OF THE ESTIMATE-SIGMA**2 =   126.94
STANDARD ERROR OF THE ESTIMATE-SIGMA =   11.267
SUM OF SQUARED ERRORS-SSE=   1015.5
MEAN OF DEPENDENT VARIABLE =   127.00
LOG OF THE LIKELIHOOD FUNCTION = -37.2922
```

VARIABLE NAME	ESTIMATED COEFFICIENT	STANDARD ERROR	T-RATIO 8 DF	P-VALUE	PARTIAL CORR.	STANDARDIZED COEFFICIENT	ELASTICITY AT MEANS
X	0.59417	0.6172E-01	9.627	0.000	0.959	0.9594	0.7953
CONSTANT	25.992	11.08	2.346	0.047	0.638	0.0000	0.2047

The above output confirms that biased estimates result when errors of measurement occur in the independent, as opposed to the dependent, variable.

To see how the explanatory variable is correlated with the error terms, refer to equation (13.5.9) and use the **PCOV** option with the **STAT** command to print the covariance matrix.

```
GENR Z=U-.6*W
STAT Z X / PCOV
```

The output follows.

```
|_GENR Z=U-.6*W
|_STAT Z X / PCOV
NAME       N    MEAN        ST. DEV      VARIANCE      MINIMUM       MAXIMUM
Z         10   0.00000       10.628       112.96       -19.631        13.407
X         10   170.00        60.850       3702.7        80.094       261.18

 COVARIANCE MATRIX OF VARIABLES -          10 OBSERVATIONS

Z          112.96
X         -21.601            3702.7
            Z                   X
```

The covariance between z and X is computed as -21.601. This confirms that, following equation (13.5.9), the assumption in the classical linear regression model that the explanatory variable is uncorrelated is violated. Inconsistent and biased OLS estimators result.

SHAZAM commands and option used in Chapter 13

DIAGNOS / RESET

DISTRIB *vars* / **TYPE=CHI DF=**

GEN1 *newvar=equation*

GENR *newvar=equation*

OLS *depvar indeps* / **LIST PREDICT RESID=**

PLOT *depvars indep* / *options*

PRINT *vars* / **WIDE**

READ(*datafile*) *vars* / *options*

SAMPLE *beg end*

STAT *vars* / **PCOV**

? Suppression of Output

Temporary variables used

$K	Number of Coefficients
$N	Number of observations used in the estimation
$R2	R-Square

14. ECONOMETRIC MODELLING II: ALTERNATIVE ECONOMETRIC METHODOLOGIES

Section 14.1 discusses Leamer's approach to model selection. However, no data is supplied (even in the original source) to replicate the regression results reported. The methodology can be followed using any set of data. The SHAZAM commands involved have been illustrated in previous chapters.

Similarly, no data is provided for the St. Louis Model in *Section 14.3*. See Chapter 17 for examples of estimating distributed lag models.

In *Section 14.3*, the data found in *Table 14.1* is used to illustrate the Davidson-MacKinnon J-Test for comparing different models. Specifically, this test is used to compare models A (14.3.3) and B (14.3.4). Note that these models contain lagged variables. That is, the values of *PDPI* and *PPCE* for the previous time period are included as independent variables in Models A and B, respectively.

The **LAG**(x) function with the **GENR** command lags a variable one time period. The function **LAG**(x,n) lags a variable n time periods.

Note that, when lagging a variable, say, one time period, observation 1 of this new variable will not be defined properly since it does not exist for the first observation. (A warning message is printed in the output). Hence, the **SAMPLE** range must be altered, after creating the lagged variable so that the first observation is dropped.

The text mentions that SHAZAM computes various model selection tests such as Amemiya's PC measure and Akaike's AIC measure. These and various other model selection tests are printed when the **ANOVA** option with the **OLS** command is used. See the *SHAZAM User's Reference Manual* for the full details.

The commands below replicate the results reported in (14.3.5) and (14.3.6). As well, the predicted values of the dependent variable are saved for use ahead.

```
TIME 1970 1
SAMPLE 1970.0 1991.0
READ(TABLE14.1) YEAR PPCE PPDI
GENR LAGPPDI=LAG(PPDI)
GENR LAGPPCE=LAG(PPCE)
* Drop first observation.
SAMPLE 1971.0 1991.0
* Estimate Model A (14.3.3) and save the predicted values of the PPCE.
OLS PPCE PPDI LAGPPDI / ANOVA RSTAT PREDICT=PPCEHATA
* Estimate Model B (13.3.4) and save the predicted values of the PPCE.
OLS PPCE PPDI LAGPPCE / ANOVA RSTAT PREDICT=PPCEHATB
```

The output, including the model selection test statistics printed with the **ANOVA** command, follows.

```
|_GENR LAGPPDI=LAG(PPDI)
..NOTE.LAG VALUE IN UNDEFINED OBSERVATIONS SET TO ZERO
|_GENR LAGPPCE=LAG(PPCE)
..NOTE.LAG VALUE IN UNDEFINED OBSERVATIONS SET TO ZERO
|_* Drop first observation.

|_SAMPLE 1971.0 1991.0
|_* Estimate Model A (14.3.3) and save the predicted values of the PPCE.

|_OLS PPCE PPDI LAGPPDI / ANOVA RSTAT PREDICT=PPCEHATA

 OLS ESTIMATION
       21 OBSERVATIONS      DEPENDENT VARIABLE = PPCE
...NOTE..SAMPLE RANGE SET TO:     2,    22

 R-SQUARE =   0.9888     R-SQUARE ADJUSTED =   0.9875
VARIANCE OF THE ESTIMATE-SIGMA**2 =    20940.
STANDARD ERROR OF THE ESTIMATE-SIGMA =   144.71
SUM OF SQUARED ERRORS-SSE= 0.37691E+06
MEAN OF DEPENDENT VARIABLE =    11119.
LOG OF THE LIKELIHOOD FUNCTION = -132.648

MODEL SELECTION TESTS - SEE JUDGE ET AL. (1985,P.242)
 AKAIKE (1969) FINAL PREDICTION ERROR - FPE =      23931.
      (FPE IS ALSO KNOWN AS AMEMIYA PREDICTION CRITERION - PC)
 AKAIKE (1973) INFORMATION CRITERION - LOG AIC =   10.081
 SCHWARZ (1978) CRITERION - LOG SC =               10.230
MODEL SELECTION TESTS - SEE RAMANATHAN (1992,P.167)
 CRAVEN-WAHBA (1979)
    GENERALIZED CROSS VALIDATION - GCV =           24430.
 HANNAN AND QUINN (1979) CRITERION =               24670.
 RICE (1984) CRITERION =                           25127.
 SHIBATA (1981) CRITERION =                        23076.
 SCHWARZ (1978) CRITERION - SC =                   27727.
 AKAIKE (1974) INFORMATION CRITERION - AIC =       23884.

VARIABLE    ESTIMATED   STANDARD    T-RATIO       PARTIAL STANDARDIZED ELASTICITY
 NAME       COEFFICIENT   ERROR      18 DF    P-VALUE CORR. COEFFICIENT  AT MEANS
PPDI        0.92041     0.1529       6.018     0.000 0.817    0.9011      1.0157
LAGPPDI     0.93141E-01 0.1476       0.6309    0.536 0.147    0.0945      0.1012
CONSTANT    -1299.1     321.7       -4.038     0.001-0.689    0.0000     -0.1168

DURBIN-WATSON = 0.8092    VON NEUMANN RATIO = 0.8497    RHO =   0.58364
RESIDUAL SUM =  0.19561E-10  RESIDUAL VARIANCE =    20940.
SUM OF ABSOLUTE ERRORS=   2422.9
R-SQUARE BETWEEN OBSERVED AND PREDICTED = 0.9888
RUNS TEST:     5 RUNS,   10 POS,    0 ZERO,    11 NEG  NORMAL STATISTIC = -2.9068
|_* Estimate Model B (13.3.4) and save the predicted values of the PPCE.

|_OLS PPCE PPDI LAGPPCE / ANOVA RSTAT PREDICT=PPCEHATB

 OLS ESTIMATION
       21 OBSERVATIONS      DEPENDENT VARIABLE = PPCE
...NOTE..SAMPLE RANGE SET TO:     2,    22
```

```
 R-SQUARE =    0.9912     R-SQUARE ADJUSTED =    0.9903
VARIANCE OF THE ESTIMATE-SIGMA**2 =    16318.
STANDARD ERROR OF THE ESTIMATE-SIGMA =    127.74
SUM OF SQUARED ERRORS-SSE=  0.29373E+06
MEAN OF DEPENDENT VARIABLE =    11119.
LOG OF THE LIKELIHOOD FUNCTION = -130.030


MODEL SELECTION TESTS - SEE JUDGE ET AL. (1985,P.242)
 AKAIKE (1969) FINAL PREDICTION ERROR - FPE =      18650.
    (FPE IS ALSO KNOWN AS AMEMIYA PREDICTION CRITERION - PC)
 AKAIKE (1973) INFORMATION CRITERION - LOG AIC =   9.8316
 SCHWARZ (1978) CRITERION - LOG SC =               9.9808
MODEL SELECTION TESTS - SEE RAMANATHAN (1992,P.167)
 CRAVEN-WAHBA (1979)
    GENERALIZED CROSS VALIDATION - GCV =        19038.
 HANNAN AND QUINN (1979) CRITERION =            19226.
 RICE (1984) CRITERION =                        19582.
 SHIBATA (1981) CRITERION =                     17984.
 SCHWARZ (1978) CRITERION - SC =                21608.
 AKAIKE (1974) INFORMATION CRITERION - AIC =    18613.


VARIABLE   ESTIMATED   STANDARD    T-RATIO         PARTIAL STANDARDIZED ELASTICITY
  NAME     COEFFICIENT   ERROR      18 DF    P-VALUE CORR. COEFFICIENT  AT MEANS
PPDI        0.71170     0.1303      5.463    0.000 0.790     0.6968      0.7853
LAGPPCE     0.29540     0.1247      2.368    0.029 0.487     0.3020      0.2904
CONSTANT   -841.86      348.8      -2.414    0.027-0.494     0.0000     -0.0757


DURBIN-WATSON = 1.0145    VON NEUMANN RATIO = 1.0652    RHO =  0.48722
RESIDUAL SUM =  0.19241E-10  RESIDUAL VARIANCE =    16318.
SUM OF ABSOLUTE ERRORS=    2084.4
R-SQUARE BETWEEN OBSERVED AND PREDICTED = 0.9912
RUNS TEST:    8 RUNS,   10 POS,    0 ZERO,   11 NEG  NORMAL STATISTIC = -1.5603
```

To apply the J-Test, the predicted values of *PPCE* estimated from Model B are included as a regressor in Model A. Similarly, the predicted values from Model A are added to Model B. The t-ratios of these variables are then examined.

```
* Estimate (14.3.7).
OLS PPCE PPDI LAGPPDI PPCEHATB / RSTAT
* Estimate (14.3.8).
OLS PPCE PPDI LAGPPCE PPCEHATA / RSTAT
```

The output follows.

```
|_* Estimate (14.3.7).

|_OLS PPCE PPDI LAGPPDI PPCEHATB / RSTAT

 OLS ESTIMATION
      21 OBSERVATIONS      DEPENDENT VARIABLE = PPCE
...NOTE..SAMPLE RANGE SET TO:     2,    22
```

```
 R-SQUARE =   0.9932    R-SQUARE ADJUSTED =   0.9920
VARIANCE OF THE ESTIMATE-SIGMA**2 =   13469.
STANDARD ERROR OF THE ESTIMATE-SIGMA =   116.06
SUM OF SQUARED ERRORS-SSE= 0.22898E+06
MEAN OF DEPENDENT VARIABLE =   11119.
LOG OF THE LIKELIHOOD FUNCTION = -127.415


VARIABLE   ESTIMATED   STANDARD   T-RATIO          PARTIAL STANDARDIZED ELASTICITY
  NAME     COEFFICIENT   ERROR      17 DF   P-VALUE CORR. COEFFICIENT  AT MEANS
PPDI      -0.70615      0.5059    -1.396    0.181-0.321   -0.6913     -0.7792
LAGPPDI   -0.43568      0.1987    -2.193    0.043-0.470   -0.4419     -0.4733
PPCEHATB   2.1335       0.6438     3.314    0.004 0.626    2.1242      2.1335
CONSTANT   1322.8       832.1      1.590    0.130 0.360    0.0000      0.1190


DURBIN-WATSON = 1.7115    VON NEUMANN RATIO = 1.7971    RHO =  0.13520
RESIDUAL SUM = -0.32784E-10  RESIDUAL VARIANCE =   13469.
SUM OF ABSOLUTE ERRORS=   1839.0
R-SQUARE BETWEEN OBSERVED AND PREDICTED = 0.9932
RUNS TEST:    8 RUNS,   10 POS,    0 ZERO,   11 NEG  NORMAL STATISTIC = -1.5603
|_* Estimate (14.3.8).

|_OLS PPCE PPDI LAGPPCE PPCEHATA / RSTAT

 OLS ESTIMATION
      21 OBSERVATIONS    DEPENDENT VARIABLE = PPCE
...NOTE..SAMPLE RANGE SET TO:    2,   22

 R-SQUARE =   0.9932    R-SQUARE ADJUSTED =   0.9920
VARIANCE OF THE ESTIMATE-SIGMA**2 =   13469.
STANDARD ERROR OF THE ESTIMATE-SIGMA =   116.06
SUM OF SQUARED ERRORS-SSE= 0.22898E+06
MEAN OF DEPENDENT VARIABLE =   11119.
LOG OF THE LIKELIHOOD FUNCTION = -127.415


VARIABLE   ESTIMATED   STANDARD   T-RATIO          PARTIAL STANDARDIZED ELASTICITY
  NAME     COEFFICIENT   ERROR      17 DF   P-VALUE CORR. COEFFICIENT  AT MEANS
PPDI       5.1177       2.013      2.542    0.021 0.525    5.0103      5.6473
LAGPPCE    0.63026      0.1902     3.314    0.004 0.626    0.6444      0.6195
PPCEHATA  -4.6777       2.133     -2.193    0.043-0.470   -4.6513     -4.6777
CONSTANT  -6549.9       2623.     -2.498    0.023-0.518    0.0000     -0.5891


DURBIN-WATSON = 1.7115    VON NEUMANN RATIO = 1.7971    RHO =  0.13520
RESIDUAL SUM =  0.15073E-09  RESIDUAL VARIANCE =   13469.
SUM OF ABSOLUTE ERRORS=   1839.0
R-SQUARE BETWEEN OBSERVED AND PREDICTED = 0.9932
RUNS TEST:    8 RUNS,   10 POS,    0 ZERO,   11 NEG  NORMAL STATISTIC = -1.5603
```

As the text notes, since the estimated coefficients for the predicted values are statistically different from zero in both models, the results indicate that neither model is well specified for explaining variations in American per capita personal consumption behavior over the period 1970 - 1991.

SHAZAM commands and options used in Chapter 14

GENR *newvar-=equation* with **LAG**(x)   **LAG**(x,n)
OLS *depvar indeps* / **ANOVA PREDICT= RSTAT**
READ (*filename*) *vars* / *options*
SAMPLE *beg end*
TIME *beg freq*

15. REGRESSION ON DUMMY VARIABLES

Chapter 15 introduces the use of dummy variables in regression analysis. They are relatively easy to use and add much flexibility to econometric modeling.

In *Section 15.1*, an example is provided, using hypothetical data, where the starting salaries of teachers are regressed on their gender. The independent variable, *DM*, is equal to 1 if the observation is for a male and zero if for a female. The commands below replicate the results provided.

```
SAMPLE 1 10
READ(TABLE15.1) Y DM
OLS Y DM
```

The output follows.

```
|_OLS Y DM

 OLS ESTIMATION
      10 OBSERVATIONS      DEPENDENT VARIABLE = Y
...NOTE..SAMPLE RANGE SET TO:    1,    10

 R-SQUARE =   0.8737    R-SQUARE ADJUSTED =    0.8579
VARIANCE OF THE ESTIMATE-SIGMA**2 =  0.48600
STANDARD ERROR OF THE ESTIMATE-SIGMA =  0.69714
SUM OF SQUARED ERRORS-SSE=   3.8880
MEAN OF DEPENDENT VARIABLE =   19.640
LOG OF THE LIKELIHOOD FUNCTION = -9.46593

VARIABLE    ESTIMATED   STANDARD   T-RATIO            PARTIAL STANDARDIZED ELASTICITY
  NAME      COEFFICIENT   ERROR      8 DF   P-VALUE CORR. COEFFICIENT  AT MEANS
DM          3.2800      0.4409     7.439   0.000 0.935    0.9347      0.0835
CONSTANT    18.000      0.3118     57.74   0.000 0.999    0.0000      0.9165
```

In the above output, the coefficient for the constant term represents the mean starting salary for females. The coefficient for the dummy variable, *DM*, added to the coefficient for the constant term is equal to the mean salary for males. That is, while females earn, on average, $18,000 per year, men enjoy an additional $3,280.

The example in *Sections 15.6* and *15.7* deals with testing for a structural break in a regression model. The hypothesis to be tested is that the intercept *and the slope* of the regression line are different for the periods of 1946 to 1954 and 1955 to 1963. First, in *Section 15.6*, a Chow Test (introduced in Chapter 8) is performed. Then, in the following section, the regression is estimated incorporating a dummy variable scheme where $D = 1$ for the first period and $D = 0$ for the second. The shift in the intercept is captured by including the dummy variable on its own. The change in the slope is captured by multiplying the explanatory variable, *X*, by the dummy variable. Hence, for the second period, $D*X$ is equal to zero. The individual t-ratios of the coefficients for the variables involving the dummy variable are examined. As well, the joint hypothesis that both these coefficients are equal to zero is tested.

In this example, the dummy variable, D, must be created. A useful command for constructing dummy variables is the **IF** command.

The **IF** Command

The **IF** command is a conditional **GENR** command. The format is:

IF(*expression*) *var=equation*

where *expression* is an expression in parentheses to be evaluated. If the expression is true, the remainder of the **IF** command is executed. *Equation* is a function which defines elements of *var*. Note that *var* has to be previously defined using a **GENR** command. Relation operators that can be used include: .EQ., .NE., .GE., .GT., LE., .LT., .AND., and .OR..

For example, the command

```
GENR X4=0
IF(X1.GE.0) X4=SQRT(X1)
```

assigns the value of the square root of $X1$ to $X4$ if $X1$ is greater than or equal to zero. Recall that the variable $X4$ must be previously defined.

The commands below estimate the model for the entire sample period and compute a Chow Test statistic testing for a structural break between the reconstruction period (1946 to 1954) and the post-reconstruction period (1957 to 1963).

```
TIME 1946 1
SAMPLE 1946.0 1963.0
READ(TABLE15.2) YEAR SAVINGS INCOME
OLS SAVINGS INCOME
DIAGNOS / CHOWONE=9
```

The pertinent output follows.

```
|_OLS SAVINGS INCOME

 OLS ESTIMATION
       18 OBSERVATIONS      DEPENDENT VARIABLE = SAVINGS
...NOTE..SAMPLE RANGE SET TO:    1,    18

 R-SQUARE =     0.9185    R-SQUARE ADJUSTED =    0.9134
VARIANCE OF THE ESTIMATE-SIGMA**2 =   0.35764E-01
STANDARD ERROR OF THE ESTIMATE-SIGMA =   0.18911
SUM OF SQUARED ERRORS-SSE=  0.57223
MEAN OF DEPENDENT VARIABLE =   0.77333
LOG OF THE LIKELIHOOD FUNCTION =   5.49644

VARIABLE     ESTIMATED   STANDARD    T-RATIO         PARTIAL STANDARDIZED ELASTICITY
  NAME      COEFFICIENT   ERROR      16 DF  P-VALUE CORR. COEFFICIENT  AT MEANS
INCOME      0.11785     0.8774E-02   13.43    0.000 0.958     0.9584      2.3992
CONSTANT   -1.0821      0.1452       -7.455   0.000-0.881     0.0000     -1.3992
|_DIAGNOS / CHOWONE=9

DEPENDENT VARIABLE = SAVINGS           18 OBSERVATIONS
REGRESSION COEFFICIENTS
    0.117845048596      -1.08207148733

SEQUENTIAL CHOW AND GOLDFELD-QUANDT TESTS
   N1    N2    SSE1       SSE2        CHOW    PVALUE    G-Q      DF1  DF2 PVALUE
    9    9  0.13965    0.19312      5.0371    0.022 0.7231      7    7 0.340

            CHOW TEST - F DISTRIBUTION WITH DF1=   2 AND DF2=  14
```

Since the Chow Test statistic computed, 5.0371, is greater than the 5% $F_{2,14}$ critical value of 3.74 , the hypothesis that the savings function is the same in both periods can be rejected. The p-value of 0.022 bolsters this conclusion.

Following *Section 15.7*, the dummy variable approach for testing for structural stability will now be used. First, the dummy variable, *D*, and the interactive variable, *DX*, will be created. Then, the **TEST** command will be used to test the joint hypothesis that the coefficients for these variables are zero. That is, is the hypothesis $\alpha_2 = \beta_2 = 0$ true?

```
GENR D=1
IF(YEAR.GT.1954)D=0
GENR DX=D*INCOME
PRINT YEAR D DX
* Equation (15.7.4)
OLS SAVINGS D INCOME DX
TEST
TEST D=0
TEST DX=0
END
```

The output follows.

```
|_PRINT YEAR D DX
     YEAR              D                DX
   1946.000         1.000000         8.800000
   1947.000         1.000000         9.400000
   1948.000         1.000000         10.00000
   1949.000         1.000000         10.60000
   1950.000         1.000000         11.00000
   1951.000         1.000000         11.90000
   1952.000         1.000000         12.70000
   1953.000         1.000000         13.50000
   1954.000         1.000000         14.30000
   1955.000         0.0000000        0.0000000
   1956.000         0.0000000        0.0000000
   1957.000         0.0000000        0.0000000
   1958.000         0.0000000        0.0000000
   1959.000         0.0000000        0.0000000
   1960.000         0.0000000        0.0000000
   1961.000         0.0000000        0.0000000
   1962.000         0.0000000        0.0000000
   1963.000         0.0000000        0.0000000

|_OLS SAVINGS D INCOME DX

 OLS ESTIMATION
      18 OBSERVATIONS        DEPENDENT VARIABLE = SAVINGS
...NOTE..SAMPLE RANGE SET TO:     1,    18


 R-SQUARE =    0.9526      R-SQUARE ADJUSTED =    0.9425
VARIANCE OF THE ESTIMATE-SIGMA**2 =   0.23769E-01
STANDARD ERROR OF THE ESTIMATE-SIGMA =   0.15417
SUM OF SQUARED ERRORS-SSE=   0.33277
MEAN OF DEPENDENT VARIABLE =   0.77333
LOG OF THE LIKELIHOOD FUNCTION =   10.3752
```

VARIABLE NAME	ESTIMATED COEFFICIENT	STANDARD ERROR	T-RATIO 14 DF	P-VALUE	PARTIAL CORR.	STANDARDIZED COEFFICIENT	ELASTICITY AT MEANS
D	1.4839	0.4704	3.155	0.007	0.645	1.1877	0.9594
INCOME	0.15045	0.1629E-01	9.238	0.000	0.927	1.2236	3.0630
DX	-0.10342	0.3326E-01	-3.109	0.008	-0.639	-0.9626	-0.7593
CONSTANT	-1.7502	0.3319	-5.273	0.000	-0.816	0.0000	-2.2632

```
|_TEST
|_TEST D=0
|_TEST DX=0
|_END
F STATISTIC =    5.0370595    WITH    2 AND   14 D.F.  P-VALUE= 0.02249
WALD CHI-SQUARE STATISTIC =    10.074119    WITH    2 D.F.  P-VALUE= 0.00649
UPPER BOUND ON P-VALUE BY CHEBYCHEV INEQUALITY = 0.19853
```

Notice that the F-statistic computed and the implied conclusions are identical to the Chow Test above.

Finally, separate regressions will be estimated for the two time periods.

```
* Equation (15.7.5).
SAMPLE 1946.0 1954.0
OLS SAVINGS INCOME
* Equation (15.7.6).
SAMPLE 1955.0 1963.0
OLS SAVINGS INCOME
```

The output follows.

```
|_* Equation (15.7.5).
|_SAMPLE 1946.0 1954.0

|_OLS SAVINGS INCOME

OLS ESTIMATION
        9 OBSERVATIONS     DEPENDENT VARIABLE = SAVINGS
...NOTE..SAMPLE RANGE SET TO:    1,    9

 R-SQUARE =    0.3092     R-SQUARE ADJUSTED =   0.2105
VARIANCE OF THE ESTIMATE-SIGMA**2 =  0.19950E-01
STANDARD ERROR OF THE ESTIMATE-SIGMA =  0.14124
SUM OF SQUARED ERRORS-SSE=  0.13965
MEAN OF DEPENDENT VARIABLE =  0.26778
LOG OF THE LIKELIHOOD FUNCTION =  5.97582

VARIABLE   ESTIMATED  STANDARD   T-RATIO        PARTIAL STANDARDIZED ELASTICITY
  NAME    COEFFICIENT  ERROR        7 DF    P-VALUE CORR. COEFFICIENT  AT MEANS
INCOME    0.47028E-01 0.2657E-01   1.770    0.120 0.556     0.5561      1.9943
CONSTANT -0.26625      0.3054      -0.8719   0.412-0.313     0.0000     -0.9943
|_* Equation (15.7.6).
|_SAMPLE 1955.0 1963.0

|_OLS SAVINGS INCOME

OLS ESTIMATION
        9 OBSERVATIONS     DEPENDENT VARIABLE = SAVINGS
...NOTE..SAMPLE RANGE SET TO:   10,    18

 R-SQUARE =    0.9131     R-SQUARE ADJUSTED =   0.9007
VARIANCE OF THE ESTIMATE-SIGMA**2 =  0.27589E-01
STANDARD ERROR OF THE ESTIMATE-SIGMA =  0.16610
SUM OF SQUARED ERRORS-SSE=  0.19312
MEAN OF DEPENDENT VARIABLE =   1.2789
LOG OF THE LIKELIHOOD FUNCTION =  4.51704

VARIABLE   ESTIMATED  STANDARD   T-RATIO        PARTIAL STANDARDIZED ELASTICITY
  NAME    COEFFICIENT  ERROR        7 DF    P-VALUE CORR. COEFFICIENT  AT MEANS
INCOME    0.15045     0.1755E-01   8.575    0.000 0.956     0.9555      2.3685
CONSTANT -1.7502      0.3576      -4.895    0.002-0.880     0.0000     -1.3685
```

Section 15.8 further illustrates the use of dummy variables in testing for structural stability in regression models. The commands below replicate the results provided for *Example 15.5.*

```
TIME 1958 4
SAMPLE 1958.4 1971.2
READ(TABLE15A.1) PERIOD UN V D DV
SAMPLE 1958.4 1966.3
PLOT UN V
SAMPLE 1966.4 1971.2
PLOT UN V
SAMPLE 1958.4 1971.2
* Equation (15.8.2).
OLS UN D V DV
```

The output follows.

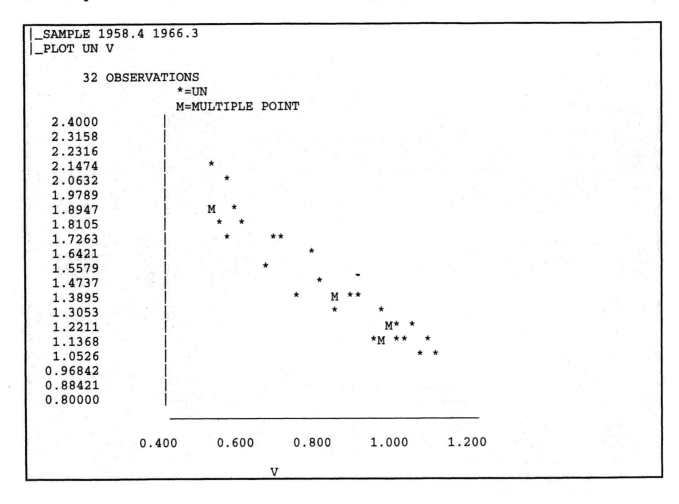

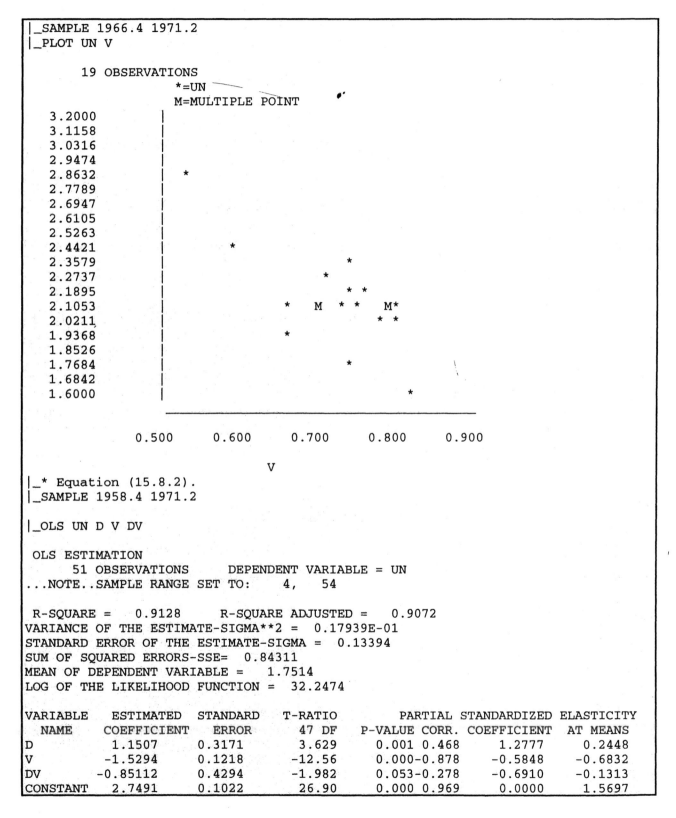

```
|_SAMPLE 1966.4 1971.2
|_PLOT UN V

      19 OBSERVATIONS
                 *=UN
                 M=MULTIPLE POINT
     3.2000    |
     3.1158    |
     3.0316    |
     2.9474    |
     2.8632    |   *
     2.7789    |
     2.6947    |
     2.6105    |
     2.5263    |
     2.4421    |        *
     2.3579    |              *
     2.2737    |            *
     2.1895    |              *  *
     2.1053    |      *   M   * *    M*
     2.0211    |                   *  *
     1.9368    |      *
     1.8526    |
     1.7684    |            *
     1.6842    |
     1.6000    |                 *

            _____
          0.500    0.600    0.700    0.800    0.900

                            V
|_* Equation (15.8.2).
|_SAMPLE 1958.4 1971.2

|_OLS UN D V DV

 OLS ESTIMATION
      51 OBSERVATIONS      DEPENDENT VARIABLE = UN
...NOTE..SAMPLE RANGE SET TO:    4,    54

 R-SQUARE =   0.9128    R-SQUARE ADJUSTED =   0.9072
 VARIANCE OF THE ESTIMATE-SIGMA**2 =  0.17939E-01
 STANDARD ERROR OF THE ESTIMATE-SIGMA =  0.13394
 SUM OF SQUARED ERRORS-SSE=  0.84311
 MEAN OF DEPENDENT VARIABLE =   1.7514
 LOG OF THE LIKELIHOOD FUNCTION =  32.2474
```

VARIABLE NAME	ESTIMATED COEFFICIENT	STANDARD ERROR	T-RATIO 47 DF	P-VALUE	PARTIAL CORR.	STANDARDIZED COEFFICIENT	ELASTICITY AT MEANS
D	1.1507	0.3171	3.629	0.001	0.468	1.2777	0.2448
V	-1.5294	0.1218	-12.56	0.000	-0.878	-0.5848	-0.6832
DV	-0.85112	0.4294	-1.982	0.053	-0.278	-0.6910	-0.1313
CONSTANT	2.7491	0.1022	26.90	0.000	0.969	0.0000	1.5697

As the text notes, the individual t-ratios for the differential intercept and slope coefficients allow for the conclusion that these parameters are statistically different from zero at a 95% significance level. The hypothesis that the coefficients for the differential intercept and slope variables are jointly equal to zero will now be tested.

```
TEST
TEST D=0
TEST DV=0
END
```

The output follows.

```
F STATISTIC =     87.881033     WITH     2 AND    47 D.F.   P-VALUE= 0.00000
WALD CHI-SQUARE STATISTIC =    175.76207     WITH    2 D.F.   P-VALUE= 0.00000
UPPER BOUND ON P-VALUE BY CHEBYCHEV INEQUALITY = 0.01138
```

Since the F-statistic computed, 87.881, is clearly above the 99% $F_{2,47}$ critical value (hence, the very low p-value), the hypothesis that the coefficients are jointly equal to zero can be rejected. Therefore, the inclusion of the dummy variables is statistically justified.

The use of dummy variables in seasonal analysis is the topic of *Section 15.10*. Three dummy variables for the second, third, and four quarters (*D2*, *D3*, and *D4*) of the sample period are included in the model. First, equation (15.10.2) is estimated. Based on their low t-ratios, the dummy variables *D3* and *D4* are dropped and equation (15.10.3) is estimated.

```
TIME 1965 4
SAMPLE 1965.1 1970.4
READ(TABLE15A.2) PERIOD PROFITS SALES D2 D3 D4
* Equation (15.10.2).
OLS PROFITS D2 D3 D4 SALES
* Equation (15.10.3).
OLS PROFITS D2 SALES
```

The output follows.

```
|_* Equation (15.10.2).
_OLS PROFITS D2 D3 D4 SALES

 OLS ESTIMATION
      24 OBSERVATIONS      DEPENDENT VARIABLE = PROFITS
...NOTE..SAMPLE RANGE SET TO:     1,    24


 R-SQUARE =   0.5255    R-SQUARE ADJUSTED =   0.4256
VARIANCE OF THE ESTIMATE-SIGMA**2 =  0.11800E+07
STANDARD ERROR OF THE ESTIMATE-SIGMA =   1086.3
SUM OF SQUARED ERRORS-SSE=  0.22420E+08
MEAN OF DEPENDENT VARIABLE =    12839.
LOG OF THE LIKELIHOOD FUNCTION = -199.023
```

VARIABLE NAME	ESTIMATED COEFFICIENT	STANDARD ERROR	T-RATIO 19 DF	P-VALUE	PARTIAL CORR.	STANDARDIZED COEFFICIENT	ELASTICITY AT MEANS
D2	1322.9	638.5	2.072	0.052	0.429	0.4083	0.0258
D3	-217.81	632.3	-0.3445	0.734	-0.079	-0.0672	-0.0042
D4	183.86	654.3	0.2810	0.782	0.064	0.0567	0.0036
SALES	0.38246E-01	0.1148E-01	3.331	0.004	0.607	0.5503	0.4539
CONSTANT	6688.4	1711.	3.908	0.001	0.668	0.0000	0.5210

```
|_* Equation (15.10.3).
|_OLS PROFITS D2 SALES


 OLS ESTIMATION
      24 OBSERVATIONS      DEPENDENT VARIABLE = PROFITS
...NOTE..SAMPLE RANGE SET TO:    1,   24


 R-SQUARE =   0.5155    R-SQUARE ADJUSTED =   0.4693
VARIANCE OF THE ESTIMATE-SIGMA**2 =  0.10902E+07
STANDARD ERROR OF THE ESTIMATE-SIGMA =   1044.1
SUM OF SQUARED ERRORS-SSE=  0.22894E+08
MEAN OF DEPENDENT VARIABLE =    12839.
LOG OF THE LIKELIHOOD FUNCTION = -199.275
```

VARIABLE NAME	ESTIMATED COEFFICIENT	STANDARD ERROR	T-RATIO 21 DF	P-VALUE	PARTIAL CORR.	STANDARDIZED COEFFICIENT	ELASTICITY AT MEANS
D2	1331.4	493.0	2.700	0.013	0.508	0.4109	0.0259
SALES	0.39310E-01	0.1057E-01	3.717	0.001	0.630	0.5656	0.4666
CONSTANT	6515.6	1623.	4.014	0.001	0.659	0.0000	0.5075

The validity of the restrictions ($D3 = 0$ and $D4 = 0$) will now be tested.

```
?OLS PROFITS D2 D3 D4 SALES
TEST
TEST D3=0
TEST D4=0
END
```

The pertinent output follows.

```
F STATISTIC =  0.20089315      WITH    2 AND   19 D.F.  P-VALUE= 0.81972
WALD CHI-SQUARE STATISTIC =   0.40178630     WITH    2 D.F.  P-VALUE= 0.81800
UPPER BOUND ON P-VALUE BY CHEBYCHEV INEQUALITY = 1.00000
```

Since the F-statistic, 0.20089, is below the 95% $F_{2,19}$ critical value of 3.52, it can be concluded that the restrictions are indeed justified. That is, the hypothesis that the coefficients for $D3$ and $D4$ are jointly equal to zero cannot be rejected. Therefore, it can be concluded that dropping the variables $D3$ and $D4$ is statistically justified.

Equation (15.10.2) could also be estimated by dropping the constant term using the **NOCONSTANT** option and including four dummy variables, one for each quarter. The **SEAS**(*nob*, *nseas*) function with the **MATRIX** command can be used to create the necessary dummy variables. The **SEAS**(*nob*, *nseas*) function creates a series of seasonal dummy variables where *nobs* is the number of observations and *nseas* represents the number of seasons.

```
MATRIX DMAT=SEAS(24,4)
PRINT DMAT
OLS PROFITS DMAT SALES / NOCONSTANT
```

The output follows.

```
|_PRINT DMAT
   DMAT
  24 BY     4 MATRIX
   1.000000      0.0000000      0.0000000      0.0000000
   0.0000000     1.000000       0.0000000      0.0000000
   0.0000000     0.0000000      1.000000       0.0000000
   0.0000000     0.0000000      0.0000000      1.000000
   1.000000      0.0000000      0.0000000      0.0000000
   0.0000000     1.000000       0.0000000      0.0000000
   0.0000000     0.0000000      1.000000       0.0000000
   0.0000000     0.0000000      0.0000000      1.000000
   1.000000      0.0000000      0.0000000      0.0000000
   0.0000000     1.000000       0.0000000      0.0000000
   0.0000000     0.0000000      1.000000       0.0000000
   0.0000000     0.0000000      0.0000000      1.000000
   1.000000      0.0000000      0.0000000      0.0000000
   0.0000000     1.000000       0.0000000      0.0000000
   0.0000000     0.0000000      1.000000       0.0000000
   0.0000000     0.0000000      0.0000000      1.000000
   1.000000      0.0000000      0.0000000      0.0000000
   0.0000000     1.000000       0.0000000      0.0000000
   0.0000000     0.0000000      1.000000       0.0000000
   0.0000000     0.0000000      0.0000000      1.000000
   1.000000      0.0000000      0.0000000      0.0000000
   0.0000000     1.000000       0.0000000      0.0000000
   0.0000000     0.0000000      1.000000       0.0000000
   0.0000000     0.0000000      0.0000000      1.000000

|_OLS PROFITS DMAT SALES / NOCONSTANT

 OLS ESTIMATION
      24 OBSERVATIONS      DEPENDENT VARIABLE = PROFITS
...NOTE..SAMPLE RANGE SET TO:    1,   24

 R-SQUARE =   0.5255    R-SQUARE ADJUSTED =   0.4256
VARIANCE OF THE ESTIMATE-SIGMA**2 =  0.11800E+07
STANDARD ERROR OF THE ESTIMATE-SIGMA =   1086.3
SUM OF SQUARED ERRORS-SSE=  0.22420E+08
MEAN OF DEPENDENT VARIABLE =   12839.
LOG OF THE LIKELIHOOD FUNCTION = -199.023
RAW MOMENT R-SQUARE =   0.9944
```

VARIABLE NAME	ESTIMATED COEFFICIENT	STANDARD ERROR	T-RATIO 19 DF	P-VALUE	PARTIAL CORR.	STANDARDIZED COEFFICIENT	ELASTICITY AT MEANS
DMAT	6688.4	1711.	3.908	0.001	0.668	2.0641	0.1302
DMAT	8011.3	1827.	4.384	0.000	0.709	2.4724	0.1560
DMAT	6470.6	1789.	3.617	0.002	0.639	1.9969	0.1260
DMAT	6872.2	1892.	3.632	0.002	0.640	2.1208	0.1338
SALES	0.38246E-01	0.1148E-01	3.331	0.004	0.607	0.5503	0.4539

The first DMAT term listed in the output corresponds to the dummy variable for the first quarter. Notice that it is equivalent to the CONSTANT term in equation (15.10.2). Hence, the constant term acted implicitly as a dummy variable for the first quarter. As well, the coefficients reported for $D2$, $D3$, and $D4$ reflect the shifts away from the constant term. The coefficients for the DMAT coefficients listed above explicitly include the value of the constant term for each quarter.

Using the hypothetical data found in *Table 15.3*, a total cost function is estimated where it is assumed that the slope changes at the output level of 5,550 units.

A dummy variable, D, is created by first generating a vector of zeros and using an **IF** statement to set the values to 1 for observations of *TCOST* greater than or equal to 5,500. The interactive term is constructed by multiplying $X1$ and D. The model is then estimated.

```
SAMPLE 1 10
READ(TABLE15.3) TCOST X
GENR X1=X-5500
GENR D=0
IF(X.GE.5500) D=1
PRINT X X1 D
GENR X1D=X1*D
* Equation (15.11.4).
OLS TCOST X X1D
```

The output follows.

```
|_PRINT X X1 D
         X                 X1                  D
   1000.000        -4500.000         0.0000000
   2000.000        -3500.000         0.0000000
   3000.000        -2500.000         0.0000000
   4000.000        -1500.000         0.0000000
   5000.000        -500.0000         0.0000000
   6000.000         500.0000         1.000000
   7000.000         1500.000         1.000000
   8000.000         2500.000         1.000000
   9000.000         3500.000         1.000000
   10000.00         4500.000         1.000000
|_GENR X1D=X1*D

|_* Equation (15.11.4).

|_OLS TCOST X X1D

OLS ESTIMATION
      10 OBSERVATIONS      DEPENDENT VARIABLE = TCOST
...NOTE..SAMPLE RANGE SET TO:    1,    10

R-SQUARE =    0.9737     R-SQUARE ADJUSTED =    0.9662
VARIANCE OF THE ESTIMATE-SIGMA**2 =    34075.
```

```
STANDARD ERROR OF THE ESTIMATE-SIGMA =    184.59
SUM OF SQUARED ERRORS-SSE=  0.23852E+06
MEAN OF DEPENDENT VARIABLE =   1507.6
LOG OF THE LIKELIHOOD FUNCTION = -64.5875
```

VARIABLE NAME	ESTIMATED COEFFICIENT	STANDARD ERROR	T-RATIO 7 DF	P-VALUE	PARTIAL CORR.	STANDARDIZED COEFFICIENT	ELASTICITY AT MEANS
X	0.27913	0.4601E-01	6.067	0.001	0.917	0.8418	1.0183
X1D	0.94500E-01	0.8255E-01	1.145	0.290	0.397	0.1588	0.0784
CONSTANT	-145.72	176.7	-0.8245	0.437	-0.298	0.0000	-0.0967

As the t-ratio and high p-value in the above output indicate, the interactive dummy variable, X1D, is not significantly different from zero. That is, as the text notes, the dummy variable could, for all practical purposes, be dropped from the equation.

Section 15.12 provides an example of using dummy variables when combining time series and cross-sectional data. After reading in the data, the **SAMPLE** range will be used to create a dummy variable, D, equal to 1 for the first 20 observations (GM) and 0 for observations 21 to 40 (Westinghouse).

Note that the data file TABLE15.4 is set up differently than shown in Table 15.4. The data for GM, Westinghouse, and GE is stacked. That is, the file is 60 observations long and contains 4 variables, YEAR, I (=Y), F (=X2), and C(=X3).

```
SAMPLE 1 60
READ(TABLE15.4) YEAR Y X2 X3
* Use the SAMPLE command to create a dummy variable (D=1 for GM, D=0 for West).
SAMPLE 21 40
GENR D=0
SAMPLE 1 20
GENR D=1
SAMPLE 1 40
* Equation (15.12.5).
OLS Y X2 X3 D / RSTAT
```

The output follows.

```
|_* Estimate model (15.12.5).
|_* Use the SAMPLE command to create a dummy variable (D=1 for GM, D=0 for West).
|_SAMPLE 21 40
|_GENR D=0
|_SAMPLE 1 20
|_GENR D=1
|_SAMPLE 1 40
```

```
|_PRINT YEAR Y D
      YEAR               Y                 D
   1935.000         317.6000          1.000000
   1936.000         391.8000          1.000000
   1937.000         410.6000          1.000000
   1938.000         257.7000          1.000000
   1939.000         330.8000          1.000000
   1940.000         461.2000          1.000000
   1941.000         512.0000          1.000000
   1942.000         448.0000          1.000000
   1943.000         499.6000          1.000000
   1944.000         547.5000          1.000000
   1945.000         561.2000          1.000000
   1946.000         688.1000          1.000000
   1947.000         568.9000          1.000000
   1948.000         529.2000          1.000000
   1949.000         555.1000          1.000000
   1950.000         642.9000          1.000000
   1951.000         755.9000          1.000000
   1952.000         891.2000          1.000000
   1953.000         1304.400          1.000000
   1954.000         1486.700          1.000000
   1935.000         12.93000          0.0000000
   1936.000         25.90000          0.0000000
   1937.000         35.05000          0.0000000
   1938.000         22.89000          0.0000000
   1939.000         18.84000          0.0000000
   1940.000         28.57000          0.0000000
   1941.000         48.51000          0.0000000
   1942.000         43.34000          0.0000000
   1943.000         37.02000          0.0000000
   1944.000         37.81000          0.0000000
   1945.000         39.27000          0.0000000
   1946.000         53.46000          0.0000000
   1947.000         55.56000          0.0000000
   1948.000         49.56000          0.0000000
   1949.000         32.04000          0.0000000
   1950.000         32.24000          0.0000000
   1951.000         54.38000          0.0000000
   1952.000         71.78000          0.0000000
   1953.000         90.08000          0.0000000
   1954.000         68.60000          0.0000000

|_OLS Y X2 X3 D / RSTAT

 OLS ESTIMATION
      40 OBSERVATIONS      DEPENDENT VARIABLE = Y
 ...NOTE..SAMPLE RANGE SET TO:     1,    40


 R-SQUARE =    0.9679    R-SQUARE ADJUSTED =    0.9652
 VARIANCE OF THE ESTIMATE-SIGMA**2 =    4479.4
 STANDARD ERROR OF THE ESTIMATE-SIGMA =    66.928
 SUM OF SQUARED ERRORS-SSE=   0.16126E+06
 MEAN OF DEPENDENT VARIABLE =    325.46
 LOG OF THE LIKELIHOOD FUNCTION = -222.795
```

```
VARIABLE    ESTIMATED   STANDARD    T-RATIO           PARTIAL STANDARDIZED ELASTICITY
  NAME      COEFFICIENT   ERROR      36 DF    P-VALUE CORR. COEFFICIENT  AT MEANS
X2          0.11213     0.1832E-01   6.120    0.000 0.714    0.6142       0.8622
X3          0.37163     0.2694E-01   13.79    0.000 0.917    0.5447       0.4191
D          -54.763      65.53       -0.8357   0.409-0.138   -0.0773      -0.0841
CONSTANT   -64.168      18.86       -3.403    0.002-0.493    0.0000      -0.1972

DURBIN-WATSON = 0.8658    VON NEUMANN RATIO = 0.8880    RHO =  0.54357
RESIDUAL SUM =  0.32685E-11  RESIDUAL VARIANCE =    4479.4
SUM OF ABSOLUTE ERRORS=   1930.9
R-SQUARE BETWEEN OBSERVED AND PREDICTED = 0.9679
RUNS TEST:     8 RUNS,    21 POS,     0 ZERO,    19 NEG  NORMAL STATISTIC = -4.1594
```

As the text notes, since the differential intercept dummy, D, is not statistically different from zero (p-value = 0.409), it can be concluded that the GM and Westinghouse investment functions have statistically the same intercepts.

The log-linear model in *Section 15.13* will be used to demonstrate falling into the "Dummy Variable Trap." First, the model will be estimated with a constant term and the dummy variable, *DMALE*, equal to 1 for males and 0 for females. Second, a dummy variable, *DFEMALE*, equal to 1 for females and 0 otherwise, will be added. The **NOCONSTANT** option will be used to drop the constant term and, hence, avoid the "Dummy Variable Trap."

```
SAMPLE 1 15
READ(TABLE15.5) Y X2 DMALE
GENR LNY=LOG(Y)
* Equation (15.13.2).
OLS LNY X2 DMALE / RSTAT LOGLIN
* Drop the constant from the regression and, instead, add a dummy variable.
GENR DFEMALE=1-DMALE
OLS LNY DMALE DFEMALE X2 / NOCONSTANT RSTAT
```

The output follows.

```
|_* Equation (15.13.2).

|_OLS LNY X2 DMALE / RSTAT LOGLIN

 OLS ESTIMATION
     15 OBSERVATIONS       DEPENDENT VARIABLE = LNY
...NOTE..SAMPLE RANGE SET TO:    1,    15


 R-SQUARE =   0.9958    R-SQUARE ADJUSTED =    0.9950
VARIANCE OF THE ESTIMATE-SIGMA**2 =  0.89359E-04
STANDARD ERROR OF THE ESTIMATE-SIGMA =  0.94530E-02
SUM OF SQUARED ERRORS-SSE=  0.10723E-02
MEAN OF DEPENDENT VARIABLE =    3.2254
LOG OF THE LIKELIHOOD FUNCTION(IF DEPVAR LOG) =  1.93048
```

```
VARIABLE    ESTIMATED   STANDARD   T-RATIO         PARTIAL STANDARDIZED ELASTICITY
  NAME      COEFFICIENT   ERROR      12 DF   P-VALUE CORR. COEFFICIENT  AT MEANS
X2          0.54612E-01 0.1130E-02   48.34    0.000 0.997     0.9155     0.2330
DMALE       0.13408     0.4925E-02   27.22    0.000 0.992     0.5157     0.0626
CONSTANT    2.9298      0.6084E-02   481.5    0.000 1.000     0.0000     2.9298

DURBIN-WATSON = 2.5101    VON NEUMANN RATIO = 2.6894    RHO = -0.39050
RESIDUAL SUM =  0.35600E-14  RESIDUAL VARIANCE =  0.89359E-04
SUM OF ABSOLUTE ERRORS=  0.10157
R-SQUARE BETWEEN OBSERVED AND PREDICTED = 0.9958
R-SQUARE BETWEEN ANTILOGS OBSERVED AND PREDICTED = 0.9962
RUNS TEST:    7 RUNS,    8 POS,    0 ZERO,    7 NEG  NORMAL STATISTIC = -0.7898
|_* Drop the constant from the regression and, instead, add a dummy variable.

|_GENR DFEMALE=1-DMALE

|_OLS LNY DMALE DFEMALE X2 / NOCONSTANT RSTAT

 OLS ESTIMATION
     15 OBSERVATIONS    DEPENDENT VARIABLE = LNY
...NOTE..SAMPLE RANGE SET TO:    1,   15

 R-SQUARE =   0.9958    R-SQUARE ADJUSTED =   0.9950
VARIANCE OF THE ESTIMATE-SIGMA**2 =  0.89359E-04
STANDARD ERROR OF THE ESTIMATE-SIGMA =  0.94530E-02
SUM OF SQUARED ERRORS-SSE=  0.10723E-02
MEAN OF DEPENDENT VARIABLE =   3.2254
LOG OF THE LIKELIHOOD FUNCTION =  50.3109
RAW MOMENT R-SQUARE =   1.0000

VARIABLE    ESTIMATED   STANDARD   T-RATIO         PARTIAL STANDARDIZED ELASTICITY
  NAME      COEFFICIENT   ERROR      12 DF   P-VALUE CORR. COEFFICIENT  AT MEANS
DMALE       3.0639      0.5761E-02   531.8    0.000 1.000    11.7833     0.4433
DFEMALE     2.9298      0.6084E-02   481.5    0.000 1.000    11.2676     0.4845
X2          0.54612E-01 0.1130E-02   48.34    0.000 0.997     0.9155     0.0722

DURBIN-WATSON = 2.5101    VON NEUMANN RATIO = 2.6894    RHO = -0.39050
RESIDUAL SUM = -0.26645E-14  RESIDUAL VARIANCE =  0.89359E-04
SUM OF ABSOLUTE ERRORS=  0.10157
R-SQUARE BETWEEN OBSERVED AND PREDICTED = 0.9958
RUNS TEST:    7 RUNS,    8 POS,    0 ZERO,    7 NEG  NORMAL STATISTIC = -0.7898
```

Note that, as in the previous example, the coefficients for *DMALE* and *DFEMALE* in the second regression represent the intercepts for each gender.

A constant term will now be included to demonstrate SHAZAM output when falling into the "Dummy Variable Trap."

```
OLS LNY DMALE DFEMALE X2 / LOGLIN RSTAT
```

The output follows.

```
|_OLS LNY DMALE DFEMALE X2 / LOGLIN RSTAT

 OLS ESTIMATION
      15 OBSERVATIONS       DEPENDENT VARIABLE = LNY
...NOTE..SAMPLE RANGE SET TO:    1,   15
...MATRIX IS NOT POSITIVE DEFINITE..FAILED IN ROW     4
```

As the output shows, if the user does fall into the "Dummy Variable Trap", SHAZAM output will read "MATRIX NOT POSITIVE-DEFINITE." This problem arises because there exists perfect collinearity between two or more of the variables. In this case, perfect collinearity exists between the constant term and the two dummy variables. People probably find themselves in a such predicament more often than they will admit.

The final set of commands replicate the results provided in the last part of *Section 15.13*. This example continues with the mean starting salaries of male and female college professors example found in *Section 15.3*. It follows the preceding methodology in that it creates two dummy variables and drops the constant term from the regression to avoid perfect collinearity.

```
SAMPLE 1 10
READ(TABLE15.1) Y D2
GENR D3=1-D2
OLS Y D2 D3
```

The output follows.

```
|_OLS Y D2 D3 / NOCONSTANT

 OLS ESTIMATION
      10 OBSERVATIONS       DEPENDENT VARIABLE = Y
...NOTE..SAMPLE RANGE SET TO:    1,   10

 R-SQUARE =   0.8737    R-SQUARE ADJUSTED =   0.8579
VARIANCE OF THE ESTIMATE-SIGMA**2 =  0.48600
STANDARD ERROR OF THE ESTIMATE-SIGMA =  0.69714
SUM OF SQUARED ERRORS-SSE=   3.8880
MEAN OF DEPENDENT VARIABLE =   19.640
LOG OF THE LIKELIHOOD FUNCTION = -9.46593
RAW MOMENT R-SQUARE =   0.9990
```

VARIABLE NAME	ESTIMATED COEFFICIENT	STANDARD ERROR	T-RATIO 8 DF	P-VALUE	PARTIAL CORR.	STANDARDIZED COEFFICIENT	ELASTICITY AT MEANS
D2	21.280	0.3118	68.26	0.000	0.999	6.0643	0.5418
D3	18.000	0.3118	57.74	0.000	0.999	5.1296	0.4582

SHAZAM commands and options used in Chapter 15

DIAGNOS / **CHOWONE=**
END
GENR *newvar=equation*   with   **LOG**(x)
IF(*expression***)** *var=equation*
MATRIX *newmat=equation*   with   **SEAS(***nobs,nseas***)**
OLS *depvar indeps* / **LOGLIN   NOCONSTANT   RSTAT**
PLOT *depvars   indep*
PRINT *vars*
READ (*filename*) *vars*   / **BYVAR**
SAMPLE *beg   end*
TEST *equation*
TIME *beg   freq*
?   Suppression of Output

16. REGRESSION ON DUMMY DEPENDENT VARIABLE: THE LPM, LOGIT, PROBIT, AND TOBIT MODELS

Chapter 16 discusses regression models in which the dependent variable is a dummy variable, taking a value of 0 or 1. There are certain problems associated with estimating such models.

Sections 16.1 to *16.3* outline the Linear Probability Model (LPM). This modeling approach is the simplest method to use given that it can be estimated using Ordinary Least Squares. However, as the text stresses, there are several limitations to using the LPM. Among the concerns is the fact that an estimated probability could lie outside the 0-1 bounds. As well, the model assumes that the conditional probabilities increase or decrease linearly with the values of the explanatory variables. In addition, the residual errors from the LPM model are usually heteroscedastic.

The numerical example provided in *Section 16.4* illustrates the LPM. Using the hypothetical data from *Table 16.1*, the objective is to determine the probability of a family owning a home given a certain income level. The dependent variable, Y, equals 1 if the family owns a home and zero otherwise. The independent variable, X, represents household income. The commands below estimate equation (16.4.1). The estimated coefficients are then used to estimate the probability of owning a house given a household income of \$12,000 ($X = 12$). The predicted values of the dependent variable are saved for prediction. The SHAZAM commands are:

```
SAMPLE 1 40
READ(TABLE16.1) FAMILY OWNHOME INCOME
OLS OWNHOME INCOME / PREDICT=YHAT COEF=C
GEN1 PROB=C(2)+12*C(1)
PRINT PROB
```

The output follows.

```
|_OLS OWNHOME INCOME / PREDICT=YHAT COEF=C

 OLS ESTIMATION
      40 OBSERVATIONS        DEPENDENT VARIABLE = OWNHOME

 R-SQUARE =    0.8048     R-SQUARE ADJUSTED =   0.7996
VARIANCE OF THE ESTIMATE-SIGMA**2 =   0.51250E-01
STANDARD ERROR OF THE ESTIMATE-SIGMA =   0.22638
SUM OF SQUARED ERRORS-SSE=   1.9475
MEAN OF DEPENDENT VARIABLE =   0.52500
LOG OF THE LIKELIHOOD FUNCTION =   3.68906
```

VARIABLE NAME	ESTIMATED COEFFICIENT	STANDARD ERROR	T-RATIO 38 DF	P-VALUE	PARTIAL CORR.	STANDARDIZED COEFFICIENT	ELASTICITY AT MEANS
INCOME	0.10213	0.8160E-02	12.52	0.000	0.897	0.8971	2.8013
CONSTANT	-0.94569	0.1228	-7.698	0.000	-0.781	0.0000	-1.8013

```
|_GEN1 PROB=C(2)+12*C(1)
|_PRINT PROB
   PROB
  0.2798857
```

Thus, the LPM concludes that the probability of a family owning a home given an income of $12,000 is approximately 28%.

The data found in *Table 16.2* will be replicated using the commands below. In an attempt to correct for heteroscedasticity (assuming that variances increase as household incomes increase), the model will be estimated using Weighted Least Squares (WLS). Note that the observations where the predicted probabilities are either negative or greater than one, the weight variable, w, will be negative. Hence, these observations must be dropped from the WLS regression. This can be done using the **SKIPIF** command.

The **SKIPIF** Command

The **SKIPIF** command is used to specify conditions under which observations are to be skipped for most commands. The general format is:

SKIPIF(*expression***)**

where *expression* may use arithmetic or logical operators such as those described for the **IF** command. The observation will be **SKIP**ped **IF** the expression is true.

Recall that, when using the **WEIGHT=** option with the **OLS** command, SHAZAM multiplies the dependent and independent variables by the square root of the weight variable. In order to follow the WLS methodology of *dividing* the variables by the square root of w, w must be inverted.

```
GENR W=YHAT*(1-YHAT)
IF(W.LT.0)W=0
GENR SQRTW=SQRT(W)
PRINT OWNHOME YHAT W SQRTW
SKIPIF((YHAT.LT.0).OR.(YHAT.GT.1))
GENR INVW=1/W
OLS OWNHOME INCOME / WEIGHT=INVW
```

The output follows.

```
|_PRINT OWNHOME YHAT W SQRTW
     OWNHOME              YHAT                 W                 SQRTW
    0.0000000          -0.1286383          0.0000000          0.0000000
    1.000000            0.6884096          0.2145018          0.4631434
    1.000000            0.8926715          0.9580908E-01       0.3095304
    0.0000000           0.1777547          0.1461580          0.3823061
    0.0000000           0.2798857          0.2015497          0.4489428
    1.000000            0.9948025          0.5170491E-02       0.7190613E-01
    1.000000            1.096933           0.0000000          0.0000000
    0.0000000           0.3820166          0.2360799          0.4858806
    0.0000000          -0.2650728E-01      0.0000000          0.0000000
    0.0000000           0.7562370E-01      0.6990476E-01       0.2643951
    1.000000            0.7905405          0.1655862          0.4069228
    1.000000            0.8926715          0.9580908E-01       0.3095304
    0.0000000           0.4841476          0.2497487          0.4997486
    1.000000            1.096933           0.0000000          0.0000000
    0.0000000          -0.3329002          0.0000000          0.0000000
    1.000000            0.9948025          0.5170491E-02       0.7190613E-01
    1.000000            0.6884096          0.2145018          0.4631434
    0.0000000           0.7562370E-01      0.6990476E-01       0.2643951
    0.0000000          -0.1286383          0.0000000          0.0000000
    1.000000            0.8926715          0.9580908E-01       0.3095304
    1.000000            1.301195           0.0000000          0.0000000
    1.000000            0.6884096          0.2145018          0.4631434
    0.0000000           0.2798857          0.2015497          0.4489428
    0.0000000           0.1777547          0.1461580          0.3823061
    1.000000            0.6884096          0.2145018          0.4631434
    0.0000000           0.1777547          0.1461580          0.3823061
    1.000000            1.096933           0.0000000          0.0000000
    1.000000            0.8926715          0.9580908E-01       0.3095304
    0.0000000           0.1777547          0.1461580          0.3823061
    0.0000000           0.7562370E-01      0.6990476E-01       0.2643951
    1.000000            0.7905405          0.1655862          0.4069228
    0.0000000           0.3820166          0.2360799          0.4858806
    1.000000            1.199064           0.0000000          0.0000000
    1.000000            1.096933           0.0000000          0.0000000
    0.0000000           0.1777547          0.1461580          0.3823061
    0.0000000          -0.1286383          0.0000000          0.0000000
    1.000000            0.7905405          0.1655862          0.4069228
    1.000000            0.6884096          0.2145018          0.4631434
    0.0000000          -0.2307692          0.0000000          0.0000000
    1.000000            0.7905405          0.1655862          0.4069228
|_SKIPIF((YHAT.LT.0).OR.(YHAT.GT.1))
OBSERVATION     1 WILL BE SKIPPED
OBSERVATION     7 WILL BE SKIPPED
OBSERVATION     9 WILL BE SKIPPED
OBSERVATION    14 WILL BE SKIPPED
OBSERVATION    15 WILL BE SKIPPED
OBSERVATION    19 WILL BE SKIPPED
OBSERVATION    21 WILL BE SKIPPED
OBSERVATION    27 WILL BE SKIPPED
OBSERVATION    33 WILL BE SKIPPED
OBSERVATION    34 WILL BE SKIPPED
OBSERVATION    36 WILL BE SKIPPED
OBSERVATION    39 WILL BE SKIPPED
```

```
|_GENR INVW=1/W
|_OLS OWNHOME INCOME / WEIGHT=INVW

 OLS ESTIMATION
      28 OBSERVATIONS       DEPENDENT VARIABLE = OWNHOME
...NOTE..SAMPLE RANGE SET TO:    1,   40
SUM OF LOG(SQRT(ABS(WEIGHT)))  =  -12.385

 R-SQUARE =   0.9214     R-SQUARE ADJUSTED =   0.9183
VARIANCE OF THE ESTIMATE-SIGMA**2 =   0.12111E-01
STANDARD ERROR OF THE ESTIMATE-SIGMA =   0.11005
SUM OF SQUARED ERRORS-SSE=  0.31488
MEAN OF DEPENDENT VARIABLE =   0.82708
LOG OF THE LIKELIHOOD FUNCTION =  10.7129

VARIABLE   ESTIMATED   STANDARD    T-RATIO          PARTIAL STANDARDIZED ELASTICITY
  NAME     COEFFICIENT   ERROR      26 DF    P-VALUE CORR. COEFFICIENT  AT MEANS
INCOME     0.11959    0.6852E-02   17.45    0.000 0.960     0.9599      2.5060
CONSTANT  -1.2456     0.1206      -10.33    0.000-0.897     0.0000     -1.5060
```

As the above output shows, warning statements listing the observations skipped are automatically printed when observations are skipped. Given a large number of skipped observations, it may be desirable to suppress these warning statements. This can be done using the **SET** command.

The **SET** Command

SET commands make it possible to turn certain options on or off. The format of the **SET** command to turn options on is:

SET *option*

To turn options off, the format is

SET NO*option*

where *option* is the desired option.

The **SET NOWARNSKIP** command suppresses the warning statements that are automatically printed when observations are skipped using the **SKIPIF** command. In addition, the **SET NOSKIP** command can be used to turn off **SKIPIF** commands.

Section 15.8 discusses estimating LOGIT models. As the text notes, using data at the micro level, such as observations for individual families, equation (16.8.1) cannot be estimated using OLS. Rather, the Method of Maximum Likelihood must be used.

Example 16.5 provides results when the Method of Maximum Likelihood is used (no data is included).

The numerical example in *Section 16.9* uses the "group" data from *Table 16.4*. That is, the number of homeowners for every income range, rather than observations for individual families, is compiled. A LOGIT model using such data can be estimated using OLS. The commands below follow the steps outlined in the text for estimating equations (15.9.1) and (15.9.2).

In keeping with the notation in the text, the **SET NOLCUC** command will be used so that SHAZAM distinguishes between upper and lower case forms of the letter "n." By default, SHAZAM converts all **L**ower **C**ase characters into **U**pper **C**ase before processing. When the **SET NOLCUC** command is used, SHAZAM distinguishes between upper and lower case. The **SET LCUC** command turns this command off.

```
SET NOLCUC
SAMPLE 1 10
READ(TABLE16.4) X N n
* First, do the computations to create Table 16.5.
* Use Equation (16.8.2) to compute PHAT (the numerator).
GENR PHAT=n/N
* Construct the denominator.
GENR DENOM=(1-PHAT)
* Construct the ratio.
GENR RATIO=PHAT/DENOM
* Put the ratio in logs (i.e. Equation (16.8.3)).
GENR LHAT=LOG(RATIO)
* Create the weight, W (i.e. Column (8) of Table 16.5)
GENR W=N*PHAT*DENOM
* Take the square root of W (i.e. Column (9)).
GENR SQRTW=SQRT(W)
* Create LHATSTAR (i.e. Column (10)).
GENR LHATSTAR=LHAT*SQRTW
* Finally, create XSTAR (Column (11)).
GENR XSTAR=X*SQRTW
* Print the variables found in Table 16.5.
PRINT X N n PHAT
PRINT DENOM RATIO LHAT W
PRINT SQRTW LHATSTAR XSTAR
* Estimate Equation (16.9.1).
OLS LHATSTAR SQRTW XSTAR / NOCONSTANT
* Estimate the unweighted regression, equation (16.9.2).
OLS LHAT X
```

The output follows.

```
|_PRINT X N n PHAT
      X                 N                 n              PHAT
    6.000000         40.00000          8.000000       0.2000000
    8.000000         50.00000          12.00000       0.2400000
   10.00000          60.00000          18.00000       0.3000000
   13.00000          80.00000          28.00000       0.3500000
   15.00000          100.0000          45.00000       0.4500000
   20.00000          70.00000          36.00000       0.5142857
   25.00000          65.00000          39.00000       0.6000000
   30.00000          50.00000          33.00000       0.6600000
   35.00000          40.00000          30.00000       0.7500000
   40.00000          25.00000          20.00000       0.8000000
|_PRINT DENOM RATIO LHAT W
    DENOM             RATIO             LHAT              W
   0.8000000         0.2500000        -1.386294        6.400000
   0.7600000         0.3157895        -1.152680        9.120000
   0.7000000         0.4285714        -0.8472979       12.60000
   0.6500000         0.5384615        -0.6190392       18.20000
   0.5500000         0.8181818        -0.2006707       24.75000
   0.4857143         1.058824         0.5715841E-01    17.48571
   0.4000000         1.500000         0.4054651        15.60000
   0.3400000         1.941176         0.6632942        11.22000
   0.2500000         3.000000         1.098612         7.500000
   0.2000000         4.000000         1.386294         4.000000
|_PRINT SQRTW LHATSTAR XSTAR
    SQRTW            LHATSTAR          XSTAR
   2.529822         -3.507078         15.17893
   3.019934         -3.481016         24.15947
   3.549648         -3.007609         35.49648
   4.266146         -2.640912         55.45990
   4.974937         -0.9983241        74.62406
   4.181592         0.2390132         83.63185
   3.949684         1.601459          98.74209
   3.349627         2.221788          100.4888
   2.738613         3.008674          95.85145
   2.000000         2.772589          80.00000
|_* Estimate Equation (16.9.1).

|_OLS LHATSTAR SQRTW XSTAR / NOCONSTANT

 OLS ESTIMATION
       10 OBSERVATIONS      DEPENDENT VARIABLE = LHATSTAR
...NOTE..SAMPLE RANGE SET TO:    1,    10


 R-SQUARE =   0.9637     R-SQUARE ADJUSTED =    0.9591
VARIANCE OF THE ESTIMATE-SIGMA**2 =   0.29208
STANDARD ERROR OF THE ESTIMATE-SIGMA =  0.54045
SUM OF SQUARED ERRORS-SSE=   2.3367
MEAN OF DEPENDENT VARIABLE = -0.37914
LOG OF THE LIKELIHOOD FUNCTION = -6.92009
RAW MOMENT R-SQUARE =    0.9645
```

VARIABLE NAME	ESTIMATED COEFFICIENT	STANDARD ERROR	T-RATIO 8 DF	P-VALUE	PARTIAL CORR.	STANDARDIZED COEFFICIENT	ELASTICITY AT MEANS
SQRTW	-1.5932	0.1115	-14.29	0.000	-0.981	-0.5418	14.5229
XSTAR	0.78669E-01	0.5448E-02	14.44	0.000	0.981	0.9363	-13.7698

```
|_* Estimate the unweighted regression, equation (16.9.2).

|_OLS LHAT X

 OLS ESTIMATION
      10 OBSERVATIONS        DEPENDENT VARIABLE = LHAT
...NOTE..SAMPLE RANGE SET TO:     1,    10


 R-SQUARE =   0.9786     R-SQUARE ADJUSTED =    0.9759
VARIANCE OF THE ESTIMATE-SIGMA**2 =  0.21690E-01
STANDARD ERROR OF THE ESTIMATE-SIGMA =  0.14728
SUM OF SQUARED ERRORS-SSE=  0.17352
MEAN OF DEPENDENT VARIABLE = -0.59516E-01
LOG OF THE LIKELIHOOD FUNCTION =  6.08077

VARIABLE    ESTIMATED   STANDARD    T-RATIO         PARTIAL STANDARDIZED ELASTICITY
  NAME      COEFFICIENT   ERROR      8 DF    P-VALUE CORR. COEFFICIENT   AT MEANS
X          0.79166E-01 0.4143E-02   19.11   0.000 0.989      0.9892     -26.8694
CONSTANT   -1.6587      0.9578E-01  -17.32   0.000-0.987      0.0000      27.8694
```

As mentioned in the text, SHAZAM can estimate LOGIT models based on individual micro data using the Method of Maximum Likelihood.

The **LOGIT** Command

The **LOGIT** command can be used to estimate LOGIT regressions by the Method of Maximum Likelihood. The general formula is:

LOGIT *devpar indeps* / *options*

where *devpar* is a 0-1 dummy variable, *indeps* is a list of independent variables, and *options* is a list of options.

Note that the **LOGIT** command cannot be used with the student version of SHAZAM, SHAZY.

The **SAMPLE** command will be used to construct the "individual" micro data based on the information found in *Table 16.4*. The new vectors must first be dimensioned using the **DIM** command. Once the necessary variables are created, the **SAMPLE** command is set to the full range of observations and the LOGIT model is estimated. Study the commands below very carefully so that you understand how the data is constructed.

```
DIM INCOME 580 OWNHOME 580
SAMPLE 1 580
GENR OWNHOME=0
SAMPLE 1 40
GENR INCOME=6
SAMPLE 1 8
GENR OWNHOME=1
SAMPLE 41 90
GENR INCOME=8
SAMPLE 41 52
GENR OWNHOME=1
SAMPLE 91 150
GENR INCOME=10
SAMPLE 91 108
GENR OWNHOME=1
SAMPLE 151 230
GENR INCOME=13
SAMPLE 151 178
GENR OWNHOME=1
SAMPLE 231 330
GENR INCOME=15
SAMPLE 231 275
GENR OWNHOME=1
SAMPLE 331 400
GENR INCOME=20
SAMPLE 331 366
GENR OWNHOME=1
SAMPLE 401 465
GENR INCOME=25
SAMPLE 401 439
GENR OWNHOME=1
SAMPLE 466 515
GENR INCOME=30
SAMPLE 466 498
GENR OWNHOME=1
SAMPLE 516 555
GENR INCOME=35
SAMPLE 516 545
GENR OWNHOME=1
SAMPLE 556 580
GENR INCOME=40
SAMPLE 556 575
GENR OWNHOME=1
SAMPLE 1 580
* Estimate the model.
LOGIT OWNHOME INCOME
```

The output follows.

```
|_LOGIT OWNHOME INCOME

 LOGIT ANALYSIS       DEPENDENT VARIABLE =OWNHOME   CHOICES =  2
     580. TOTAL OBSERVATIONS
     269. OBSERVATIONS AT ONE
     311. OBSERVATIONS AT ZERO
   25 MAXIMUM ITERATIONS
```

```
CONVERGENCE TOLERANCE =0.00100

                          ASYMPTOTIC                          WEIGHTED
VARIABLE    ESTIMATED     STANDARD     T-RATIO    ELASTICITY   AGGREGATE
  NAME      COEFFICIENT    ERROR                  AT MEANS    ELASTICITY

INCOME       0.79066E-01  0.10108E-01   7.8222     0.78175     0.68036
CONSTANT     -1.6023      0.20397      -7.8558    -0.85837    -0.75866

LOG-LIKELIHOOD FUNCTION =   -365.30
```

For further details on the **LOGIT** command, see the *SHAZAM User's Reference Manual*.

Section 16.11 discusses the PROBIT model and the method of estimating such a model using OLS. As is the case with LOGIT models, SHAZAM can estimate PROBIT models using the Method of Maximum Likelihood. This will be demonstrated ahead. First, the steps outlined in *Section 16.11* will be followed and equations (16.12.1) and (16.12.2) will be estimated.

The **INVERSE** option with the **DISTRIB** command returns the critical values of the distributions instead of the probabilities. Note that the data must be in probabilities. The **CRITICAL=** option saves the critical values in the variable specified when the **INVERSE** option is used. In the case of a normal distribution, SHAZAM returns critical values X such that $\Pr(z>X)$ = probability.

Following the text, obtain the index I by computing the inverse of the empirical measure of the probabilities, *PHAT*. Since SHAZAM assumes probabilities for the **INVERSE** option are in the form 1-CDF, it is necessary to reverse the sign of I to conform to *Table 16.7*.

```
SAMPLE 1 10
DISTRIB PHAT / TYPE=NORMAL INVERSE CRITICAL=I
GENR I=-I
PRINT PHAT I
* Estimate equation (16.12.1).
OLS I X
* Generate the variable PROBIT and estimate (16.12.2).
GENR PROBIT=I+5
OLS PROBIT X
```

The output follows.

```
|_DISTRIB PHAT / TYPE=NORMAL INVERSE CRITICAL=I
NORMAL DISTRIBUTION - MEAN=  0.00000     VARIANCE=    1.0000

              PROBABILITY CRITICAL VALUE    PDF
    PHAT
ROW    1      0.20000      0.84156       0.27998
ROW    2      0.24000      0.70626       0.31088
```

```
ROW     3    0.30000     0.52437      0.34770
ROW     4    0.35000     0.38530      0.37040
ROW     5    0.45000     0.12566      0.39581
ROW     6    0.51429    -0.35819E-01  0.39869
ROW     7    0.60000    -0.25334      0.38634
ROW     8    0.66000    -0.41244      0.36641
ROW     9    0.75000    -0.67445      0.31779
ROW    10    0.80000    -0.84155      0.27998
|_GENR I=-I
|_PRINT PHAT I
     PHAT            I
  0.2000000    -0.8415570
  0.2400000    -0.7062550
  0.3000000    -0.5243720
  0.3500000    -0.3853020
  0.4500000    -0.1256570
  0.5142857     0.3581871E-01
  0.6000000     0.2533370
  0.6600000     0.4124430
  0.7500000     0.6744500
  0.8000000     0.8415500
|_* Estimate equation (16.12.1).

|_OLS I X

 OLS ESTIMATION
      10 OBSERVATIONS    DEPENDENT VARIABLE = I

 R-SQUARE =   0.9790    R-SQUARE ADJUSTED =   0.9763
VARIANCE OF THE ESTIMATE-SIGMA**2 =  0.79683E-02
STANDARD ERROR OF THE ESTIMATE-SIGMA =  0.89265E-01
SUM OF SQUARED ERRORS-SSE=  0.63747E-01
MEAN OF DEPENDENT VARIABLE = -0.36554E-01
LOG OF THE LIKELIHOOD FUNCTION =  11.0877


VARIABLE    ESTIMATED   STANDARD   T-RATIO        PARTIAL STANDARDIZED ELASTICITY
 NAME       COEFFICIENT  ERROR       8 DF   P-VALUE CORR. COEFFICIENT  AT MEANS
X           0.48463E-01 0.2511E-02  19.30   0.000 0.989    0.9894    -26.7807
CONSTANT   -1.0155      0.5805E-01 -17.49   0.000-0.987    0.0000     27.7807
|_* Generate the variable PROBIT and estimate (16.12.2).
|_GENR PROBIT=I+5

|_OLS PROBIT X

 OLS ESTIMATION
      10 OBSERVATIONS    DEPENDENT VARIABLE = PROBIT

 R-SQUARE =   0.9790    R-SQUARE ADJUSTED =   0.9763
VARIANCE OF THE ESTIMATE-SIGMA**2 =  0.79683E-02
STANDARD ERROR OF THE ESTIMATE-SIGMA =  0.89265E-01
SUM OF SQUARED ERRORS-SSE=  0.63747E-01
MEAN OF DEPENDENT VARIABLE =   4.9634
LOG OF THE LIKELIHOOD FUNCTION =  11.0877


VARIABLE    ESTIMATED   STANDARD   T-RATIO        PARTIAL STANDARDIZED ELASTICITY
 NAME       COEFFICIENT  ERROR       8 DF   P-VALUE CORR. COEFFICIENT  AT MEANS
X           0.48463E-01 0.2511E-02  19.30   0.000 0.989    0.9894     0.1972
CONSTANT    3.9845      0.5805E-01  68.64   0.000 0.999    0.0000     0.8028
```

Note that the output above differs slightly from the results reported in the text because the text uses the rounded *I*'s found in *Table 16.8*.

The **PROBIT** command will now be used with the "individual" data to estimate the PROBIT model using the Method of Maximum Likelihood.

The **PROBIT** Command

The **PROBIT** command can be used to estimate PROBIT regressions. The general formula is:

PROBIT *devpar indeps / options*

where *devpar* is a 0-1 dummy variable, *indeps* is a list of independent variables, and *options* is a list of options.

Note that the **PROBIT** command cannot be used with the student version of SHAZAM, SHAZY.

```
SAMPLE 1 580
PROBIT OWNHOME INCOME
```

The output follows.

```
|_PROBIT OWNHOME INCOME

PROBIT ANALYSIS      DEPENDENT VARIABLE =OWNHOME   CHOICES =  2
    580. TOTAL OBSERVATIONS
    269. OBSERVATIONS AT ONE
    311. OBSERVATIONS AT ZERO
  25 MAXIMUM ITERATIONS
CONVERGENCE TOLERANCE =0.00100

                            ASYMPTOTIC                        WEIGHTED
VARIABLE     ESTIMATED      STANDARD     T-RATIO    ELASTICITY   AGGREGATE
  NAME       COEFFICIENT      ERROR                 AT MEANS    ELASTICITY

INCOME        0.48586E-01  0.59858E-02   8.1169      0.76847     0.68717
CONSTANT     -0.98812      0.12234      -8.0769     -0.84677    -0.76712

LOG-LIKELIHOOD FUNCTION =  -365.30
```

When comparing the LOGIT and PROBIT models, one can look at the value of the log-likelihood function (LLF). The model with the highest LLF can then be considered more appropriate. However, in this case, the LLF from LOGIT model (-365.30) is identical to the LLF from the PROBIT model so either model can be chosen.

Section 16.14 discusses the TOBIT model. However, no data is provided to replicate the empirical example. As the text notes, SHAZAM can estimate TOBIT models.

The **TOBIT** Command

The **TOBIT** command is available for regressions with limited dependent variables. In general, the format of the **TOBIT** command is:

TOBIT *depvar   indeps   /   options*

where *depvar* is the dependent variable, *indeps* is a list of independent variables, and *options* is a list of desired options.

Note that the **TOBIT** command cannot be used with the student version of SHAZAM, SHAZY.

SHAZAM commands and options used in Chapter 16

DIM *var   size   var   size   ...*
DISTRIB *vars* / **CRITICAL= INVERSE TYPE=NORMAL**
GEN1 *newvar=equation*
GENR *newvar=equation* with **LOG**(x) **SQRT**(x)
IF(*expression*) *var=equation*
LOGIT *depvar   indeps* / *options*
OLS *depvar   indeps* / **COEF= NOCONSTANT PREDICT= WEIGHT=**
PRINT *vars* / *options*
PROBIT *depvar   indeps* / *options*
READ(*datafile*) *vars* / *options*
SAMPLE *beg   end*
SET with **NOLCUP NOWARNSKIP NOSKIP NOLCUC LCUP**
SKIPIF(*expression*)
TOBIT *depvar   indeps* / *options*

17. DYNAMIC ECONOMETRIC MODEL: AUTOREGRESSIVE AND DISTRIBUTED LAG MODELS

Chapter 17 discusses autoregressive and distributed lag models, often used when analyzing time series data. A distributed lag model is a regression which contains explanatory variables that are lagged one or more periods. A model is said to be autoregressive if it includes lagged values of the dependent variable.

Section 17.4 introduces the Koyck approach to distributed lag models. The empirical example at the end of this section was estimated in Chapter 14 using the **LAG**(x) function with the **GENR** command to lag the variable *PPCE*. However, when estimating distributed lag models, it is more convenient to use the following form of the **OLS** command:

OLS *depvar indep(first.last,order,endcon) / options*

where *depvar* is the name of the dependent variable and *indep* is the name of an independent variable (which may include lagged values of the dependent variable). The terms *first* and *last* are separated by a dot (".") and specify the first and last periods to use for lags. For example, (0.3) indicates that the current period (0) and lags t=1,2,3 are to be used. The *order* parameter specifies the order of the polynomial in an Almon lag model (see the example below from *Section 17.13* for a demonstration of this feature). The *endcon* parameter specifies the endpoint restrictions (discussed at the end of *Section 17.13*) as follows:

   0 = No endpoint restrictions.

   1 = Endpoint restrictions on the left side of the polynomial.

   2 = Endpoint restrictions on the right side of the polynomial.

   3 = Endpoint restrictions on both left and right sides of the polynomial.

If *order* and *endcon* are not specified, an unrestricted lag is used.

Recall that, when using the **LAG**(x,n) function with the **GENR** command, the **SAMPLE** range must be changed to drop the first n observations since these variables are undefined. An advantage to using the above format of the **OLS** command when lagging variables is that SHAZAM will automatically delete the necessary number of observations corresponding to any lagged variables undefined at the beginning of the data. Hence, the **SAMPLE** command must not be used to skip these observations.

The following commands estimate the consumption-expenditure model in *Example 17.5.*

```
TIME 1970 1
SAMPLE 1970.0 1991.0
READ(TABLE14.1) YEAR PPCE PPDI
* Equation (17.4.11).
OLS PPCE PPCE(1.1) PPDI / RSTAT DLAG COEF=C
GEN1 LAMBDA=C(1)
GEN1 MEDLAG=-LOG(2)/LOG(LAMBDA)
GEN1 MEANLAG=LAMBDA/(1-LAMBDA)
PRINT LAMBDA MEDLAG MEANLAG
```

The output follows.

```
|_* Equation (17.4.11).
|_OLS PPCE PPCE(1.1) PPDI / RSTAT DLAG COEF=C

 OLS ESTIMATION
      21 OBSERVATIONS      DEPENDENT VARIABLE = PPCE
...NOTE..SAMPLE RANGE SET TO:    2,    22


 R-SQUARE =   0.9912    R-SQUARE ADJUSTED =   0.9903
VARIANCE OF THE ESTIMATE-SIGMA**2 =   16318.
STANDARD ERROR OF THE ESTIMATE-SIGMA =   127.74
SUM OF SQUARED ERRORS-SSE=  0.29373E+06
MEAN OF DEPENDENT VARIABLE =   11119.
LOG OF THE LIKELIHOOD FUNCTION = -130.030


VARIABLE    SUM OF LAG COEFS    STD ERROR       T-RATIO       MEAN LAG
PPCE          0.29540          0.12474         2.3681         1.0000


VARIABLE    ESTIMATED   STANDARD   T-RATIO         PARTIAL STANDARDIZED ELASTICITY
  NAME      COEFFICIENT   ERROR     18 DF   P-VALUE CORR. COEFFICIENT  AT MEANS
PPCE         0.29540     0.1247     2.368    0.029 0.487    0.3020      0.2904
PPDI         0.71170     0.1303     5.463    0.000 0.790    0.6968      0.7853
CONSTANT     -841.86     348.8     -2.414    0.027-0.494    0.0000     -0.0757


DURBIN-WATSON = 1.0145    VON NEUMANN RATIO = 1.0652    RHO =  0.48722
RESIDUAL SUM = -0.22595E-11  RESIDUAL VARIANCE =     16318.
SUM OF ABSOLUTE ERRORS=   2084.4
R-SQUARE BETWEEN OBSERVED AND PREDICTED = 0.9912
RUNS TEST:    8 RUNS,   10 POS,    0 ZERO,   11 NEG  NORMAL STATISTIC = -1.5603
DURBIN H STATISTIC (ASYMPTOTIC NORMAL) =   2.7212
|_GEN1 LAMBDA=C(1)
|_GEN1 MEDLAG=-LOG(2)/LOG(LAMBDA)
|_GEN1 MEANLAG=LAMBDA/(1-LAMBDA)
|_PRINT LAMBDA MEDLAG MEANLAG
    LAMBDA
  0.2954044
    MEDLAG
  0.5684283
    MEANLAG
  0.4192538
```

The Durbin-h statistic is used to test for autocorrelation in autoregressive models. The example in *Section 17.11* illustrates how to construct this statistic following the steps outlined in *Section 17.10.* Recall that the Durbin-h statistic is printed when the **RSTAT** option is specified with the **AUTO** command, a command used to estimate certain types of autoregressive models. When using the **OLS** command to estimate **Distributed LAG** models, the **DLAG** option is used to print the Durbin-h statistic. Note that the lagged dependent variable *must* be the first independent variable listed .

The following commands estimate the money demand model in *Section 17.11*.

```
TIME 1948 1
SAMPLE 1948.0 1964.0
READ(EXER725.DAT) YEAR NOMM NOMNI IPD R
* Convert the nominal variables to real and take logs of the variables.
GENR LNM=LOG(NOMM/IPD)
GENR LNY=LOG(NOMNI/IPD)
GENR LNR=LOG(R)
* Equation (17.11.6).
OLS LNM LNM(1.1) LNR LNY / DLAG STDERR=SE RSTAT COEF=C
GEN1 GAMMA=1-C(1)
PRINT GAMMA
```

The output follows.

```
|_* Equation (17.11.6).

|_OLS LNM LNM(1.1) LNR LNY / DLAG STDERR=SE RSTAT COEF=C

 OLS ESTIMATION
      16 OBSERVATIONS      DEPENDENT VARIABLE = LNM
...NOTE..SAMPLE RANGE SET TO:    2,   17


 R-SQUARE =   0.9379    R-SQUARE ADJUSTED =   0.9224
VARIANCE OF THE ESTIMATE-SIGMA**2 =  0.33527E-02
STANDARD ERROR OF THE ESTIMATE-SIGMA =  0.57903E-01
SUM OF SQUARED ERRORS-SSE=  0.40233E-01
MEAN OF DEPENDENT VARIABLE =   3.1149
LOG OF THE LIKELIHOOD FUNCTION =  25.1823

VARIABLE   SUM OF LAG COEFS    STD ERROR        T-RATIO        MEAN LAG
LNM            0.52974          0.20134          2.6311         1.0000

VARIABLE   ESTIMATED  STANDARD   T-RATIO         PARTIAL STANDARDIZED ELASTICITY
   NAME    COEFFICIENT  ERROR    12 DF   P-VALUE CORR. COEFFICIENT  AT MEANS
LNM        0.52974    0.2013     2.631   0.022 0.605     0.4957      0.5246
LNR       -0.10413    0.3710    -0.2807  0.784-0.081    -0.0640     -0.0455
LNY        0.68589    0.3859     1.777   0.101 0.457     0.5519      0.0238
CONSTANT   1.5484     0.8336     1.857   0.088 0.473     0.0000      0.4971

DURBIN-WATSON = 1.8801    VON NEUMANN RATIO = 2.0054    RHO =  0.02823
RESIDUAL SUM =  0.62728E-14  RESIDUAL VARIANCE =  0.33527E-02
SUM OF ABSOLUTE ERRORS=  0.63085
R-SQUARE BETWEEN OBSERVED AND PREDICTED = 0.9379
RUNS TEST:   10 RUNS,    8 POS,    0 ZERO,    8 NEG  NORMAL STATISTIC =  0.5175
```

```
DURBIN H STATISTIC (ASYMPTOTIC NORMAL) =   0.19051
|_GEN1 GAMMA=1-C(1)
|_PRINT GAMMA
    GAMMA
  0.4702618
```

As an exercise, the Durbin-h statistic is computed the "long way" using equation (17.10.1). Recall that **$RHO** is a dummy variable for the estimated first-order serial correlation, ρ.

```
GEN1 DURBINH=$RHO*SQRT($N/(1-$N*(SE(1)**2)))
PRINT DURBINH
```

The output follows.

```
|_GEN1 DURBINH=$RHO*SQRT($N/(1-$N*(SE(1)**2)))
..NOTE..CURRENT VALUE OF $RHO =   0.28233E-01
..NOTE..CURRENT VALUE OF $N   =    16.000
..NOTE..CURRENT VALUE OF $N   =    16.000
|_PRINT DURBINH
    DURBINH
  0.1905114
```

As expected, the Durbin-h statistic above is identical to the one printed using the **DLAG** option with the **OLS** command.

The numerical example in *Section 17.13* illustrates the Almon approach to distributed lag models discussed in this section. The following commands first estimate equation (17.13.14) and save the estimated coefficients. Following equation (17.13.8), these coefficients, the $\hat{a}$'s, are then used to construct the $\hat{\beta}$'s.

```
TIME 1955 1
SAMPLE 1955.0 1974.0
READ(TABLE17.3) YEAR Y X Z0 Z1 Z2
* Equation (17.13.14).
SAMPLE 1958.0 1974.0
OLS Y Z0 Z1 Z2 / COEF=AHAT
* Construct the betahats from the estimated coefficients above.
GEN1 B0HAT=AHAT(1)
GEN1 B1HAT=AHAT(1)+AHAT(2)+AHAT(3)
GEN1 B2HAT=AHAT(1)+2*AHAT(2)+4*AHAT(3)
GEN1 B3HAT=AHAT(1)+3*AHAT(2)+9*AHAT(3)
PRINT B0HAT B1HAT B2HAT B3HAT
```

The output follows.

```
|_* Equation (17.13.14).
|_SAMPLE 1958.0 1974.0

|_OLS Y Z0 Z1 Z2 / COEF=AHAT

 OLS ESTIMATION
      17 OBSERVATIONS        DEPENDENT VARIABLE = Y
 ...NOTE..SAMPLE RANGE SET TO:    4,    20

 R-SQUARE =    0.9968     R-SQUARE ADJUSTED =    0.9961
 VARIANCE OF THE ESTIMATE-SIGMA**2 =   0.30887E+07
 STANDARD ERROR OF THE ESTIMATE-SIGMA =    1757.5
 SUM OF SQUARED ERRORS-SSE=   0.40153E+08
 MEAN OF DEPENDENT VARIABLE =    81869.
 LOG OF THE LIKELIHOOD FUNCTION = -148.859
```

VARIABLE NAME	ESTIMATED COEFFICIENT	STANDARD ERROR	T-RATIO 13 DF	P-VALUE	PARTIAL CORR.	STANDARDIZED COEFFICIENT	ELASTICITY AT MEANS
Z0	0.66125	0.1655	3.996	0.002	0.742	1.1760	1.3576
Z1	0.90205	0.4831	1.867	0.085	0.460	2.1317	2.6351
Z2	-0.43216	0.1665	-2.596	0.022	-0.584	-2.3193	-2.9055
CONSTANT	-7140.8	1993.	-3.583	0.003	-0.705	0.0000	-0.0872

```
|_* Construct the betahats from the estimated coefficients above.
|_GEN1 B0HAT=AHAT(1)
|_GEN1 B1HAT=AHAT(1)+AHAT(2)+AHAT(3)
|_GEN1 B2HAT=AHAT(1)+2*AHAT(2)+4*AHAT(3)
|_GEN1 B3HAT=AHAT(1)+3*AHAT(2)+9*AHAT(3)
|_PRINT B0HAT B1HAT B2HAT B3HAT
   B0HAT
  0.6612482
   B1HAT
   1.131142
   B2HAT
  0.7367252
   B3HAT
 -0.5220014
```

Equation (17.13.15) is now estimated. The quick and easy way to estimate an Almon lag model does not use constructed variables. Instead, the direct approach is used where the model is specified on the **OLS** command. Note that the Almon scheme used here assumes a second-order polynomial lag. Hence, inside the parentheses, *order* = 2. The estimated coefficients will be saved for use ahead.

```
SAMPLE 1955.0 1974.0
OLS Y X(0.3,2) / COEF=CFS
```

The output follows.

```
|_SAMPLE 1955.0 1974.0

|_OLS Y X(0.3,2) / COEF=CFS
 LAG FOR X        RANGE =  0   3 ORDER= 2 ENDCON=0

 OLS ESTIMATION
      17 OBSERVATIONS       DEPENDENT VARIABLE = Y
 ...NOTE..SAMPLE RANGE SET TO:    4,   20
 F TEST ON RESTRICTIONS= 0.31052E-01 WITH    1 AND   12 DF  P-VALUE= 0.86306


  R-SQUARE =   0.9968     R-SQUARE ADJUSTED =   0.9961
 VARIANCE OF THE ESTIMATE-SIGMA**2 =   0.30887E+07
 STANDARD ERROR OF THE ESTIMATE-SIGMA =   1757.5
 SUM OF SQUARED ERRORS-SSE=  0.40153E+08
 MEAN OF DEPENDENT VARIABLE =    81869.
 LOG OF THE LIKELIHOOD FUNCTION = -148.859

 VARIABLE    SUM OF LAG COEFS     STD ERROR         T-RATIO         MEAN LAG
 X               2.0071         0.63303E-01          31.706          0.51745

 VARIABLE    ESTIMATED   STANDARD   T-RATIO        PARTIAL STANDARDIZED ELASTICITY
   NAME      COEFFICIENT   ERROR     13 DF    P-VALUE CORR. COEFFICIENT AT MEANS
 X            0.66125     0.1655     3.996    0.002 0.742    0.3674      0.3730
 X            1.1311      0.1800     6.284    0.000 0.867    0.5267      0.5947
 X            0.73673     0.1643     4.485    0.001 0.779    0.2970      0.3642
 X           -0.52200     0.2348    -2.223    0.045-0.525   -0.1919     -0.2448
 CONSTANT    -7140.8      1993.     -3.583    0.003-0.705    0.0000     -0.0872
```

The above output confirms the initial computations of the $\hat{\beta}$'s using the $\hat{a}$'s estimated from equation (17.13.14).

Note that, when estimating a distributed lag model using the **OLS** command, the output includes the summation of the estimated coefficients for the lagged variables as well as their standard errors and t-ratios.

Figure 17.7 will be replicated using the following commands.

```
SAMPLE 1 4
GENR LAGTIME=TIME(-1)
PLOT CFS LAGTIME
```

The output follows.

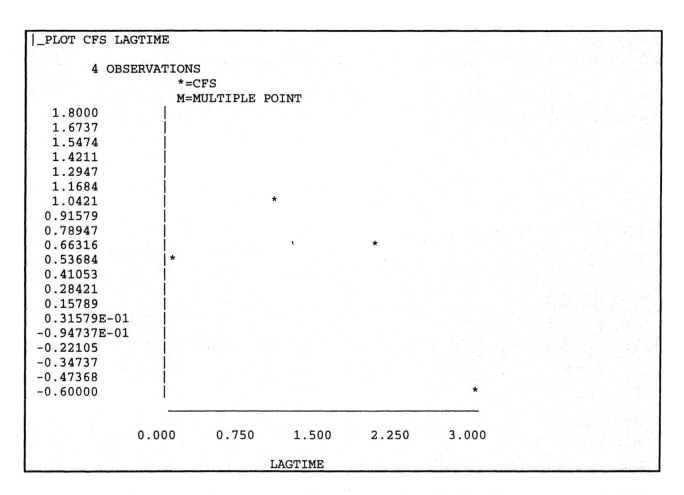

```
|_PLOT CFS LAGTIME

        4 OBSERVATIONS
                      *=CFS
                      M=MULTIPLE POINT
    1.8000          |
    1.6737          |
    1.5474          |
    1.4211          |
    1.2947          |
    1.1684          |
    1.0421          |                  *
   0.91579          |
   0.78947          |
   0.66316          |              '           *
   0.53684          |*
   0.41053          |
   0.28421          |
   0.15789          |
  0.31579E-01       |
 -0.94737E-01       |
  -0.22105          |
  -0.34737          |
  -0.47368          |
  -0.60000          |                              *


                 _____
              0.000    0.750    1.500    2.250    3.000

                               LAGTIME
```

Section 17.14 discusses the question of causation. Specifically, the issue is to find the direction of causality between two variables. The text introduces the Granger test as a method for testing the direction of causation. The GNP-money supply example (see equation (17.14.1)) will be used to illustrate how the Granger test is constructed. Although no data is provided, the following commands will compute an F-statistic testing whether the variable *MONEY* Granger causes *GNP*. A lag of four quarters is considered (i.e. M = 4).

```
TIME 1960 4
SAMPLE 1960.1 1980.4
READ(SOMEFILE) QUARTER GNP MONEY
* Test if M Granger causes GNP.
* Estimate the restricted regression and save the residual sum of squares.
?OLS GNP GNP(1.4) / NOCONSTANT
GEN1 RSSR=$SSE
* Estimate the unrestricted regression and save the residual sum of squares.
?OLS GNP GNP(1.4) MONEY(1.4) / NOCONSTANT
GEN1 RSSUR=$SSE
* Construct the F-test statistic (see equation (8.7.9)).
GEN1 F=((RSSR-RSSUR)/4)/(RSSUR/($N-$K))
PRINT F
```

The test statistic follows the F-distribution with M and N-K degrees of freedom. M is the number of lag terms considered, N is the number of observations used in the estimations, and K is the number of parameters estimated in the unrestricted regression. If the test statistic is greater than the critical value for an F[M, N-K] distribution, the null hypothesis that the coefficients for ιhe lagged terms in the unrestricted regression are jointly equal to zero can be rejected. Thus, it can be concluded that *MONEY* Granger causes *GNP*.

Exercise 17.28 discusses the use of Schwarz's Criterion (SC) in determining lag length. The **ANOVA** option with an estimation command prints this statistic.

SHAZAM commands and options used in Chapter 17

GEN1 *newvar=equation*   with   **LOG**(x)   **SQRT**(x)

GENR *newvar=equation*   with   **LOG**(x)   **TIME**(x)   **LAG**(x)   **LAG**(x,n)

OLS *depvar*   *indeps(first.last,order.endcon)*   /   **COEF=   DLAG   NOCONSTANT**
                                              RSTAT   STDERR=

PLOT *depvars*   *indep*   /   *options*

PRINT *vars*   /   *options*

READ(*datafile*) *vars*   /   *options*

SAMPLE *beg   end*

TIME *beg   freq*

?   Suppression of Output

Temporary variables used

$K	Number of Coefficients
$N	Number of observations used in the estimation
$RHO	Residual Autocorrelation coefficient, ρ
$SSE	Sum of Squared Errors

18. SIMULTANEOUS EQUATION MODELS

Chapter 18 discusses the implications of estimating models involving simultaneous equations. The interdependence between the dependent and explanatory variables poses a number of problems for regression estimation. In particular, this chapter explores the idea that parameters estimated using OLS will be biased and inconsistent. This outcome results because some of the explanatory variables are determined simultaneously and thus, are endogenous (i.e. not independent). As a result, they are correlated with the error term. As well, in these types of models, it is often difficult to determine if the "correct" coefficients have been estimated. This is called the identification problem and is discussed in *Chapter 19*.

Example 18.1, in *Section 18.2*, illustrates the difficulties in distinguishing between demand and supply curves when only the price and quantity variables are known. The data provided in *Table 20.1* will be used to run a simple OLS regression of quantity (Q) on price (P).

```
TIME 1970 1
SAMPLE 1970.0 1991.0
READ(TABLE20.1) PERIOD Q P X
OLS Q P
```

The output follows.

```
|_OLS Q P

OLS ESTIMATION
     22 OBSERVATIONS      DEPENDENT VARIABLE = Q
...NOTE..SAMPLE RANGE SET TO:      1,    22


 R-SQUARE =    0.4345    R-SQUARE ADJUSTED =    0.4063
VARIANCE OF THE ESTIMATE-SIGMA**2 =    91.228
STANDARD ERROR OF THE ESTIMATE-SIGMA =    9.5513
SUM OF SQUARED ERRORS-SSE=   1824.6
MEAN OF DEPENDENT VARIABLE =    100.86
LOG OF THE LIKELIHOOD FUNCTION = -79.8152


VARIABLE    ESTIMATED   STANDARD   T-RATIO        PARTIAL STANDARDIZED ELASTICITY
  NAME      COEFFICIENT   ERROR      20 DF    P-VALUE CORR. COEFFICIENT  AT MEANS
P            0.32717    0.8346E-01   3.920     0.001 0.659     0.6592     0.3539
CONSTANT     65.172       9.329      6.986     0.000 0.842     0.0000     0.6461
```

The above regression results partially illustrate the identification problem. It cannot be determined from the OLS results whether the demand or supply curve has been estimated. Although the slope coefficient is positive, this does not imply that the supply curve has been found. As the text notes, this may simply indicate that the regression is estimating a movement of the two curves. In *Chapters 19* and *20*, it will be shown that more information is needed in order to estimate either the demand or supply curve.

Example 18.6 shows that structural equations in a simultaneous equation model cannot be estimated using the OLS method if there are endogenous variables on the right-hand side of the equations. The model presented in this example is known as *Klein's Model I*. The data for this example is found in *Table 20.5*. The commands below run three OLS regressions to estimate the structural equations.

```
TIME 1920 1
SAMPLE 1920.0 1941.0
READ(TABLE20.5) YEAR C P W I KLAG X WP G T
GENR W2=W+WP
GENR LAGP=LAG(P)
GENR LAGX=LAG(X)
SAMPLE 1921.0 1941.0
* The Consumption Function.
OLS C P W2 LAGP
* The Investment Function.
OLS I P LAGP KLAG
* Demand for Labor Function.
OLS W X LAGX YEAR
```

The output follows.

```
|_* The Consumption Function.
|_OLS C P W2 LAGP

OLS ESTIMATION
      21 OBSERVATIONS        DEPENDENT VARIABLE = C

 R-SQUARE =  0.9810     R-SQUARE ADJUSTED =  0.9777
VARIANCE OF THE ESTIMATE =     1.0517
STANDARD ERROR OF THE ESTIMATE =    1.0255
LOG OF THE LIKELIHOOD FUNCTION = -28.1086

VARIABLE      ESTIMATED      STANDARD     T-RATIO    PARTIAL STANDARDIZED ELASTICITY
NAME         COEFFICIENT     ERROR        17 DF      CORR.   COEFFICIENT  AT MEANS

P            0.19293        0.91210E-01   2.1153     0.4565  0.11868      0.060353
W2           0.79622        0.39944E-01   19.933     0.9793  0.87687      0.61168
LAGP         0.89885E-01 0.90648E-01     0.99158    0.2338  0.52773E-01  0.027261
CONSTANT     16.237         1.3027        12.464     0.9494  0.0          0.30070
|_* The Investment Function.

|_OLS I P LAGP KLAG

OLS ESTIMATION
      21 OBSERVATIONS        DEPENDENT VARIABLE = I

 R-SQUARE =  0.9313     R-SQUARE ADJUSTED =  0.9192
VARIANCE OF THE ESTIMATE =     1.0190
STANDARD ERROR OF THE ESTIMATE =    1.0094
```

```
LOG OF THE LIKELIHOOD FUNCTION = -27.7764

VARIABLE     ESTIMATED    STANDARD    T-RATIO    PARTIAL STANDARDIZED ELASTICITY
  NAME       COEFFICIENT    ERROR      17 DF       CORR.  COEFFICIENT  AT MEANS

P            0.47964     0.97115E-01   4.9389     0.7677  0.56987      6.3957
LAGP         0.33304     0.10086       3.3020     0.6251  0.37769      4.3057
KLAG        -0.11179     0.26728E-01  -4.1827    -0.7122 -0.31218    -17.696
CONSTANT    10.126       5.4655        1.8527     0.4099  0.0          7.9940
|_* Demand for Labor Function.

|_OLS W X LAGX YEAR

OLS ESTIMATION
      21 OBSERVATIONS      DEPENDENT VARIABLE = W

 R-SQUARE =  0.9874      R-SQUARE ADJUSTED =  0.9852
VARIANCE OF THE ESTIMATE =  0.58851
STANDARD ERROR OF THE ESTIMATE =  0.76715
LOG OF THE LIKELIHOOD FUNCTION = -22.0124

VARIABLE     ESTIMATED    STANDARD    T-RATIO    PARTIAL STANDARDIZED ELASTICITY
  NAME       COEFFICIENT    ERROR      17 DF       CORR.  COEFFICIENT  AT MEANS

X            0.43948     0.32408E-01   13.561     0.9568  0.74012      0.72586
LAGX         0.14609     0.37423E-01   3.9037     0.6875  0.20667      0.23297
YEAR         0.13025     0.31910E-01   4.0816     0.7035  0.12819      0.039401
CONSTANT     0.64346E-01 1.1518        0.055866   0.0135  0.0          0.0017696
```

Although the above three equations are identified, the estimates are biased because endogenous variables appear on the right-hand side of the equations. The bias remains even with large sample sizes (i.e. the OLS estimator is inconsistent).

Section 18.4 provides an empirical example illustrating the concepts of simultaneous-equation bias and inconsistency discussed in *Section 18.3.* A Monte Carlo study (see Chapter 11) is performed using the Keynesian model of income determination.

The first step is to generate a random error term, u_t, assuming a normal distribution. Furthermore, it is assumed that:

$$\text{E}(u_t) = 0, \text{E}(u_t u_{t+j}) = 0 \; (j \neq 0), \text{var}(u_t) = \sigma^2 = 0.04, \text{ and } \text{cov}(u_t, I_t) = 0.$$

As is shown in the appendix to Chapter 11, the random error term u_t, given the above assumptions, can be generated using the command:

GENR U=NOR(0.2)

where 0.2 is the assumed standard error. The u_t, listed in *Table 18.1*, was generated in a similar fashion.

It is assumed that the values of the true parameters for the consumption function (18.2.3) are $\beta_0 = 2$ and $\beta_1 = 0.8$. The income variable, Y_t, is constructed following equation (18.3.1). Given that Y_t, along with β_0, β_1 and u_t, are known, values of consumption, C_t, can be generated following equation (18.2.3).

```
SAMPLE 1 20
READ(TABLE18.1) I U
GEN1 BETA1=.8
GEN1 BETA0=2
* Generate Y following equation (18.3.1).
GENR Y=BETA0/(1-BETA1)+(1/(1-BETA1))*I+(1/(1-BETA1))*U
* Generate C following equation (18.2.3).
GENR C=2+BETA1*Y+U
PRINT Y C I U
```

The output follows.

```
|_PRINT Y C I U
      Y               C             I              U
   18.15697        16.15697      2.000000      -0.3686055
   19.59980        17.59980      2.000000      -0.8004084E-01
   21.93468        19.73468      2.200000       0.1869357
   21.55145        19.35145      2.200000       0.1102906
   21.88427        19.48427      2.400000      -0.2314535E-01
   22.42648        20.02648      2.400000       0.8529544E-01
   25.40940        22.80940      2.600000       0.4818807
   22.69523        20.09523      2.600000      -0.6095481E-01
   24.36465        21.56465      2.800000       0.7292983E-01
   24.39334        21.59334      2.800000       0.7866819E-01
   24.09215        21.09215      3.000000      -0.1815703
   24.87451        21.87451      3.000000      -0.2509900E-01
   25.31580        22.11580      3.200000      -0.1368398
   26.30465        23.10465      3.200000       0.6092946E-01
   25.78235        22.38235      3.400000      -0.2435298
   26.08018        22.68018      3.400000      -0.1839638
   27.24440        23.64440      3.600000      -0.1511200
   28.00963        24.40963      3.600000       0.1926739E-02
   30.89301        27.09301      3.800000       0.3786015
   28.98706        25.18706      3.800000      -0.2588852E-02
```

As the text mentions, since the true β_0 and β_1 are known and the sample errors are exactly the same as the "true errors" (by design), an OLS estimation regressing C_t on Y_t should result in $\beta_0 = 2$ and $\beta_1 = .8$ if OLS is unbiased. However, as equation (18.3.7) shows, since the regressor Y_t is correlated with the error term u_t, the results will be biased. The predicted value of the biased β_1 is computed following equation (18.3.7). The size and direction of the anticipated bias is then calculated. First, $\Sigma y_t u_t$ and Σy_t^2 must be computed.

```
STAT Y C I U / PCPDEV CPDEV=DEV PCOV
MATRIX SIGMAYU=DEV(1,4)
MATRIX SIGMAYY=DEV(1,1)
PRINT SIGMAYU SIGMAYY
* Compute the predicted beta1 following (18.3.7).
GEN1 PREDB1=BETA1+SIGMAYU/SIGMAYY
PRINT PREDB1
* Compute the predicted bias.
GEN1 PREDBIAS=PREDB1-BETA1
PRINT PREDBIAS
```

The output follows.

```
|_STAT Y C I U / PCPDEV CPDEV=DEV PCOV
NAME          N     MEAN          ST. DEV      VARIANCE       MINIMUM       MAXIMUM
Y            20    24.500          3.1119         9.6842        18.157        30.893
C            20    21.600          2.5608         6.5579        16.157        27.093
I            20    2.9000         0.58938        0.34737        2.0000        3.8000
U            20    0.53500E-08    0.20000        0.40000E-01   -0.36861       0.48188
 COVARIANCE MATRIX OF VARIABLES -          20 OBSERVATIONS

Y         9.6842
C         7.9474         6.5579
I         1.7368         1.3895        0.34737
U         0.20000        0.20000      -0.26053E-08   0.40000E-01
              Y              C              I              U

CROSSPRODUCT MATRIX IN DEVIATIONS -           20 OBSERVATIONS

Y         184.00
C         151.00        124.60
I         33.000         26.400        6.6000
U         3.8000         3.8000       -0.49500E-07   0.76000
              Y              C              I              U
|_MATRIX SIGMAYU=DEV(1,4)
|_MATRIX SIGMAYY=DEV(1,1)
|_PRINT SIGMAYU SIGMAYY
    SIGMAYU
  3.800000
    SIGMAYY
  184.0000
|_* Compute the predicted beta1 following (18.3.7).
|_GEN1 PREDB1=BETA1+SIGMAYU/SIGMAYY
|_PRINT PREDB1
    PREDB1
  0.8206522
|_* Compute the predicted bias.
|_GEN1 PREDBIAS=PREDB1-BETA1
|_PRINT PREDBIAS
    PREDBIAS
  0.2065217E-01
```

Note that the covariance matrix printed above confirms that $E(u_t) = 0$, $var(u_t) = 0.04$, and $cov(u_t, I_t) = 0$.

According to equation (18.3.7), the β_1 estimated using OLS will be biased upward by 0.02065. The model is now estimated using OLS and the anticipated bias will be compared to the actual one.

```
OLS C Y / COEF=BETAOLS
* Now compute the bias when OLS is used.
GEN1 BIAS=BETAOLS(1)-BETA1
PRINT BIAS
```

The output follows.

```
|_* Estimate the model using OLS.

|_OLS C Y / COEF=BETAOLS

 OLS ESTIMATION
      20 OBSERVATIONS       DEPENDENT VARIABLE = C
...NOTE..SAMPLE RANGE SET TO:     1,    20

 R-SQUARE =    0.9945     R-SQUARE ADJUSTED =    0.9942
VARIANCE OF THE ESTIMATE-SIGMA**2 =  0.37862E-01
STANDARD ERROR OF THE ESTIMATE-SIGMA =  0.19458
SUM OF SQUARED ERRORS-SSE=  0.68152
MEAN OF DEPENDENT VARIABLE =    21.600
LOG OF THE LIKELIHOOD FUNCTION = 5.41282

VARIABLE    ESTIMATED   STANDARD   T-RATIO        PARTIAL STANDARDIZED ELASTICITY
  NAME      COEFFICIENT   ERROR      18 DF    P-VALUE CORR. COEFFICIENT  AT MEANS
Y           0.82065     0.1434E-01  57.21     0.000 0.997     0.9973      0.9308
CONSTANT    1.4940      0.3541       4.219    0.001 0.705     0.0000      0.0692
|_* Now compute the bias when OLS is used.
|_GEN1 BIAS=BETAOLS(1)-BETA1
|_PRINT BIAS
   BIAS
 0.2065217E-01
```

As expected, β_1 estimated using OLS is biased by exactly the value predicted in equation (18.4.1).

SHAZAM commands and options used in Chapter 18

GEN1 *newvar=equation*

GENR *newvar=equation*   with   **LAG**(x)   **NOR**(x)

MATRIX *newmat=equation*

OLS *depvar indeps* / **COEF=**

PRINT *vars* / *options*

READ(*datafile*) *vars* / *options*

SAMPLE *beg end*

STAT *vars* / **CPDEV= PCOV PCPDEV**

TIME *beg freq*

19. THE IDENTIFICATION PROBLEM

Chapter 19 explores the problem of identification when estimating a simultaneous equation model. The issue is whether or not it is possible to obtain unique numerical estimates of the parameters of a structural equation from the estimated reduced form coefficients. If this is possible, the equation is said to be identified. If this cannot be done, the equation is either under or overidentified.

The first three sections of *Chapter 19* outline the theoretical underpinnings of the identification problem. In particular, *Section 19.3* summarizes the rules for determining the identification of an equation in a system of equations.

The Indirect Least Squares (ILS) method of estimating regression coefficients will be used to illustrate the problem of identification in simultaneous equation models. When an equation is "just identified," the method of ILS can be used to compute the parameter estimates based on the results from reduced form regressions. (*Section 20.3* outlines the steps involved). The data from *Table 18.1* will be used to demonstrate this.

In order to show how to use ILS, return to the Keynesian model of income determination. Equations (18.2.3) and (18.2.4) are the structural equations which describe the consumption and income functions. By substituting (18.2.3) into (18.2.4), the reduced-form equation for Y (income) can be found. This is shown in equation (19.1.2). From this result, the reduced-form equation for C, given by equation (19.1.4), may be derived.

To obtain the ILS estimates for this example, it is necessary to estimate the two reduced-form equations using OLS. The coefficient estimates from each regression are saved for later use.

```
SAMPLE 1 20
READ(TABLE18.1) I U
GEN1 BETA1=.8
GEN1 BETA0=2
GENR Y=2/(1-BETA1)+(I/(1-BETA1))+(U/(1-BETA1))
GENR C=2+BETA1*Y+U
OLS Y I / COEF=PIY
OLS C I / COEF=PIC
```

The output follows.

```
|_OLS Y I / COEF=PIY

OLS ESTIMATION
      20 OBSERVATIONS       DEPENDENT VARIABLE = Y
```

```
  R-SQUARE =  0.8967     R-SQUARE ADJUSTED =  0.8910
VARIANCE OF THE ESTIMATE =    1.0556
STANDARD ERROR OF THE ESTIMATE =    1.0274
LOG OF THE LIKELIHOOD FUNCTION = -27.8658

VARIABLE    ESTIMATED   STANDARD    T-RATIO          PARTIAL STANDARDIZED ELASTICITY
  NAME      COEFFICIENT   ERROR      18 DF   P-VALUE CORR. COEFFICIENT  AT MEANS

I           5.0000       .3999       12.50    .000   .947    .9470      .5918
CONSTANT   10.000       1.182        8.458    .000   .894    .0000      .4082

 | OLS C I / COEF=PIC

OLS ESTIMATION
        20 OBSERVATIONS      DEPENDENT VARIABLE = C

  R-SQUARE =  0.8475     R-SQUARE ADJUSTED =  0.8390
VARIANCE OF THE ESTIMATE =    1.0556
STANDARD ERROR OF THE ESTIMATE =    1.0274
LOG OF THE LIKELIHOOD FUNCTION = -27.8658

VARIABLE    ESTIMATED   STANDARD    T-RATIO          PARTIAL STANDARDIZED ELASTICITY
  NAME      COEFFICIENT   ERROR      18 DF   P-VALUE CORR. COEFFICIENT  AT MEANS

I           4.0000       .3999       10.00    .000   .921    .9206      .5370
CONSTANT   10.000       1.182        8.458    .000   .894    .0000      .4630
```

The coefficients from the reduced-form equations, the Π's, are called the impact or short-run multipliers. These multipliers may be used to find the true coefficients of the model. Using equations (19.1.3) and (19.1.5), it can easily be seen that $\beta_0 = \Pi_0/\Pi_1$. Once β_0 is known, β_1 can be found as $\beta_1/\beta_0 = \Pi_3/\Pi_2$. The commands below perform these operations.

```
GEN1 BETA0=PIY(2)/PIY(1)
GEN1 BETA1=(PIC(1)/PIC(2))*BETA0
PRINT BETA0 BETA1
STOP
```

The output follows.

```
 | PRINT BETA0 BETA1
    BETA0
   2.000000
    BETA1
   0.8000000
```

Because unique values for the parameters can be found by using the reduced-form equations, the above model is "just identified."

A model is said to be "underidentified" when no solution exists for the structural parameters in terms of the reduced form parameters. To illustrate this case, return to the demand-supply model presented in *Example 18.1*. Equations (19.2.2) and (19.2.5) describe the reduced-form equations for *P* and *Q*, respectively. Note that only a constant accompanies the disturbance term in both equations. Run two OLS regressions on the reduced-form equations.

```
TIME 1970 1
SAMPLE 1970.0 1991.0
READ(TABLE20.1) PERIOD Q P X
OLS P
OLS Q
```

The output follows.

```
|_OLS P

 OLS ESTIMATION
        22 OBSERVATIONS      DEPENDENT VARIABLE = P
...NOTE..SAMPLE RANGE SET TO:    1,    22

 R-SQUARE =   0.0000     R-SQUARE ADJUSTED =   0.0000
VARIANCE OF THE ESTIMATE-SIGMA**2 =    623.71
STANDARD ERROR OF THE ESTIMATE-SIGMA =   24.974
SUM OF SQUARED ERRORS-SSE=   13098.
MEAN OF DEPENDENT VARIABLE =    109.09
LOG OF THE LIKELIHOOD FUNCTION = -101.497

VARIABLE    ESTIMATED   STANDARD   T-RATIO           PARTIAL STANDARDIZED ELASTICITY
  NAME     COEFFICIENT   ERROR      21 DF    P-VALUE CORR. COEFFICIENT  AT MEANS
CONSTANT    109.09       5.324      20.49    0.000 0.976    0.0000      1.0000

|_OLS Q

 OLS ESTIMATION
        22 OBSERVATIONS      DEPENDENT VARIABLE = Q
...NOTE..SAMPLE RANGE SET TO:    1,    22

 R-SQUARE =   0.0000     R-SQUARE ADJUSTED =   0.0000
VARIANCE OF THE ESTIMATE-SIGMA**2 =    153.65
STANDARD ERROR OF THE ESTIMATE-SIGMA =   12.395
SUM OF SQUARED ERRORS-SSE=   3226.6
MEAN OF DEPENDENT VARIABLE =    100.86
LOG OF THE LIKELIHOOD FUNCTION = -86.0862

VARIABLE    ESTIMATED   STANDARD   T-RATIO           PARTIAL STANDARDIZED ELASTICITY
  NAME     COEFFICIENT   ERROR      21 DF    P-VALUE CORR. COEFFICIENT  AT MEANS
CONSTANT    100.86       2.643      38.17    0.000 0.993    0.0000      1.0000
```

In *Section 19.2*, it is shown that the above coefficients estimated from the OLS regressions cannot be used to find the true coefficients. Therefore, this model is "underidentified."

Suppose now that the demand function for the above example is also a function of *I*, as described in equation (19.2.12). With this slight modification, the supply function is identified. It may appear slightly odd that adding an exogenous variable to the demand function can help identify the supply function.

First, estimate the two new reduced-form equations for P and Q as given by equations (19.2.15) and (19.2.17). The impact multipliers may now be used, as in equation (19.2.19), to obtain the desired coefficient estimates.

```
OLS P X / COEF=PIP
OLS Q X / COEF=PIQ
GEN1 B1=PIQ(1)/PIP(1)
GEN1 B0=PIQ(2)-B1*PIP(2)
PRINT B1 B0
```

The output follows.

```
|_OLS P X / COEF=PIP

 OLS ESTIMATION
      22 OBSERVATIONS      DEPENDENT VARIABLE = P
...NOTE..SAMPLE RANGE SET TO:    1,   22


 R-SQUARE =   0.4930    R-SQUARE ADJUSTED =   0.4677
VARIANCE OF THE ESTIMATE-SIGMA**2 =   332.00
STANDARD ERROR OF THE ESTIMATE-SIGMA =   18.221
SUM OF SQUARED ERRORS-SSE=   6640.0
MEAN OF DEPENDENT VARIABLE =   109.09
LOG OF THE LIKELIHOOD FUNCTION = -94.0247


VARIABLE    ESTIMATED    STANDARD    T-RATIO          PARTIAL STANDARDIZED ELASTICITY
  NAME      COEFFICIENT    ERROR      20 DF    P-VALUE CORR. COEFFICIENT  AT MEANS
X           0.43430E-02 0.9847E-03    4.410     0.000 0.702     0.7022     0.3372
CONSTANT    72.309        9.200       7.859     0.000 0.869     0.0000     0.6628

|_OLS Q X / COEF=PIQ

 OLS ESTIMATION
      22 OBSERVATIONS      DEPENDENT VARIABLE = Q
...NOTE..SAMPLE RANGE SET TO:    1,   22


 R-SQUARE =   0.4172    R-SQUARE ADJUSTED =   0.3881
VARIANCE OF THE ESTIMATE-SIGMA**2 =   94.021
STANDARD ERROR OF THE ESTIMATE-SIGMA =   9.6965
SUM OF SQUARED ERRORS-SSE=   1880.4
MEAN OF DEPENDENT VARIABLE =   100.86
LOG OF THE LIKELIHOOD FUNCTION = -80.1470


VARIABLE    ESTIMATED    STANDARD    T-RATIO          PARTIAL STANDARDIZED ELASTICITY
  NAME      COEFFICIENT    ERROR      20 DF    P-VALUE CORR. COEFFICIENT  AT MEANS
X           0.19829E-02 0.5240E-03    3.784     0.001 0.646     0.6459     0.1665
CONSTANT    84.070        4.896      17.17      0.000 0.968     0.0000     0.8335
|_GEN1 B1=PIQ(1)/PIP(1)
|_GEN1 B0=PIQ(2)-B1*PIP(2)
```

```
|_PRINT B1 B0
   B1
  0.4565685
   B0
   51.05616
```

Although both β_1 and β_0 can be identified uniquely in this model, this is not the case for α_1 and α_0.

The demand equation may be identified if a new exogenous variable is added to the supply function. Consider equation (19.2.24). The new variable which has been added to the supply function is the lagged price, P_{t-1}. The new reduced form equations are described in equations (19.2.24) and (19.2.26). As above, the new reduced form regressions are estimated to obtain the impact multipliers. All six structural coefficients may now be calculated using equations (19.2.25) and (19.2.27).

```
GENR PLAG=LAG(P)
SAMPLE 1971.0 1991.0
OLS P X PLAG / COEF=PIP2
OLS Q X PLAG / COEF=PIQ2
GEN1 BET1=PIQ2(1)/PIP2(1)
GEN1 BET0=PIQ2(3)-BET1*PIP2(3)
GEN1 BET2=PIQ2(2)-(PIP2(2)*PIQ2(2))/PIP2(1)
GEN1 ALPHA1=PIQ2(2)/PIP2(2)
GEN1 ALPHA0=PIQ2(3)-ALPHA1*PIP2(3)
GEN1 ALPHA2=PIQ2(1)-(PIP2(1)*PIQ2(2))/PIP2(2)
PRINT BET1 BET0 BET2 ALPHA0 ALPHA1 ALPHA2
```

The output follows.

```
|_SAMPLE 1971.0 1991.0

|_OLS P X PLAG / COEF=PIP2

 OLS ESTIMATION
      21 OBSERVATIONS        DEPENDENT VARIABLE = P
...NOTE..SAMPLE RANGE SET TO:     2,   22


 R-SQUARE =   0.7562     R-SQUARE ADJUSTED =    0.7291
VARIANCE OF THE ESTIMATE-SIGMA**2 =    131.17
STANDARD ERROR OF THE ESTIMATE-SIGMA =   11.453
SUM OF SQUARED ERRORS-SSE=    2361.1
MEAN OF DEPENDENT VARIABLE =    111.81
LOG OF THE LIKELIHOOD FUNCTION = -79.3826

VARIABLE    ESTIMATED   STANDARD    T-RATIO         PARTIAL STANDARDIZED ELASTICITY
  NAME      COEFFICIENT   ERROR      18 DF    P-VALUE CORR. COEFFICIENT  AT MEANS
X         0.68031E-03 0.9135E-03   0.7447     0.466  0.173    0.1223      0.0531
PLAG      0.68184     0.1437       4.745      0.000  0.745    0.7790      0.6592
CONSTANT  32.172      11.68        2.754      0.013  0.545    0.0000      0.2877
```

```
| OLS Q X PLAG / COEF=PIQ2

 OLS ESTIMATION
      21 OBSERVATIONS      DEPENDENT VARIABLE = Q
...NOTE..SAMPLE RANGE SET TO:    2,   22

 R-SQUARE =   0.5411    R-SQUARE ADJUSTED =   0.4901
VARIANCE OF THE ESTIMATE-SIGMA**2 =   67.047
STANDARD ERROR OF THE ESTIMATE-SIGMA =   8.1882
SUM OF SQUARED ERRORS-SSE=   1206.8
MEAN OF DEPENDENT VARIABLE =   102.00
LOG OF THE LIKELIHOOD FUNCTION = -72.3357

VARIABLE    ESTIMATED   STANDARD   T-RATIO            PARTIAL STANDARDIZED ELASTICITY
  NAME      COEFFICIENT   ERROR      18 DF    P-VALUE CORR. COEFFICIENT AT MEANS
X           0.52590E-03 0.6531E-03  0.8052     0.431 0.186     0.1814      0.0450
PLAG        0.27204      0.1027      2.648      0.016 0.529     0.5964      0.2883
CONSTANT    68.007       8.351       8.144      0.000 0.887     0.0000      0.6667
  GEN1 BET1=PIQ2(1)/PIP2(1)
  GEN1 BET0=PIQ2(3)-BET1*PIP2(3)
  GEN1 BET2=PIQ2(2)-(PIP2(2)*PIQ2(2))/PIP2(1)
  GEN1 ALPHA1=PIQ2(2)/PIP2(2)
  GEN1 ALPHA0=PIQ2(3)-ALPHA1*PIP2(3)
  GEN1 ALPHA2=PIQ2(1)-(PIP2(1)*PIQ2(2))/PIP2(2)
  PRINT BET1 BET0 BET2 ALPHA0 ALPHA1 ALPHA2
    BET1
  0.7730307
    BET0
   43.13716
    BET2
  -188.5799
    ALPHA0
   55.17109
    ALPHA1
  0.3989755
    ALPHA2
  0.2544748E-03
```

Since all six structural coefficients can be defined uniquely in this model, it is now considered to be "just identified."

Finally, it is possible for a model to be "overidentified." In this case, more than one solution for the structural parameters in terms of the reduced form parameters is possible. No unique estimates of the structural parameters exist.

Section 19.4 discusses the problem of simultaneity. This problem arises when some of the right-hand side variables are endogenous. That is, their values are determined within the model. As a result, these variables are likely to be correlated with the error term.

If there is no simultaneous equation bias, OLS estimation will provide consistent and efficient estimators. However, if simultaneity is present, OLS estimators will not even be consistent. Conversely, if alternate methods of estimation are used (see *Chapter 20*) when there is no simultaneity, these methods yield estimators which are consistent but not efficient. Hence, it may be important to test for simultaneity.

The method introduced for testing for endogeneity is Hausman's Specification Test. Essentially, this procedure tests whether an endogenous regressor is correlated with the error term. *Example 19.5* illustrates this method. The simultaneous equation model is as follows:

$$EXP_i = \beta_1 + \beta_2\ AID_i + \beta_3\ INC_i + \beta_4\ POP_i + u_i \qquad (19.4.8)$$

$$AID_i = \delta_1 + \delta_2\ EXP_i + \delta_3\ PS_i + v_i \qquad (19.4.9)$$

where *EXP* = state and local government public expenditures, *AID* = level of federal grants-in-aid, *INC* = income of states, *POP* = state population, *PS* = population of primary and secondary schoolchildren, and *u* and *v* are error terms. The data for this example was taken from the original source (Pindyck and Rubinfeld, *Econometric Models and Economic Forecasts, Third Edition*, McGraw-Hill, 1991, pp. 155-156).

The first step is to estimate the following reduced form regression:

$$AID_i = \Pi_0 + \Pi_1\ INC_i + \Pi_2\ POP_i + \Pi_3\ PS_i + w_i$$

The estimated residuals, *w*, are added as a regressor to equation (19.4.8). If the estimated coefficient for *w* is statistically significant, there is evidence of a simultaneity problem.

```
SAMPLE 1 50
READ(EXAMP195.DAT) EXP AID POP INC PS / BYVAR
OLS AID INC POP PS / RESID=W
* Estimate equation (19.4.10).
OLS EXP AID INC POP W
```

The output follows.

```
|_OLS AID INC POP PS / RESID=W

 OLS ESTIMATION
      50 OBSERVATIONS        DEPENDENT VARIABLE = AID
...NOTE..SAMPLE RANGE SET TO:     1,    50


 R-SQUARE =    0.9348     R-SQUARE ADJUSTED =    0.9306
VARIANCE OF THE ESTIMATE-SIGMA**2 =    49255.
STANDARD ERROR OF THE ESTIMATE-SIGMA =    221.94
SUM OF SQUARED ERRORS-SSE=  0.22657E+07
MEAN OF DEPENDENT VARIABLE =    692.80
LOG OF THE LIKELIHOOD FUNCTION = -338.982
```

```
VARIABLE    ESTIMATED   STANDARD    T-RATIO           PARTIAL STANDARDIZED ELASTICITY
  NAME     COEFFICIENT    ERROR      46 DF     P-VALUE CORR.  COEFFICIENT  AT MEANS
INC        0.36337E-04 0.1336E-04    2.719     0.009 0.372      0.9602      0.9889
POP        0.17509      0.1255       1.395     0.170 0.201      0.9145      1.0487
PS        -0.83355      0.3850      -2.165     0.036-0.304     -0.9210     -1.0977
CONSTANT  41.615       49.72         0.8370    0.407 0.122      0.0000      0.0601
|_* Estimate equation (19.4.10).

|_OLS EXP AID INC POP W

 OLS ESTIMATION
      50 OBSERVATIONS      DEPENDENT VARIABLE = EXP
...NOTE..SAMPLE RANGE SET TO:    1,    50

 R-SQUARE =   0.9935    R-SQUARE ADJUSTED =   0.9929
VARIANCE OF THE ESTIMATE-SIGMA**2 =  0.13488E+06
STANDARD ERROR OF THE ESTIMATE-SIGMA =   367.25
SUM OF SQUARED ERRORS-SSE=  0.60694E+07
MEAN OF DEPENDENT VARIABLE =    3316.2
LOG OF THE LIKELIHOOD FUNCTION = -363.616

VARIABLE    ESTIMATED   STANDARD    T-RATIO           PARTIAL STANDARDIZED ELASTICITY
  NAME     COEFFICIENT    ERROR      45 DF     P-VALUE CORR.  COEFFICIENT  AT MEANS
AID        4.5006       0.7643       5.889     0.000 0.660      0.8695      0.9403
INC        0.12928E-03 0.4222E-04    3.062     0.004 0.415      0.6599      0.7351
POP       -0.51814      0.1118      -4.633     0.000-0.568     -0.5228     -0.6484
W         -1.3911       0.8023      -1.734     0.090-0.250     -0.0686      0.0000
CONSTANT -89.415       86.02        -1.040     0.304-0.153      0.0000     -0.0270
```

As the output shows, the coefficient for w is not statistically different from zero at the 5% level of significance. Therefore, it can be concluded that no simultaneity problem exists. However, the p-value of 0.09 reflects the fact that the coefficient is statistically different from zero at the 10 percent level of significance, indicating that some simultaneity may exist.

For comparison, equation (19.4.8) is estimated using OLS.

```
* Estimate the OLS regression (19.4.11).
OLS EXP AID INC POP
```

The output follows.

```
|_* Estimate the OLS regression (19.4.11).

|_OLS EXP AID INC POP

 OLS ESTIMATION
      50 OBSERVATIONS      DEPENDENT VARIABLE = EXP
...NOTE..SAMPLE RANGE SET TO:    1,    50

 R-SQUARE =   0.9930    R-SQUARE ADJUSTED =   0.9926
```

```
VARIANCE OF THE ESTIMATE-SIGMA**2 =  0.14076E+06
STANDARD ERROR OF THE ESTIMATE-SIGMA =    375.18
SUM OF SQUARED ERRORS-SSE=  0.64749E+07
MEAN OF DEPENDENT VARIABLE =    3316.2
LOG OF THE LIKELIHOOD FUNCTION = -365.232
```

VARIABLE NAME	ESTIMATED COEFFICIENT	STANDARD ERROR	T-RATIO 46 DF	P-VALUE	PARTIAL CORR.	STANDARDIZED COEFFICIENT	ELASTICITY AT MEANS
AID	3.2382	0.2374	13.64	0.000	0.895	0.6256	0.6765
INC	0.19068E-03	0.2348E-04	8.120	0.000	0.767	0.9733	1.0841
POP	-0.59662	0.1045	-5.710	0.000	-0.644	-0.6020	-0.7465
CONSTANT	-46.805	84.21	-0.5558	0.581	-0.082	0.0000	-0.0141

Section 19.5 shows how the Hausman test can be used to test for endogeneity. Since no empirical example is provided, the model in *Exercise 16.9* will be considered. The model is constructed as follows:

Money Demand: $M^d_t = \beta_0 + \beta_1 Y_t + \beta_2 R_t + \beta_3 P_t + u_{1t}$

Money Supply: $M^s_t = \alpha_0 + \alpha_1 Y_t + u_{2t}$

where M = money, Y = income, R = rate of interest, P = price, and the u's are error terms. It is assumed that R and P are exogenous and M and Y are endogenous.

Using the procedure described in *Section 19.5*, the hypothesis that Y is indeed endogenous will be tested. The first step is to estimate the reduced form equation for Y and save the predicted values. These values are then included as regressors in the Money Supply equation. If the estimated coefficient for these predicted values is statistically different from zero, it can be concluded that the variable Y is indeed endogenous. Note that the data for this example is stored in the file *EXER1916.DAT*.

```
TIME 1970 1
SAMPLE 1970.0 1991.0
READ(EXER1916.DAT) YEAR M Y R P
* Estimate the reduced form equation for Y. Save the predicted values of Y.
?OLS Y R P / PREDICT=YHAT RESID=W
* Test for the endogeneity of Y.
OLS M Y YHAT
```

The output follows.

```
|_* Test for the endogeneity of Y.

|_OLS M Y YHAT

 OLS ESTIMATION
      22 OBSERVATIONS      DEPENDENT VARIABLE = M
...NOTE..SAMPLE RANGE SET TO:    1,    22
```

```
 R-SQUARE =    0.9967      R-SQUARE ADJUSTED =    0.9963
VARIANCE OF THE ESTIMATE-SIGMA**2 =    3289.0
STANDARD ERROR OF THE ESTIMATE-SIGMA =    57.350
SUM OF SQUARED ERRORS-SSE=    62490.
MEAN OF DEPENDENT VARIABLE =    1889.9
LOG OF THE LIKELIHOOD FUNCTION = -118.686
```

VARIABLE NAME	ESTIMATED COEFFICIENT	STANDARD ERROR	T-RATIO 19 DF	P-VALUE	PARTIAL CORR.	STANDARDIZED COEFFICIENT	ELASTICITY AT MEANS
Y	0.42877	0.7859E-01	5.456	0.000	0.781	0.6978	0.6851
YHAT	0.18636	0.7902E-01	2.358	0.029	0.476	0.3017	0.2978
CONSTANT	32.308	27.62	1.170	0.257	0.259	0.0000	0.0171

Since the coefficient for the predicted values of Y, $YHAT$, is statistically different from zero (p-value = 0.02922), it can be concluded that Y is endogenous in the money demand model .

SHAZAM commands and options used in Chapter 19

GEN1 *newvar=equation*

GENR *newvar=equation* with **LAG**(x)

OLS *depvar indeps* / **COEF= PREDICT= RESID=**

PRINT *vars* / *options*

READ(*datafile*) *vars* / **BYVAR**

SAMPLE *beg end*

TIME *beg freq*

? Suppression of Output

20. SIMULTANEOUS EQUATION METHODS

Chapter 20 discusses some of the methods that can be used to estimate simultaneous equation models. The first method described is that of Indirect Least Squares (ILS). The method of estimation by Two-Stage Least Squares (2SLS) is then introduced.

When an equation is exactly identified, the method of ILS can be used for estimation. The steps involved are outlined in *Section 20.3*. First, the reduced form equations are estimated using OLS. This is possible since all the right-hand side variables in these equations are exogenous. Hence, the resulting estimators are consistent. The reduced form coefficients (Π) can then be used to construct the ILS estimators.

The following commands replicate the empirical results provided in *Section 20.3.*

```
TIME 1970 1
SAMPLE 1970.0 1991.0
READ(TABLE20.1) YEAR Q P X
* Estimate the reduced form equations and save the coefficients.
* Equation (20.3.11).
OLS P X / COEF=C1
* Equation (20.3.12).
OLS Q X / COEF=C2
* Following equations (20.3.9) and (20.3.10), construct the ILS estimates for
* the supply function, beta0 and beta1.
GEN1 B1HAT=C2(1)/C1(1)
GEN1 B0HAT=C2(2)-B1HAT*C1(2)
PRINT B0HAT B1HAT
* For comparison, estimate the supply function using OLS equation (20.3.16).
OLS Q P
```

The output follows.

```
|_* Estimate the reduced form equations and save the coefficients.
|_* Equation (20.3.11).

|_OLS P X / COEF=C1

 OLS ESTIMATION
     22 OBSERVATIONS     DEPENDENT VARIABLE = P
...NOTE..SAMPLE RANGE SET TO:    1,    22


 R-SQUARE =   0.4930     R-SQUARE ADJUSTED =    0.4677
VARIANCE OF THE ESTIMATE-SIGMA**2 =    332.00
STANDARD ERROR OF THE ESTIMATE-SIGMA =    18.221
SUM OF SQUARED ERRORS-SSE=   6640.0
MEAN OF DEPENDENT VARIABLE =    109.09
LOG OF THE LIKELIHOOD FUNCTION = -94.0247
```

```
VARIABLE    ESTIMATED   STANDARD    T-RATIO          PARTIAL STANDARDIZED ELASTICITY
  NAME      COEFFICIENT   ERROR       20 DF   P-VALUE CORR. COEFFICIENT  AT MEANS
X           0.43430E-02 0.9847E-03   4.410    0.000 0.702    0.7022       0.3372
CONSTANT    72.309        9.200       7.859    0.000 0.869    0.0000       0.6628
|_* Equation (20.3.12).

|_OLS Q X / COEF=C2

 OLS ESTIMATION
      22 OBSERVATIONS      DEPENDENT VARIABLE = Q
...NOTE..SAMPLE RANGE SET TO:     1,    22


 R-SQUARE =    0.4172     R-SQUARE ADJUSTED =    0.3881
VARIANCE OF THE ESTIMATE-SIGMA**2 =     94.021
STANDARD ERROR OF THE ESTIMATE-SIGMA =   9.6965
SUM OF SQUARED ERRORS-SSE=    1880.4
MEAN OF DEPENDENT VARIABLE =    100.86
LOG OF THE LIKELIHOOD FUNCTION = -80.1470


VARIABLE    ESTIMATED   STANDARD    T-RATIO          PARTIAL STANDARDIZED ELASTICITY
  NAME      COEFFICIENT   ERROR       20 DF   P-VALUE CORR. COEFFICIENT  AT MEANS
X           0.19829E-02 0.5240E-03   3.784    0.001 0.646    0.6459       0.1665
CONSTANT    84.070        4.896      17.17     0.000 0.968    0.0000       0.8335
|_* Following equations (20.3.9) and (20.3.10), construct the ILS estimates for
|_* the supply function, beta0 and beta1.
|_GEN1 B1HAT=C2(1)/C1(1)
|_GEN1 B0HAT=C2(2)-B1HAT*C1(2)
|_PRINT B0HAT B1HAT
   B0HAT
  51.05616
   B1HAT
  0.4565685
|_* For comparison, estimate the supply function using OLS equation (20.3.16).

|_OLS Q P

 OLS ESTIMATION
      22 OBSERVATIONS      DEPENDENT VARIABLE = Q
...NOTE..SAMPLE RANGE SET TO:     1,    22


 R-SQUARE =    0.4345     R-SQUARE ADJUSTED =    0.4063
VARIANCE OF THE ESTIMATE-SIGMA**2 =     91.228
STANDARD ERROR OF THE ESTIMATE-SIGMA =   9.5513
SUM OF SQUARED ERRORS-SSE=    1824.6
MEAN OF DEPENDENT VARIABLE =    100.86
LOG OF THE LIKELIHOOD FUNCTION = -79.8152

VARIABLE    ESTIMATED   STANDARD    T-RATIO          PARTIAL STANDARDIZED ELASTICITY
  NAME      COEFFICIENT   ERROR       20 DF   P-VALUE CORR. COEFFICIENT  AT MEANS
P           0.32717     0.8346E-01   3.920    0.001 0.659    0.6592       0.3539
CONSTANT    65.172        9.329       6.986    0.000 0.842    0.0000       0.6461
```

Note though that a shortcoming of the ILS approach is that this method is not capable of providing unique estimators in models that are overidentified. However, the method of 2SLS, described in *Section 20.4*, is able to provide unique parameter estimates for overidentified equations.

The **2SLS** Command

The **2SLS** command can be used to estimate a single linear equation by Two-Stage Least Squares. The general format is:

2SLS *depvar   rhsvars   (exogs)   /   options*

where *depvar* is the dependent variable, *rhsvars* is a list of the right-hand-side variables in the equation, *exogs* is a list of the exogenous variables in the system and *options* is a list of options.

The R^2 statistic in 2SLS is not well defined and may be negative, usually indicating that the model does not fit the data well.

Of course, 2SLS can also be used to estimate exactly identified models. For example, the above ILS estimators will also be computed using the **2SLS** command.

```
2SLS Q P (X)
```

The output follows.

```
|_2SLS Q P (X)
 TWO STAGE LEAST SQUARES - DEPENDENT VARIABLE = Q
  1 EXOGENOUS VARIABLES
  2 POSSIBLE ENDOGENOUS VARIABLES
      22 OBSERVATIONS

 R-SQUARE =    0.3666     R-SQUARE ADJUSTED =    0.3349
VARIANCE OF THE ESTIMATE-SIGMA**2 =    102.19
STANDARD ERROR OF THE ESTIMATE-SIGMA =    10.109
SUM OF SQUARED ERRORS-SSE=    2043.9
MEAN OF DEPENDENT VARIABLE =    100.86
```

VARIABLE NAME	ESTIMATED COEFFICIENT	STANDARD ERROR	T-RATIO 20 DF	P-VALUE	PARTIAL CORR.	STANDARDIZED COEFFICIENT	ELASTICITY AT MEANS
P	0.45657	0.1258	3.629	0.002	0.630	0.9199	0.4938
CONSTANT	51.056	13.89	3.675	0.002	0.635	0.0000	0.5062

As the 2SLS output shows, the parameters estimated are identical to the above ILS estimators. The **2SLS** command has an advantage in that it provides a full set of statistics (such as standard errors, etc.) for the model.

The example provided in *Section 20.5* will first be estimated the "long way" following the steps outlined. The **2SLS** command will then be used to confirm the results.

```
TIME 1970 1
SAMPLE 1970.0 1991.0
READ(TABLE20.2) YEAR Y1 Y2 X1 X2 X3
* Regress Y1 on all the exogenous variables in the system (i.e. equation
* (20.5.1)) and save the predicted values.
OLS Y1 X1 X2 / PREDICT=YHAT1
* Now replace Y1 with Yhat1 and estimate equation (20.5.2). Save the standard
* errors and estimated coefficients for use ahead.
OLS Y2 YHAT1 / STDERR=SE COEF=SECONDBS
```

The output follows.

```
|_* Regress Y1 on all the exogenous variables in the system (i.e. equation
|_* (20.5.1)) and save the predicted values.

|_OLS Y1 X1 X2 / PREDICT=YHAT1

 OLS ESTIMATION
      22 OBSERVATIONS       DEPENDENT VARIABLE = Y1
...NOTE..SAMPLE RANGE SET TO:    1,    22


 R-SQUARE =   0.9948     R-SQUARE ADJUSTED =    0.9943
VARIANCE OF THE ESTIMATE-SIGMA**2 =    13403.
STANDARD ERROR OF THE ESTIMATE-SIGMA =    115.77
SUM OF SQUARED ERRORS-SSE=  0.25465E+06
MEAN OF DEPENDENT VARIABLE =    3020.0
LOG OF THE LIKELIHOOD FUNCTION = -134.139


VARIABLE     ESTIMATED    STANDARD    T-RATIO          PARTIAL STANDARDIZED ELASTICITY
  NAME       COEFFICIENT    ERROR      19 DF    P-VALUE CORR. COEFFICIENT  AT MEANS
X1           0.51695       0.4151      1.245     0.228 0.275    0.0783      0.0850
X2           3.8126        0.2602      14.65     0.000 0.958    0.9216      0.8726
CONSTANT     128.04        62.35       2.053     0.054 0.426    0.0000      0.0424
|_* Now replace Y1 with Yhat1 and estimate equation (20.5.2). Save the standard
|_* errors and estimated coefficients for use ahead.

|_OLS Y2 YHAT1 / STDERR=SE COEF=SECONDBS

 OLS ESTIMATION
      22 OBSERVATIONS       DEPENDENT VARIABLE = Y2
...NOTE..SAMPLE RANGE SET TO:    1,    22


 R-SQUARE =   0.9954     R-SQUARE ADJUSTED =    0.9951
VARIANCE OF THE ESTIMATE-SIGMA**2 =    4318.6
STANDARD ERROR OF THE ESTIMATE-SIGMA =    65.716
SUM OF SQUARED ERRORS-SSE=    86372.
MEAN OF DEPENDENT VARIABLE =    1890.1
LOG OF THE LIKELIHOOD FUNCTION = -122.246


VARIABLE     ESTIMATED    STANDARD    T-RATIO          PARTIAL STANDARDIZED ELASTICITY
  NAME       COEFFICIENT    ERROR      20 DF    P-VALUE CORR. COEFFICIENT  AT MEANS
YHAT1        0.61440       0.9370E-02  65.57     0.000 0.998    0.9977      0.9817
CONSTANT     34.580        31.58       1.095     0.286 0.238    0.0000      0.0183
```

As the text notes, the standard errors computed for equation (20.5.2) need to be corrected. The following commands use the information provided in *Section 20.2A* in *Appendix 20A* to do this.

```
GEN1 SIG2STAR=$SIG2
GENR U2=Y2-SECONDBS(2)-SECONDBS(1)*Y1
MATRIX SIG2=U2'U2/($N-$K)
* Now construct the corrected t-stats. Since the vectors SECONDBS and SE
* are 2 observations long, alter the SAMPLE range.
SAMPLE 1 2
GENR NEWSE=SE*(SQRT(SIG2))/(SQRT(SIG2STAR))
GENR NEWT=SECONDBS/NEWSE
PRINT SECONDBS NEWSE NEWT
```

The pertinent output follows.

```
|_PRINT SECONDBS NEWSE NEWT
     SECONDBS           NEWSE            NEWT
    0.6144038       0.9062894E-02      67.79333
    34.57999         30.54156         1.132228
```

Note that the **2SLS** command automatically uses the corrected standard errors when computing the output statistics. The commands below will confirm this.

```
SAMPLE 1970.0 1991.0
2SLS Y2 Y1 (X1 X2)
```

The output follows.

```
|_2SLS Y2 Y1 (X1 X2)
 TWO STAGE LEAST SQUARES - DEPENDENT VARIABLE = Y2
  2 EXOGENOUS VARIABLES
  2 POSSIBLE ENDOGENOUS VARIABLES
      22 OBSERVATIONS


 R-SQUARE =    0.9957     R-SQUARE ADJUSTED =    0.9955
VARIANCE OF THE ESTIMATE-SIGMA**2 =    4040.4
STANDARD ERROR OF THE ESTIMATE-SIGMA =    63.564
SUM OF SQUARED ERRORS-SSE=    80807.
MEAN OF DEPENDENT VARIABLE =    1890.1
```

VARIABLE NAME	ESTIMATED COEFFICIENT	STANDARD ERROR	T-RATIO 20 DF	P-VALUE	PARTIAL CORR.	STANDARDIZED COEFFICIENT	ELASTICITY AT MEANS
Y1	0.61440	0.9063E-02	67.79	0.000	0.998	1.0003	0.9817
CONSTANT	34.580	30.54	1.132	0.271	0.245	0.0000	0.0183

The money supply model is now estimated using OLS.

```
* Equation (20.5.4).
OLS Y2 Y1
```

The output follows.

```
|_OLS Y2 Y1

 OLS ESTIMATION
      22 OBSERVATIONS      DEPENDENT VARIABLE = Y2
...NOTE..SAMPLE RANGE SET TO:      1,    22

 R-SQUARE =   0.9957    R-SQUARE ADJUSTED =   0.9955
VARIANCE OF THE ESTIMATE-SIGMA**2 =    4034.9
STANDARD ERROR OF THE ESTIMATE-SIGMA =   63.521
SUM OF SQUARED ERRORS-SSE=    80697.
MEAN OF DEPENDENT VARIABLE =    1890.1
LOG OF THE LIKELIHOOD FUNCTION = -121.498

VARIABLE    ESTIMATED   STANDARD   T-RATIO        PARTIAL STANDARDIZED ELASTICITY
  NAME     COEFFICIENT   ERROR      20 DF   P-VALUE CORR. COEFFICIENT  AT MEANS
Y1          0.61291     0.9033E-02  67.85    0.000 0.998    0.9978      0.9793
CONSTANT    39.081      30.46       1.283    0.214 0.276    0.0000      0.0207
```

The Hausman test, testing for simultaneity, is now performed.

```
?OLS Y1 X1 X2 / RESID=V PREDICT=Y1HAT
OLS Y2 Y1HAT V
```

The output follows.

```
|_?OLS Y1 X1 X2 / RESID=V PREDICT=Y1HAT

|_OLS Y2 Y1HAT V

 OLS ESTIMATION
      22 OBSERVATIONS      DEPENDENT VARIABLE = Y2
...NOTE..SAMPLE RANGE SET TO:      1,    22

 R-SQUARE =   0.9968    R-SQUARE ADJUSTED =   0.9965
VARIANCE OF THE ESTIMATE-SIGMA**2 =    3130.4
STANDARD ERROR OF THE ESTIMATE-SIGMA =   55.950
SUM OF SQUARED ERRORS-SSE=    59477.
MEAN OF DEPENDENT VARIABLE =    1890.1
LOG OF THE LIKELIHOOD FUNCTION = -118.142

VARIABLE    ESTIMATED   STANDARD   T-RATIO        PARTIAL STANDARDIZED ELASTICITY
  NAME     COEFFICIENT   ERROR      19 DF   P-VALUE CORR. COEFFICIENT  AT MEANS
Y1HAT       0.61440     0.7977E-02  77.02    0.000 0.998    0.9977      0.9817
V           0.32499     0.1109      2.931    0.009 0.558    0.0380      0.0000
CONSTANT    34.580      26.88       1.286    0.214 0.283    0.0000      0.0183
```

Since the coefficient for *V* is statistically different from zero, it can be concluded that GDP (*Y1*) and the money supply (*Y2*) are mutually dependent.

Section 20.6 provides some illustrated examples of simultaneous equation estimations. In particular, the data supplied in *Table 20.5* will be used to replicate the regression results reported in *Table 20.6*.

```
* Section 20.6 - Illustrated Examples.
TIME 1920 1
SAMPLE 1920.0 1941.0
READ(TABLE20.5) YEAR C P W I LAGK X WP G T
GENR W2=W+WP
GENR LAGP=LAG(P)
GENR LAGX=LAG(X)
* Adjust the SAMPLE range to drop the undefined lagged variables.
SAMPLE 1921.0 1941.0
* First the OLS estimates.
OLS C P W2 LAGP / RSTAT
OLS I P LAGP LAGK / RSTAT
OLS W X LAGX YEAR / RSTAT
* Now the reduced form equations.
OLS P LAGP LAGK LAGX YEAR T G / RSTAT
OLS W2 LAGP LAGK LAGX YEAR T G / RSTAT
OLS X LAGP LAGK LAGX YEAR T G / RSTAT
* Finally, the 2SLS estimations.
2SLS C P W2 LAGP (LAGP LAGK LAGX YEAR T G)
2SLS I P LAGP LAGK (LAGP LAGK LAGX YEAR T G)
2SLS W X LAGX YEAR (LAGP LAGK LAGX YEAR T G)
```

The OLS output follows.

```
|_OLS C P W2 LAGP / RSTAT

 OLS ESTIMATION
       21 OBSERVATIONS      DEPENDENT VARIABLE = C
...NOTE..SAMPLE RANGE SET TO:    2,   22


 R-SQUARE =   0.9810     R-SQUARE ADJUSTED =    0.9777
VARIANCE OF THE ESTIMATE-SIGMA**2 =   1.0517
STANDARD ERROR OF THE ESTIMATE-SIGMA =   1.0255
SUM OF SQUARED ERRORS-SSE=   17.879
MEAN OF DEPENDENT VARIABLE =    53.995
LOG OF THE LIKELIHOOD FUNCTION = -28.1086

VARIABLE    ESTIMATED    STANDARD    T-RATIO          PARTIAL STANDARDIZED ELASTICITY
  NAME      COEFFICIENT    ERROR      17 DF    P-VALUE CORR. COEFFICIENT  AT MEANS
P           0.19293      0.9121E-01   2.115     0.049 0.456    0.1187      0.0604
W2          0.79622      0.3994E-01   19.93     0.000 0.979    0.8769      0.6117
LAGP        0.89885E-01  0.9065E-01   0.9916    0.335 0.234    0.0528      0.0273
CONSTANT    16.237       1.303        12.46     0.000 0.949    0.0000      0.3007

DURBIN-WATSON = 1.3675    VON NEUMANN RATIO = 1.4358    RHO =   0.24630
RESIDUAL SUM = -0.13856E-12   RESIDUAL VARIANCE =    1.0517
SUM OF ABSOLUTE ERRORS=   14.951
R-SQUARE BETWEEN OBSERVED AND PREDICTED = 0.9810
RUNS TEST:   11 RUNS,   10 POS,    0 ZERO,   11 NEG  NORMAL STATISTIC = -0.2137
```

```
|_OLS I P LAGP LAGK / RSTAT

 OLS ESTIMATION
      21 OBSERVATIONS      DEPENDENT VARIABLE = I
...NOTE..SAMPLE RANGE SET TO:      2,    22

 R-SQUARE =    0.9313    R-SQUARE ADJUSTED =    0.9192
VARIANCE OF THE ESTIMATE-SIGMA**2 =    1.0190
STANDARD ERROR OF THE ESTIMATE-SIGMA =    1.0094
SUM OF SQUARED ERRORS-SSE=   17.323
MEAN OF DEPENDENT VARIABLE =    1.2667
LOG OF THE LIKELIHOOD FUNCTION = -27.7764


VARIABLE    ESTIMATED   STANDARD    T-RATIO        PARTIAL STANDARDIZED ELASTICITY
  NAME      COEFFICIENT   ERROR      17 DF   P-VALUE CORR. COEFFICIENT  AT MEANS
P           0.47964     0.9711E-01   4.939   0.000 0.768    0.5699      6.3957
LAGP        0.33304     0.1009       3.302   0.004 0.625    0.3777      4.3057
LAGK       -0.11179     0.2673E-01  -4.183   0.001-0.712   -0.3122    -17.6955
CONSTANT   10.126       5.466        1.853   0.081 0.410    0.0000      7.9940


DURBIN-WATSON = 1.8102    VON NEUMANN RATIO = 1.9007    RHO =   0.08425
RESIDUAL SUM =  0.14977E-12  RESIDUAL VARIANCE =    1.0190
SUM OF ABSOLUTE ERRORS=   13.931
R-SQUARE BETWEEN OBSERVED AND PREDICTED = 0.9313
RUNS TEST:    9 RUNS,   12 POS,    0 ZERO,    9 NEG  NORMAL STATISTIC = -1.0460

|_OLS W X LAGX YEAR / RSTAT

 OLS ESTIMATION
      21 OBSERVATIONS      DEPENDENT VARIABLE = W
...NOTE..SAMPLE RANGE SET TO:      2,    22

 R-SQUARE =    0.9874    R-SQUARE ADJUSTED =    0.9852
VARIANCE OF THE ESTIMATE-SIGMA**2 =    0.58851
STANDARD ERROR OF THE ESTIMATE-SIGMA =    0.76715
SUM OF SQUARED ERRORS-SSE=   10.005
MEAN OF DEPENDENT VARIABLE =    36.362
LOG OF THE LIKELIHOOD FUNCTION = -22.0124


VARIABLE    ESTIMATED   STANDARD    T-RATIO        PARTIAL STANDARDIZED ELASTICITY
  NAME      COEFFICIENT   ERROR      17 DF   P-VALUE CORR. COEFFICIENT  AT MEANS
X           0.43948     0.3241E-01   13.56      0.000 0.957    0.7401      0.7259
LAGX        0.14609     0.3742E-01   3.904      0.001 0.688    0.2067      0.2330
YEAR        0.13025     0.3191E-01   4.082      0.001 0.704    0.1282      0.0394
CONSTANT   0.64346E-01  1.152       0.5587E-01  0.956 0.014    0.0000      0.0018


DURBIN-WATSON = 1.9584    VON NEUMANN RATIO = 2.0564    RHO = -0.08334
RESIDUAL SUM =  0.85043E-13  RESIDUAL VARIANCE =   0.58851
SUM OF ABSOLUTE ERRORS=   12.096
R-SQUARE BETWEEN OBSERVED AND PREDICTED = 0.9874
RUNS TEST:   10 RUNS,   11 POS,    0 ZERO,   10 NEG  NORMAL STATISTIC = -0.6626
```

Next are the reduced-form regression results.

```
|_OLS P LAGP LAGK LAGX YEAR T G / RSTAT


 OLS ESTIMATION
      21 OBSERVATIONS      DEPENDENT VARIABLE = P
 ...NOTE..SAMPLE RANGE SET TO:    2,   22


  R-SQUARE =    0.8261    R-SQUARE ADJUSTED =    0.7515
 VARIANCE OF THE ESTIMATE-SIGMA**2 =   4.4253
 STANDARD ERROR OF THE ESTIMATE-SIGMA =    2.1036
 SUM OF SQUARED ERRORS-SSE=    61.955
 MEAN OF DEPENDENT VARIABLE =    16.890
 LOG OF THE LIKELIHOOD FUNCTION = -41.1575
```

VARIABLE NAME	ESTIMATED COEFFICIENT	STANDARD ERROR	T-RATIO 14 DF	P-VALUE	PARTIAL CORR.	STANDARDIZED COEFFICIENT	ELASTICITY AT MEANS
LAGP	0.80981	0.4469	1.812	0.091	0.436	0.7730	0.7852
LAGK	-0.21308	0.6744E-01	-3.160	0.007	-0.645	-0.5008	-2.5293
LAGX	0.18815E-01	0.2538	0.7415E-01	0.942	0.020	0.0398	0.0646
YEAR	0.29549	0.1549	1.907	0.077	0.454	0.4344	0.1924
T	-0.92782	0.3921	-2.366	0.033	-0.534	-0.4467	-0.3738
G	0.43999	0.3757	1.171	0.261	0.299	0.2484	0.1249
CONSTANT	46.212	10.91	4.236	0.001	0.750	0.0000	2.7360

```
 DURBIN-WATSON = 1.8372    VON NEUMANN RATIO = 1.9291    RHO =  0.07059
 RESIDUAL SUM = -0.14433E-14  RESIDUAL VARIANCE =    4.4253
 SUM OF ABSOLUTE ERRORS=    30.749
 R-SQUARE BETWEEN OBSERVED AND PREDICTED = 0.8261
 RUNS TEST:   10 RUNS,   11 POS,    0 ZERO,   10 NEG  NORMAL STATISTIC = -0.6626

 |_OLS W2 LAGP LAGK LAGX YEAR T G / RSTAT


 OLS ESTIMATION
      21 OBSERVATIONS      DEPENDENT VARIABLE = W2
 ...NOTE..SAMPLE RANGE SET TO:    2,   22


  R-SQUARE =    0.9648    R-SQUARE ADJUSTED =    0.9497
 VARIANCE OF THE ESTIMATE-SIGMA**2 =   2.8741
 STANDARD ERROR OF THE ESTIMATE-SIGMA =    1.6953
 SUM OF SQUARED ERRORS-SSE=    40.237
 MEAN OF DEPENDENT VARIABLE =    41.481
 LOG OF THE LIKELIHOOD FUNCTION = -36.6255
```

VARIABLE NAME	ESTIMATED COEFFICIENT	STANDARD ERROR	T-RATIO 14 DF	P-VALUE	PARTIAL CORR.	STANDARDIZED COEFFICIENT	ELASTICITY AT MEANS
LAGP	0.82083	0.3601	2.279	0.039	0.520	0.4376	0.3241
LAGK	-0.14411	0.5435E-01	-2.652	0.019	-0.578	-0.1892	-0.6966
LAGX	0.11759	0.2045	0.5750	0.574	0.152	0.1388	0.1644
YEAR	0.88073	0.1249	7.054	0.000	0.883	0.7233	0.2336
T	-0.57119	0.3160	-1.807	0.092	-0.435	-0.1536	-0.0937
G	0.85941	0.3028	2.838	0.013	0.604	0.2710	0.0993
CONSTANT	40.192	8.791	4.572	0.000	0.774	0.0000	0.9689

```
 DURBIN-WATSON = 2.3832    VON NEUMANN RATIO = 2.5024    RHO = -0.23229
 RESIDUAL SUM =  0.26201E-12  RESIDUAL VARIANCE =    2.8741
 SUM OF ABSOLUTE ERRORS=    24.551
 R-SQUARE BETWEEN OBSERVED AND PREDICTED = 0.9648
 RUNS TEST:   12 RUNS,   10 POS,    0 ZERO,   11 NEG  NORMAL STATISTIC =  0.2351
```

```
|_OLS X LAGP LAGK LAGX YEAR T G / RSTAT

 OLS ESTIMATION
     21 OBSERVATIONS       DEPENDENT VARIABLE = X
...NOTE..SAMPLE RANGE SET TO:    2,   22


 R-SQUARE =   0.9178    R-SQUARE ADJUSTED =   0.8826
VARIANCE OF THE ESTIMATE-SIGMA**2 =   13.237
STANDARD ERROR OF THE ESTIMATE-SIGMA =   3.6382
SUM OF SQUARED ERRORS-SSE=   185.31
MEAN OF DEPENDENT VARIABLE =    60.057
LOG OF THE LIKELIHOOD FUNCTION = -52.6616
```

VARIABLE NAME	ESTIMATED COEFFICIENT	STANDARD ERROR	T-RATIO 14 DF	P-VALUE	PARTIAL CORR.	STANDARDIZED COEFFICIENT	ELASTICITY AT MEANS
LAGP	1.7225	0.7729	2.229	0.043	0.512	0.6535	0.4697
LAGK	-0.31915	0.1166	-2.736	0.016	-0.590	-0.2981	-1.0654
LAGX	0.96390E-01	0.4389	0.2196	0.829	0.059	0.0810	0.0931
YEAR	0.87574	0.2679	3.268	0.006	0.658	0.5118	0.1604
T	-0.55827	0.6782	-0.8231	0.424	-0.215	-0.1068	-0.0633
G	1.3116	0.6498	2.018	0.063	0.475	0.2944	0.1047
CONSTANT	78.124	18.87	4.141	0.001	0.742	0.0000	1.3008

```
DURBIN-WATSON = 2.0436    VON NEUMANN RATIO = 2.1457    RHO = -0.04388
RESIDUAL SUM =  0.54845E-13  RESIDUAL VARIANCE =   13.237
SUM OF ABSOLUTE ERRORS=   51.664
R-SQUARE BETWEEN OBSERVED AND PREDICTED = 0.9178
RUNS TEST:   10 RUNS,   11 POS,   0 ZERO,   10 NEG  NORMAL STATISTIC = -0.6626
```

The 2SLS estimations using the same set of six exogenous variables follow.

```
|_2SLS C P W2 LAGP (LAGP LAGK LAGX YEAR T G)
 TWO STAGE LEAST SQUARES - DEPENDENT VARIABLE = C
   6 EXOGENOUS VARIABLES
   3 POSSIBLE ENDOGENOUS VARIABLES
      21 OBSERVATIONS


 R-SQUARE =   0.9767     R-SQUARE ADJUSTED =   0.9726
VARIANCE OF THE ESTIMATE-SIGMA**2 =   1.2905
STANDARD ERROR OF THE ESTIMATE-SIGMA =   1.1360
SUM OF SQUARED ERRORS-SSE=   21.938
MEAN OF DEPENDENT VARIABLE =   53.995
```

VARIABLE NAME	ESTIMATED COEFFICIENT	STANDARD ERROR	T-RATIO 17 DF	P-VALUE	PARTIAL CORR.	STANDARDIZED COEFFICIENT	ELASTICITY AT MEANS
P	0.16946E-01	0.1313	0.1291	0.899	0.031	0.0104	0.0053
W2	0.81037	0.4476E-01	18.11	0.000	0.975	0.8925	0.6226
LAGP	0.21632	0.1193	1.814	0.087	0.403	0.1270	0.0656
CONSTANT	16.552	1.469	11.27	0.000	0.939	0.0000	0.3065

```
|_2SLS I P LAGP LAGK (LAGP LAGK LAGX YEAR T G)
 TWO STAGE LEAST SQUARES - DEPENDENT VARIABLE = I
   6 EXOGENOUS VARIABLES
   2 POSSIBLE ENDOGENOUS VARIABLES
      21 OBSERVATIONS
```

```
R-SQUARE =    0.8846    R-SQUARE ADJUSTED =    0.8643
VARIANCE OF THE ESTIMATE-SIGMA**2 =    1.7124
STANDARD ERROR OF THE ESTIMATE-SIGMA =    1.3086
SUM OF SQUARED ERRORS-SSE=   29.111
MEAN OF DEPENDENT VARIABLE =    1.2667
```

VARIABLE NAME	ESTIMATED COEFFICIENT	STANDARD ERROR	T-RATIO 17 DF	P-VALUE	PARTIAL CORR.	STANDARDIZED COEFFICIENT	ELASTICITY AT MEANS
P	0.14932	0.1928	0.7746	0.449	0.185	0.1774	1.9911
LAGP	0.61672	0.1811	3.405	0.003	0.637	0.6994	7.9733
LAGK	-0.15791	0.4020E-01	-3.928	0.001	-0.690	-0.4410	-24.9955
CONSTANT	20.306	8.393	2.419	0.027	0.506	0.0000	16.0311

```
|_2SLS W X LAGX YEAR (LAGP LAGK LAGX YEAR T G)
 TWO STAGE LEAST SQUARES - DEPENDENT VARIABLE = W
   6 EXOGENOUS VARIABLES
   2 POSSIBLE ENDOGENOUS VARIABLES
      21 OBSERVATIONS


 R-SQUARE =    0.9874    R-SQUARE ADJUSTED =    0.9852
VARIANCE OF THE ESTIMATE-SIGMA**2 =    0.58854
STANDARD ERROR OF THE ESTIMATE-SIGMA =    0.76716
SUM OF SQUARED ERRORS-SSE=   10.005
MEAN OF DEPENDENT VARIABLE =    36.362
```

VARIABLE NAME	ESTIMATED COEFFICIENT	STANDARD ERROR	T-RATIO 17 DF	P-VALUE	PARTIAL CORR.	STANDARDIZED COEFFICIENT	ELASTICITY AT MEANS
X	0.43864	0.3961E-01	11.07	0.000	0.937	0.7387	0.7245
LAGX	0.14688	0.4317E-01	3.402	0.003	0.636	0.2078	0.2342
YEAR	0.13045	0.3239E-01	4.028	0.001	0.699	0.1284	0.0395
CONSTANT	0.66518E-01	1.153	0.5767E-01	0.955	0.014	0.0000	0.0018

The above *Klein Model I* is frequently used to illustrate simultaneous equation estimations. However, there is some controversy surrounding the list of variables considered exogenous. The generally used method includes seven exogenous variables in the 2SLS estimation (W2 being considered exogenous). For more details, see H. Theil's *Principles of Econometrics*, (Wiley, 1971).

SHAZAM commands and options used in Chapter 20

2SLS *depvar indeps* (*exogs*) / *options*
GEN1 *newvar=equation*
GENR *newvar=equation* with **LAG**(x) **SQRT**(x)
MATRIX *newmat=equation*
OLS *depvar indeps* / **COEF= PREDICT= RESID= RSTAT STDERR=**
PRINT *vars* / *options*
READ(*datafile*) *vars* / *options*
SAMPLE *beg end*
TIME *beg freq*
? Suppression of Output

Temporary variables used

$N	Number of observations in the estimation
$SIG2	Variance of the Estimate - **SIGMA****2
$K	Number of Coefficients

21. TIME SERIES ECONOMETRICS I: STATIONARITY, UNIT ROOTS AND COINTEGRATION

The initial focus of *Chapter 21* is on the concept of stationarity in time series data and the methods available to test for it. As *Section 21.2* notes, a time series is said to be stationary if its mean, variance, and autocovariance (at various lags) are constant throughout the sample period.

Figure 21.1 (and *Figure 21.5* ahead) were replicated using GNUPLOT, a graphics program interfaced with SHAZAM. For details on GNUPLOT, see the *SHAZAM User's Reference Manual.*

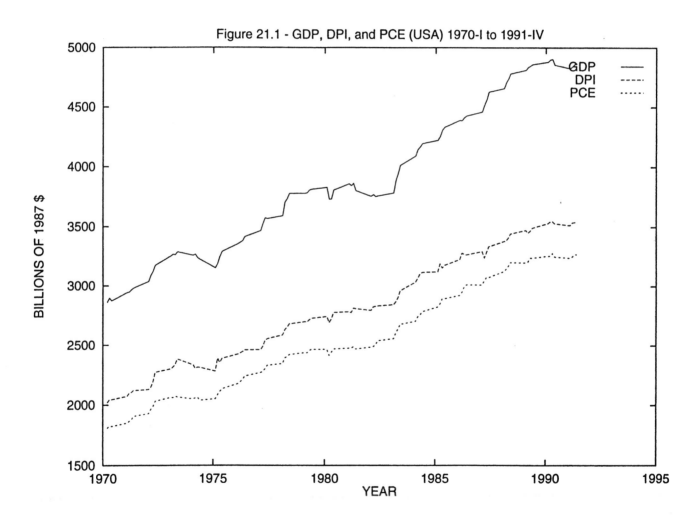

Figure 21.1 - GDP, DPI, and PCE (USA) 1970-I to 1991-IV

As the text notes, the time series plotted in *Figure 21.1* all trend upwards. It appears that these time series are non-stationary. The tests that follow confirm this initial conclusion.

Section 21.3 shows how to test for stationarity based on the sample autocorrelation function (ACF). The **ARIMA** command can be used to compute the ACF, plot the correlogram, and print the Ljung-Box statistic described in equation (21.3.6).

The **ARIMA** Command

The **ARIMA** command provides features for the Box-Jenkins approach to the analysis of **A**uto**R**egressive **I**ntegrated **M**oving **A**verage models of univariate time series (see *Section 22.3*). The general format of the **ARIMA** command is:

ARIMA *var* / *options*

where *var* is a time series variable and *options* is a list of desired options.

Note that the **ARIMA** command is not available with the student version of SHAZAM, SHAZY.

The **PLOTAC** option with the **ARIMA** command **PLOT**s the **A**uto**C**orrelation function (i.e. the correlogram)Correlogram The number of lags to be considered is specified using the **NLAG=** option. The default is 24. Note that high quality plots of the correlogram can be made using GNUPLOT (see Chapter 22 for an example).

For a time series z_t, $t=1,\ldots,N$ with sample mean $\bar{z}$ the sample autocovariances are:

$$c_j = \frac{1}{N} \sum_{t=j+1}^{N} \left[(z_t - \bar{z})(z_{t-j} - \bar{z}) \right] \quad j=0,1,2,\ldots \tag{21.3.2}$$

The sample autocorrelations at lag j are:

$$r_j = c_j/c_0 \quad j=1,2,\ldots \tag{21.3.4}$$

A plot of the r_j gives the sample correlogram.

In the text, the confidence bounds printed with the ACF correlogram are constructed based on the variance of the autocorrelations using the formula $1/N$ where N is the sample size. This assumes that the autocorrelations are individually equal to zero (which is not the case for this example). SHAZAM plots confidence intervals for the ACF computing the variance as follows:

$$\left(1 + 2\sum_{j=1}^{q} r_j^2\right) / N$$

Note that, if the sample autocorrelations are indeed zero, the formula becomes $1/N$. If the plotted autocorrelations exceed these confidence bounds, it can be concluded that the model exhibits higher order-autocorrelation.

Judge *et al.* state that confidence bounds computing the variance based on the formula $1/N$ are appropriate for the *partial* autocorrelations (*Introduction to the Theory and Practice of Econometrics, Second Edition*, Wiley, 1988, p. 683). In fact, SHAZAM does this when plotting the correlogram for the partial autocorrelation function (see Chapter 22).

The following commands replicate the correlogram printed in *Figure 21.4*.

```
TIME 1970 4
SAMPLE 1970.1 1991.4
READ(TABLE21.1) PERIOD GDP DPI PCE PROFITS DIVIDEND
ARIMA GDP / PLOTAC NLAG=25
```

The output follows.

```
|_ARIMA GDP / PLOTAC NLAG=25
     ARIMA MODEL
NUMBER OF OBSERVATIONS =   88
...NOTE..SAMPLE RANGE SET TO:      1,      88

     IDENTIFICATION SECTION - VARIABLE=GDP
NUMBER OF AUTOCORRELATIONS =   25
NUMBER OF PARTIAL AUTOCORRELATIONS =   12

SERIES  (1-B) (1-B  )  GDP

  NET NUMBER OF OBSERVATIONS =    88
MEAN=     3865.6        VARIANCE=    0.39694E+06    STANDARD DEV.=      630.03

  LAGS                      AUTOCORRELATIONS                          STD ERR
  1 -12    0.97 0.94 0.90 0.87 0.83 0.79 0.75 0.71 0.67 0.64 0.60 0.57   0.11
 13 -24    0.53 0.50 0.47 0.44 0.41 0.37 0.34 0.31 0.28 0.25 0.21 0.18   0.42
 25 -25    0.15                                                          0.46

MODIFIED BOX-PIERCE (LJUNG-BOX-PIERCE) STATISTICS  (CHI-SQUARE)
    LAG    Q     DF  P-VALUE        LAG    Q     DF  P-VALUE
     1   85.46   1   .000          13   731.56  13   .000
     2  166.02   2   .000          14   758.29  14   .000
     3  241.72   3   .000          15   782.02  15   .000
     4  312.39   4   .000          16   803.03  16   .000
     5  378.10   5   .000          17   821.35  17   .000
     6  438.57   6   .000          18   837.24  18   .000
     7  493.85   7   .000          19   850.79  19   .000
```

```
   8   544.11    8   .000        20   862.17   20   .000
   9   589.77    9   .000        21   871.39   21   .000
  10   631.12   10   .000        22   878.65   22   .000
  11   668.33   11   .000        23   884.22   23   .000
  12   701.65   12   .000        24   888.31   24   .000
                                 25   891.25   25   .000

  LAGS                    PARTIAL AUTOCORRELATIONS                    STD ERR
  1 -12    0.97 -.06 -.02 -.05 -.02 -.06 -.03 -.02 0.01 -.01 -.02 -.01    0.11


                                                    0      0 0
AUTOCORRELATION FUNCTION OF THE SERIES      (1-B) (1-B )   GDP

  1 0.97 .                           +      RRRRRRRRRRRRRRRRRRRRRRRRRRRRRRRR.
  2 0.94 .                       +          RRRRRRRRRRRRRRRRRRRRRRRRRRRRRRRR .
  3 0.90 .                     +            RRRRRRRRRRRRRRRRRRRRRRRRRRRRRRR  .
  4 0.87 .                   +              RRRRRRRRRRRRRRRRRRRRRRRRRRRRRR   .
  5 0.83 .                 +                RRRRRRRRRRRRRRRRRRRRRRRRRRRRR    .
  6 0.79 .               +                  RRRRRRRRRRRRRRRRRRRRRRRRRRRR     .
  7 0.75 .              +                   RRRRRRRRRRRRRRRRRRRRRRRRRRR      .
  8 0.71 .            +                     RRRRRRRRRRRRRRRRRRRRRRRRR+       .
  9 0.67 .           +                      RRRRRRRRRRRRRRRRRRRRRRRR  +      .
 10 0.64 .          +                       RRRRRRRRRRRRRRRRRRRRRRR    +     .
 11 0.60 .          +                       RRRRRRRRRRRRRRRRRRRRR      +     .
 12 0.57 .        +                         RRRRRRRRRRRRRRRRRRRR       +     .
 13 0.53 .       +                          RRRRRRRRRRRRRRRRRR          +    .
 14 0.50 .       +                          RRRRRRRRRRRRRRRRR           +    .
 15 0.47 .     +                            RRRRRRRRRRRRRRRR             +   .
 16 0.44 .     +                            RRRRRRRRRRRRRRR              +   .
 17 0.41 .     +                            RRRRRRRRRRRRRR               +   .
 18 0.37 .   +                              RRRRRRRRRRRRR                 +  .
 19 0.34 .   +                              RRRRRRRRRRRR                  +  .
 20 0.31 .   +                              RRRRRRRRRRR                   +  .
 21 0.28 .   +                              RRRRRRRRR                     +  .
 22 0.25 .   +                              RRRRRRRR                      +  .
 23 0.21 .   +                              RRRRRRR                        + .
 24 0.18 . +                                RRRRRR                         +.
 25 0.15 . +                                RRRRR                          +.
```

The output shows that the sample ACF declines slowly at higher lags indicating that the GDP time series is not stationary. In fact, the ACF exceeds the 95% confidence bounds (denoted with "+") for the first seven quarters implying that the model exhibits higher-order autocorrelation. In addition, Ljung-Box statistic based on 25 lags (labelled LJUNG-BOX-PIERCE in the output) is clearly significant (p-value = 0). Hence, it can be concluded that the autocorrelations are not jointly equal to zero.

Section 21.4 introduces another method used for testing for stationarity, the Dickey-Fuller (DF) unit root test.Unit RootsThe **COINT** command can be used to compute the various forms of the DF unit root tests described in this section.

The **COINT** Command

The **COINT** command implements tests for unit roots and **COINT**egration including Dickey-Fuller unit root tests, Phillips-Perron unit root tests, and tests on the residuals of a cointegrating regression. The general format of the **COINT** command is:

COINT *vars* / *options*

where *vars* is a list of variable names and *options* is a list of desired options.

The text describes four different forms of DF tests in equations (21.4.3), (21.4.5), (21.4.6), and (21.4.7). The **COINT** command uses the following forms of the "augmented" Dickey-Fuller (ADF) regressions:

$$(1) \quad \Delta Y_t = \alpha_o + \alpha_1 Y_{t-1} + \sum_{j=1}^{p} \gamma_j \Delta Y_{t-j} + \varepsilon_t$$

$$(2) \quad \Delta Y_t = \alpha_o + \alpha_1 Y_{t-1} + \alpha_2 t + \sum_{j=1}^{p} \gamma_j \Delta Y_{t-j} + \varepsilon_t$$

where ε_t for $t = 1, \ldots, N$ is assumed to be Gaussian White Noise. Equation (1) is with-constant, no-trend and (2) is with-constant, with-trend. The number of lagged terms p is set to the highest significant lag order (using an approximate 95% confidence interval) from either the autocorrelation function or the partial autocorrelation function. The **NLAG=** option with the **COINT** command is used to over-ride this default and specify the number of lags to be considered in the ADF regressions.

Note that the two ADF regressions above are generalized forms of the DF regression forms described in the text. For example, a DF regression without a time trend and no lagged ΔY_{t-j} terms (i.e. the "non-augmented" DF regression) in the right-hand side of the equation can be estimated by setting the number of lags for the ΔY_{t-j} terms to zero using the **NLAG=** option. Hence, the ΔY_{t-j} term drops out and equation (1) above becomes equivalent to equation (21.4.3).

The focus of the various DF regressions reported in the text is on the t-ratio for the lagged dependent variable, Y_{t-1}. If the coefficient for Y_{t-1} equals zero, the time series Y is non-stationary. That is, it can be concluded that a unit root exists.

In the **COINT** output, the t-ratio in question is defined as "A(1)=0 T-TEST." In addition, SHAZAM reports the appropriate asymptotic τ (*tau*) critical values at a 10% level of significance. The **SIGLEVEL=** option on the **COINT** command can be used to over-ride this default and specify 1% or 5% levels of significance for the critical values.

First, the DF tests in *Section 21.4* will be performed using the **OLS** command. Since the first observation of the lagged *GDP* variable is undefined, this observation must be dropped from the sample range. (When the **COINT** command is used, the necessary number of observations are automatically dropped).

```
GENR LAGGDP=LAG(GDP)
GENR DGDP=GDP-LAGGDP
GENR LAGDGDP=LAG(DGDP)
SAMPLE 1970.2 1991.4
GENR T=TIME(0)
* Estimate equation (21.4.8) (i.e. the DF regression without a time trend).
OLS DGDP LAGGDP / RSTAT
* Estimate equation (21.4.9) (i.e. the DF regression with a time trend).
OLS DGDP T LAGGDP / RSTAT
* Estimate the augmented Dickey-Fuller regression (ADF) equation (21.4.10).
SAMPLE 1970.3 1991.4
OLS DGDP T LAGGDP LAGDGDP / RSTAT
* Although it is not done in the text, estimate another ADF equation but
* omit the time trend from (21.4.10).
OLS DGDP LAGGDP LAGDGDP / RSTAT
```

The output follows.

```
|_SAMPLE 1970.2 1991.4
|_* Estimate equation (21.4.8) (i.e. the DF regression without a time trend).

|_OLS DGDP LAGGDP / RSTAT

 OLS ESTIMATION
       87 OBSERVATIONS      DEPENDENT VARIABLE = DGDP
...NOTE..SAMPLE RANGE SET TO:    2,    88

 R-SQUARE =    0.0006    R-SQUARE ADJUSTED =  -0.0112
VARIANCE OF THE ESTIMATE-SIGMA**2 =    1305.7
STANDARD ERROR OF THE ESTIMATE-SIGMA =    36.135
SUM OF SQUARED ERRORS-SSE= 0.11099E+06
MEAN OF DEPENDENT VARIABLE =    22.933
LOG OF THE LIKELIHOOD FUNCTION = -434.528

VARIABLE     ESTIMATED    STANDARD    T-RATIO        PARTIAL STANDARDIZED ELASTICITY
  NAME      COEFFICIENT    ERROR       85 DF    P-VALUE CORR. COEFFICIENT  AT MEANS
LAGGDP     -0.13679E-02 0.6242E-02  -0.2192      0.827-0.024    -0.0238     -0.2299
CONSTANT    28.205       24.37        1.158      0.250 0.125     0.0000      1.2299
```

```
DURBIN-WATSON = 1.3520    VON NEUMANN RATIO = 1.3677    RHO =  0.31747
RESIDUAL SUM = -0.65370E-12  RESIDUAL VARIANCE =   1305.7
SUM OF ABSOLUTE ERRORS=   2289.6
R-SQUARE BETWEEN OBSERVED AND PREDICTED = 0.0006
RUNS TEST:   29 RUNS,   47 POS,    0 ZERO,   40 NEG  NORMAL STATISTIC = -3.3039
|_* Estimate equation (21.4.9) (i.e. the DF regression with a time trend).

|_OLS DGDP T LAGGDP / RSTAT

  OLS ESTIMATION
       87 OBSERVATIONS    DEPENDENT VARIABLE = DGDP
...NOTE..SAMPLE RANGE SET TO:    2,   88

  R-SQUARE =    0.0305    R-SQUARE ADJUSTED =    0.0074
VARIANCE OF THE ESTIMATE-SIGMA**2 =    1281.7
STANDARD ERROR OF THE ESTIMATE-SIGMA =   35.801
SUM OF SQUARED ERRORS-SSE=  0.10766E+06
MEAN OF DEPENDENT VARIABLE =    22.933
LOG OF THE LIKELIHOOD FUNCTION = -433.204

VARIABLE    ESTIMATED   STANDARD    T-RATIO        PARTIAL STANDARDIZED ELASTICITY
  NAME      COEFFICIENT   ERROR      84 DF    P-VALUE CORR. COEFFICIENT  AT MEANS
T            1.4776      0.9172      1.611    0.111 0.173     1.0386      2.8994
LAGGDP      -0.60317E-01 0.3711E-01 -1.625    0.108-0.175    -1.0479    -10.1366
CONSTANT     188.91      102.6       1.841    0.069 0.197     0.0000      8.2372

DURBIN-WATSON = 1.3147    VON NEUMANN RATIO = 1.3300    RHO =  0.33755
RESIDUAL SUM =  0.28422E-12  RESIDUAL VARIANCE =   1281.7
SUM OF ABSOLUTE ERRORS=   2273.3
R-SQUARE BETWEEN OBSERVED AND PREDICTED = 0.0305
RUNS TEST:   29 RUNS,   48 POS,    0 ZERO,   39 NEG  NORMAL STATISTIC = -3.2781
|_* Estimate the augmented Dickey-Fuller regression (ADF) equation (21.4.10).
|_SAMPLE 1970.3 1991.4

|_OLS DGDP T LAGGDP LAGDGDP / RSTAT

  OLS ESTIMATION
       86 OBSERVATIONS    DEPENDENT VARIABLE = DGDP
...NOTE..SAMPLE RANGE SET TO:    3,   88

  R-SQUARE =    0.1526    R-SQUARE ADJUSTED =    0.1216
VARIANCE OF THE ESTIMATE-SIGMA**2 =    1134.5
STANDARD ERROR OF THE ESTIMATE-SIGMA =   33.682
SUM OF SQUARED ERRORS-SSE=   93026.
MEAN OF DEPENDENT VARIABLE =    23.345
LOG OF THE LIKELIHOOD FUNCTION = -422.439

VARIABLE    ESTIMATED   STANDARD    T-RATIO        PARTIAL STANDARDIZED ELASTICITY
  NAME      COEFFICIENT   ERROR      82 DF    P-VALUE CORR. COEFFICIENT  AT MEANS
T            1.8922      0.8792      2.152    0.034 0.231     1.3147      3.6879
LAGGDP      -0.78661E-01 0.3551E-01 -2.215    0.030-0.238    -1.3543    -13.0246
LAGDGDP      0.35579     0.1027      3.465    0.001 0.357     0.3573      0.3526
CONSTANT     233.08      97.73       2.385    0.019 0.255     0.0000      9.9840

DURBIN-WATSON = 2.0859    VON NEUMANN RATIO = 2.1104    RHO = -0.04912
RESIDUAL SUM = -0.28670E-11  RESIDUAL VARIANCE =   1134.5
SUM OF ABSOLUTE ERRORS=   2085.1
```

```
R-SQUARE BETWEEN OBSERVED AND PREDICTED = 0.1526
RUNS TEST:   48 RUNS,   49 POS,    0 ZERO,   37 NEG  NORMAL STATISTIC = 1.0705
|_* Although it is not done in the text, estimate another ADF equation but
|_* omit the time trend from (21.4.10).

|_OLS DGDP LAGGDP LAGDGDP / RSTAT

OLS ESTIMATION
      86 OBSERVATIONS      DEPENDENT VARIABLE = DGDP
...NOTE..SAMPLE RANGE SET TO:    3,    88

 R-SQUARE =    0.1047    R-SQUARE ADJUSTED =    0.0832
VARIANCE OF THE ESTIMATE-SIGMA**2 =   1184.1
STANDARD ERROR OF THE ESTIMATE-SIGMA =   34.411
SUM OF SQUARED ERRORS-SSE=   98281.
MEAN OF DEPENDENT VARIABLE =   23.345
LOG OF THE LIKELIHOOD FUNCTION = -424.802


VARIABLE   ESTIMATED   STANDARD   T-RATIO        PARTIAL STANDARDIZED ELASTICITY
  NAME     COEFFICIENT   ERROR      83 DF    P-VALUE CORR. COEFFICIENT AT MEANS
LAGGDP    -0.33039E-02 0.6038E-02 -0.5472     0.586-0.060    -0.0569    -0.5471
LAGDGDP    0.31971     0.1035      3.089      0.003 0.321     0.3211     0.3169
CONSTANT   28.719      23.65       1.214      0.228 0.132     0.0000     1.2302


DURBIN-WATSON = 2.0405    VON NEUMANN RATIO = 2.0646    RHO = -0.02362
RESIDUAL SUM = -0.37659E-12  RESIDUAL VARIANCE =   1184.1
SUM OF ABSOLUTE ERRORS=   2127.9
R-SQUARE BETWEEN OBSERVED AND PREDICTED = 0.1047
RUNS TEST:   40 RUNS,   50 POS,    0 ZERO,   36 NEG  NORMAL STATISTIC = -0.6377
```

The output shows that the t-ratios testing the hypothesis that $\delta = 0$ (i.e. the coefficients for GDP_{t-1} are all below the τ critical values). Hence, it can be concluded that the GDP time series exhibits a unit root and is thus non-stationary. This confirms the conclusion based on the correlogram above.

The **COINT** command will now be used to perform the above DF and ADF tests. Note, as mentioned above, that the **COINT** command automatically sets the sample range to drop the undefined observations. Since equations (21.4.8) and (21.4.9) are not ADF regressions, the **NLAG=** option is set to zero so that the ΔY_{t-j} term is dropped from the regressions.

```
SAMPLE 1970.1 1991.4
* The DF regressions equivalent to equation (21.4.8) and (21.4.9).
COINT GDP / NLAG=0
* The ADF regressions equivalent to (21.4.10) and the added regression.
COINT GDP / NLAG=1
```

The output follows.

```
|_SAMPLE 1970.1 1991.4
* The DF regressions equivalent to equation (21.4.8) and (21.4.9).

|_COINT GDP / NLAG=0
...NOTE..SAMPLE RANGE SET TO:      1,     88


TOTAL NUMBER OF OBSERVATIONS =    88


VARIABLE : GDP
DICKEY-FULLER TESTS - NO.LAGS =   0    NO.OBS =    87

      NULL              TEST        ASY. CRITICAL
    HYPOTHESIS        STATISTIC      VALUE 10%
------------------------------------------------------------------
CONSTANT, NO TREND
A(1)=0  Z-TEST       -0.11901       -11.2
A(1)=0  T-TEST       -0.21916       -2.57
A(0)=A(1)=0           17.545         3.78
                                          AIC =      7.197
                                          SC =       7.254
------------------------------------------------------------------
CONSTANT, TREND
A(1)=0  Z-TEST       -5.2476        -18.2
A(1)=0  T-TEST       -1.6253        -3.13
A(0)=A(1)=A(2)=0      12.781         4.03
A(1)=A(2)=0           1.3221         5.34
                                          AIC =      7.190
                                          SC =       7.275
------------------------------------------------------------------

|_* The ADF regressions equivalent to (21.4.10) and the added regression.

|_COINT GDP / NLAG=1
...NOTE..SAMPLE RANGE SET TO:      1,     88


TOTAL NUMBER OF OBSERVATIONS =    88


VARIABLE : GDP
DICKEY-FULLER TESTS - NO.LAGS =   1    NO.OBS =    86

      NULL              TEST        ASY. CRITICAL
    HYPOTHESIS        STATISTIC      VALUE 10%
------------------------------------------------------------------
CONSTANT, NO TREND
A(1)=0  T-TEST       -0.54721       -2.57
A(0)=A(1)=0           6.7200         3.78
                                          AIC =      7.111
                                          SC =       7.197
------------------------------------------------------------------
CONSTANT, TREND
A(1)=0  T-TEST       -2.2153        -3.13
A(0)=A(1)=A(2)=0      6.2201         4.03
A(1)=A(2)=0           2.4724         5.34
                                          AIC =      7.079
                                          SC =       7.193
------------------------------------------------------------------
```

Note that the T-TEST values reported for the hypothesis A(1)=0 are identical to the t-ratios computed for the coefficients for the GDP_{t-1} variable in the above regressions. The appropriate τ critical values at the 10% level of significance are reported in the next column.

The commands below test if the first-differenced GDP series (ΔGDP) is stationary. First, the ΔGDP series will be plotted using GNUPLOT.

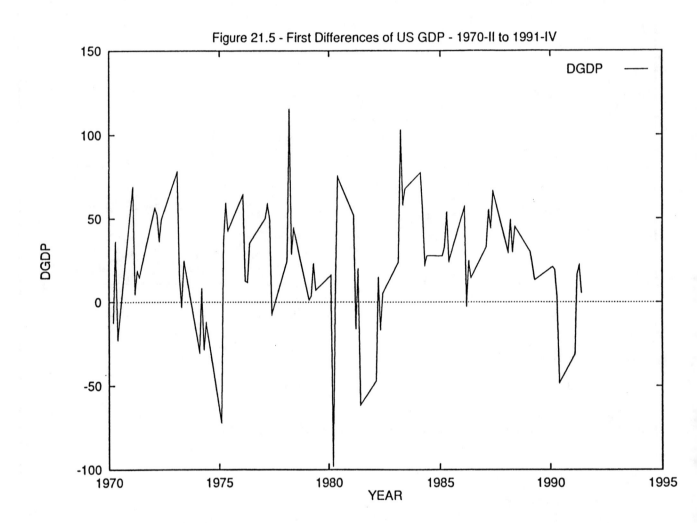

Figure 21.5 appears to indicate that the first-differenced GDP time series is stationary. This conclusion will be tested using DF regressions.

The **SIGLEVEL=** option is set to 1 so that the τ critical values at the 1% (instead of 10%) level of significance are reported. Again, since the ΔY_{t-j} term is dropped from the ADF regression (i.e. the non-augmented DF regression is run), **NLAG=** is set to zero.

```
* Estimate equation (21.4.11).
GENR DDGDP=DGDP-LAGDGDP
SAMPLE 1970.3 1991.4
OLS DDGDP LAGDGDP
* Perform the DF tests using the COINT command.
SAMPLE 1970.2 1991.0
COINT DGDP / NLAG=0 SIGLEVEL=1
```

The output follows.

```
|_* Estimate equation (21.4.11).
|_GENR DDGDP=DGDP-LAGDGDP
|_SAMPLE 1970.3 1991.4
|_OLS DDGDP LAGDGDP

 OLS ESTIMATION
      86 OBSERVATIONS        DEPENDENT VARIABLE = DDGDP


 R-SQUARE =   0.3436     R-SQUARE ADJUSTED =   0.3357
VARIANCE OF THE ESTIMATE-SIGMA**2 =    1174.2
STANDARD ERROR OF THE ESTIMATE-SIGMA =  34.267
SUM OF SQUARED ERRORS-SSE=   98636.
MEAN OF DEPENDENT VARIABLE =  0.20698
LOG OF THE LIKELIHOOD FUNCTION = -424.957


VARIABLE   ESTIMATED   STANDARD   T-RATIO         PARTIAL STANDARDIZED ELASTICITY
  NAME     COEFFICIENT   ERROR      84 DF   P-VALUE CORR. COEFFICIENT  AT MEANS
LAGDGDP   -0.68276     0.1030    -6.630     0.000-0.586   -0.5861    -76.3274
CONSTANT   16.005      4.397      3.640     0.000 0.369    0.0000     77.3274
|_* Perform the DF tests using the COINT command.
|_SAMPLE 1970.2 1991.4
|_COINT DGDP / NLAG=0 SIGLEVEL=1
...NOTE..SAMPLE RANGE SET TO:      2,     88


TOTAL NUMBER OF OBSERVATIONS =    87


VARIABLE : DGDP
DICKEY-FULLER TESTS - NO.LAGS =    0   NO.OBS =    86


      NULL            TEST      ASY. CRITICAL
   HYPOTHESIS       STATISTIC    VALUE  1%
-------------------------------------------------------------------------
CONSTANT, NO TREND
A(1)=0  Z-TEST       -58.718     -20.6
A(1)=0  T-TEST       -6.6303      -3.43
A(0)=A(1)=0           21.982       6.43
                                            AIC =     7.091
                                            SC =      7.148

-------------------------------------------------------------------------
CONSTANT, TREND
A(1)=0  Z-TEST       -58.691     -29.4
A(1)=0  T-TEST       -6.5884      -3.96
A(0)=A(1)=A(2)=0      14.498       6.09
A(1)=A(2)=0           21.746       8.27
                                            AIC =     7.114
                                            SC =      7.200
-------------------------------------------------------------------------
```

Again, note that, in the regression with CONSTANT, NO TREND, the T-TEST value testing the hypothesis A(1)=0, -6.6303, is identical to the t-ratio for the coefficient for $DGDP_{t-1}$ in equation (21.4.11). Furthermore, since it is below the τ 1% critical value, it can be concluded that the first-differenced GDP series is stationary.

Section 21.6 examines the problem of spurious regressions which may result when a time series variable is regressed on another time series variable. Despite a high R^2 statistic, no meaningful relationship may exist between the variables.

As an example of a potentially spurious regression, from *Table 21*, personal consumption expenditure (*PCE*) is regressed on personal disposable income (*DPI*) (equation 21.6.1).

```
* Equation (21.6.1).
SAMPLE 1970.1 1991.4
OLS PCE DPI / RSTAT
```

The output follows.

```
|_* Equation (21.6.1).
|_SAMPLE 1970.1 1991.4
|_OLS PCE DPI / RSTAT

 OLS ESTIMATION
      88 OBSERVATIONS      DEPENDENT VARIABLE = PCE

 R-SQUARE =   0.9941    R-SQUARE ADJUSTED =   0.9940
VARIANCE OF THE ESTIMATE-SIGMA**2 =   1290.8
STANDARD ERROR OF THE ESTIMATE-SIGMA =   35.928
SUM OF SQUARED ERRORS-SSE=  0.11101E+06
MEAN OF DEPENDENT VARIABLE =   2537.0
LOG OF THE LIKELIHOOD FUNCTION = -439.029


VARIABLE    ESTIMATED   STANDARD   T-RATIO       PARTIAL STANDARDIZED ELASTICITY
  NAME      COEFFICIENT  ERROR      86 DF    P-VALUE CORR. COEFFICIENT  AT MEANS
DPI         0.96725     0.8069E-02  119.9    0.000 0.997     0.9970      1.0676
CONSTANT   -171.44      22.92       -7.481   0.000-0.628     0.0000     -0.0676


DURBIN-WATSON = 0.5316    VON NEUMANN RATIO = 0.5377    RHO =  0.72469
RESIDUAL SUM =  0.20048E-10  RESIDUAL VARIANCE =   1290.8
SUM OF ABSOLUTE ERRORS=   2439.8
R-SQUARE BETWEEN OBSERVED AND PREDICTED = 0.9941
RUNS TEST:   17 RUNS,   50 POS,   0 ZERO,   38 NEG  NORMAL STATISTIC = -5.9405
```

As the text notes, the results appear to be "fabulous." The R^2 statistic is high as are the t-ratios. However, the Durbin-Watson statistic clearly indicates the problem of model misspecification.

The commands below test if the PCE and DPI series are stationary.

```
* Generate the first-difference variables for PCE and DPI.
GENR LAGPCE=LAG(PCE)
GENR LAGDPI=LAG(DPI)
GENR DPCE=PCE-LAGPCE
GENR DDPI=DPI-LAGDPI
SAMPLE 1970.2 1991.4
* Equation (21.6.2) (i.e. DF test with a time trend).
OLS DPCE T LAGPCE
* Equation (21.6.3) (i.e. DF test with a time trend).
OLS DDPI T LAGDPI
```

The output follows.

```
|_SAMPLE 1970.2 1991.4
|_* Equation (21.6.2) (i.e. DF test with a time trend).

|_OLS DPCE T LAGPCE

 OLS ESTIMATION
        87 OBSERVATIONS      DEPENDENT VARIABLE = DPCE
...NOTE..SAMPLE RANGE SET TO:    2,    88

 R-SQUARE =    0.0221     R-SQUARE ADJUSTED =   -0.0012
VARIANCE OF THE ESTIMATE-SIGMA**2 =    334.94
STANDARD ERROR OF THE ESTIMATE-SIGMA =    18.301
SUM OF SQUARED ERRORS-SSE=    28135.
MEAN OF DEPENDENT VARIABLE =    16.903
LOG OF THE LIKELIHOOD FUNCTION = -374.829
```

VARIABLE NAME	ESTIMATED COEFFICIENT	STANDARD ERROR	T-RATIO 84 DF	P-VALUE	PARTIAL CORR.	STANDARDIZED COEFFICIENT	ELASTICITY AT MEANS
T	0.79872	0.5871	1.360	0.177	0.147	1.1030	2.1263
LAGPCE	-0.44464E-01	0.3231E-01	-1.376	0.172	-0.148	-1.1157	-6.6514
CONSTANT	93.392	55.67	1.678	0.097	0.180	0.0000	5.5250

```
|_* Equation (21.6.3) (i.e. DF test with a time trend).

|_OLS DDPI T LAGDPI

 OLS ESTIMATION
        87 OBSERVATIONS      DEPENDENT VARIABLE = DDPI
...NOTE..SAMPLE RANGE SET TO:    2,    88

 R-SQUARE =    0.0757     R-SQUARE ADJUSTED =    0.0537
VARIANCE OF THE ESTIMATE-SIGMA**2 =    738.08
STANDARD ERROR OF THE ESTIMATE-SIGMA =    27.168
SUM OF SQUARED ERRORS-SSE=    61998.
MEAN OF DEPENDENT VARIABLE =    17.895
LOG OF THE LIKELIHOOD FUNCTION = -409.197
```

VARIABLE NAME	ESTIMATED COEFFICIENT	STANDARD ERROR	T-RATIO 84 DF	P-VALUE	PARTIAL CORR.	STANDARDIZED COEFFICIENT	ELASTICITY AT MEANS
T	2.8752	1.136	2.531	0.013	0.266	2.6003	7.2299
LAGDPI	-0.15694	0.6064E-01	-2.588	0.011	-0.272	-2.6594	-24.4822
CONSTANT	326.63	118.6	2.755	0.007	0.288	0.0000	18.2523

Again, the **COINT** command will be used to perform the above DF tests. As can be seen, using the **COINT** command is much easier than the "long way".

```
SAMPLE 1970.1 1991.4
COINT PCE DPI / NLAG=0
```

The output follows.

```
|_SAMPLE 1970.1 1991.4
|_COINT PCE DPI / NLAG=0
...NOTE..SAMPLE RANGE SET TO:    1,    88


TOTAL NUMBER OF OBSERVATIONS =   88


VARIABLE : PCE
DICKEY-FULLER TESTS - NO.LAGS =   0   NO.OBS =   87

        NULL            TEST        ASY. CRITICAL
      HYPOTHESIS      STATISTIC       VALUE 10%
------------------------------------------------------------
CONSTANT, NO TREND
A(1)=0  Z-TEST      -0.77962E-01  -11.2
A(1)=0  T-TEST      -0.20736      -2.57
A(0)=A(1)=0          36.762        3.78
                                              AIC =     5.847
                                              SC =      5.903
------------------------------------------------------------
CONSTANT, TREND
A(1)=0  Z-TEST      -3.8683       -18.2
A(1)=0  T-TEST      -1.3761       -3.13
A(0)=A(1)=A(2)=0     25.370        4.03
A(1)=A(2)=0          0.94711       5.34
                                              AIC =     5.848
                                              SC =      5.933
------------------------------------------------------------
VARIABLE : DPI
DICKEY-FULLER TESTS - NO.LAGS =   0   NO.OBS =   87

        NULL            TEST        ASY. CRITICAL
      HYPOTHESIS      STATISTIC       VALUE 10%
------------------------------------------------------------
CONSTANT, NO TREND
A(1)=0  Z-TEST      -0.37301      -11.2
A(1)=0  T-TEST      -0.67158      -2.57
A(0)=A(1)=0          17.971        3.78
                                              AIC =     6.688
                                              SC =      6.745
------------------------------------------------------------
CONSTANT, TREND
A(1)=0  Z-TEST      -13.654       -18.2
A(1)=0  T-TEST      -2.5883       -3.13
A(0)=A(1)=A(2)=0     14.878        4.03
A(1)=A(2)=0          3.4422        5.34
                                              AIC =     6.638
                                              SC =      6.723
------------------------------------------------------------
```

Since the relevant DF test statistics are below the appropriate τ critical levels, the hypothesis that the PCE and DPI series exhibit a unit root (i.e. are non-stationary) can not be rejected.

The next step is to test if the first-differenced PCE (ΔPCE) and DPI (ΔDPI) series are stationary.

```
SAMPLE 1970.2 1991.4
COINT DDPI DPCE
```

The output follows.

```
|_SAMPLE 1970.2 1991.4

|_COINT DDPI DPCE
...NOTE..SAMPLE RANGE SET TO:      2,     88

...NOTE..TEST LAG ORDER AUTOMATICALLY SET

TOTAL NUMBER OF OBSERVATIONS =    87

VARIABLE : DDPI
DICKEY-FULLER TESTS - NO.LAGS =   3   NO.OBS =    83

      NULL            TEST        ASY. CRITICAL
   HYPOTHESIS       STATISTIC       VALUE 10%
-----------------------------------------------------------------
CONSTANT, NO TREND
A(1)=0   T-TEST      -4.1247        -2.57
A(0)=A(1)=0           8.5132         3.78
                                              AIC =      6.787
                                              SC  =      6.932
-----------------------------------------------------------------
CONSTANT, TREND
A(1)=0   T-TEST      -4.1126        -3.13
A(0)=A(1)=A(2)=0      5.6510         4.03
A(1)=A(2)=0           8.4699         5.34
                                              AIC =      6.809
                                              SC  =      6.984
-----------------------------------------------------------------


VARIABLE : DPCE
DICKEY-FULLER TESTS - NO.LAGS =   2   NO.OBS =    84

      NULL            TEST        ASY. CRITICAL
   HYPOTHESIS       STATISTIC       VALUE 10%
-----------------------------------------------------------------
CONSTANT, NO TREND
A(1)=0   T-TEST      -3.4127        -2.57
A(0)=A(1)=0           5.8239         3.78
                                              AIC =      5.800
                                              SC  =      5.916
-----------------------------------------------------------------
```

```
CONSTANT, TREND
A(1)=0   T-TEST        -3.3884      -3.13
A(0)=A(1)=A(2)=0        3.8984       4.03
A(1)=A(2)=0             5.8468       5.34
                                            AIC =     5.821
                                            SC  =     5.966
---------------------------------------------------------------------
```

Since the pertinent DF test statistics are above the appropriate τ-critical values, it can be concluded that the first-differenced PCE and DPI series do not exhibit a unit root and, thus, are indeed stationary. That is, they are I(1) (i.e. integrated of order 1).

Section 21.7 discusses the issue of cointegration. Although the PCE and DPI series are individually non-stationary, it is possible that a linear combination is stationary. If this is the case, they are said to be cointegrated.

To test for cointegration, the text estimates a DF regression based on the estimated residuals from the regression of *PCE* on *PDI* (equation (21.6.1)). The following commands do this.

```
* Perform a DF test on the residuals from (21.6.1).
?OLS PCE DPI / RESID=U
GENR LAGU=LAG(U)
GENR DU=U-LAGU
SAMPLE 1970.2 1991.4
OLS DU LAGU / RSTAT NOCONSTANT
```

The output follows.

```
|_OLS DU LAGU / RSTAT NOCONSTANT

 OLS ESTIMATION
       87 OBSERVATIONS      DEPENDENT VARIABLE = DU
...NOTE..SAMPLE RANGE SET TO:    2,    88


 R-SQUARE =    0.1422    R-SQUARE ADJUSTED =    0.1422
VARIANCE OF THE ESTIMATE-SIGMA**2 =    588.52
STANDARD ERROR OF THE ESTIMATE-SIGMA =   24.259
SUM OF SQUARED ERRORS-SSE=    50612.
MEAN OF DEPENDENT VARIABLE = -0.40588
LOG OF THE LIKELIHOOD FUNCTION = -400.371
RAW MOMENT R-SQUARE =    0.1424


VARIABLE    ESTIMATED   STANDARD   T-RATIO        PARTIAL STANDARDIZED ELASTICITY
  NAME      COEFFICIENT   ERROR      86 DF   P-VALUE CORR. COEFFICIENT  AT MEANS
LAGU       -0.27531    0.7285E-01  -3.779     0.000-0.377      -0.3774    -0.0875


DURBIN-WATSON = 2.2775    VON NEUMANN RATIO = 2.3040    RHO = -0.13957
RESIDUAL SUM =  -38.401       RESIDUAL VARIANCE =    588.52
SUM OF ABSOLUTE ERRORS=    1568.4
R-SQUARE BETWEEN OBSERVED AND PREDICTED = 0.1425
RUNS TEST:    45 RUNS,    38 POS,    0 ZERO,    49 NEG  NORMAL STATISTIC =  0.2621
```

The **COINT** command can be used to test for cointegration. The **TYPE=** option with the **COINT** command specifies the type of tests to perform. When **TYPE=RESD** is specified, Dickey-Fuller tests are computed on the **RESiDuals** of the cointegrating regressions. The default is **TYPE=DF** which performs augmented Dickey-Fuller tests.

Testing for cointegration is done by constructing test statistics from the residuals of a cointegrating regression. With M time series $Y_{t1}, \ldots, Y_{tM}$, each of which is I(1), two forms of the cointegrating regression equations are:

$$(A) \quad Y_{t1} = \beta_0 + \sum_{j=2}^{M} \beta_j Y_{tj} + u_t$$

$$(B) \quad Y_{t1} = \beta_0 + \beta_1 t + \sum_{j=2}^{M} \beta_j Y_{tj} + u_t$$

Equation (A) is no-trend and equation (B) is with-trend. A test for no cointegration is given by a test for a unit root in the estimated residuals $\hat{u}_t$. The augmented Dickey-Fuller regression equation is:

$$\Delta\hat{u}_t = \alpha_* \hat{u}_{t-1} + \sum_{j=1}^{p} \phi_j \Delta\hat{u}_{t-j} + v_t$$

The text focuses on the "non-augmented" DF test. That is, the lagged first-differenced term is dropped. Again, this can be done by setting **NLAG=0**.

The following commands test for cointegration between *PCE* and *DPI*, including the DF test performed above.

```
SAMPLE 1970.1 1991.4
COINT PCE DPI / TYPE=RESD NLAG=0
```

The output follows.

```
|_SAMPLE 1970.1 1991.4

|_COINT PCE DPI / TYPE=RESD NLAG=0
...NOTE..SAMPLE RANGE SET TO:      1,     88

COINTEGRATING REGRESSION - CONSTANT, NO TREND    NO.OBS =    88
REGRESSAND : PCE

 R-SQUARE = 0.9941          DURBIN-WATSON = 0.5316
```

```
DICKEY-FULLER TESTS ON RESIDUALS - NO.LAGS =  0   M =  2

                        TEST      ASY. CRITICAL
                        STATISTIC    VALUE 10%
--------------------------------------------------------------
NO CONSTANT, NO TREND
        Z-TEST      -23.952      -17.1
        T-TEST      -3.7791      -3.04
                                          AIC =      6.389
                                          SC =       6.417
--------------------------------------------------------------

COINTEGRATING REGRESSION - CONSTANT, TREND     NO.OBS =   88
REGRESSAND : PCE

 R-SQUARE = 0.9941        DURBIN-WATSON = 0.5814

 DICKEY-FULLER TESTS ON RESIDUALS - NO.LAGS =  0   M =  2

                        TEST      ASY. CRITICAL
                        STATISTIC    VALUE 10%
--------------------------------------------------------------
NO CONSTANT, NO TREND
        Z-TEST      -26.097      -23.4
        T-TEST      -3.9633      -3.50
                                          AIC =      6.459
                                          SC =       6.488
--------------------------------------------------------------
```

Since the test statistics are above the appropriate τ critical values, it can be concluded that the estimated residuals from (21.6.1) do not exhibit a unit root (i.e. are stationary). Hence, it can be concluded that the PCE and DPI series are cointegrated.

Section 21.8 estimates a regression with the two cointegrated series using the error correction mechanism as described in equation (21.8.1). The following commands replicate the results for this regression reported in equation (21.8.2).

```
* Equation (21.8.2).
SAMPLE 1970.2 1991.4
OLS DPCE DDPI LAGU / RSTAT
```

The output follows.

```
|_* Equation (21.8.2).
|_SAMPLE 1970.2 1991.4
|_OLS DPCE DDPI LAGU / RSTAT

 OLS ESTIMATION
      87 OBSERVATIONS     DEPENDENT VARIABLE = DPCE
...NOTE..SAMPLE RANGE SET TO:    2,    88
```

```
 R-SQUARE =    0.1686     R-SQUARE ADJUSTED =    0.1488
VARIANCE OF THE ESTIMATE-SIGMA**2 =    284.76
STANDARD ERROR OF THE ESTIMATE-SIGMA =    16.875
SUM OF SQUARED ERRORS-SSE=   23920.
MEAN OF DEPENDENT VARIABLE =    16.903
LOG OF THE LIKELIHOOD FUNCTION = -367.767


VARIABLE    ESTIMATED   STANDARD   T-RATIO          PARTIAL STANDARDIZED ELASTICITY
  NAME     COEFFICIENT    ERROR      84 DF   P-VALUE CORR. COEFFICIENT  AT MEANS
DDPI        .28791      .6976E-01   4.127     .000  .411    .4396       .3048
LAGU       -.81936E-01  .5482E-01  -1.495     .139 -.161   -.1592       .0006
CONSTANT    11.741      2.199       5.338     .000  .503    .0000       .6946


DURBIN-WATSON = 1.9262    VON NEUMANN RATIO = 1.9486    RHO =    .03015
RESIDUAL SUM =    .20250E-12  RESIDUAL VARIANCE =    284.76
SUM OF ABSOLUTE ERRORS=    1132.7
R-SQUARE BETWEEN OBSERVED AND PREDICTED =   .1686
RUNS TEST:    47 RUNS,    43 POS,    0 ZERO,    44 NEG  NORMAL STATISTIC =  0.5405
```

SHAZAM commands and options used in Chapter 21

ARIMA *var* / **NLAG=** **PLOTAC**

COINT *vars* / **NLAG=** **SIGLEVEL=** **TYPE=DF** **TYPE=RESID**

GENR *newvar=equation* with **LAG**(x) **TIME**(x)

OLS *depvar indeps* / **RSTAT** **RESID=** **NOCONSTANT**

READ(*datafile*) *vars* / *options*

SAMPLE *beg end*

TIME *beg freq*

? Suppression of Output

22. TIME SERIES ECONOMETRICS II: FORECASTING WITH ARIMA AND VAR MODELS

Chapter 21 discussed and illustrated methods used to test for stationarity in time series data. *Chapter 22* now looks at methods of modeling stationary time series. The first part of the chapter outlines the Box-Jenkins approach to the analysis of Autoregressive Integrated Moving Average (ARIMA) models of univariate time series.

As explained in *Section 22.2*, an autoregressive process of order p, AR(p), describes a process in which the value of a variable, Y, depends on its value at time t and its value to time t - p. With an autoregressive and moving average process with autoregressive order of p and a moving average order of q, ARMA(p, q), Y again depends on its time t to t-p values. However, now the value of Y also depends on a moving average of the time t to time t-q error terms. If p = 0, then Y follows an MA(q) process. Now, if Y follows an ARIMA(p, d, q) process, this indicates that Y is integrated of order d. In other words, d differences must be taken in order to make Y stationary. Once differences are taken, the ARMA model can then be estimated.

As *Section 22.3* explains, the Box-Jenkins approach to ARIMA modeling involves four stages. The first involves identifying the type of process the time series follows. That is, the values of p, d, and q must be determined. In the second stage, the identified model is estimated. The third stage constructs diagnostic tests on the estimated model. Once an appropriate model is defined, forecasting can be performed.

The main instruments used for identification are the autocorrelation function (ACF) and the partial autocorrelation function (PACF). As illustrated in Chapter 21, the **PLOTAC** option with the **ARIMA** command plots the correlogram of the ACF. Similarly, the **PLOTPAC** option **PLOT**s the **PACF**. The default number of lags of the PACF plotted is 12. The **NLAGP=** option is used to over-ride this setting.

Using the GDP series from *Table 21.1*, the commands below plot the correlograms found in *Figure 22.1*.

```
TIME 1970 4
SAMPLE 1970.1 1991.4
READ(TABLE21.1) PERIOD GDP DPI PCE PROFITS DIVIDEND
* Figure 22.1.
ARIMA GDP / PLOTAC NLAG=25 PLOTPAC NLAGP=25
```

The output follows.

```
|_ARIMA GDP / PLOTAC NLAG=25 PLOTPAC NLAGP=25
    ARIMA MODEL
NUMBER OF OBSERVATIONS =   88
...NOTE..SAMPLE RANGE SET TO:       1,      88
```

```
        IDENTIFICATION SECTION - VARIABLE=GDP
NUMBER OF AUTOCORRELATIONS =  25
NUMBER OF PARTIAL AUTOCORRELATIONS =  25


              0     0 0
SERIES  (1-B) (1-B  )  GDP


  NET NUMBER OF OBSERVATIONS =   88
MEAN=    3865.6       VARIANCE=   0.39694E+06    STANDARD DEV.=     630.03

  LAGS                        AUTOCORRELATIONS                     STD ERR
   1 -12     0.97 0.94 0.90 0.87 0.83 0.79 0.75 0.71 0.67 0.64 0.60 0.57    0.11
  13 -24     0.53 0.50 0.47 0.44 0.41 0.37 0.34 0.31 0.28 0.25 0.21 0.18    0.42
  25 -25     0.15                                                           0.46


MODIFIED BOX-PIERCE (LJUNG-BOX-PIERCE) STATISTICS  (CHI-SQUARE)
    LAG    Q      DF  P-VALUE       LAG    Q      DF  P-VALUE
      1   85.46   1   .000          13  731.56   13   .000
      2  166.02   2   .000          14  758.29   14   .000
      3  241.72   3   .000          15  782.02   15   .000
      4  312.39   4   .000          16  803.03   16   .000
      5  378.10   5   .000          17  821.35   17   .000
      6  438.57   6   .000          18  837.24   18   .000
      7  493.85   7   .000          19  850.79   19   .000
      8  544.11   8   .000          20  862.17   20   .000
      9  589.77   9   .000          21  871.39   21   .000
     10  631.12  10   .000          22  878.65   22   .000
     11  668.33  11   .000          23  884.22   23   .000
     12  701.65  12   .000          24  888.31   24   .000
                                    25  891.25   25   .000

  LAGS                   PARTIAL AUTOCORRELATIONS                  STD ERR
   1 -12     0.97 -.06 -.02 -.05 -.02 -.06 -.03 -.02 0.01 -.01 -.02 -.01    0.11
  13 -24     0.02 -.01 -.02 0.00 -.04 0.00 -.04 -.02 -.07 -.02 -.01 -.02    0.11
  25 -25     0.02                                                           0.11

                                          0     0 0
AUTOCORRELATION FUNCTION OF THE SERIES   (1-B) (1-B  )  GDP

 1 0.97 .                            +     RRRRRRRRRRRRRRRRRRRRRRRRRRRRRRRRRRR.
 2 0.94 .                          +       RRRRRRRRRRRRRRRRRRRRRRRRRRRRRRRRRRR .
 3 0.90 .                        +         RRRRRRRRRRRRRRRRRRRRRRRRRRRRRRRRRR  .
 4 0.87 .                      +           RRRRRRRRRRRRRRRRRRRRRRRRRRRRRRRRR   .
 5 0.83 .                    +             RRRRRRRRRRRRRRRRRRRRRRRRRRRRRRRR    .
 6 0.79 .                  +               RRRRRRRRRRRRRRRRRRRRRRRRRRRRRRR     .
 7 0.75 .                +                 RRRRRRRRRRRRRRRRRRRRRRRRRRRRR       .
 8 0.71 .              +                   RRRRRRRRRRRRRRRRRRRRRRRRRRR+        .
 9 0.67 .             +                    RRRRRRRRRRRRRRRRRRRRRRRRR  +        .
10 0.64 .           +                      RRRRRRRRRRRRRRRRRRRRRRR      +      .
11 0.60 .           +                      RRRRRRRRRRRRRRRRRRRRR        +      .
12 0.57 .          +                       RRRRRRRRRRRRRRRRRRR          +      .
13 0.53 .         +                        RRRRRRRRRRRRRRRRR             +     .
14 0.50 .         +                        RRRRRRRRRRRRRRRR              +     .
15 0.47 .       +                          RRRRRRRRRRRRRRR                +    .
16 0.44 .       +                          RRRRRRRRRRRRRR                 +    .
17 0.41 .       +                          RRRRRRRRRRRRR                   +  .
18 0.37 .     +                            RRRRRRRRRRRRR                    + .
```

```
19 0.34 .   +                                    RRRRRRRRRRRR                        +  .
20 0.31 .   +                                    RRRRRRRRRRR                         +  .
21 0.28 .   +                                    RRRRRRRRR                           +  .
22 0.25 .   +                                    RRRRRRRR                            +  .
23 0.21 .   +                                    RRRRRRR                             +  .
24 0.18 . +                                      RRRRRR                             +  .
25 0.15 . +                                      RRRRR                              +  .

                                                           0      0 0
PARTIAL AUTOCORRELATION FUNCTION OF THE SERIES  (1-B) (1-B   )   GDP

 1 0.97 .                                  +        RRRRRRRRRRRRRRRRRRRRRRRRRRRRRRRRRRRR.
 2 -.06 .                                  +     RRR       +                                .
 3 -.02 .                                  +     RR        +                                .
 4 -.05 .                                  +     RRR       +                                .
 5 -.02 .                                  +     RR        +                                .
 6 -.06 .                                  +     RRR       +                                .
 7 -.03 .                                  +     RR        +                                .
 8 -.02 .                                  +     RR        +                                .
 9 0.01 .                                  +     R         +                                .
10 -.01 .                                  +     R         +                                .
11 -.02 .                                  +     RR        +                                .
12 -.01 .                                  +     R         +                                .
13 0.02 .                                  +     RR        +                                .
14 -.01 .                                  +     R         +                                .
15 -.02 .                                  +     RR        +                                .
16 0.00 .                                  +     R         +                                .
17 -.04 .                                  +     RR        +                                .
18 0.00 .                                  +     R         +                                .
19 -.04 .                                  +     RR        +.                               .
20 -.02 .                                  +     RR        +                                .
21 -.07 .                                  +     RRR       +                                .
22 -.02 .                                  +     RR        +                                .
23 -.01 .                                  +     R         +                                .
24 -.02 .                                  +     RR        +                                .
25 0.02 .                                  +     RR        +                                .
```

Two things can be seen from the above correlograms. First, the ACF decays very slowly implying that the series is not stationary. Second, the PACF decays very quickly. In fact, only the PACF for lag 1 is outside the 95% confidence bounds.

The **NDIFF=** option with the **ARIMA** command is used to specify the order of differencing when transforming the data. Note that the sample range is adjusted automatically.

The next command takes first-differences of the GDP series and plots the ACF and PACF found in *Figure 22.2*.

```
ARIMA GDP / NDIFF=1 PLOTAC NLAG=25 PLOTPAC NLAGP=25
```

The output follows.

```
|_ARIMA GDP / NDIFF=1 PLOTAC NLAG=25  PLOTPAC NLAGP=25
     ARIMA MODEL
NUMBER OF OBSERVATIONS =  88
...NOTE..SAMPLE RANGE SET TO:      1,     88
DEGREE OF DIFFERENCING =   1


      IDENTIFICATION SECTION - VARIABLE=GDP
NUMBER OF AUTOCORRELATIONS =  25
NUMBER OF PARTIAL AUTOCORRELATIONS =  25


           1    0 0
SERIES  (1-B) (1-B ) GDP


  NET NUMBER OF OBSERVATIONS =   87
MEAN=    22.933      VARIANCE=     1291.3      STANDARD DEV.=     35.934

  LAGS                    AUTOCORRELATIONS                         STD ERR
  1 -12     0.32 0.19 0.05 0.05 -.01 -.02 -.07 -.29 -.07 0.02 0.04 -.24    0.11
 13 -24     -.12 -.20 -.13 -.04 -.06 0.01 -.04 0.07 0.08 0.04 -.07 -.03    0.13
 25 -25     0.01                                                           0.14

MODIFIED BOX-PIERCE (LJUNG-BOX-PIERCE) STATISTICS  (CHI-SQUARE)
    LAG    Q    DF  P-VALUE      LAG    Q    DF  P-VALUE
     1   9.01   1   .003        13   29.31  13   .006
     2  12.17   2   .002        14   33.71  14   .002
     3  12.39   3   .006        15   35.47  15   .002
     4  12.63   4   .013        16   35.61  16   .003
     5  12.64   5   .027        17   35.96  17   .005
     6  12.67   6   .049        18   35.97  18   .007
     7  13.19   7   .068        19   36.20  19   .010
     8  21.38   8   .006        20   36.69  20   .013
     9  21.82   9   .009        21   37.52  21   .015
    10  21.85  10   .016        22   37.70  22   .020
    11  21.99  11   .024        23   38.26  23   .024
    12  27.89  12   .006        24   38.38  24   .032
                                25   38.41  25   .042


  LAGS               PARTIAL AUTOCORRELATIONS                     STD ERR
  1 -12     0.32 0.10 -.04 0.03 -.03 -.02 -.06 -.28 0.13 0.10 -.01 -.31    0.11
 13 -24     0.01 -.11 -.05 -.02 -.02 0.12 -.07 -.13 0.09 -.06 -.12 -.04    0.11
 25 -25     0.09                                                           0.11


                                      1    0 0
AUTOCORRELATION FUNCTION OF THE SERIES    (1-B) (1-B ) GDP


 1 0.32 .                    +      RRRRRRRRRRR              .
 2 0.19 .                    +      RRRRRR +                 .
 3 0.05 .                    +      RRR    +                 .
 4 0.05 .                    +      RRR    +                 .
 5 -.01 .                    +       R     +                 .
 6 -.02 .                    +      RR     +                 .
 7 -.07 .                    +     RRR     +                 .
 8 -.29 .             RRRRRRRRRR          +                  .
 9 -.07 .                    +     RRR      +                .
10 0.02 .                    +      RR      +                .
11 0.04 .                    +      RR      +                .
12 -.24 .                +RRRRRRRRR         +                .
```

```
13 -.12 .                         +      RRRRR          +                          .
14 -.20 .                         + RRRRRRR             +                          .
15 -.13 .                         +      RRRRR          +                          .
16 -.04 .                      +       RR          +                               .
17 -.06 .                      +       RRR         +                               .
18 0.01 .                      +        R          +                               .
19 -.04 .                      +       RRR         +                               .
20 0.07 .                      +         RRR       +                               .
21 0.08 .                      +         RRRR      +                               .
22 0.04 .                      +        RR         +                               .
23 -.07 .                      +       RRR         +                               .
24 -.03 .                      +        RR         +                               .
25 0.01 .                      +         R         +                               .


                                                    1      0 0
PARTIAL AUTOCORRELATION FUNCTION OF THE SERIES  (1-B) (1-B  )  GDP

 1 0.32 .                              +        RRRRRRRRRRR                         .
 2 0.10 .                              +        RRRR   +                            .
 3 -.04 .                              +     RR      +                              .
 4 0.03 .                              +     RR      +                              .
 5 -.03 .                              +     RR      +                              .
 6 -.02 .                              +     RR      +                              .
 7 -.06 .                              +    RRR      +                              .
 8 -.28 .                         RRRRRRRRRR         +                              .
 9 0.13 .                              +       RRRRR +                              .
10 0.10 .                              +       RRRR  +                              .
11 -.01 .                              +      R      +                              .
12 -.31 .                         RRRRRRRRRRR        +                              .
13 0.01 .                              +      R      +                              .
14 -.11 .                              +   RRRRR     +                              .
15 -.05 .                              +    RRR      +                              .
16 -.02 .                              +     RR      +                              .
17 -.02 .                              +     RR      +                              .
18 0.12 .                              +       RRRRR +                              .
19 -.07 .                              +    RRR      +                              .
20 -.13 .                              +   RRRRR     +                              .
21 0.09 .                              +       RRRR  +                              .
22 -.06 .                              +    RRR      +                              .
23 -.12 .                              +   RRRRR     +                              .
24 -.04 .                              +     RR      +                              .
25 0.09 .                              +       RRRR  +                              .
```

Since both the ACF and PACF at lags 1, 8, and 12 extend past the 95 % confidence bounds, the text concludes that the appropriate model to estimate is an AR(12). As well, given that the PACF is not statistically different from zero at lags other than 1, 8, and 12, only these lags are included in the regression.

It appears that equation (22.5.2) is estimated using OLS. The commands below will estimate this model. Recall that, when estimating models containing lagged variables using the **OLS** command which follows the format below, the necessary number of observations are automatically dropped (in this case 13). The residuals and estimated coefficients are saved for use ahead.

```
GENR DGDP=GDP-LAG(GDP)
SAMPLE 1970.2 1991.4
OLS DGDP DGDP(1.1) DGDP(8.8) DGDP(12.12)  / RSTAT RESID=E COEF=CF DLAG
```

The output follows.

```
|_OLS DGDP DGDP(1.1) DGDP(8.8) DGDP(12.12)  / RSTAT RESID=E COEF=CF DLAG


 OLS ESTIMATION
      75 OBSERVATIONS      DEPENDENT VARIABLE = DGDP
...NOTE..SAMPLE RANGE SET TO:    14,     88


 R-SQUARE =   0.2931     R-SQUARE ADJUSTED =    0.2633
VARIANCE OF THE ESTIMATE-SIGMA**2 =    984.72
STANDARD ERROR OF THE ESTIMATE-SIGMA =   31.380
SUM OF SQUARED ERRORS-SSE=   69915.
MEAN OF DEPENDENT VARIABLE =    21.529
LOG OF THE LIKELIHOOD FUNCTION = -362.829


VARIABLE    SUM OF LAG COEFS     STD ERROR        T-RATIO          MEAN LAG
DGDP          -0.22107           0.17290          -1.2786           23.637

VARIABLE     ESTIMATED   STANDARD   T-RATIO        PARTIAL STANDARDIZED ELASTICITY
  NAME       COEFFICIENT   ERROR      71 DF    P-VALUE CORR. COEFFICIENT  AT MEANS
DGDP         0.34277     0.9879E-01   3.470    0.001 0.381     0.3476      0.3582
DGDP        -0.29947     0.1016      -2.948    0.004-0.330    -0.2952     -0.3555
DGDP        -0.26437     0.9858E-01  -2.682    0.009-0.303    -0.2680     -0.3122
CONSTANT    28.194       5.577        5.056    0.000 0.514     0.0000      1.3095


DURBIN-WATSON = 1.7663    VON NEUMANN RATIO = 1.7902    RHO =   0.10276
RESIDUAL SUM = -0.43343E-12  RESIDUAL VARIANCE =    984.72
SUM OF ABSOLUTE ERRORS=   1757.3
R-SQUARE BETWEEN OBSERVED AND PREDICTED = 0.2931
RUNS TEST:   33 RUNS,   41 POS,   0 ZERO,   34 NEG  NORMAL STATISTIC = -1.2136
DURBIN H STATISTIC (ASYMPTOTIC NORMAL) =  1.7191
```

In the above case, it is possible to use OLS to estimate the model. The **ARIMA** command provides a full range of options to estimate more complex models. For example, the **NAR=** option is used to specify the order of the AR process, p. The **NMA=** option is used to specify the order of the MA process, q. Also, as mentioned above, the **NDIFF=** option is used to specify the number of differences to be taken, d.

In *Section 22.6*, the ACF and PACF based on the residuals computed from (22.5.2) are plotted. The commands below will compute these autocorrelations and partial autocorrelations. However, this time the correlograms will be plotted using GNUPLOT, the graphics program interfaced with SHAZAM. For more details on GNUPLOT, see the *SHAZAM User's Reference Manual*.

```
SAMPLE 1973.2 1991.4
ARIMA E / NLAG=25 NLAGP=25 GNU DEVICE=POSTSCRIPT OUTPUT=PS1
```

The output follows.

```
|_ARIMA E / NLAG=25 NLAGP=25
   ARIMA MODEL
NUMBER OF OBSERVATIONS =  75
...NOTE..SAMPLE RANGE SET TO:     14,     88

     IDENTIFICATION SECTION - VARIABLE=E
NUMBER OF AUTOCORRELATIONS =  25
NUMBER OF PARTIAL AUTOCORRELATIONS =  25


            0      0 0
SERIES  (1-B) (1-B  )  E

  NET NUMBER OF OBSERVATIONS =    75
MEAN=  -0.54556E-14   VARIANCE=    944.80        STANDARD DEV.=    30.738

  LAGS                      AUTOCORRELATIONS                    STD ERR
  1 -12     0.10 0.09 0.05 -.10 -.02 0.03 0.01 -.08 0.13 0.13 0.12 -.06   0.12
 13 -24     0.05 -.16 -.21 -.01 -.20 0.03 0.00 -.11 0.04 0.00 -.07 -.08   0.13
 25 -25     -.08                                                          0.14

MODIFIED BOX-PIERCE (LJUNG-BOX-PIERCE) STATISTICS  (CHI-SQUARE)
     LAG    Q    DF  P-VALUE      LAG    Q     DF  P-VALUE
      1   0.82    1  .365         13    8.06   13  .840
      2   1.42    2  .493         14   10.48   14  .726
      3   1.62    3  .654         15   14.74   15  .470
      4   2.50    4  .645         16   14.76   16  .542
      5   2.53    5  .771         17   18.93   17  .332
      6   2.59    6  .858         18   19.00   18  .392
      7   2.60    7  .919         19   19.00   19  .457
      8   3.17    8  .923         20   20.19   20  .446
      9   4.70    9  .860         21   20.33   21  .500
     10   6.25   10  .794         22   20.33   22  .562
     11   7.51   11  .757         23   20.92   23  .586
     12   7.86   12  .796         24   21.58   24  .604
                                  25   22.39   25  .613

  LAGS                  PARTIAL AUTOCORRELATIONS                STD ERR
  1 -12     0.10 0.08 0.04 -.12 -.01 0.05 0.02 -.11 0.15 0.14 0.09 -.16   0.12
 13 -24     0.07 -.13 -.18 -.01 -.14 0.07 -.05 -.17 0.07 0.00 -.07 -.05   0.12
 25 -25     0.00                                                          0.12
```

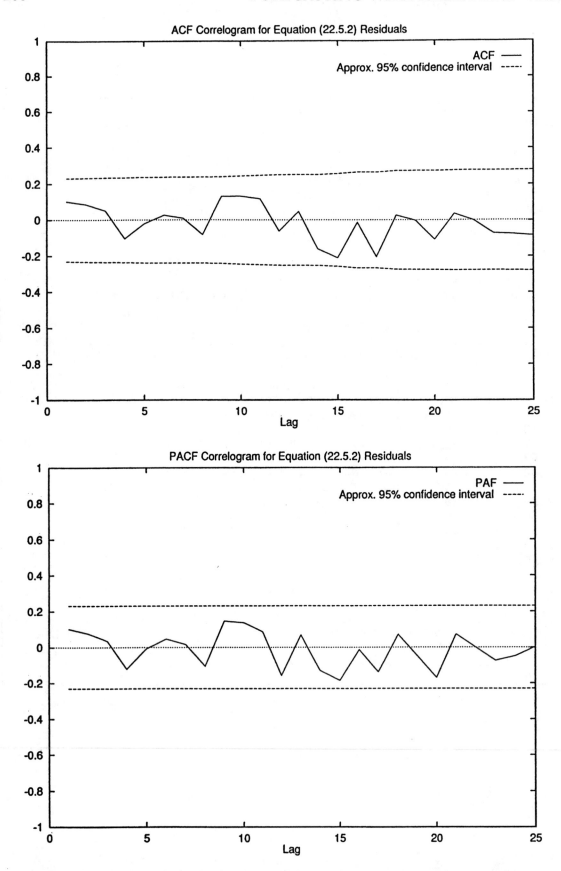

Note that the ACF and PACF both remain inside the 95% confidence bounds.

In *Section 22.7*, the parameters estimated from (22.5.2) are used to forecast GDP for the first quarter of 1992. In the process, the first-differences are "undone." This is a fairly straight forward procedure. The commands below perform the computations involved.

```
GEN1 A1=CF(4)
GEN1 A2=CF(1)
GEN1 A2PLUS1=A2+1
GEN1 A3=CF(2)
GEN1 A4=CF(3)
GENR Y=GDP
GENR LAGY=LAG(GDP)
GENR LAG2Y=LAG(GDP,2)
GENR LAG8Y=LAG(GDP,8)
GENR LAG9Y=LAG(GDP,9)
GENR LAG12Y=LAG(GDP,12)
GENR LAG13Y=LAG(GDP,13)
SAMPLE 1991.4 1991.4
PRINT Y LAGY LAG8Y LAG9Y LAG12Y LAG13Y / WIDE
PRINT A1 A2 A2PLUS1 A3 A4
GENR GDP921=A1+A2PLUS1*Y-A2*LAGY+A3*LAG8Y-A3*LAG9Y+A4*LAG12Y-A4*LAG13Y
PRINT GDP921
```

The output follows.

```
|_P Y LAGY LAG8Y LAG9Y LAG12Y LAG13Y / WIDE
      Y                 LAGY              LAG8Y             LAG9Y             LAG12Y
LAG13Y
    4868.000         4862.700          4859.700          4845.600          4779.700
4734.500
|_P A1 A2 A2PLUS1 A3 A4
   A1
   28.19371
   A2
  0.3427683
   A2PLUS1
   1.342768
   A3
 -0.2994664
   A4
 -0.2643712
|_GENR GDP921=A1+A2PLUS1*Y-A2*LAGY+A3*LAG8Y-A3*LAG9Y+A4*LAG12Y-A4*LAG13Y
|_PRINT GDP921
    GDP921
    4881.838
```

While the above forecast is quite simple to compute, the **ARIMA** command provides many features for forecasting when more complex forecasts are desired.

The rest of *Chapter 22* discusses Vector Autoregression (VAR) models. However, no data is provided for the illustrated examples.

VAR model estimation involves estimating two equations simultaneously. The **SYSTEM** command provides features for joint estimation of a set of linear equations. See the *SHAZAM User's Reference Manual* for details and examples.

SHAZAM commands and options used in Chapter 22.

ARIMA *var* / **DEVICE=POSTSCRIPT GNU NAR= NDIFF= NLAG= NLAGP= NMA= OUTPUT= PLOTAC PLOTPAC**

GENR *newvar=equation* with **LAG**(x)

OLS *depvar indeps* / **COEF= DLAG RESID= RSTAT**

PRINT *vars* / **WIDE**

READ (*filename*) *vars*

SAMPLE *beg end*

TIME *beg freq*

SUMMARY OF SYMBOLS

+   Addition

-      Subtraction

*   Multiplication

/   Division

* *   Exponentiation

?   Suppression of Output

*   Comment if in Column1, otherwise Multiplication

&   Continuation of SHAZAM Command to another line

$ Indicates Temporary Variable

     $ANF,$DF,$DW,$K,$LLF,$N,$RHO,$SIG2,$SSE,$SSR,$SST

ABS()   Absolute Value

SQRT()   Square Root

LAG()   Lag a Variable

LOG()   Natural Log

EXP()   Antilogs

INV()   Invert Matrix

INTRODUCING

THE SHAZAM FREQUENT REGRESSORS CLUB

SHAZAM is now the first Econometrics Computer Program to give bonus awards for Frequent Regressors.

Save all your old regressions for valuable awards. The more regressions you run the more awards you can receive. Members receive 1 point for each regression run.

AWARD SCHEDULE

10,000 pts.: Regression upgrade. Run **OLS**; get output for **Two Stage Least Squares.**
20,000 pts.: One free Computer Handbook for Econometrics.
30,000 pts.: One free **SHAZAM** manual.
40,000 pts.: One free **SHAZAM** t-shirt.
50,000 pts.: 10% off on purchase of your next version of **SHAZAM.**

Now for a limited time only you will start off with 3,000 points just for joining the Frequent Regressors Club.

Now, you can accumulate regressions even faster with SHAZAM bonus awards:

1. *Obtain double points for all regressions run in Version 7.0 (up to 100 bonus points allowed).*
2. *500 bonus points for regressions run while flying on United Airlines or Canadian Airlines (up to 1000 bonus points allowed).*
3. *Systems of equations yield multiple points. For example, a 3 equation system will yield 3 points.*
4. *1000 bonus points for running* **SHAZAM** *regressions at over 100 different* **SHAZAM** *installations. Select from nearly 2000 worldwide.*
5. *Receive 1 bonus point for every R^2 over .99 (up to 100 bonus points allowed).*

Now, SHAZAM is the only program with penalty points:

1. *Subtract 1 point for every negative R^2.*
2. *Subtract 2 points for every stepwise regression.*
3. *Subtract 3 points for every non-linear model that doesn't converge.*

How do I enroll?

It's easy! Simple fill out the application form on the reverse and mail it in. You may start running regressions as soon as your form is postmarked.

How do I claim my awards?

It's simple! When you have run enough regressions to qualify simply send copies of the regressions to the **SHAZAM** *processing center. Your award will be mailed as soon as your output is verified. To receive your 10,000 point award regression upgrade you should also send your data.*

What does it cost to join?

This is the best part! Enrollment is free.

How do I keep track of my points?

It's simple! Just count them.

Do all regressions count?

No. Only regressions run with **SHAZAM** *are eligible. Each regression must be different; duplicate results are not allowed. Regressions run in* **DO** *loops are also not eligible. All other regressions are eligible, even simple regressions.*

How much time do I have to accumulate regressions?

At present, there is no time limit. However, **SHAZAM** *reserves the right to modify the rules and awards and introduce new award levels.*

ENROLL NOW! Don't let any of your regressions go to waste.

_____

Date: _____

Name: _____

Address: _____

_____

_____

Phone: _____

Send this form to:

SHAZAM
#997-1873 East Mall
Vancouver, British Columbia
V6T 1Z1
Canada

SHAZAM ORDER FORM

Date: _____

Name: _____

Address: _____

_____

Telephone:_____ FAX:_____ Electronic Mail Address:_____

SOFTWARE PRICES

SHAZAME, SHAZAMW, SHAZAMO, NeXT, POWERMAC, or SPARC Single Copy Rate ....US$ 395.00

SHAZAMN or Macintosh Single Copy Rate ....US$ 295.00

IBM, VAX/ALPHA, UNIX, CDC, or GENERIC Mainframe/Workstaton Rate ....US$ 500.00

Site License Rate for first Operating System ....US$ 1200.00

Site License Rate for each additional Operating System ....US$ 400.00

SITE LICENSE		SINGLE COPY	RATE	VERSIONS
_____	/	_____	x _____	**SHAZAME** (DOS-E) requires 80386/80387 or 80486DX and 4 MB RAM.
_____	/	_____	x _____	**SHAZAMN** (MS-DOS) require a hard disk and 640K RAM.
_____	/	_____	x _____	**SHAZAMW** (WINDOWS) requires 80286, 80386, or 80486 and 4 MB RAM.
_____	/	_____	x _____	**SHAZAMO/SHAZAMP** (OS/2) requires 80386 or 80486 and 4 MB RAM.
_____	/	_____	x _____	**Macintosh** requires 1 MB RAM and a hard disk.
_____	/	_____	x _____	**POWERMAC** (Power Macintosh).
_____	/	_____	x _____	**NeXT** 68040.
_____	/	_____	x _____	**Sun SPARCstation/Sun Solaris.**
_____	/	_____	x _____	**IBM** with MVS/VM/CMS/TSO operating system on MS-DOS high density disk.
_____	/	_____	x _____	**VAX/ALPHA** with VMS or ULTRIX operating system on MS-DOS high density disk.
_____	/	_____	x _____	**UNIX** on MS-DOS high density disk.
_____	/	_____	x _____	**CDC** with NOS and NOSVE operating systems on MS-DOS high density disk.
_____	/	_____	x _____	**GENERIC** (all other machines) on MS-DOS high density disk.

Computer & Operating System: _____

COPIES RATE COMMAND AND DATA DISKETTES FOR THE FOLLOWING BOOKS:

COPIES	RATE	
_____	x US$35.00	E.R. Berndt, *The Practice Of Econometrics*, Addison-Wesley, 1990.
_____	x US$35.00	W.H. Greene, *Econometric Analysis, Second Edition*, Macmillan, 1993.
_____	x US$35.00	D.N. Gujarati, *Basic Econometrics, Second Edition*, McGraw-Hill, 1988.
_____	x US$35.00	Judge et al., *Introduction To The Theory And Practice of Econometrics*, Wiley, 1988.
_____	x US$35.00	Judge et al., *The Theory And Practice Of Econometrics*, Wiley, 1985.
_____	x US$35.00	G.S. Maddala, *Introduction To Econometrics, Second Edition*, Macmillan, 1992.
_____	x US$35.00	R.S. Pindyck and D.L. Rubinfeld, *Econometric Models & Economic Forecasts*, McGraw-Hill, 1991.
_____	x US$35.00	R. Ramanathan, *Introductory Econometrics with Applications, Second Edition*, Harcourt Brace Jovanovich, 1992.
_____	x US$35.00	T.D. Wallace and J.L. Silver, *Econometrics: An Introduction*, Addison-Wesley, 1988.

Disk Type: 3.5 inch _____ 5.25 inch _____ Computer Type: For MSDOS _____ For Macintosh _____

$_____ **TOTAL (US Dollars)**

Send this form and payment to:

SHAZAM
UBC Economics
#997 - 1873 East Mall
Vancouver, BC V6T 1Z1
CANADA
Tel: 1-604-822-5062   FAX: 1-604-822-5915
EMAIL : info@shazam.econ.ubc.ca

CREDIT CARD PAYMENT:
NAME(Please Print):_____
MASTERCARD NO:_____
VISA NO:_____
EXPIRY DATE:_____
BANK ISSUED CARD:_____
SIGNATURE:_____

Cheques payable to: UNIVERSITY OF BRITISH COLUMBIA, 5-55885
Be sure that your order and payment are sent to the full address above.
ORDERS WILL NOT BE SHIPPED UNTIL PAYMENT IS RECEIVED.

FLEXIBLE DISKETTE
Care and Handling Guide

1. Do not touch or attempt to clean the exposed diskette surface (the brown vinyl-like material inside the jacket).
2. Do not eat, drink or smoke while handling the diskette.
3. Do not use any magnetized objects near the diskette. Some common sources of magnetic fields are telephones, any recording equipment, magnets, etc. Pieces of the program or data can be lost if the diskettes are exposed to a magnetic field.
4. Do not place heavy objects on top of the diskette.
5. Do not expose the diskette to excessive heat or sunlight. Heat will distort the recording medium or protective jacket: if distorted, it will not run in your disk drive.
6. Do not fold or bend the diskette. Do not use paper clips, rubber bands or tape on the diskette.
7. Do not use a ball point to mark a label already applied to the diskette. Write on a label before you place it on the diskette. If you must mark a label that is already adhered to the diskette, use only a felt tip pen with light pressure applied.
8. Do not expose the diskette to a dusty environment or near where erasures are being made. Any particles of dust or grit on a diskette will not only make for a shorter life, but will contaminate the Read/Write head in your disk drive. You may permanently damage that head, causing costly repairs.
9. Should the diskette become damaged as outlined above, it would be wise to have it replaced rather than risk damage to your computer equipment.
10. Always replace the diskette in its protective sleeve after removing it from a disk drive Diskettes may be stored horizontally (using the caution above) or vertically if not allowed to sag or lean.
11. Should the diskette be exposed to excessive heat or cold, allow it to acclimate to room temperature for at least 30 minutes before using it.

LICENSE AGREEMENT FOR McGRAW-HILL SOFTWARE

This agreement gives you, the customer, certain benefits, rights and obligations. By using the software, you indicate that you have read, understood, and will comply with the terms.

TERMS OF AGREEMENT:

1. McGraw-Hill licenses and authorizes you to use the software specified below only on a micro-computer located within your own facilities.
2. You will abide by the Copyright Law of the United States. This law provides you with the right to make only one back-up copy. It prohibits you from making any additional copies, except as expressly provided by McGraw-Hill. In the event that the software is protected against copying in such a way that it cannot be duplicated, McGraw-Hill will provide you with one back-up copy at minimal cost or no charge.
3. You will not prepare derivative works based on the software because that is also not permitted under Copyright Law. For example, you cannot prepare an alternative hardware version or format based on the existing software.
4. If you have a problem with the operation of our software or believe it is defective, contact your nearest McGraw-Hill Book Company office about securing a replacement. We cannot, however, offer free replacement of diskettes damaged through normal wear and tear, or lost while in your possession. Nor does McGraw-Hill warrant that the software will satisfy your requirements, that the operation of the software will be uninterrupted or error-free, or that program defects in the software can be corrected. Except as described in this agreement, software and diskettes are distributed "as is" without warranties of any kind, either express or implied, including, but not limited to, implied warranties of merchantability and fitness for a particular purpose or use.
5. Additional rights and benefits may come with the specific software package you have purchased. Consult the support materials that come with this program, or contact the nearest McGraw-Hill Book Company office in your area.

NOTES

NOTES

NOTES

NOTES

NOTES

NOTES

NOTES

NOTES

NOTES

NOTES